YOUNG CHILDREN WITH SPECIAL NEEDS

A Developmental and Ecological Approach

S. Kenneth Thurman
Temple University

Anne H. Widerstrom
University of Colorado, Denver

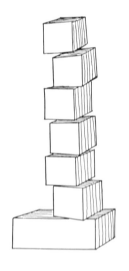

ALLYN AND BACON, INC.
Boston London Sydney Toronto

To our children
Shane and Anne
And to children everywhere

Library of Congress Cataloging in Publication Data

Thurman, S. Kenneth.
  Young children with special needs.

  Bibliography: p.
  Includes index.
  1. Handicapped children—Education (Preschool)
2. Child & development. 3. Mainstreaming in education.
I. Widerstrom, Anne H. II. Title.
LC4019.2.T48   1985   371.9   84–6403
ISBN 0–205–08143–6

Printed in the United States of America

10 9 8 7 6 5 4 3 2 1 89 88 87 86 85 84

Contents

Preface

This book was written in response to a long-felt need on the part of both authors for a scholarly and comprehensive text on infants and young children with special needs. As the commitment grows to appropriately educate special needs children beginning in infancy, the need for well-trained teachers and other specialists to work in intervention programs will increase. At present the number of university-level programs for training such people is multiplying rapidly, and we have often heard the lament, indeed have expressed it ourselves, that there is a lack of good text material for the courses we teach, especially those for upper division and graduate students. This book presents a thorough examination of major issues related to intervention with handicapped infants and young children.

The book is organized around two basic premises which we consider to be of vital importance. First, to be effective interventionists with young special needs children, professionals require firm grounding in normal development. Second, professionals need to recognize the ecology of which the child is part. Normal development is a yardstick by which to measure expectations and performance. An ecological perspective suggests that the child is part of a system and, as such, is in constant interaction with it. The child's interactions with the system can be a target for intervention.

Each of these perspectives, developmental and ecological, dominates portions of the book. Section One is devoted to an examination of general issues affecting young children with special needs and to discussions of normal and abnormal development in cognitive, language, social, and motor areas. It is hoped that readers will pay close attention to the material on normal development and consider it a foundation for their knowledge of handicapping conditions. The material on abnormal development is then presented in contrast to the normal sequences.

In Section Two, screening and assessment, an ecological approach is taken to evaluating young, handicapped children. The child's total environment—home and family, preschool or day care, and community—is taken into account in the diagnostic process. In its focus on programming, Section Three also takes an ecological perspective with emphasis on the child's fit or congruence with his or her surroundings. The final section addresses models of intervention and culminates with a chapter on the implications of mainstreaming special needs children at the preschool level.

We hope that our book proves to be a useful resource for teachers, psychologists, counselors, members of the medical profession, and other professionals. We have included the latest theory and research to present a perspective which is somewhat different from that of other texts in this area. Because we see our book as a beginning to the learning process and not an end, we have included a comprehensive list of references at the end of the book. In addition, each chapter begins with a few questions to be kept in mind not only while reading the chapters but also when practicing as a professional.

While this book is our responsibility and its shortcomings may be assigned to us, we would be remiss if we were not to acknowledge the contributions of several people to this effort. First, we would like to acknowledge Dr. Terry D. Meddock. His help in early conceptualizations of this book was invaluable to its formation. He contributed significantly to the scope and structure of the book and without his contribution this book probably would never have come to pass. He was also a contributing author to Chapter 7. We appreciate his contribution.

We would also like to thank Dr. Allen Sandler who displayed his scholarship and ability as the author of Chapter 10. His lucid writing style and comprehensive coverage of material are truly appreciated.

We owe a debt of gratitude to Dr. Debbie May who went above and beyond the call of duty in reviewing earlier drafts of our book. Her insight and suggestions were indeed meaningful and useful to us.

Finally, each of us has special thanks for family members, colleagues and students who have been especially helpful to us during the preparation of this book. One of us (SKT) would like to thank his wife, Marcia, and son, Shane, for their never-ending love and support during the time when this book was being written. They both on occasion became frustrated at always hearing about "the book." Nonetheless, they always bore with me, and Marcia even generously helped to prepare the final manuscript. Both of them will continue to have my gratitude and my love. The other (AHW) owes a debt of gratitude to Diane Bryen, Bob Hofmeister, and Ken Thurman, who guided her doctoral study and introduced her to the pleasures of writing and conducting systematic inquiry. We both wish to thank our graduate students at Temple University and the University of Colorado at Denver who used early drafts of the book as a course text and provided us with valuable feedback.

S. K. T.
A. H. W.

PERSPECTIVES
AND ISSUES

one

A Perspective on Young Children with Special Needs

1. What are some challenges of early intervention besides those mentioned in this chapter?
2. In what ways are a developmental and an ecological perspective compatible with each other?
3. What do you see as the personal rewards you may gain as an early interventionist?

This book is about children from birth to age six. It is about children whose developmental patterns lie outside the range considered "normal." It is about children whose environments and social settings place them at risk. It is about children who have special needs.

Special needs are those that require care or intervention beyond that normally required to assure the best possible developmental outcome in young children. All young children require stimulating, nurturing environments. All young children require love and trust. Children with special needs in addition require specialized treatment and interventions. Low birth weight infants, for example, may be required to spend the first weeks of life in an intensive care nursery. A three-and-a-half-year-old who is not talking may require language therapy. A five-year-old whose behavior is oppositional may require a behavior-management program in order to be ready for public school. As you read this book you will become familiar with the various types of problems and special needs that young children may have. You will also learn about ways in which these special needs can be addressed to minimize or remediate their effects.

THE CHALLENGES
OF EARLY INTERVENTION

The challenges of early intervention for young children with special needs include:

1. Provision of programs without stigmatizing through labels
2. Inclusion of family members in programs without destroying family integrity
3. Financial maintenance of programs in times of declining resources
4. Development of personnel from a variety of disciplines who understand children both with and without special needs

Each of these challenges is elaborated below.

Early intervention must counteract the effects of special needs without creating self-fulfilling prophecies regarding the developmental outcomes and potentials of these children. Thus, the first challenge is to identify and provide programs for young children with special needs without labeling the children. In order to do this, early interventionists must be aware that children with special needs fall outside of the accepted parameters of normalcy; but they must also resist placing inhibiting labels on these children. Thurman and Lewis (1979) have pointed out how the early labeling of children may actually contribute to the development of prejudice towards them. Thurman and Lewis contend that early intervention programs should stress the confrontation of difference in a positive way and, by so doing, reduce the possibilities of developing negative prejudices. In fact, early intervention programs, if properly designed, should reduce the probability of a child receiving a label. Take, for example, the case of the oppositional five-year-old mentioned above. This child has a pattern of behavior that, if left alone, could result in his being labeled as behavior-disordered or emotionally disturbed in first grade. Proper intervention designed to make the child less oppositional could prevent such labeling. In cases where labeling is unavoidable, early intervention can be useful in reducing the severity of the label. For example, a child born without arms is destined to be labeled. Early intervention, however, can minimize the child's disability and, therefore, his label, at say age six.

A second challenge for early intervention programs is family involvement. It is accepted practice to involve their families in intervention programs for young children with special needs. Some programs, in fact (see Chapter 11), are actually structured so that parents are responsible for any intervention that a child receives. Too often, however, interventionists have failed to recognize that families that include young children with special needs are families with special needs. While it is not unreasonable to expect families to put forth additional effort on behalf of their special-needs children, it must be remembered that each family is different and has individual members whose ability to respond and be effective varies greatly. Turnbull and Turnbull (1982) have suggested that professionals tend to respond to parents with a standardized set of expectations. They go on to point out the problems with such an approach. The early interventionist would do well to remember that individual family members are as different from each other as are individual special-needs children. The principle that special-needs children should be responded to as individuals is especially applicable to responding to their families. Chapter 10 addresses the needs and involvement of families with special-needs children.

A third challenge facing the early interventionist is the financial maintenance of programs. This challenge is salient in times of declining federal and state support. Early interventionists must provide cost-efficient programs and use each resource to its maximum. Effective use of volunteers, for example, may reduce overall program cost. Staff-made materials often are less costly than mass-produced ones and at the same time can be more responsive to the individual needs of the children. The financial stability of a program is critical if high-quality services are to be maintained. When direct-intervention staff are constantly concerned with whether there will be money to run the program their morale and effectiveness decline. The challenge to provide financial solvency lies primarily with program administrators, who should be prepared to tap a variety of different funding sources. One mistake often made by program administrators is to rely too heavily on a single source of funds. Generally, a program ought not to rely on one source for more than 25 to 30 percent of its operating funds. While this is not always possible, the challenge of financial solvency can be more readily met if programs are developed with multiple funding bases. As you read the program descriptions in Chapter 11, you may want to recall this point and think how well each program seems to be meeting the challenge of financial solvency through the use of cost-effective methods and multiple funding bases.

The fourth challenge to be discussed deals with the development of personnel to provide early intervention to young children with special needs. These people need to come from a wide variety of disciplines including special education, psychology, early childhood education, speech and language pathology, occupational therapy, physical therapy, nursing, social work, and pediatrics. These professionals must be provided with expertise on the needs of children both with and without special needs. While it is up to colleges, universities, and professional schools to offer pre-service programs to train early interventionists, it is not their responsibility alone. Individual early intervention programs must take the responsibility for providing meaningful, ongoing staff development programs. These programs should inform staff of the latest theories and techniques as they are applicable to young children with special needs. The bases of both pre-service and in-service training should be familiarity with the normal theories of development and their relationship to intervention with young children who have special needs. Our commitment to this belief, in fact, is manifest in this book which has as one of its major foci normal developmental patterns in children from birth to age six.

Each individual professional involved in early intervention must take up the challenge of his own professional development. Interventionists must think of themselves as self-directed learners and must stay abreast of the field by reading professional literature and by attending conferences. At the same time, they must use their own programs as a source of knowledge and professional development. They can learn not only from peers but also from the children and families for whom they provide services. Careful record keeping and data collection can provide important information about the effectiveness of various techniques and procedures. Systematic observation can provide valuable insight into children's development as well as into their patterns of interaction with their environments. Many of these themes are further elaborated in later chapters of this book.

The future of early intervention programs for children with special needs depends on how well we are able to respond to these four challenges. We hope that through reading this book you will become better able to meet the challenges of early intervention. The knowledge that you gain should be a point of departure and not an end to your own professional development. To that end each chapter, including this one, begins with a series of thought questions designed to let you continue to think about the issues raised in each chapter.

A DEVELOPMENTAL
ECOLOGICAL PERSPECTIVE

As you read this book, you will find that it approaches young children with special needs from two separate yet interrelated perspectives. On the one hand, the first section of the book is developmental in approach. Our concern is to provide the reader with a knowledge of normal patterns of development as they characterize cognitive, language, social/emotional, and motor functions. In addition, specific problems that may occur in children from birth to age six are addressed. Our focus on development stems from our belief that one of the major functions of early intervention is to facilitate development and a second, as will be discussed in the next chapter, is to reduce risk to young children. Effective early intervention, then, should improve the quality of development beyond the point that would be expected were intervention not provided. To improve it, we must understand development and the problems that may occur in normal developmental patterns.

An equally important perspective that characterizes this book is an ecological one. An ecological perspective recognizes that a child is not a free-floating developing human being but assumes rather that she is part of an ecological system. An ecological approach is concerned with the child as a developing organism *in interaction with* the environment. *Ecology* is defined as the study of an organism's interaction with its environment. In an ecological approach, attention must be given to the goodness-of-fit between the child and the environment. To elucidate goodness-of-fit, Thurman (1977) developed the concept of ecological congruence (the degree to which an individual and his environment are mutually tolerant). This tolerance is in part a function of the developmental status of the individual child.

An ecological approach complements a developmental one because it provides the context within which developmental intervention occurs. Development can only be improved in some context. The ecological system provides the context. So, while it should be designed to improve the developmental status of a child, early intervention should also be designed to recognize that the child's development has meaning only within its ecological context. Chapters 8 and 9 discuss the ecological congruence model in detail and describe how to design early interventions that develop a higher level of tolerance or congruence within the ecological system. In short, to be concerned with a child's development without having equal concern for the ecological system is to overlook a major aspect of early intervention. It is only in a well-balanced ecology that development is facilitated and maintained.

SUMMARY AND CONCLUSION

This brief chapter was designed to familiarize the reader with the perspectives and orientation of this book. The book is a resource, a beginning point for the student who is concerned with early intervention for special needs children. Readers are urged to use the thought questions at the beginning of each chapter and to extend their knowledge by consulting sources from the references at the end of the book which relate to their own areas of interest. The challenges of early intervention are great. A commitment to meeting those challenges can result in meaningful personal rewards. It is to be hoped that those rewards will be yours.

Determinants of Risk in Young Children

1. What factors can put a young child at risk?
2. Does being at risk necessarily imply a negative outcome?
3. What are the implications of incidence and prevalence for the study of young children at risk?
4. Why is it important for interventionists to understand the concept of risk?

The purpose of this chapter is to identify the determinants of risk and disability in young children. The concepts to be discussed are derived from psychology, sociology, and medicine. Simply, this chapter addresses factors that help determine the degree of risk experienced by children in infancy and early childhood. It also provides perspective on the pervasiveness of developmental problems in young children through a discussion of incidence and prevalence.

THE CONCEPT OF BEING AT RISK

In one sense, we are all at risk. That is, every time we get into a moving automobile, cross a street, or participate in sports, we are risking personal injury or even death. Most of the risks we take as well-adjusted adults are voluntary risks. No one forces us to play football or jog across a busy street. As a matter of fact, most of us have a point beyond which we will not take risks. For example, you may be perfectly willing to drive your car down the highway at 55 miles per hour but not at 100 miles per hour, since the latter speed would not only increase your likelihood of receiving a stiff fine but would also put you at a much greater risk of injuring or killing yourself. Essentially, we are all at risk to a certain extent but at at the same time we have a certain amount of control over the degree of risk to which we are exposed.

Unfortunately, the same thing could not have been said about us during prenatal and early postnatal periods. While it is obvious that we are exposed to risk every day, being at risk actually begins with the moment of conception. Developmental risk that occurs either prenatally or in the first several years of life provides the most basic rationale for early developmental intervention. The roots of much of our early developmental programming for young children are found in the desire to decrease exposure to risk for these children. Thus, we have established special programs for those young children whom we consider to be especially at risk. By reducing the risk to which a child is exposed, we maximize the probability that she will develop to the fullest extent possible. Typically, the greater the degree of perceived risk, the more intensive the intervention.

FACTORS CONTRIBUTING TO RISK

Solnit and Provence (1979) have suggested that the degree of potential risk is determined in part by the *vulnerability* of the child. They suggest that "vulnerability refers particularly to the weaknesses, deficits, or defects of the child, whereas risk refers to the interaction of the environment and the child" (p. 800). This section examines a number of factors related to the vulnerability of infants and young children as well as to the risk they may encounter in their environments. These factors include socioeconomic status, prematurity and low birth weight, hereditary and genetic conditions, prenatal factors, and events during birth and delivery.

Socioeconomic Status

Socioeconomic status (SES) relates more often to vulnerability and risk than does any other identifiable variable. For example, lower SES mothers are more likely than higher SES mothers to give birth to premature infants (Butler & Alberman, 1969; Guthrie et el., 1977) and SES remains the single best predictor of later IQ scores (McCall, Hogarty, & Hurlburt, 1972). Put another way, infants and young children born and reared in lower SES environments have a greater risk of exhibiting lower IQ scores in subsequent years than do their higher SES peers.

Generally, children born into lower SES environments tend to be more vulnerable throughout infancy and preschool years than those born into higher SES environments. This is true, of course, if we base our conclusions solely on statistical evidence, for the statistics show that such factors as nutrition, mother/child interaction patterns, and language experience in lower SES families are less promoting of optimal development than in middle and upper class families (Golden & Birns, 1976). Nevertheless, it would be false to assume that middle and upper income families by definition are better at caring for their children than are lower income families, or that lower SES parents may automatically be categorized as producing at-risk children. Obviously, many disabled children are identified from all SES groups. Vulnerability and risk must be considered on an individual basis.

Prematurity and Low Birth Weight

Prematurity and low birth weight contribute to the risk of infants by increasing their vulnerability in different ways. *Prematurity* refers to a relatively short gestational period, usually less than 37 weeks. Infants born prematurely most often have below average birth weights; however, their weights at birth are appropriate for their gestational ages.

Another group of infants who manifest low birth weights are those whose gestational period is within normal limits (39 to 41 weeks), but whose birth weight is substantially below that of the normal full term infant (less than 2500 grams or 5 1/2 pounds). These infants are typically referred to as *small for date*. Before the mid-1960s it was common practice to treat both of these types of infants, that is, premature and low birth weight infants, as a single group (cf., Gruenwald, 1965).

More recently, Robinson and Robinson (1976) and Fox (1978) suggested that the validity of research with low birth weight infants has been compromised by the inclusion of both premature and small for date babies in experimental samples. Fox (1978) reports that small for date babies, as compared to premature infants, "are associated with . . . higher rates of seizure and mental retardation in the absence of cerebral palsy, but lower rates of spastic diplegia [a type of cerebral palsy] and deafness" (p. 2).

Further complicating matters, however, is the fact that infants may be simultaneously premature and gestationally small for date. Hunt (1976) suggested that any baby, whether premature or full term, may be considered small for date if he is three standard deviations below the average birth weight for the gestational age. These babies, although not specifically addressed in the literature, are probably subject to more risk than are babies who are either premature or small for date.

At any rate, an examination of existing literature shows an improving prognosis for low birth weight infants, especially those below 1500 grams, since the early 1970s. For example, Drillien's (1964) data demonstrated a negative correlation between birth weight and developmental status at four years of age. Studies published in the 1970s (for example, Rawlings et al., 1971; Fitzhardinge & Ramsay, 1973) show much more favorable outcomes. This shift toward more favorable developmental outcomes can be attributed to improved medical and educational intervention, which accelerated significantly in the 1970s.

Now these medical services, centered in intensive care neonatal nurseries, are available to more infants of low birth weight than previously. For example, Children's Hospital in Denver, a pioneer in neonatal care, serves a region comprising 500 square miles. High risk, low birth weight infants are flown to the hospital's neonatal unit and are given twenty-four-hour individual care, sometimes for many months. Respirators are routinely provided, since nearly all low birth weight infants require respiratory aid because their lungs are not fully developed. The babies are fed intravenously if necessary, and remain in warmed bassinettes, often under ultraviolet lights to treat jaundice, also a common condition in low birth weight infants. The neonatal unit has a high nurse/infant ratio, and the babies' blood pressure, heart rate, and respiration are regularly monitored.

This neonatal program, like others across the country, has been remarkably successful in both preventing deaths of infants weighing less than 1500 grams at birth and in preventing disabilities that in the past were considered an inherent risk of extreme prematurity. For example, of infants admitted to the hospital weighing from 1000 grams (2 pounds, 3 ounces) to 1500 grams (3 pounds, 5 ounces), most survive and about one-third are developmentally normal. Those weighing less than 1000 grams generally have some developmental problems, primarily involving vision, hearing, or motor function. Low IQ later in life is not necessarily associated with the low birth weight.

At Children's Hospital in Denver infants as small as 600 grams (1 pound, 5 ounces) are treated. However, the survival rate is lower for these than for bigger babies and developmental problems more numerous in the survivors. For example, in 1981, the year for which the foregoing data were gathered, only one infant weighing less than 600 grams survived.

Complications seen in these premature and small for date infants include respiratory distress syndrome (RDS), hyperbilirubinemia, neuromotor disorders, and retina damage from too much oxygen. *RDS*, also known as *Hyaline membrane disease*, is a condition in which the infant lacks the special protein substance that wets the membrane lining the lungs. The infant generally has great difficulty with lung expansion as a result. *Hyperbilirubinemia* is caused by abnormally large amounts of bilirubin, a red bile pigment, in the circulating blood, causing jaundice.

Regardless of the cause, low birth weight represents a condition of relative immaturity in the infant. Since physiological and anatomical maturation are the main events of the fetal period of prenatal development, it is reasonable to assume that low birth weights come about because of an interference with the maturational process. Logic suggests that any organism which is immature is more vulnerable than that which is not and so subject to greater risk. Stewart et al. (1977) clearly demonstrate the increased vulnerability of low birth weight infants. They studied 148 infants born between 1966 and 1975 and weighing less than 1000 grams. Only 26 percent of their sample survived the first year of life. In addition, 23 percent of those surviving the first year had some degree of identifiable disability during follow-up assessments.

Prematurity and low birth weight are not themselves responsible for poor developmental outcomes (i.e., increased risk). They are associated with conditions such an anoxia (lack of oxygen), jaundice, and other perinatal complications, which account for increased developmental risk. Parmelee and Haber (1973), in fact, suggest that the premature infant who experiences no additional trauma during the prenatal or newborn periods will fare just as well as a full term infant raised in a comparable environment (Sameroff, 1979). However, it must be assumed that Parmelee and Haber were referring to premature infants whose weight and gestational age do not vary greatly from the norm.

Genetic Factors

Between 15 and 25 percent of developmental disorders in young children are related to genetic factors. By genetic factors we mean abnormalities in the makeup of either genes or chromosomes.

The *gene* is the functional unit of heredity, the means by which characteristics of parents are transmitted to their children. Each gene occupies a specific place on a *chromosome*. Chromosomes are arranged in pairs and are present in every cell of the body. There are 23 pairs of chromosomes in the normal human being. Of these 23 pairs, 22 pairs are called *autosomal*. The other pair is referred to as the *sex chromosomes*. The sex chromosomes are labeled XX for females and XY for males. Genetic material, coded on the chromosomes, is contained in molecules of DNA (deoxyribonucleic acid). When additional chromosomal material is present or when a certain amount is lacking, the infant is at risk of developmental disorder or delay.

When describing genetic disorders we refer to them as either autosomal or X-linked and dominant or recessive. A child whose parent carries a gene for a dominant disorder has a higher likelihood of inheriting that disorder than does one whose parent carries a gene for a recessive disorder. In other words, the child is at greater risk for disability. This means the child is more likely to manifest the abnormal condition since the dominant gene takes precedence over the other parent's recessive gene. For example, tuberous sclerosis is a genetic disorder related to a dominant gene. If one parent carries this dominant gene, the child faces a 50 percent risk of inheriting tuberous sclerosis. However, if both parents carry the gene the risk increases to 100 percent. Hurler's syndrome, on the other hand, is an autosomal, recessive disorder. Autosomal, recessive disorders are the most commonly seen of the genetic disorders, although they carry a lower risk factor than do dominant ones. When only one parent carries the abnormal gene, the other parent's normal dominant gene takes precedence. Of course if both parents carry this recessive gene the risk greatly increases. Muscular dystrophy is an example of a sex-linked chromosomal disorder. It occurs on the X chromosome and so is more commonly seen in boys than girls, since boys have only one X chromosome. In girls the harmful action of genes on one X chromosome is usually suppressed by dominant genes on the other X chromosome.

Many genetic disorders manifest themselves in metabolic dysfunction. That is, due to genetic error the infant is born with a lack of a certain enzyme. Infants with galactosemia, for example, lack the enzyme necessary to convert galactose, a milk sugar, into glucose. Many metabolic disorders can now be controlled by dietary means or through enzyme replacement therapy.

While some genetic disorders are inherited through either dominant or recessive genes, others are due to chromosome abnormalities. These abnormalities, resulting from additions or deletions of chromosomal material, are referred to as *cytogenetic conditions*. Unlike dominant and recessive conditions, cytogenetic conditions are not typically passed from generation to generation. That is, they are not inheritable. Several of the better known cytogenetic conditions that place infants and young children at risk for developmental delays are Down's syndrome (Trisomy 21), Trisomy 18, and Cri du Chat syndrome.

Recent advances in medical techniques have made it possible to identify many genetic disorders prenatally. Through such procedures as amniocentesis, sonar scanning, and fetoscopy, parents can be informed of potential problems before birth. *Amniocentesis* involves removing a sample of amniotic fluid from the womb and analyzing it for a variety of possible birth defects. Tay Sachs disease, for example, can be identified through this method. *Sonar scanning* uses ultrasound detection to identify possible problems in the developing fetus, and fetoscopy consists of viewing the fetus in utero by means of an endoscope for viewing the womb internally. Another diagnostic technique is the analysis of the levels of alpha fetoprotein (AFP) in maternal blood samples taken during the second trimester of pregnancy. Increased levels of AFP indicate a neural tube defect (spina bifida), for example (Hayden & Beck, 1982).

Parents whose infants are at risk for developmental disorders may receive genetic counseling, which includes diagnosis, an appraisal of risk factors, discussions relating to etiology of various conditions, and information concerning alternatives. Sixty percent of first trimester abortions, for example, are performed on women whose infants would be born with serious chromosomal abnormalities. In other cases, the counseling may result in the pregnancy proceeding with appropriate therapy either during pregnancy or immediately following birth.

The foregoing section provides only a basic understanding of the relationship between being at risk and the genetic endowment of individuals. There are many other conditions related to genetic factors that may be associated with significant risk of developmental delay. The interested reader should consult Carter (1975) for a more comprehensive coverage of these and other genetically related conditions.

Prenatal Risk Factors

While it provides maximum protection for the rather vulnerable organism within it, the uterus does not provide an absolutely safe environment. Every fetus is at some degree of risk during the prenatal period. A number of specific factors that can occur during a pregnancy place the developing fetus at risk. Infants who are born as a result of a pregnancy including such factors are usually more vulnerable than infants deriving from normal pregnancies.

Two types of factors can account for placing the fetus at risk prenatally. First are those related to the physical and health status of the mother and the general quality of the uterus. These factors include age, level of nutrition, and specific health problems like hypertension and diabetes. The second group of factors are those that interfere more directly with the developmental progress of the fetus regardless of the conditions of the general intrauterine environment. These factors include radiation, prenatal anoxia, various drugs, and viral and bacterial infections.

AGE   Maternal age has a direct relationship to the degree of risk associated with pregnancy. Increased maternal (over 35 years) and paternal age significantly increase the risk of giving birth to a Down's syndrome infant or an infant who manifests other types of chromosomal abnormalities (Abroms & Bennett, 1980). For example, the incidence of Down's syndrome births in the general population is about 1 in 600 (cf., Hirshhorn, 1973) but the incidence in women under 30 is 1 in 1500 as compared with 1 in 65 for mothers over 45 (Smith & Wilson, 1973). Lilienfeld and Pasamanick (1956) also report an increased risk of children with mental retardation resulting from mothers under 20 years of age and mothers over 35 years of age.

MATERNAL NUTRITION   The major studies of maternal nutrition have been done with animals since the ethical considerations in manipulating animal diets during pregnancy are fewer than those in the manipulation of human diets during similar times. Winick and Rosso (1973), for example, have demonstrated retarded fetal and placental growth and a reduction in the number of brain cells in rats whose mothers' protein intake was restricted during pregnancy.

An in-depth study of pregnancies during the siege of Leningrad (Anatov, 1947) indicated that the poor nutrition of the mothers resulted in only slightly reduced birth weights but significant increases in spontaneous abortion and premature births. However, a later follow-up of babies born during the food blockade of Holland in 1944 showed few identifiable developmental defects (Stein et al., 1972).

Winick (1970) has pointed out that a major factor in fetal malnutrition is incomplete development of the placenta. Thus, inadequate nutrition in the fetus may be related to the structure and function of the placenta itself or, as discussed above, to the general nutritional status of the mother during pregnancy.

SPECIFIC HEALTH PROBLEMS   Hypertension or high blood pressure during pregnancy places both the mother and infant at risk. Robinson and Robinson (1976, p. 121) suggest that 20 percent of all pregnancy-related maternal deaths can be accounted for by disorders related to high blood pressure in the third trimester of pregnancy. At the same time, Hellman and Pritchard (1971) estimated that as many as 25,000 fetal deaths a year occur because of maternal hypertension.

While it increases the likelihood that mothers will become hypertensive during pregnancy, diabetes in mothers can also put the fetus at risk by affecting the development of the placenta. Mothers with diabetes have often developed vascular problems, which manifest themselves in inadequate nutritional exchange via the placenta. Diabetic mothers are also prone to have larger babies, which may result in birth complications. These babies are often hypoglycemic. Although techniques for managing diabetes have improved over time and have reduced the risk to both mother and fetus during pregnancy, it is still the case that diabetic women experience greater risks during pregnancy than do women who are non-diabetic.

The interaction between mother and fetus is a complex one and includes many factors related to risk in pregnancy. The specific effects of these factors are, at best, difficult to measure. In general, age, health, and nutritional status of the mother before and during pregnancy can contribute to the overall development of the child. Other factors are more specifically linked to risk in prenatal development and to later behavioral deficits.

RADIATION   Radiation can contribute to risk during prenatal development. Its hazard is related to its ability to alter genetic structures and cause mutations (or changes in the genes) to occur. Radiation is most dangerous during early pregnancy. It is most unfortunate that many women do not even realize they are pregnant when these effects can be greatest. Microcephaly is a common manifestation of prenatal radiation. Although Wilson (1974) has suggested that less than 1 percent of all developmental defects can be linked to radiation, it is imperative that women who even suspect they are pregnant relate this to the physician prior to submitting to an X ray of any kind. Recent advances in technology have developed the ultrasound technique of diagnosis, which appears not to have the negative effects of X rays on the fetus. It has been used more and more commonly to assess the prenatal condition of the uterus, placenta, and fetus during pregnancy.

PRENATAL ANOXIA   Prenatal anoxia can damage the central nervous system. *Anoxia* is the deprivation of oxygen for some period of time. Prenatal anoxia may occur several ways. First, a pregnant woman's oxygen supply may be cut off through accident or suffocation. If prolonged, this can also result in the fetus experiencing an anoxic condition. Women with deficient hearts are prone to produce anoxic conditions in fetuses during pregnancy. One possible result of anoxia is anacephaly or total absence of a differentiated brain. A second factor that can result in prenatal anoxia is the closing off of the umbilical cord. This can occur through accident to the pregnant woman or through premature separation of the placenta from the uterine wall. In rare instances the fetus may actually become entangled in the umbilical cord and anoxia can result. In any event, prenatal anoxia greatly increases the risk to the fetus during pregnancy.

DRUGS   Ingestion of drugs, whether prescribed, over the counter, or illicit, can place the developing fetus at risk. Wilson (1973) has reported that over 600 drugs have been related to later birth defects in animals, although only about 20 have been linked to similar effects in human beings. Wilson (1974) has estimated that only 2 to 3 percent of the defects present in human populations can be related to drugs taken during pregnancy. In addition to drugs, it is quite likely that increased amounts of environmental pollutants are increasing the risk to which many fetuses are exposed. Cassarett and Doull (1975), for example, have reported the effects of mercury pollution on mothers and their offspring. The combined risk of drugs and pollutants and of various drugs with each other is virtually unexamined in spite of reports indicating that 92 percent of all women surveyed used drugs during pregnancy (Apgar, 1965) and that on the average women recall the use of four different medications during pregnancy (Barnes, 1968). More recently Stewart, Cluff, and Philp (1977) reported that mothers consumed a mean of 11 different drugs during pregnancy. Hill, Craig, Chaney, Tennyson, and McCulley (1977) surveyed 241 upper middle class, pregnant women who reported taking a mean of 9.6 different drugs, of which an average 6.4 were prescribed by physicians.

Perhaps the most famous cause of a drug creating significant risk during prenatal development is thalidomide, reported by Mellin and Katzenstein (1962). This report linked the use of the relatively mild tranquilizer to a number of babies born in Europe with physical anomalies. About 20 percent of the children whose mothers took the drug during critical periods of pregnancy were affected (Robinson & Robinson, 1976, p. 123). While their mental development did not seem to be affected in most cases, these children certainly experienced increased risk of severe developmental problems because of the prenatal influence of the drug.

Other drugs have also been shown to increase risk to the fetus during prenatal development. Mothers addicted to heroin, morphine, or methodone during pregnancy create additional risk to their offspring. The infants are quite often born addicted and must undergo the trauma of withdrawal. Nicotine, too, has effects on fetal heart rate and overall blood supply to the placenta and subsequently to the fetus, thus creating an increased risk of malnutrition and low birth weight.

Alcholic mothers also put their infants at risk. Their infants often develop what has come to be recognized as fetal alcohol syndrome (Furey, 1982; Jones et al., 1973; Umbreit & Ostrow, 1980). Manifestations of the syndrome are retarded physical and mental development, microcephaly, short eye slits, and possible limb and cardiac anomalies. About 40 percent of the children born to chronically alcoholic mothers display fetal alcohol syndrome (Green, 1974; Jones & Smith, 1974). Green (1974) points out, however, that many alcoholic mothers are also subject to environmental factors (for example, low SES, poor nutrition, anxiety, and the like), which themselves are prone to place a fetus at risk.

There is ample evidence that maternal exposure to drugs and other types of chemical agents increase the risk to the fetus during pregnancy. Professionals concerned with decreasing the risk of developmental difficulties to young children should provide information about the hazards of drug use during pregnancy to women likely to become pregnant. In general, pregnant women would be well advised to use any kind of drug prudently, if at all, and only with the advice of a physician.

Maternal Infection

There are many bacterial and viral infections that if contracted during pregnancy can place the fetus at significant risk of later developmental problems.

Rubella, or German measles, is one of the best known conditions having such an effect on prenatal development, since its effects were first recognized four decades ago (Gregg, 1941). Typically, rubella is very mild in childhood and results in few, if any, complications. Unfortunately, contracting rubella during pregnancy can have devastating effects on the developing fetus. This is especially true if the disease occurs during the first trimester of pregnancy. Children exposed prenatally to rubella are often profoundly mentally and physically disabled (Cooper & Krugman, 1966). Although the advent of rubella vaccine has decreased the incidence of the disease in the general population, women contemplating pregnancy must determine whether or not they need the vaccine prior to conceiving. Simple blood tests can answer this question.

Another preventive function of blood tests is in screening for the presence of spirochete bacteria that cause syphilis. In spite of improved detection techniques, the incidence of syphilis is on the rise. Syphilis is not only potentially fatal to the person contracting it, but it can also have grave effects on a developing fetus. A woman who has syphilis can pass the infection to her fetus, possibly resulting in visual handicaps and insult to the central nervous system and even death depending upon the progress of the disease. Using antibiotics, syphilis can be cured in the mother and the risk to the fetus can be dramatically reduced prior to approximately the eighteenth week of gestation.

At least two other, more chronic viruses have been linked to increased risk to the fetus if contracted by the mother during pregnancy. One is *cytomegalic inclusion disease* which may result in a wide variety of developmental disorders. Another virus, *herpes virus hominus*, while leaving mild manifestation in adults can, like rubella, greatly increase the risk to the fetus by introducing a higher incidence of brain lining infections. The mortality rate for herpes infants is 50 percent.

Pregnant women should, of course, take precautions against contracting any infections during pregnancy, since the degree of risk created by other microbic agents is not well understood.

Perinatal Risk Factors

Not all factors that increase the risk of later developmental difficulties occur during pregnancy. A number of factors occurring during birth, infancy, and early childhood may contribute to developmental problems. The perinatal period lasts from the twenty-eighth week of gestation to the seventh day after delivery.

Birth complications most often can result in *anoxia* or lack of oxygen. In a breech birth, for example, the infant is born buttocks first rather than head first. While it is often possible for the obstetrician to turn the baby with instruments, use of instruments contributes to the risk of direct damage to the baby's head. The risk of anoxia occurs in breech birth because the umbilical cord can rather easily become wrapped around the infant's neck.

Precipitous labor, that is, labor of less than two hours, often sets the stage for anoxia. In this situation, anoxia results from premature separation of the placenta from the uterine wall. Prolonged labor may also lead to anoxia through an incomplete separation of the placenta.

Drugs used during labor may also affect the infant. Heavy anesthesia used during delivery may not only affect the woman but also her baby since anesthetic crosses the placental barrier quickly. Exposure to anesthetic may reduce the ability of the infant to breathe independently and cause a general depression of the central nervous system (Brackbill, 1979). After an in-depth analysis of the use of drugs during birth, Brackbill (1979, p. 109) draws the conclusion that "drugs given to mothers during labor and delivery have subsequent effects on infant behavior and no study has demonstrated functional enhancement following obstetrical medication." In addition, these effects may persist into the first year of life. Suffice it to say that, as with prenatal drugs, drugs administered during labor and delivery do affect the risk status of infants and thus should be used judiciously.

Prematurity also greatly increases the chances of anoxia. Premature infants tend to lack the physiological maturity within their respiratory systems to breathe independently. Thus, when the umbilical cord is severed the child may become anoxic and need assistance in breathing.

While a number of birth complications can lead to anoxia, it is not well established just how much anoxia an infant can withstand before irreparable nervous system damage has occurred. Generally, even brief episodes of anoxia should be avoided at birth to decrease the risk of later developmental problems.

INFANT STATUS AT BIRTH   Because labor and delivery increase the risk to the infant making the transition from the uterine environment to the outside world, the infant's status must be assessed immediately after birth. The status of the infant is an index of vulnerability and consequently is important in identifying infants who are significantly at risk just after birth. The most widely used measure of determining an infant's status at birth is the Apgar Scale (Apgar, 1953), discussed in Chapter 7. While low Apgar scores seem to predict neonatal death rates in groups of infants (Apgar et al., 1958; Apgar & James, 1962), they may or may not predict behavioral outcomes or death for a given infant (Self & Horowitz, 1979).

DEFINING RISK

No single factor can adequately predict the degree of risk to which an infant is exposed. Recognition of this fact led Parmelee, Sigman, Kopp, and Haber (1975) to develop the concept of cumulative risk. Their method of identifying infants at risk uses multiple assessments at different ages and measures a wide range of variables. The cumulative risk score system devised by Parmelee and colleagues is composed of certain items related to each period, as follows:

Neonatal risk score items
1. obstetric complications
2. postnatal events
3. newborn neurological examination
4. visual attention
5. sleep polygraph

Three and four month risk score items
1. pediatric events and examination
2. Gesell test
3. visual attention
4. sleep polygraph

Eight and nine months risk score items
1. pediatric events and examination
2. Gesell test
3. cognitive test
4. hand precision/sensory-motor schemes
5. exploratory behavior

Parmelee, Sigman, Kopp, and Haber (1976) provided a more complete description of these items to which the interested reader is referred.

Simply defined, risk is a prediction of the manifestation of later developmental disability. Parmelee and others (1975) asserted that the greater number of predictor variables the more accurately risk status can be assigned to an individual infant. This argument, however, is only one half of the story, for Parmelee's system is designed to measure only the biological status of the infant, that is, the child's vulnerability. However, Parmelee and colleagues do recognize that "one important recurring observation is that outcome measures are strongly influenced by the socio-economic circumstances of the children's environments, and this influence is often stronger than that of earlier biological events" (Parmelee et al., 1975, p. 114).

As we stated earlier in this chapter, being at risk is a function of the child's biological status in interaction with the environment. Thus, as Anastasi (1958) suggested two decades ago and as Bixler (1980) reiterated recently, both nature and nurture contribute to a child's development and our mission is to find out how these two influences interact to place children at risk.

Sameroff and Chandler (1975) took this interactional view one step further. They suggested that neither environmental nor biological factors are static. Instead, they suggest a transactional model, one in which the biological nature of the child influences the caretaking environment which in turn influences the child. That a baby is premature for example, does not mean he will be ultimately at risk or manifest a developmental problem. On the other hand, a baby's prematurity may set the stage for transactions with the caretaking environment and thus result in developmental delay.

Kearsley (1979) has presented the concept of *iatrogenic retardation*, a syndrome of learned incompetence. His example provides an excellent illustration of the way an infant's transactions can be governed by a biological event like prematurity. In addition, he presents evidence to suggest that a modification of the transactional pattern between the infant and the caretaking environment can significantly alter the course of the child's development. Kearsley's argument demonstrates the way labeling a child as vulnerable can create a self-fulfilling prophecy by establishing an over-protective and under-stimulating set of transactions. In such cases, it may be the label "prematurity" rather than the biological event of prematurity that contributes most to the child's risk status. Kearsley's agrument is sobering when one considers the negative effect of labels that have been recognized by sociologists (for example, Bogdan, 1980; Dexter, 1964; Farber, 1968; Mercer, 1973). Labels have significant effects on the life chances (Farber, 1968) and status (Mercer, 1973) of school-age children and adults. Apparently labels may have similar effects on infants, beginning even at birth.

In summary, we have pointed out a number of factors that can contribute to the risk status of the infant. These factors are both biological and environmental in nature and interact to define the degree of risk assigned to any infant or young child. Accepting the premise of Sameroff and Chandler (1975) allows us to see this interaction as a dynamic one and to suggest that a modification of the child's transactions with the environment may significantly alter her eventual developmental status. As we will discuss in later chapters, early developmental intervention is often the key to effective modifications in the young child's transactions with the environment, and, as a result, in the child's degree of risk and eventual developmental status.

INCIDENCE AND PREVALENCE

Now that we have examined some of the factors related to increased risk in young children, it is necessary to explore the pervasiveness of the developmental problems exhibited by preschool-age children. To accomplish this, we will consider the incidence and prevalence of various developmental problems in preschool children.

Incidence and prevalence both relate to the actual occurrence of a particular developmental problem. While the two terms are related and have often been used interchangeably, they are not synonymous. *Incidence* refers to the frequency with which something occurs within a population. For example, the expected incidence of Down's syndrome is approximately 1 in 600 births. The actual incidence, however, would be defined by how many Down's syndrome children were actually born during a particular period of time, so that the actual incidence of the condition may have been 87 Down's syndrome births out of 35,000 births in a given year. Changes in incidence figures may reflect what society is doing about preventing a particular condition. For example, the worldwide incidence of smallpox has been zero over the last several years. Essentially, society has been successful in preventing smallpox through mass immunization programs.

Prevalence refers to the actual number of individuals identified as having a particular condition at a given point in time. Thus, while the incidence of Down's syndrome has decreased due to phenomena like genetic counseling and amniocentesis, the prevalence has increased due to medical practitioners' ability to prolong the life of people with Down's syndrome. Prevalence figures tell society how much of a particular problem there is to deal with. On the other hand, incidence figures can provide the basis for predicting the need for future services.

Although a number of prevalence studies have been completed to determine the number of children with a particular disability, no studies yet provide data on specific disabling conditions in children under six years of age. The figures that are presented are based on estimates extrapolated from census data. For example, the National Advisory Committee on the Handicapped (1976) estimated that there were 1,187,000 disabled children birth to six years during the 1975–76 school year. Of these, they estimated that approximately 737,000 were unserved.

Two main reasons account for the lack of definitive prevalence data on disabled children under the age of six. First, such studies are difficult to conduct, especially at a national level, and are therefore quite costly. Second, and perhaps more important, is the difficulty in adequately defining a preschool-age, disabled population. As was seen in the first section of this chapter, a number of factors contribute to an infant or young child being at risk. However, as was also stated, being at risk does not per se make a child disabled. Since many disabilities manifest themselves, at least in part, through deficits in academic performance, it is only when children reach school age that they are clearly identified as disabled. Thus, accurate prevalence figures for school age populations are easier to develop than for preschool age ones.

In some instances, however, even preschool-age children can be identified, classified, and accounted for as disabled. These instances arise when the disabling condition has obvious physical and/or behavioral manifestations, as with birth defects or many genetically determined syndromes like those discussed above. In addition, multiply disabled, preschool children tend to be more easily accounted for than are those with single disabilities. For example, in an early prevalence study of visually impaired children, Graham (1967) was able to determine that 86 percent of the children identified under the age of six had one or more additional disabilities.

As with prevalence figures, incidence figures depend on one's ability to identify the actual condition of concern. Again, more severe and more obvious conditions are identifiable at birth. Thus, a number of incidence figures are available for the more obvious congenital anomalies and birth injuries. Table 2.1 presents incidence figures for 1973 and 1974 for a number of major birth anomalies. These figures come from a report by the National Center for Health Statistics entitled *Congential Anomalies and Birth Injuries Among Live Births—United States 1973–1974* (Taffel, 1978). This study concluded that 821 babies out of every 100,000 born had a congenital anomaly and that 216 of 100,000 born suffered a birth injury. Thus for the 1973–1974 period a total of 1037 babies per 100,000 born exhibited an identifiable characteristic at birth that placed them at increased risk. These figures are probably underreported, primarily because of "incomplete reporting on birth certificates [from which the data were gathered which] has been attributed to the failure to recognize a defect during the short interval before the certificate is filed, failure to transfer information from hospital records to birth certificates, and the recording of only the most severe anomaly when multiple anomalies were present" (Taffel, 1978, p. 2). Clearly, this statement supports the argument that an anomaly must be recognized before it can be recorded. Further underscoring this point is that a recent survey of 44 state Departments of Education found that only seven states have specific defi-

TABLE 2.1   Incidence of Selected Birth Anomalies in 1973–74, Based on 100,000 Live Births

CONGENITAL ANOMALY	1973	1974
Anencephalus	21.4	20.5
Hydrocephalus	16.2	16.3
Heart Anomalies	60.7	64.0
Congenital Cataract	2.2	2.1
Cleft Palate	36.4	29.9
Cleft Lip	25.0	22.7
Tracheo-Esophageal Fistula	8.2	4.5
Clubfoot	100.0	98.7
Reduction Deformity of Upper Limb	16.5	16.1
Reduction Deformity of Lower Limb	14.4	7.7
Other Syndromes due to Autosomal Abnormality (e.g., Cri du Chat, Trisomy 18, etc.)	3.6	5.0

Adapted from *Congenital Anomalies and Birth Injuries Among Live Births: United States 1973–1974.* Washington, D.C.: National Center for Health Statistics, DEW Publication No. Phs. 79–1909

nitions of preschool, disabled children (Lessen & Rose, 1980). Lessen and Rose concluded from their results that:

> identifying the pre-school handicapped population may seem difficult for a number of reasons including variability in normal development, questionable identification and diagnostic instruments, and variability in quality and quantity of environmental experiences. Because of these difficulties, the identification and definition and accounting for this population is at best tenuous. [1980, p. 469]

CONCLUSION

The conclusion that can be drawn from this discussion is that we have only rough estimates of the number of disabled children under the age of six. Until more precise and sensitive means for identifying infants and young children with developmental disabilities are established, it will continue to be difficult to account for them accurately. At present, the best solution would seem to be to continue research efforts to determine the degree of risk to which an individual child is exposed and to continue to develop assessment mechanisms that truly differentiate the child who is at risk from the one who has a true disability. In the final analysis, however, intervention strategies must continue to be developed and implemented so that preschool-age children who are at risk will be provided the maximum opportunity to overcome that risk, and so that those children who indeed have disabilities will minimize the effects of the disabilities in future years. Such efforts, if successful, should lead to concomitant declines in the prevalence of disabled, school-age children and adults in subsequent years.

Considerations for Cognitive Development

1. What is the role of the central nervous system in the development of cognition?
2. Can one theoretical position explain cognitive development?
3. What is the relationship between basic cognitive processes and problems in cognitive development?
4. What are the similarities and differences in the manifestations of mental retardation and learning disabilities in the period between three and five years of age?

Cognition can be defined as the process of knowing. What we know and, in a sense, how we know it represents our cognition. While each of us knows more about some things than others, we all came to know our world through an orderly sequence of development. This sequence remains relatively constant from individual to individual. Thus, the development of cognition is an orderly, predictable process by which we come to know and understand the world.

The study of cognition is mainly based on hypothetical constructs inferred from the behavior of young children. Thus, while it is difficult to deny the existence of cognition, it is equally difficult to directly observe it in young children, or in anyone else for that matter. It is possible to observe some cognitive processes, however. For example, memory is an important cognitive process. We are all conscious of our memory failing us from time to time, like when a shopping list is necessary for a trip to the grocery store or when we forget the name of someone we've just met. We can conclude, therefore, that there is a relationship between behavior and cognition and we can infer that this relationship exists in early childhood.

Of course, it is also true that behavior shapes cognition. That is, a child's level of cognition is directly related to the degree of behavioral experience the child has had in the world. The unfortunate aspect of this argument is that cognition is typically measured through behavioral assessments. Therefore, the case could be made that the amount of behavior exhibited at point A is a function of the degree of experience the child has had prior to arriving at point A and that the level of function is not necessarily related to the child's existing level of cognition. The circularity of the definition is difficult to overcome. The degree to which behavior occurs is said to be related to the level of cognitive function. Simultaneously, however, cognitive function is inferred from the behavior. Consider the example of discrimination, a cognitive function. We observe a child who can match red objects and green objects with samples of each of these colors. The child behaves as though she can discriminate. Thus, we infer that the child has acquired the necessary cognitive structures to discriminate. The circularity is manifest, however, when we pose the question, "Why is the child able to match red with red and green with green?" The apparent answer is "she has the cognitive structures necessary to do so." We have defined behavior in terms of cognition while simultaneously defining cognition in terms of behavior.

Cognition in young infants is tied closely to perceptual processing, which has been presumed to have certain physiological correlates. These physiological measures provide another means of defining cognitive processes. These measures include: eye fixation, electroencephalographic measure, heart rate, habituation, and skin potentials. For example, heart rate will increase in infants in a fearful situation such as perception of a stranger (Provost & Decarie, 1974) or decrease when the child perceives visual and auditory displays (Lewis et al., 1966; Lewis & Spaulding, 1967) or discrepant stimuli (Kagan, 1968; Lewis & Goldberg, 1969).

Interestingly, these physiological measures may not be congruent with some behavioral measures. Zelazo's (1979) preliminary data suggest that certain children who display deficits in cognitive development when measured with standardized behaviorally based measures like the Bayley Scales of Infant Development (Bayley, 1969) may not show deficits when measured with other more physiologically based criteria (for example, heart rate, visual fixation, and habituation). Zelazo suggests that the former measures are greatly affected by environmental and cultural influences. Zelazo appears to believe that physiological measures of perceptual-cognitive processes are somehow more valid or pure than behaviorally based ones. As Berg and Berg argue, however, "there are not grounds for a clear functional distinction nor for a hierarchical one in which one type of response (i.e., behavioral or physiological) is considered to be a priori more valid or direct [and that] both are types of behaviors differing only in the extent to which they are overt or covert" (1979, p. 283). In short, a fuller understanding of cognition is provided by a combination of overt and covert methods.

How cognition is measured in a given situation will remain a function of the specific questions being asked about cognition and the particular bias of the individual who is responsible for its measurement.

ORIGINS OF COGNITION

When we view human development in an evolutionary sense, we see that human beings were predestined to develop a high level of cognition. This is because the human neurological system was genetically endowed for such intellectual activity and because, in evolutionary terms, human beings have been successful in adapting to a variety of environments. According to Scarr-Salapatek (1976) cognition emerged in humans initially as a result of *canalization* or genetic predisposition on the one hand and *developmental adaptation* on the other. Developmental adaptation is the process by which a genotype adapts to varied environments and produces a variety of phenotypes, ensuring survival. Cognition emerges, then, not only because of predetermined genetic endowments resulting in the human neurological structures but also from the ability of those structures to perform in a flexible manner depending on the environment.

Underlying the development of cognition, as the previous discussion would suggest, are the basic neurological structures of the young child. These structures are the hardware through which cognition emerges. They are programmed through interaction with the environment. Put another way, the environment provides the software of cognition. Cognitive abilities develop in young children because of the interplay between neurological structures and cultural/environmental influences. Cross-cultural studies reveal both similarities and differences in cognitive development in different cultures. The differences in general are in the rate of development of specific cognitive abilities and *not* in the sequence. For example, the cognitive abilities described by Piaget (1954), seriation, classification, and conservation, develop in all young children in the same sequence, that is, a child is able to arrange objects in order of size before he is able to conserve. Sensorimotor abilities such as reaching for objects, smiling at them, or searching for them when they are hidden also emerge in a uniform sequence in normally developing infants (Widerstrom, 1979, 1982). However, the rate of acquisition varies depending on the characteristics of the child. Mentally disabled children, for example, follow the same sequence in their development of conservation, but their rate of development is slower (Gallagher & Reid, 1981).

All cultures may be seen as having certain common elements. Like genetic predeterminants, these cultural elements account for the development of the structure and sequence of cognitive function. For example, all cultures expose children to objects, usually to counting, matching, or stacking them. One-to-one mathematical correspondence is a cognitive concept learned by nearly all children everywhere, because their cultures provide the necessary exposure to objects. Specific cultural differences are related to differences in the content of cognition rather than to its sequence and structure. For example, Inuit children generally know a good deal more about snow than do Hawaiian children.

This argument can be carried one step further and be applied to human environments in general. That is to say, all environments inhabited by human beings have certain common elements which define the general course of development. At the same time, every environment has unique features which help to account for the individual variations in cognitive function. Development at any point in time is a function of both environmental and biological factors. Normal development depends on a set of standard biological and environmental conditions.

The current functional level of any individual originates from past and present biological and environmental factors. To the extent that these factors are within normal limits, cognitive function will be developed and maintained within normal limits.

Figure 3.1 provides a matrix for classifying various factors that affect cognitive development. Each cell of the matrix contains examples of biological or environmental factors. The factors are divided into those that may have affected the child's cognitive development in the past and those that may be affecting it presently. These factors not only account independently for development but also, and more importantly, they account for development through interaction with each other.

It should be clear that we will never be able to isolate all of the factors represented by this matrix. To the extent that we are able to isolate these factors and to demonstrate their interrelationships we will understand the origins of cognition and subsequent cognitive functions.

	Biological	*Environmental*
Past	Phylogenetic antecedents Failure to breathe at birth Genotype Low birth weight Malnutrition during infancy	Father absent during first 3 years of life Involvement in day care Maternal attention to inappropriate behavior Confinement to a playpen
Present	Overweight Hunger Increased adrenalin Tiredness Need to defecate Not feeling thirsty	Positive reinforcement for attending to day care teacher A bright cheerful room Verbal disapproval (punishment) for talking out A Holly Hobby doll Mother & father in the same room

FIGURE 3.1   A Matrix for Classifying Factors Accounting for Cognitive Development and Function

COGNITION AND THE
CENTRAL NERVOUS SYSTEM

No discussion of the origins of cognition can proceed very far without a discussion of the central nervous system. While an extremely detailed discussion of the structure and function of the central nervous system (CNS) is beyond the scope of this chapter, some basic understanding of the CNS is necessary to understand cognition. The nature of the human CNS is determined by the genetic uniqueness of human beings. Without the underlying structure of the CNS, human cognition would develop in a very different manner. In considering the CNS, it is convenient to begin with the smallest functional unit, the neuron, and proceed to the largest functional unit, the brain.

The Neuron

The *neuron* or *nerve cell* is the most basic functional unit within the CNS. Like most of the body's cells, the neuron is comprised of a nucleus and cell body (see Figure 3.2). Each neuron has appendages, which perform specialized functions. *Dendrites* pick up impulses and bring them into the neuron. *Axons* transmit impulses to adjacent neurons. The space between the axon of one neuron and the dendrite of the next is the *synapse*. Nerve impulses are passed across the synapse by means of chemical substances called *neural transmitters*. These neural trans-

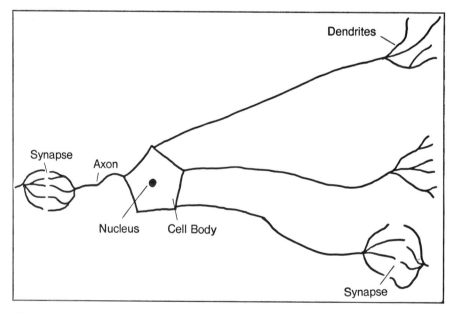

FIGURE 3.2   The Structure of a Neuron

mitters are critical in keeping the nerve impulses moving through the nervous system. At the same time, other substances called *neural inhibitors* prevent impulses from "backing up" through the system. The complementary function of transmitters and inhibitors keeps impulses moving through the CNS in a systematic and orderly manner.

As the CNS matures a process called myelinization occurs. Myelinization results from the build-up of a fatty substance called *myelin*, which surrounds axons and protects them by insulating them. Most of this myelinization process occurs during the first postnatal year.

A unique feature of neurons that significantly affects cognitive development is their inability to reproduce. That is, once a neuron is lost through accident or disease it is lost permanently. When a significant number of neurons is lost, impairment in cognitive function or development is likely to follow.

The major period for growth of neurons is the prenatal period, particularly around four and five fetal months (Smith, 1976). New cells are being added well into postnatal life, however, especially during the first six postnatal months. Once the CNS is completely formed—by the end of the second postnatal year—the number of neurons never increases, although the number may be decreased as a result of insult to the CNS.

As the CNS matures the nerve cells grow in size and develop increasingly complex interconnections with each other. As these interconnections increase, cognitive development proceeds.

A theory of neurophysiological development postulated by Hebb (1949) is particularly helpful in elucidating the relationship between neurological structures and cognitive development. Hebb's theory, although first developed in the late 1940s, is still relevant today. It is useful, too, in demonstrating how environmental stimuli provide the basis for the software of cognitive development. Through sensory input beginning at birth, Hebb suggests that repeated firing of adjacent neurons causes them to form units or *cell assemblies*. By firing we mean the transmittal of a neural impulse through the neuron, from the synapse along dendrites and axon to the cell nucleus and then across another synapse to the next neuron (see Figure 3.2).

As more and more stimulation of the CNS continues, these cell assemblies are integrated into larger units, which Hebb refers to as *phase sequences*. Phase sequences grow out of repeated experiences employing cell assemblies and provide the basis of perceptual integration. Finally, perceptual association and concepts emerge as the repeated use of phase sequences leads to the formation of *phase cycles*. Phase cycles contain the cognitive structures associated with higher order cognitive functions like concept formation and reasoning.

It is important to point out that Hebb believes not only that early stimulation is necessary for the development of cell assemblies, phase sequences, and phase cycles, but that it is necessary to continue their stimulation to maintain their maximum function. Thus, Hebb's theory supports the need to provide young children with environments that stimulate cognitive growth. Such environments are even more necessary for the development of children whose nervous systems may not be intact due to insults or whose nervous systems do not operate as efficiently as possible. Thus, Hebb's theory provides a rationale for early intervention with young children.

This notion has been underscored by research demonstrating that deprived environments can not only affect later perceptual processes but may indeed alter anatomical structures in young organisms. Held and Hein (1963) demonstrated that young kittens deprived of certain visual motor experiences early in life showed impairments in the visual motor domain as adults. More startling perhaps is the research of Riesen (1965) whose studies revealed actual atrophy of visual structures in monkeys reared in environments devoid of meaningful visual stimuli and reduced levels of light. Although ethical concerns would prevent researchers from conducting such experiments with human infants, there is certainly evidence to suggest that environments that deprive infants and young children of sensory and affective experiences lead to performance deficits on tests designed to assess cognitive function (Dennis & Najarian, 1957; Kearsley, 1979; Skeels & Dye, 1939). However, these authors also demonstrate that remediation is possible if environments become more enriching. At the same time continued environmental deprivation can be related to ongoing deficits in cognitive function (Tizard & Tizard, 1971). It should be noted, too, that it is not the *quantity* of stimulation that is important for cognitive growth to take place, but rather the *quality* of stimulation. It is certainly true that some environments, for example, noisy, disorganized, or cluttered ones might provide too much of the wrong kind of stimulation for optimal cognitive development.

The Spinal Cord

The spinal cord is a major component of the central nervous system and provides the main nerve pathway from various areas of the body to the brain. The function of the spinal cord in cognitive development is to relay nerve impulses to and from the brain. Major nerves of the body feed into the spinal cord, which in turn passes information to the brain. Similarly, information from the brain passes down the spinal cord and into various regions of the body. The latter impulses account for many human behavioral responses. For example, walking depends on neural impulses traveling from the brain to muscles of the legs and feet. So in a sense, the spinal cord provides the link between the cognitive programming of an individual and his motor responses.

Although cognition does not reside in the spinal cord, the spinal cord is intimately involved in establishing the relationship between the behavior of a person and her cognitive structures. A spina bifida child, for example, born with an incompletely formed spinal cord, cannot walk even though the joints and muscles of the legs are perfectly normal. The inability of the neural impulses to travel across the injured spinal cord from brain to legs results in a child's inability to walk.

The Brain

The brain consists of three major sections, the *medula oblongata*, the *cerebellum*, and the *cerebral cortex*. These three sections are linked together through the *reticular formation*, which regulates and coordinates the functions of the brain. Whereas the cerebellum and medulla are primarily responsible for postural and basic motor coordination and various autonomic functions, the cortex is responsible for cognitive function. Perception and memory, two of the basic cognitive functions, reside in the cortex and provide the basis for further cognitive development. Brain growth is extremely rapid in infancy, especially during the first six months after birth. Growth is almost complete by two years of age, with the brain reaching 80 percent of its adult size by this age (Smith, 1976).

The cortex is made up of neurons supported structurally by *glial cells*. These glial cells are responsible for the myelinization process. Seen from the top, the cortex appears as two nearly identical halves, split down the middle and bridged by a massive set of nerve fibers called the *corpus callosum*. The two cortical halves, called *right* and *left hemispheres*, communicate with each other primarily by means of the corpus callosum.

Brain researchers have noted with interest that each hemisphere of the cortex is divided into distinct regions called *lobes* (see Figure 3.3). At the front of the brain we find left and right frontal lobes, whereas to the rear are located left and right occipital lobes. Some cortical functions, notably those involving the processing of sensory information, are specific to certain lobes, whereas others are apparently more general. For example, vision appears to be a function of the occipital lobe, hearing is localized in the temporal lobe, and tactile information is

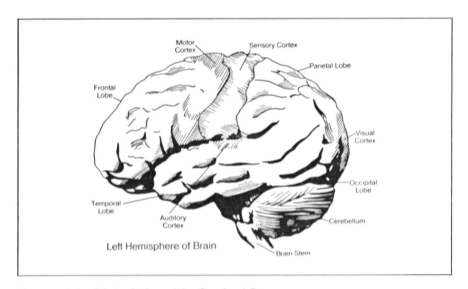

FIGURE 3.3   Major Lobes of the Cerebral Cortex

processed in the parietal lobe. On the other hand, memory is apparently more generally located in several regions of the brain. Verbal language is commonly found in the left hemisphere, while nonverbal language is found in the right hemisphere.

Despite years of research and much recent new knowledge concerning the brain, much of its structure and function remains a mystery (Lindsay & Norman, 1977). Nevertheless, some interesting research has illuminated the specialization of the two hemispheres. This research comes from two sources: laboratory experiments on animals (primarily rats) and clinical observations of people who have suffered brain damage. The present discussion is based on the reporting of Cohen and Martin (1975), Gazzaniga and Blakemore (1975), Levy (1974), Levy, Trevarthen, and Sperry (1972), Lindsay and Norman (1977), and Sperry (1974). Results indicate that the brain consists of two fully equipped central processing systems joined by a very efficient communication system (the corpus callosum). While each hemisphere receives only part of the sensory information arriving from the various sensory receptors, the communicating fibers of the corpus callosum seem to be used to transfer the missing parts of the message to each cortex, so that each half of the brain has a complete representation of the environment. For example, the left side of the brain receives its input from the right hand, right ear, and right half of the visual field; the right brain receives its information from the left side of the body. Thus, the two hemispheres create duplicate memories in a learning task, even when the sensory messages are restricted to only one hemisphere. Interestingly enough, however, when the two hemispheres are disconnected by severing the corpus callosum each is capable of functioning independently. Each half can acquire and store the information needed to perform a learning task, even though each hemisphere is receiving only part of the environmental information. Congenital brain damage affecting the corpus callosum does not produce serious impairment of perceptual or intellectual abilities. Language abilities, however, *will* be affected as we shall see in the following discussion.

Human beings have a higher degree of specialization in hemispheric function than do other species. A great deal of evidence has accumulated in recent years to show that the left and right hemispheres, although physically symmetrical, are not identical in their capabilities or organization (Springer & Deutsch, 1981). The left hemisphere is evidently more skilled at analytical processing, especially the production and understanding of language, and it appears to process input in a sequential manner. The right hemisphere, on the other hand, is more adept at simultaneously processing input, which makes it well suited to deal with visual-spatial tasks. The right hemisphere is said to be more holistic or synthetic in contrast to the analytic character of the left hemisphere (Cohen & Martin, 1975; Levy, 1974). For example, serious disturbances in orientation and awareness have been noted in patients with right hemisphere damage. These patients performed poorly on tasks involving form, distance, depth perception, and other space relationships such as map reading, visual puzzles, and part-whole relationships (Springer & Deutsch, 1981). Musical ability also seems to be a specialty of the right hemisphere, since patients who suffer left hemisphere damage lose their ability to speak but not to sing.

Another difference between the hemispheres is the way they are organized. Right hemisphere processes are distributed over larger regions of brain tissue than left hemisphere processes. This may be associated with the differences in function, analytic versus synthetic, noted above. For example, we would expect the left brain to be better at mathematical concepts requiring analysis and the right brain to be more efficient at processing concepts requiring a holistic approach.

Are there differences in brain asymmetry between right-handed and left-handed people? According to Springer and Deutsch (1981), 95 percent of right-handers and 70 percent of left-handers have left hemisphere control of speech and language. Of the remaining left-handers, half have right hemisphere control and half have bilateral control of speech and language. It is not known why this is so, nor why most people are right handed. The right hemisphere seems able to recognize some language, such as concrete nouns (but not verbs) but cannot *produce* language (Gazzaniga, 1970).

The preceding discussion illustrates that the brain is an incredibly complex and flexible organ. The two halves share many functions and either can take over should an emergency arise. The flexibility is greater in a young child than in an adult, as might be expected. After age 12 the brain loses much of this flexibility (Lindsay & Norman, 1977). The younger the child when brain injury occurs, the better chance for the intact hemisphere to take over the functions of the injured one. The more language has been developed, the more difficult is this process (Gazzaniga & LeDoux, 1978).

In summary, the nervous system plays a vital role in cognitive function. Using a computer as an analog, one might suggest that the structure of the nervous system provides the hardware for programming of cognition. Just like a computer, the nervous system provides the general limits of the cognitive program and accepts its programming only in certain forms. Thus, the nervous system provides the framework for the development of cognition. We will return to this analogy of the computer when we discuss the information processing model of cognition.

BASIC COGNITIVE PROCESSES

Having briefly examined the way the nervous system works, we will now examine some basic cognitive processes, namely attention, perception, and memory. These processes are the most basic forms of cognitive activity from which all others grow. In addition, problems in cognition are most often related to deficits in these areas. Essentially the development of cognitive structures can be related to the efficiency with which the central nervous system performs its function (Benoit, 1959). Inefficiency, of course, results from both biological and environmental factors.

Attention

Attention may be defined as the process by which one focuses awareness. What is not directly attended to will not be perceived or remembered. As Bourne, Dominowski, and Loftus suggest, "Attention is associated with the conscious, active processing required for example, whenever we perceive some event and then remember it later on" (1979, p. 35). Zeaman and his associates (Zeaman & House, 1963, 1979; Fisher & Zeaman, 1973) suggested the cognitive problems of mentally retarded persons may be associated with deficits in attentional processes. They suggest that cognitively retarded persons have difficulty learning to which cues they should attend. Such deficits in attention interfere with movement of information from the sensory input level to short-term memory. Zeaman and colleagues suggest that manipulation of cues and reinforcement of outcomes can help improve these problems. It is important for young children with developmental delays, especially in cognitive areas, to be given the necessary cues and prompts so that their attentional processes can be used to the fullest. Indeed, teaching young, delayed children to tune in to relevant information and to screen out irrelevant stimuli is a major educational goal of most early childhood programs. This basic step, the ability to focus attention on the relevant, which we take for granted as adults, is actually an important prerequisite for successful cognitive development in young, handicapped children.

Perception

John (1976) suggested that human beings are capable of several levels of information processing. The two most basic levels, he suggests, are *sensation* and *perception.* He defines sensations as "patterns of information arriving in the central nervous system" as a result of activity in one of the sense organs of sight, smell, hearing, and the like. "Perceptions," he says, "are the interpretation of the meaning of sensations in the context of stored information about previous experiences" (John, 1976, p. 3). Perception is therefore a cognitive process, because it provides meaning or knowledge of the world to the individual perceiver.

Sensation, while not a cognitive process, is the basis for perception. It is all but impossible to experience sensations without attaching meaning to them. In attaching meaning, perception is taking place.

Very young infants are capable of perception and as Pick relates, "research has been accumulating that suggests that infants are more perceptually precocious than ever imagined" (1976, p. 78). He further suggests that, unlike the qualitative changes found in cognitive development (as discussed later in this chapter), perception does not undergo significant qualitative changes over time. Rather, Pick asserts, the infant's and young child's perceptual processes become increasingly integrated leading to complex perceptual development. Thus, while the basic perceptual processes remain relatively unchanged, the child develops the ability to apply these processes in a more integrated manner.

MODES OF PERCEPTION Each sensory system (visual, auditory, haptic, olfactory, and gustatory) can be associated with a mode of perception. The most commonly studied mode of perception, especially in infants, is the visual mode (Cohen, DeLoache, & Strauss, 1979). This is because it is the easiest mode to study since as Kagan, Kearsley, and Zelazo suggest, "the child announces his attentional investment in an event by orienting his eyes toward it" (1978, p. 62). Because of the extensive study, the visual modality provides the basis for most models of perception. Auditory and haptic perception have been studied to a lesser degree and the smallest amount of attention has been directed to the olfactory and gustatory modes.

Within each mode of perception different perceptual abilities emerge. For example, in the visual mode we find such abilities as perception of depth, size, shape, color, brightness, and movement. In the auditory mode there is perception of pitch, loudness, and language. What aspect of a particular stimulus is perceived, that is, how it is perceived, depends upon the process of attention, which is the means by which perception is directed.

MODELS OF PERCEPTION   Neisser (1976) has contrasted two models of perception. One grows from a traditional view of perception based on an information processing model, the other represents a more active view of perception based upon what Neisser calls anticipatory schema. The information processing model is described as being rather static; the active model, or perceptual cycle, is said to be more dynamic in character.

Neisser (1976) asserts that, in the information processing model,

> the image is not looked at but *processed*. Certain specific mechanisms in the visual system, called *detectors*, are assumed to initiate neural messages in response to certain equally specific features of the image. Information about these features is then passed on to higher stages of the brain. At the higher stages it is collated and combined with previously stored information in a series of processes that eventually results in perceptual experience. [p. 16]

This process is known as *feature analysis*. Figure 3.4 is a representation of the information processing model of perception. Essentially, the perceptual process

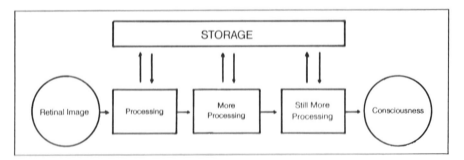

FIGURE 3.4   The Information-Processing Model of Perception. From *Cognition and reality: Principles and implications of cognitive psychology* by U. Neisser. Copyright 1976 by W. H. Freeman and Company. All rights reserved.

defined in the information processing model is a static one. Simply, no change occurs in the perceptual process; environmental stimuli are sensed and perceived.

Neisser (1976) proposes a dynamic model of perception based upon anticipatory schema. Neisser asserts that

> at each moment the perceiver is constructing anticipations of certain kinds of information that enable him to accept it as it becomes available. Often he must actively explore the optic array to make it available, by moving his eyes or his head or his body. These explorations are directed by the anticipatory schemata, which are plans for perceptual action as well as readinesses for particular kinds of optical structure. The outcomes of the explorations—the information picked up—modifies the original schema. Thus modified, it directs further exploration and becomes ready for more information. [pp. 20–21]

This process is called a *perceptual cycle* and is the mechanism that assures continuity of perception over time (Neisser, 1976, p. 22). Figure 3.5 shows the perceptual cycle as outlined by Neisser. An example of a perceptual cycle follows.

A young child sitting by himself in his playing area has called out for his

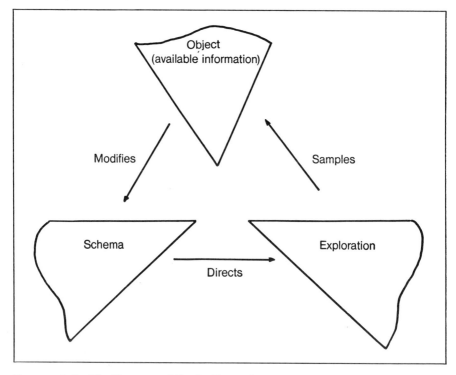

FIGURE 3.5   The Perceptual Cycle. From *Cognition and reality: Principles and implications of cognitive psychology* by U. Neisser. Copyright 1976 by W.H. Freeman and Company. All rights reserved.

mother. The perceptual cycle begins as he looks toward the door in anticipation of her appearance. At the same time he listens for her footsteps. His anticipatory schemata, as Neisser (1976) calls them, direct his visual and auditory explorations. Now mother approaches the room and her appearance in the doorway confirms the child's expectation. The information he expected—his mother's person and voice within his perceptual field—does not require a modification of his anticipatory schemata since her presence has confirmed them. But suppose not mother but father enters through another doorway of the room in response to the call. The child's perceptual cycle must now include a modification to take into account the unexpected, unanticipated visual and auditory information that his father's appearance provides. He has anticipated mother, but his perceptual abilities tell him it is father who has entered; therefore, he must modify his anticipatory schemata to now expect father's voice and father's touch. In this way the cycle is continual, causing the child to constantly anticipate, explore, assess information, and modify anticipations.

Both of these models have as their base the assignment of meaning to the world. Both provide the basis for interpretation of environmental events and so fit our earlier definitions of both cognition and perception.

It is clear that attention and perception are the most basic cognitive processes, and that all information gained from the environment stems from initial perceptual processing. Neonatal infants apparently have the ability to perceive and make sense of their environments to some degree. For perception to occur, schema or stored information in the nervous system must exist. This is true whether one adheres to a perceptual cycle or information-processing model of perception. Thus, at birth infants must have some knowledge of the extrauterine environment even though they have had no direct experience of it. Apparently, this knowledge results from our phylogenetic heritage (cf., Freedman, 1974, Chapter 1) and the infant's interactions with her prenatal environment. In essence, then, the infant may come to the world with "memories" of phylogenetic and prenatal origins! The theories of both Hebb and Piaget, discussed in this chapter, illustrate quite well how cognitive development proceeds from this basic perceptual ability which the infant possesses at birth. To quote Neisser (1976) once again, "Perception itself depends on the skill and experience of the perceiver—on what he knows in advance" (p. 13).

In conclusion, perceptual processes provide the basis for the acquisition of knowledge about one's world (i.e., cognition). As such, perceptual processes are the most basic of all cognitive processes. Perception provides us with the link between that reality which is outside of our bodies and that which is inside, and so our resulting reality becomes whatever we perceive it to be.

Memory

Memory may be defined as the means by which information about the world is stored in the central nervous system. Robinson and Robinson (1976) have suggested that memory can be divided into three stages beginning with encoding or the basic acquisition of information by means of the sensory system (perception, if you will). Encoding is followed by storage—the retention of the information for some period of time (learning, if you will). The third stage is *retrieval* or drawing information back from storage (remembering, if you will). Since the first stage of memory (encoding) is analogous to perceptual processing, it is fair to conclude that deficits in memory may be related to deficits in perceptual abilities. Simply, if something cannot be perceived it cannot be stored in the memory. Conversely, information upon which perception is based is part of the permanent memory store of the individual. Thus, deficits in memory storage can lead to deficits in perceptual processing and vice versa. Attention, memory, and perception are intimately interwoven processes and together form the basis of all other cognitive processes. Nothing is remembered unless it is first attended to and perceived and nothing is attended to or perceived for which previously stored associations are not present. Young developmentally disabled children often exhibit cognitive deficits because of faulty attention, faulty perception, faulty memory, or faulty interaction of the systems with each other.

In a sense, like perceptual modes there are memory modes. For example, we can remember visual stimuli apart from auditory stimuli. Thus being able to remember what has been read is a visual memory skill, whereas remembering what has been said is an auditory memory skill. There are also memory modalities associated with smell, taste, and touch, but like their perceptual counterparts they have been studied to a much smaller degree than visual and auditory modalities. Also like perception, the process of memory does not really change qualitatively with time. Rather as children develop they learn to apply memory strategies in more sophisticated ways and acquire skills that facilitate memory processes.

A MODEL OF MEMORY   One of the most widely accepted models for explaining memory is that put forth by Atkinson and Shiffrin (1968). Because it is based on the input and output of information, it is called an information processing model. Figure 3.6 shows the Atkinson-Shiffrin model in schematic form. The model begins with sensory memory, which has a large capacity but lasts only a

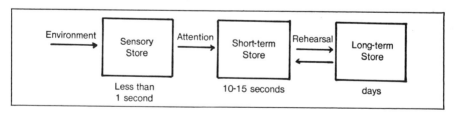

FIGURE 3.6 Schematic Representation of the Atkinson-Shiffrin Model. Adapted from Bourne, L.E., Jr., Dominowski, R.D., & Loftus, E.E. *Cognitive processes.* Englewood Cliffs, N.J.: Prentice-Hall, 1979. Reprinted with permission.

very short period of time, typically about .25 seconds. Through sensory memory initial encoding occurs and the perceptual event enters the memory system. Whether a sensory memory enters the short-term memory store depends on attention.

After entering the short-term store, information can be expected to stay there about 30 seconds. As Robinson and Robinson (1976, p. 286) have pointed out, this information will be "lost through fading or decay, unless there is a deliberate attempt to maintain it." If the material is maintained beyond the normal limit, movement to the long-term store is facilitated. This facilitation is brought about most commonly through a rehearsal mechanism. *Rehearsal* is a strategy by which information in the short-term store is repeated over and over or is practiced in some organized manner. Craik and Lockhart (1972) have suggested that only elaborative rehearsal is effective in moving information to the long-term store from the short-term store. According to these authors *elaborative rehearsal* requires processing the new information by some means that consciously associates it with or relates it to other information already in the long-term store. In essence, their model suggests that the deeper the level of analysis the more likely information is to remain in long-term memory. Rote learning or memorizing, for example, represents a fairly shallow level of analysis. Information learned in this manner is not retained very long.

Young children do not rehearse information spontaneously and consequently must be provided with repeated experiences with the same environmental events in order for long-term memory (learning) to occur. Young children with developmental delays are even less likely to learn rehearsal skills independently and, of course, will do so at a relatively later age (Ellis, 1970). Most nondelayed children will acquire the use of rehearsal strategies between seven and nine years of age. While there is some evidence that older retarded persons can improve their rehearsal skills (Belmont & Butterfield, 1971; Brown et al., 1973; Butterfield, Wambold, & Belmont, 1973), teachers of young developmentally delayed children should be concerned with helping these children learn the prerequisite skills to effective rehearsal and should create learning environments where rehearsal becomes an integral part of the teaching-learning process.

For example, a young child working a puzzle may by trial and error fit all the pieces together. The next day, however, he may not remember what pieces go where and may have to resort again to trial and error. With enough sessions of puzzle working (rehearsals), the child remembers where the pieces go and does not have to try each one out before finding its proper place. Repeated experiences with the same event thus aid learning.

In theory, once information reaches the long-term store it will remain there permanently. The long-term store holds all of the information we have learned over our lifetimes. However, for this information to be useful, it must be retrieved. Information is retrieved by transferring it from the long-term store back to the short-term store. Information is not really forgotten once it enters the long-term store; however, we may become unable to retrieve it. The ability to retrieve information depends on the cues a person is able to employ. These cues may be in the external environment or they may be internal cues in the form of images. These cues provide a means of retrieving the desired inforation with the available cue. Forgetting occurs when we are unable to associate the desired information with the available cues. The work of Tulving and his associates has been of significant importance in demonstrating the role of cues in retrieval processes (cf., Tulving & Pearlstone, 1966; Tulving & Thomason, 1971, 1973) and the interested reader is referred to these souces for additional insight. Some neurological aspects of the storage and retrieval processes are discussed below.

Since learning is a direct outgrowth of memory, any deficiency in memory processes (i.e., encoding, storage, or retrieval) can result in overall cognitive deficits. It is difficult, however, to pinpoint where deficits occur. For example, take a young child who cannot point to the color red when asked to do so. Her inability to perform this task, given the nooooooary motivation, would suggest that the child has not learned the color red. This lack of learning may be a result of any of several factors: (1) the child's inability to encode the necessary information, (2) the inability to attend to the necessary cues, (3) the inability to transfer the encoded information from short-term to long-term store, (4) the inability to retrieve the information from the long-term store.

Research into the physiological mechanisms of memory has revealed some interesting facts concerning the storage and retrieval of information in long-term and short-term memory. Scientists have long been interested in these different forms of memory. Is short-term store somehow converted into long-term store? Or are they separate functions? Is one more durable than the other? Answers to these questions are gradually being revealed. For a more detailed review of this research than the one following, the reader is referred to the excellent discussion by Lindsay and Norman (1977).

Studies of victims of retrograde amnesia, a common form of amnesia brought about by a severe jolt to the brain, such as a fall or a blow to the head, reveal that the victims forget events prior to the accident. They tend to forget more recent events completely but to remember events from long ago. Memory seems to be erased starting from the accident and extending backwards for a duration proportional to the severity of the wound. Interestingly enough, only memory for events appears to be affected. Other kinds of stored information, notably language comprehension and use, are not affected. These patients almost always recover their memories, and it is the old memories that return first.

This pattern confirms that different processes are responsible for storage and retrieval. It is the retrieval process that is disrupted by brain trauma, not the storage process. Apparently information in long-term store is very strong—quite resistant to destruction through brain damage. But the neural process for getting at it and retrieving the information is more vulnerable.

Other research has provided evidence that disruption of short-term memory interferes with storage of information in long-term memory. There is a direct relationship between short and long-term store. Information apparently enters short-term store first and then, if certain conditions take place, the information is consolidated in long-term store. One of these necessary conditions may be the synthesis of protein in the neurons and at the synaptic junctions. These new proteins may then permanently alter the responsibilities of the neuron. Thus short and long-term memory may represent different phases of activity that occur at the neuron (Lindsay & Norman, 1977). There is a time period during which only temporary (short-term) memory exists. The period of time until the permanent trace (long-term) is established is called the *consolidation period*. The precise nature of the consolidation process is not at present known.

In summary, memory, perception, and attention are basic cognitive processes that interact to provide the basis for the development of later cognitive structures. Indeed any cognitive structure is stored in memory and thus is dependent on the efficient function of memory to be useful. Deficits in one of attention, perception, or memory are likely to result in deficits in other areas of cognitive functioning.

Now is the time to examine some models of cognitive development and functioning.

THE DEVELOPMENT OF COGNITION

Buckminister Fuller relates the story of a father who, upon observing a picture drawn by his young son, inquired why the child had included both the *moon* and the *sun* in his picture since both are not in the sky at the same time. Fuller's query, which followed the anecdote, was "But indeed aren't the sun and the moon in the sky at the same time?" Although meant to show both the innocence and wisdom of childhood, Fuller's story also points up an example of the qualitative difference in children's and adults' cognition. The young child in Fuller's story was unable to see anything unusual about the moon and the sun both being in the scene which he had drawn. The father, on the other hand, had a different reality, or knowledge of the world. The issue is not who's "right" but rather the differences evident in the father's and son's views of the world (i.e., in their knowing or cognition).

Several authors have devised theoretical models to account for the development of cognition. One, Hebb's neurophysiological model, was briefly described earlier in the chapter. Another, the information-processing model, was alluded to in the discussion of perception and memory. In this section we will discuss two other models.

Piaget

Piaget devoted years of study to the changes in cognitive processes in young children. His research methodology consisted of extremely detailed observations made of the behavior of a single child. Unlike anecdotal or running records used by classroom teachers (as well as by ethologists in animal behavior research), Piaget was not content to simply observe the child's behavior as objectively as possible. Rather, his practice was to manipulate the situation in some way in order to test the child's reaction. For example, upon observing him sucking on the nipple, Piaget offered his infant son the edge of a blanket to see whether he would suck that object as vigorously.

With older children, Piaget both observed their approach to a learning task and carefully questioned them to get at their thinking processes. Piaget made at least two important contributions to cognitive psychology: (1) a theory of the construction of knowledge, which has strongly influenced educational thought in the United States, and (2) a research methodology, the *méthode clinique*, that incorporates advantages of both naturalistic and laboratory techniques of child study. Since research methodology is not the focus of the present discussion, we will confine our review to Piaget's cognitive theory.

Piaget believed that each person constructs his or her knowledge of the world through a process that involves both the external environment and internal cognitive processes. According to Piaget, a child constructs new knowledge by a process that involves *assimilating* information from the environment, combining it with previously held ideas (*accommodation*), and constructing a new understanding.

This much of Piaget's theory is fairly widely known and understood. However, certain of his concepts are often ignored or misinterpreted and erroneously applied to educational practice. For example, Piaget believed that a state of *disequilibration* or disequilibrium was necessary in order for learning to take place. Disequilibration occurs when the child assimilates information that contradicts her previously held ideas or, as Piaget would say, her existing cognitive structures. The contradiction causes her to question her previous conclusions and perhaps to alter them to accommodate the new idea. When the child reaches a new level of understanding about the matter, equilibration is reestablished. This process of disequilibration is the means by which new information is incorporated into existing cognitive structures, expanding them and increasing the child's ability for more complex functioning. Piaget describes this process as "the spiral of knowing" (Gallagher & Reid, 1981) because the assimilation of the new knowledge depends on the existence of previous structures of knowledge into which the new ideas are incorporated. It is modification of already existing concepts through interaction with the environment that brings a child to a higher, more advanced level of knowledge.

Piaget constantly refined his theory of cognitive development. He developed the concept of the spiral of knowing only a few years before his death. Although he did not intend it to replace his stage theory, he believed that the spiral concept better describes the process by which knowledge is constructed than do the strictly separate levels of functioning implicit in a stage theory.

Perhaps an example will help to clarify the equilibration process. The following is adapted from Gallagher and Reid's (1981) excellent discussion.

When a child is presented with a problem, he first tries to solve it by assimilation, that is, by using available strategies. If the strategies work, no modification of the child's cognitive structures will take place. For example, if a child who has sorted red, blue, and yellow into piles of squares and circles is then presented with a blue square, she will probably have little difficulty in placing it in the pile with the other squares. However, if she is presented with a blue triangle, the problem is not so easily solved, for there is no pile of similar shapes. The classification system breaks down. Simple assimilation will not solve the problem. The contradiction represented by trying to classify the triangle with squares and circles creates a state of disequilibrium and the child may react in several ways. She may ignore the contradiction and place the triangle in the pile of squares or place it in a new pile by itself. These solutions represent *compensations* (activities aimed at neutralizing a contradiction) which maintain the existing strategy and lead to very little accommodation or change in structure. Piaget refers to these as *alpha behaviors* (Piaget, 1977).

Instead of ignoring the problem the child may change her strategy to better accommodate the blue triangle. She may decide to group by color rather than by shape, thus compensating for the contradiction and at the same time expanding her repertoire of grouping strategies. This solution, which involves both assimilation and accommodation and therefore modification of existing structures, is called *beta behavior* (Piaget, 1977).

A third solution is that the child may have already anticipated the possibility of grouping by color or size or thickness before being presented with the triangle, and so experiences no contradiction. This anticipation of all possibilities is known as *gamma behavior* (Piaget, 1977).

These three kinds of equilibration are important in considering the educational needs of mentally retarded youngsters. While very young children generally use the simpler alpha behaviors described above, those with average cognitive functioning develop quite independently into beta and gamma equilibrations. Mentally retarded children do not. It is important for teachers to be aware of the level of responses made by young retarded children and to encourage beta behavior as much as possible, calling attention to alternative strategies, demonstrating alternatives, and so on. Teachers should also be aware that gamma behavior is very difficult for the truly retarded child. If many such behaviors are observed in a child who has been labeled mentally retarded it would be well to review the diagnosis, for the diagnosis may be incorrect.

Another area of misunderstanding encountered in Piagetian thought is that of *operations*. Piaget defines operations as actions which the child performs mentally and which are reversible (Ginsburg & Opper, 1979). By *reversible* we mean that for each particular mental action, for example, addition, the child can perform its opposition action, in this case, subtraction. Piaget divided children's construction of knowledge into two categories: those that involve the performance of operations and those that do not. Piagetian stages include two preoperational (sensorimotor and preoperational) and two operational (concrete operations and formal operations). These are discussed in some detail below.

Many people apparently believe that providing a child with opportunities for physical manipulation of objects is the key to applying Piagetian theory to education. The concept of operations tells us that this is not accurate. When he studied the child's interaction with objects, Piaget concentrated on the child's *mental* manipulations. Thinking about objects and how they work, observing transformations in them (e.g., water to ice and back to water as temperature changes), and predicting what will happen to them—these mental activities are more important to the construction of new knowledge than is actual physical manipulation.

The implication for teachers is obvious. It is important to encourage children to think about the objects and events in their environment. One way to do this is to ask open-ended questions about activities in which the child is engaged. Another is to provide opportunities for each child to experiment informally with objects. Even mentally retarded preschoolers can benefit from trial and error approaches to learning, particularly if they are guided along the way. They do require more direction from the teacher in exploring alternatives, but to assume that such children learn only by methods involving external reinforcement is to underestimate them.

Preschool children are commonly found in the sensorimotor period and the preoperational period. The normally developing child takes approximately eighteen months to two years to progress through the sensorimotor stages (beginning at birth) and about the next five years (to age seven) to complete the preoperational stage. For a more complete review of Piaget's stages of cognitive development, the reader is referred to Piaget (1952), Ginsburg and Opper (1979), or Flavell (1977).

A child with developmental delays, while progressing through the same stages and in the same order as nonhandicapped children, advances at a slower rate. Both the rate of progress and the ultimate level of development attained appear to be dependent upon the severity of the retardation (Gallagher & Reid, 1981). Mildly retarded persons usually attain concrete operations; the moderately retarded generally reach preoperations; but the severely retarded are unable to advance beyond the sensorimotor stage (Inhelder, 1968).

SENSORIMOTOR STAGE   Piaget believed that an infant is born with a neurological system of reflexes that at first operate pretty much automatically but soon come under the infant's control. The reflexive actions cause the infant to assimilate more and more information (visual, auditory, tactile) about the world and to modify her behavior as a result. For example, an infant learns to suck whatever comes in contact with her mouth. At first this is a purely reflexive action, but it is not long before the infant learns to deliberately explore new objects in this manner, and for many months she brings new objects to the mouth for examination. As she learns more and more objects, she modifies her behavior to accommodate the new information. For example, she opens her mouth wide for a large object such as a rubber ball, but closes her mouth around a small key on a keychain.

These reflexive actions are the beginning of sensorimotor intelligence, which the infant develops by physically exploring objects with hands, mouth, eyes, and ears. It will be many years before she is able to learn about the world through solely mental activity. Indeed, even as adults we continue to learn many things through physical exploration.

Piaget suggests that sensorimotor development proceeds in five distinct domains as cognitive development moves forward. These domains are object permanence, means-ends relationships, spatial relationships, imitation, and play. While the text below gives a general description of each of the six stages of the sensorimotor period, Table 3.1 provides a summary of characteristic behaviors in each of the five domains during the six stages of sensorimotor development.

Stage 1—The use of reflexes (0–1 month). At this stage the infant's reflex behaviors are modified through activity and new patterns of behavior emerge. For example, the infant is born with a strong sucking reflex and initially uses this reflex with the nipple. During Stage 1, however, he learns to use this reflex in other situations, such as sucking on the edge of his blanket.

Stage 2—Primary circular reactions (1–4 months). The infant's behavior, by chance, leads to an interesting or advantageous result which is then repeated through trial and error until it becomes a habit. For example, a circular reaction develops as the infant learns to bring his hand to his mouth and suck his thumb. These primary circular reactions are always centered on the infant's own body.

Stage 3—Secondary circular reactions (5–8 months). In Stage 3 the infant's horizons expand as she begins to crawl and manipulate objects. The circular reactions of this stage are called "secondary," since they now involve events or objects in the external environment. The secondary circular reactions are the result of the infant's ability to reproduce interesting or advantageous events that were initially discovered by chance.

Stage 4—Coordination of secondary schemes (8–12 months). At this stage the infant's behavior is more goal-directed than previously. Rather than accidentally discovering a goal as at Stage 3, the infant has the goal in mind from the beginning. Patterns of previously learned behavior are applied to new problems in order to achieve the goal. Stage 4 is sometimes known as the application of old means to new situations.

Stage 5—Discovery of new means through active experimentation (12–18 months). In Stage 5, behavior loses its emphasis on what has been previously learned, and the child who has now begun to walk begins to search for novelty. At this stage the child's interest is not focused so much on himself and those properties of an object which aid him in attaining some goal, but rather he seems curious about the object as an object, and he seems desirous of learning all he can about its nature. This interest in novelty for its own sake is called a tertiary circular reaction. Instead of simply repeating the behaviors that produced the interesting event, as at Stage 3 and 4, the child begins to experiment to produce variations in the event. New means to a goal are discovered through experimentation.

Stage 6—Invention of new means through mental combinations (18–24 months). Stage 6 is marked by the ability to use mental symbols and words to refer to absent objects. This frees the child from dependence on immediate experience and introduces the world of possibilities. Rather than needing to act out solutions to problems, the child is now beginning to be able to do problem solv-

TABLE 3.1   Major Accomplishments of the Sensorimotor Period

SENSORIMOTOR STAGE	OBJECT PERMANENCE	MEANS-END	CAUSALITY	SPATIAL	IMITATION	PLAY
I. Reflexes Slight modifications of initial reflexes (sucking, grasping, arm/leg movements).	No differentiation of developments in these areas. Behavior is at the level of exercising reflexes.				No imitation of new responses. May be stimulated to respond by external events (e.g., may start crying when hears other infants crying).	No evidence of play.
II. Primary Circular Reactions Reflexes undergo adaptations to environmental experience; coordinations between responses beginning (e.g., looking at grasped object).	There are no special adaptations as yet to the vanished object. Related developments during this period include visual pursuit of a slowly moving object by (1) following through arc of 180°; (2) reacting to disappearance of a slowly moving object by maintaining gaze at point of disappearance.	Differentiation between means-end and causality is not possible at this stage. The following are prerequisites for both: (1) visual examination of hand, (2) visually directed grasp, (3) repetition of movements which produce environmental effect, (4) refinements in reach and grasp.		Child: (1) switches gaze from one visual stimulus to another, (2) turns to localize a noise made outside the visual field, (3) looks to other end of opaque screen when object disappears at one end.	No imitation of new responses. When others imitate infants' responses, infants may repeat or intensify own responses.	Infants will repeat primary circular reactions for the pleasure of repetition (called *functional assimilation*).

III. Secondary Circular Reactions

Schemata are repeated. This systematically produces a change in, and effect on, the environment.

Child: (1) moves to look after a fallen object, (2) searches for a partly hidden object, (3) returns gaze to starting point when a slowly moving object disappears, (4) searches for object under single screen.

Child: (1) moves to object out of reach, (2) pulls a support to obtain a toy attached to the support.

Child responds to cessation of a spectacle (that she cannot reproduce) by touching the adult or the toy.

Child: (1) follows movement of rapidly moving object, (2) rotates trunk to receive object moved behind her, (3) examines objects by turning them over.

No imitation of new responses *but* infants will "imitate" model's response if that response is familiar to them *but* they can "imitate" in this way *only* responses that they can see or hear themselves perform.

Relaxed repetition of responses can be distinguished from the serious business of attempting to adapt to new experiences. Infants enjoy activity for its own sake without need for external reinforcement.

IV. Coordination of Secondary Circular Reactions

Schemata are used together for intentional results.

Child finds an object hidden under one of two screens by searching directly under the correct screen, up to three screens.

Child: (1) does not pull support if object is held above it, (2) expands pulling scheme to other tools such as strings both horizontal and vertical (vertical use requires object permanence as object is not in view).

Child responds to cessation of a spectacle, by handing the toy to the adult, but may first try to reproduce the spectacle by direct action on the toy.

Child: (1) brings functionally related objects together, i.e., cup and spoon, (2) begins container play by taking an object out of container then placing one in at a time, building to larger numbers.

Infants overcome the limitations of Stage 3. *Can* imitate simple new responses, even those they cannot see or hear themselves perform.

Infants can abandon goal-directed behavior in favor of playing with actions directed at obstacle. Engage in ritualized play (e.g., infants may act out ritual of going to sleep when they come upon their pillows).

V. Tertiary Circular Reactions

Child, through trial and error procedures, discovers new means

Child: (1) finds an object after a single invisible displacement, (2) follows

Child uses an unattached tool such as a rake to get an object.

Child: (1) lets a toy continue activity without intervention, (2) attempts

Child: (1) empties container by dumping, (2) moves around

Imitate more precisely the behaviors of a model, including more

Rapidly convert newly acquired responses to play rituals.

(continued)

TABLE 3.1 Continued

SENSORIMOTOR STAGE	OBJECT PERMANENCE	MEANS-END	CAUSALITY	SPATIAL	IMITATION	PLAY
to obtain desired goals. Requires combination of previous schemata.	objects through a series of visible displacements and searches in correct location, (3) finds an object hidden from view and taken through successive displacements.		to activate a toy after demonstration.	barriers to obtain objects, (3) builds a tower of blocks.	subtle or complex responses. Experiment with different ways of imitating different models.	
VI. Invention of New Means through Mental Combinations						
Child is assumed to solve problems representationally and then applies a solution to the problem situation.	Child searches along path in a complex problem when object is left in first location and the examiner's hand moves through the entire path. The child searches systematically until the object is found.	Child solves problem through "foresight"; for example, does not attempt to stack a solid ring on a pole.	Child displays spontaneous attempt to activate a toy.	Child recognizes absence of familiar persons.	Readily imitate complex new behaviors. Imitate actions of objects as well as people.	Engage in symbolic play (pretense or make-believe).

Adapted from C.C. Robinson and J.H. Robinson. Sensorimotor function and cognitive development. In M.E. Snell (ed.) *Systematic instruction of the moderately and severely handicapped.* Columbus: Charles Merrill, 1978; and from T.L. Kodera and S.G. Garwood. The acquisition of cognitive competence. In S.G. Garwood (ed.) *Educating young handicapped children: A developmental approach.* Reprinted by permission of Aspen Systems Corporation, © 1979.

ing through thinking. Piaget believed that this is because the child is able to represent mentally an object or action which is not perceptually represented.

PREOPERATIONAL PERIOD   Until about seven years old a child cannot perform mental operations correctly. One general characteristic of cognitive activity during this period is *centration*. The child tends to focus on a limited amount of the information available. He tends to focus on one dimension of his problem and fails to take into account other dimensions, failing to appreciate the relations between the two. He also concentrates on the *static* state of a situation rather than on a dynamic transformation. In addition, the preoperational child's thought lacks *reversibility*. By this we mean that the child is unable to perform the steps of a mental operation in reverse in order to arrive at the starting point again. These limitations on his thought processes prevent the preoperational child from making accurate observations about the physical world.

CONCRETE OPERATIONS   Between the ages of seven and nine years the child overcomes the limitations described in the previous paragraph. She learns to decenter and take into account both dimensions of a problem, and thus her mental operations become more accurate. Nevertheless, she is still bound by immediate perceptions and is not able to take into account the range of possibilities in solving a problem. Her mental operations are performed on concrete objects, which are present and observable, rather than on abstract concepts.

FORMAL OPERATIONS   As the child enters adolescence he is able to perform mental operations and arrive at conclusions without manipulating concrete objects. The adolescent makes reality secondary to possibility. He imagines that many things might occur, that many interpretations of the data might be feasible, and he is able to hypothesize various alternatives.

McCall

Piaget's approach relied on systematic observation of his own children in both naturalistic and contrived situations. McCall's (1979) approach was based on statistical analysis of psychometric data. McCall and his associates (McCall, Appelbaum, & Hogarty, 1973; McCall, Eichorn, & Hogarty, 1977) demonstrated the qualitative transitions in the cognitive development of infants and young children. Using data from the Berkeley Growth Study (Bayley, 1970), McCall, Eichorn, and Hogarty (1977) used principal components analysis to identify the major components of cognitive functioning at various times within the first two years of life. McCall (1979) concluded that five major stages of cognitive development emerge in the first two years of life. The major characteristics of these stages can be found in Table 3.2. As can be seen in Table 3.2 and Figure 3.7, the stages outlined by McCall are similar in structure to those espoused by Piaget and his colleagues (Piaget, 1951, 1952, 1954) although they are organized somewhat differently.

TABLE 3.2   Major Attributes of the Stages of Infant Cognitive Development Proposed by McCall and Piaget

	McCALL	PIAGET
Stage I	Period of the Newborn (0–2 mos.) Infant governed by internal behavior and is dependent on biological status	Use of Reflexes (0–1 mo.) Infant practices existing reflexes in various situations
Stage II	Complete Subjectivity (2–7 mos.) Infant knows world only through physical contact	Primary Circular Reactions (1–4 mos.) Infant learns to extend reflexes to involve activity centered upon her own body.
Stage III	Separation of Means from Ends (7–13 mos.) Infant recognizes his action on the world but still knows the world only through his own actions	Secondary Circular Reactions (5–8 mos.) Infant acts intentionally using schemes which become more interrelated and include objects from the external environment
Stage IV	Objectification of Environmental Entities (13–21 mos.) Infant has separated means from ends. Mental operations are present and the infant is no longer dependent on direct action to operate on the world	Object Permanence & Coordination of Secondary Schemes (8–12 mos.) Object permanence emerges. Infant shows goal-directed behavior and will attempt to influence the future
Stage V	Symbolic Relations (21+ mos.) Infant engages in symbolic representation. The infant recognizes the independences of actions and entities	Tertiary Circular Reactions (12–18 mos.) Infant uses new response patterns to bring about novel results. Infant recognizes cause-effect relationships
Stage VI		Invention of New Means through mental combinations (18–24 mos.) The infant develops foresight and plans activities. Schemes and mental symbols combined internally

Notice also that while the terminology used by McCall and Piaget are somewhat different, the *sequence* of cognitive development is essentially the same in both conceptualizations. As was mentioned earlier in this chapter, research has generally supported the notion that this sequence is relatively stable across cultures (e.g., Bovet, Dasen, & Inhelder, 1974; and Lezine, Stambek, & Casati, 1969) and with children having retarded development (e.g., Kahn, 1976; Rogers, 1977; Woodward, 1959, 1961, 1962).

In fact, such compelling evidence exists that mentally retarded children develop cognitively in the same way normally developing children do, only at a slower rate, that we believe teachers of mentally retarded children should follow a normal developmental sequence in planning curriculum.

McCall	I	II	III	IV	V
	Stage I Period of New Born	Stage II Complete Subjectivity	Stage III Separation of Means from Ends	Stage IV Objectification of the Environment	Stage V Symbolic Relations

Piaget	I	II	III	IV	V	VI
	Stage I Stabilization of Reflexes	Stage II Primary Circular Responses	Stage III Secondary Circular Responses	Stage IV Object Permanence & Coordination of Secondary Schema.	Stage V Tertiary Circular Responses	Stage VI Invention of New Means

```
 ı  ı  ı  ı  ı  ı  ı  ı  ı  ı  ı  ı  ı  ı  ı  ı  ı  ı  ı  ı  ı  ı  ı  ı
                      1  1  1  1  1  1 ·1  1  1  1  2  2  2  2  2  2  2  2
 1  2  3  4  5  6  7  8  9  0  1  2  3  4  5  6  7  8  9  0  1  2  3  4  5  6  7
```

MONTHS

FIGURE 3.7   The Emergence of Cognitive Development in the First Twenty-Four Months

PROBLEMS IN COGNITION

Problems of cognition that are manifest in the preschool years tend to be more severe in nature than do those that appear later. At the same time, these problems tend to be general, rather than specific, in nature. Mental retardation affects cognition at a general level, whereas learning disability affects cognition at a specific level. Thus on one level, a young retarded child could be said to have a general deficit in cognitive function, while a young learning disabled child could be said to have a specific deficit in perceptual or memory process.

Mental Retardation

In discussing mental retardation in children under six, it is important to distinguish between physiological and environmental factors related to cause. The etiology of severe mental retardation, usually identifiable during the perinatal period, is nearly always associated with biological factors. Milder forms of mental retardation, many of which are not identified in young children until they enter a preschool program, are generally associated with environmental deprivation. Many children labeled mildly retarded in school are not considered so at home and in the community where they live (Mercer, 1973). Children who are identified as mentally retarded before age three are usually severely enough impaired that there is little question about the appropriateness of the label. In children from three to five years, however, when milder forms are identified, there may be differences of opinion in making the diagnosis. The present discussion will focus on definitions of mental retardation and on the characteristics of mentally retarded preschool children.

DEFINITIONS   All definitions of mental retardation include references to the general cognitive or intellectual functioning of children. In addition, some of them include concepts like adaptive behavior or social competence. Adaptive behavior has to do with how well a person can adapt to and function independently in her environment. A person who demonstrates behavior that is adaptive may not be as retarded as a simple IQ score indicates. For example, adaptive behavior in young children may involve self-care skills such as feeding, toileting, and dressing self; ability to socialize with peers; and the ability to abstain from self-destructive, stereotypical behaviors.

Both adaptive behavior and social competence are relatively more difficult to assess in preschool children especially those below the age of three years. Thus, the term developmental delay rather than mental retardation is often used to describe this population. A child who is identified as developmentally delayed has an increased risk of being labeled mentally retarded later, usually upon entrance to kindergarten or first grade. Through understanding the developmental process discussed earlier in this chapter as well as the characteristics of persons labeled mentally retarded, a person concerned with preschool children can be more effective in facilitating a delayed child's development and hopefully prevent the application of the label mentally retarded at some future date.

Most early definitions of mental retardation stressed the biological or genetic causes of the condition (e.g., Ireland, 1900; Tregold, 1908; Penrose, 1949; Jervis, 1952; Benoit, 1959; Luria, 1963). It was not until the American Association on Mental Deficiency (AAMD) first produced an official definition (Heber, 1959), which it has revised periodically, that mental retardation was defined as related to environmental factors. For example, the revision of the AAMD definition (Heber, 1961) was:

> Mental retardation refers to subaverage general intellectual functioning which originates in the developmental period and is associated with impairment in adaptive behavior. [Heber, 1961, p. 3]

In 1973 the AAMD definition was revised to its present form as follows:

> Mental retardation refers to significantly subaverage general intellectual functioning existing concurrently with deficits in adaptive behavior, and manifested during the developmental period. [Grossman, 1973, p. 5]

The significance of the 1973 revisions lies first in its elimination of the borderline category since "significantly subaverage" means at least two standard deviations below the mean (i.e., IQ 70). Second, the 1973 revision clearly established the place of adaptive behavior deficits in defining mental retardation. Table 3.3 sets out the provisions of the 1973 AAMD definition.

The AAMD definition also provided criteria for deciding whether a given child should be labeled mentally retarded under the terms of the definition.

TABLE 3.3   Provisions of the 1973 AAMD Definition of Mental Retardation

General Definition: Significantly subaverage general intellectual functioning existing concurrently with deficits in adaptive behavior and manifested during the developmental period

Significantly Subaverage: Two or more standard deviations below the mean

Developmental Period: Upper age limit of 18 years

Adaptive Behavior: Defined as effectiveness or degree with which the individual meets the standards of personal independence and social responsibility expected of his age and cultural group. Adaptive behavior may be reflected in the following areas:

A. Infancy and early childhood:
   1. Sensory motor skills
   2. Communication skills
   3. Self-help skills
   4. Socialization

B. Childhood and early adolescence
   1. Application of basic academic skills to activities of daily life
   2. Application of appropriate reasoning and judgement in mastery of the environment
   3. Social skills

C. Late adolescence and adulthood
   1. Vocation and social responsibilities and performances

Levels of Mental Retardation: Mild (2–3 SD); Moderate (3–4 SD); Severe (4–5 SD); Profound (>5 SD)

*SD = standard deviation
Modified from Kauffman & Payne (1975, pp. 27–29) and reprinted with the permission of the publisher.

Standard intelligence tests were to be used to identify "subaverage intellectual functioning" and tests of adaptive behavior were developed to measure adaptive behavior.

Advances in the measurement of adaptive behavior through the publication of the AAMD Adaptive Behavior Scale (Nihara et al., 1969) was certainly instrumental in bringing about the 1973 revision. The Adaptive Behavior Scale established an objective means for measuring adaptive behavior in particular for lower functioning individuals. The original scale was revised in 1974 (Nihara et al., 1974).

An important aspect of the AAMD definitions (Heber, 1959, 1961; and Grossman, 1973) is that they are concerned with the operationalization of mental retardation. Almost all earlier definitions had been theoretical statements about the construct of mental retardation. While they guided conceptual advancements, these definitions were not of particular use in the actual identification and diagnosis of mentally retarded persons. Diagnosis is concerned with determining whether or not a particular individual fits the classification identified by a definition. For example, does person X fit into the category mentally retarded as defined by Grossman (1973)? Such a determination is made through operational measures (e.g., standard intelligence tests, adaptive behavior scales, etc.)

However, psychometrists encounter problems when applying the definition to very young children. The standardized intelligence tests most widely used for determining subaverage intellectual functioning are the Stanford-Binet and the Wechsler. Neither of these have norms for children under two years of age. A commonly used instrument for children age birth to two years is the Bayley Scales of Infant Development. However, the predictive validity of this and other infant tests is very low (Bayley, 1970; McCall, 1971; Zelazo, 1979). In a sense, the AAMD definition is not valid for children under two years of age. For this reason, many practitioners prefer to use the term developmental delays when working with infants and toddlers.

CLASSIFICATIONS Table 3.3 shows that the AAMD definition (Grossman, 1973) identifies four levels of severity associated with mental retardation. Each of these levels is defined by IQ ranges determined approximately by successive subtractions of standard deviations from the mean. Table 3.4 shows the differences in IQ range for the Stanford-Binet and Wechsler for the four levels of mental retardation. While this classification scheme is probably the most widely used today, at least two other major classification systems deserve some discussion. The first is the most commonly used educational classification system, the second is a medical classification system.

Educators have tended to use a classification that, while tied to IQ levels, also suggests the degree of educability of retarded individuals. Gearhart (1972) offers the following categories as those most accepted among American educators.

Dull/Normal	IQ 76–85
Educable Mentally Retarded (EMR)	IQ 50–75
Trainable Mentally Retarded (TMR)	IQ 30–49
Totally Dependent	IQ < 30

TABLE 3.4 IQ Ranges for AAMD Levels of Mental Retardation According to Stanford-Binet and Wechsler Scores

LEVEL	STANFORD-BINET IQ RANGE	WECHSLER IQ RANGE
Mild	68–52	69–55
Moderate	51–36	54–40
Severe	35–20	39–25
Profound	< 20	< 25

The category of totally dependent has also been termed custodial and more recently Severely Mentally Retarded (SMR) or Profoundly Mentally Retarded (PMR). The term custodial has lost more and more of its popularity because of its connotation that individuals so classified are unable to learn and merely have to be cared for. The early classification system of idiot (IQ 25), imbecile (IQ 25–50), and moron (IQ 50–75) roughly corresponds to the classification of SMR, TMR, and EMR.

As part of the definitional process, Grossman (1973) presented a classification scheme based on the medical etiology associated with a mentally retarded person. This classification system includes ten major biological conditions including: (1) infections and intoxications; (2) trauma or physical agents; (3) metabolism and nutrition; (4) gross brain disease; (5) unknown prenatal influence; (6) chromosomal abnormalities; (7) gestational disorders; (8) following psychiatric disorder; (9) environmental influences; (10) other conditions. Each of these major headings is subdivided further.

In general, classification systems provide guidelines for describing mentally retarded individuals. They do not, however, prove very useful as a means for planning or implementing specific programmatic interventions. Specific information about the behavioral functioning and present environmental system of a particular child is more useful for program planning. On the other hand, the scope of these classification systems taken as a group confirms the complex and heterogeneous nature of mental retardation.

CHARACTERISTICS   Young, mentally retarded children generally display a wide variety of characteristics. The following discussion is a brief review of those particularly seen in children below age five.

Retarded children commonly have delays in all areas of development. Language, cognitive, social, and motor skills are usually delayed to some degree. Moderately to severely retarded preschoolers generally lack expressive language except for certain single-word utterances. They also do not respond to verbal requests, often ignoring the adult who attempts interaction with them. Similarly, they have poor eye contact and they lack the ability to tune in or attend to a person or event. They often resist social interactions with adults as well as with their peers and are slow to initiate interactions.

Motor delays are usually apparent in seriously retarded youngsters. These may be complicated by the interference of primitive reflexes in the voluntary movement patterns (see Chapter 6). Even when reflex interference is minimal, these children exhibit problems in coordination, balance, and control of movement. Severely retarded children may be completely non-ambulatory, particularly if their developmental level is early sensorimotor period.

Severely retarded children may also be prone to self-stimulating or stereotypical behaviors, some of which may be self-injurious (such as biting the hand until it is raw). They generally have problems with toilet training. In temperament, moderately and severely retarded youngsters vary from the docile good nature for which Down's children are famous to the more stubborn and willful. In this sense they are very much like normally developing children.

Cognitively, these children perform at a very concrete level. They have difficulty with time concepts and do better with problems in the present than with those in the past or future. Many repetitions are necessary for new learning to be truly assimilated.

Learning Disabilities

Learning disabilities are more apt to be identified in school age children than in preschool age children. Certainly the existence of a learning disability would be difficult, if not impossible, to detect in a child under three years of age, because learning disabilities are most commonly associated with problems in reading and writing. Persons responsible for services to young children need to be aware of the characteristics of learning disabled children so that when preschool children begin to display these characteristics, the necessary interventions can be designed to remediate their difficulties. If successful, these interventions can do a great deal toward assuring the later success of these children and maximize their probability of placement in the mainstream of the educational system. Three to five year old children who exhibit these characteristics are often classified as learning disabled in the primary grades. Proper intervention reduces the risk of such labels. Unfortunately many of the characteristics of truly learning disabled children remain relatively subtle during the preschool years. It is useful, nonetheless, to briefly describe the major characteristics of learning disabilities that may be seen in children before age five. It should be noted that these may be characterics of both normally developing children and children with other handicapping conditions; their occurrence does not automatically signal the presence of a learning disability.

The first of these characteristics is *hyperactivity*. Young children are by nature highly active, but there is a level of activity apparent in some children that is far beyond normal limits. Adults who spend time with such children—especially parents—know well what that level is. Hyperactivity (also called hyperkinesis) can be identified even in infants, when it is manifested in irregular sleeping habits, irritability during waking hours, and a high activity level. Of course many such babies outgrow these characteristics. But many children who are identified as hyperactive during middle childhood have histories of such patterns reaching back to their infancy.

Two other common characteristics of children with learning disabilities are *impulsivity* and *distractibility*. Both of these are also quite commonly found in normally developing children, so again, abnormality is a matter of degree. Impulsivity refers to the child's acting before she thinks. Distractibility means that the child has difficulty attending to proper stimuli and easily allows his attention to wander off the task. Exhibition of these behaviors consistently over time might be an indication of learning disability.

Perseveration is a fourth warning signal that might be observed in a preschool child. Perseveration is carrying on an activity after it is no longer appropriate. For example, a child, in coloring a picture of stars, may decide to color one star purple. Soon the entire page is purple, for the child continued to color with the purple crayon far longer than was appropriate. In the same way, a child may repeat a series of words over and over again in a meaningless way, even though his original utterance made sense and was appropriate.

Difficulties with *spatial relations* may also characterize the learning-disabled child. This difficulty might be expressed in the child's inability to find his way even in familiar surroundings, in poor body image, or perhaps in difficulty with recognizing or reproducing different shapes.

Other characteristics include poor listening ability, difficulty in following oral directions, and problems with motor coordination. As stated above, all of these may be considered typical behaviors in very young children. Nevertheless, some children stand out from the others due to extreme forms of these behaviors. Any child who displays only one or two of the preceding eight characteristics should not be considered at risk for learning disabilities. Unless a pattern is observed over a considerable period of time involving several of the characteristics, there is probably no reason to suspect a potential learning disability.

Unlike mental retardation, learning disability has been recognized only relatively recently. Although the term learning disabilities itself was not coined until it was used by Samuel Kirk in the early 1960s (Johnson & Morasky, 1980), it is perhaps the work of Strauss and his associates in the early 1940s which was most influential in beginning to study and characterize children who had specific learning problems. Strauss and Warner (1942) identified a group of children whom they referred to as having brain damage. These children were characterized as having perceptual disorders, figure-ground confusion, perseveration, inability to organize abstract concepts, and hyperkinesia. Strauss and Lehtinen (1947) expanded on these notions and described what they saw as the educational provisions for these children. Many of the characteristics suggested by Strauss are still associated with learning disabled children and the underlying belief that the truly learning disabled child has some type of minimal brain dysfunction which accounts for her manifested characteristics remains.

Learning disabilities became formally recognized with the passage of the Learning Disabilities Act of 1969. That law defined children with learning disabilities as children who

> exhibit a disorder in one or more of the basic psychological processes involved in understanding or using spoken or written language. These may be manifested in disorders of listening, thinking, talking, reading, writing, spelling, or arithmetic. They include conditions which have been referred to as perceptual handicaps, brain injury, minimal brain dysfunction, dyslexia, developmental aphasia, etc. They *do not* include learning problems which are due primarily to visual, hearing, or motor handicaps, to mental retardation, emotional disturbance, or to environmental disadvantage.

This definition has been the mostly widely used working definition of learning disabilities and appears in Public Law 94–142 in a slightly more refined form.

P.L. 94–142 requires that a child who is classified as learning disabled show discrepancy in academic achievement or in achievement commensurate with his chronological age. In essence this definition classifies as learning disabled children whose achievement level is below that which would be predicted from intelligence test scores and which is not explained by the existence of another more general disability.

A problem with the definition is the fact the environmentally disadvantaged children are automatically excluded from being labeled learning disabled. As a result, learning disabilities are restricted primarily to white middle class, mostly suburban, children. Children from low socioeconomic backgrounds, be they rural or urban poor, do not qualify for this label and tend to be labeled mentally retarded, a much heavier load to bear.

The definition does not provide operational criteria for classifying learning disabled children. Thus, identification of children who are learning disabled depends upon the criteria established by individual agencies, school districts, and even independent practitioners. The population of children seen as learning disabled is therefore diverse in nature, and the children's learning difficulties may be the result of repeated failure by the educational system to provide them with meaningful instructional experiences rather than the result of perceptual and/or cognitive processing problems.

The group of children with processing deficits require more attention from professionals concerned with provision of services to preschool children. Unfortunately, many of the characteristics of learning disabled children are found to some extent in all children in the three to five year age range. As mentioned previously, the educational programmer must be concerned with whether children possess these characteristics to an excessive degree. The programmer is making a hypothetical statement about a child's future function based upon present performance (Keogh & Becker, 1973). As was discussed in Chapter 2, intervening variables can significantly change the predictive value that presently identified variables have for defining future conditions.

CLASSIFICATION OF LEARNING DISABILITIES According to Johnson and Morasky (1980, pp. 31–32) learning disabilities can fall into at least the following eleven areas: (1) atypical spelling errors; (2) auditory discrimination problems; (3) letter recognition problems; (4) initial sound-in-words confusion; (5) counting and number recognition difficulties; (6) auditory memory deficits; (7) visual memory deficits; (8) gross motor incoordination; (9) spatial disorientation; (10) articulation errors; (11) fine motor problems—usually perceived in handwriting. Again we see in Johnson and Morasky's list a set of "problems" which might be present in many cognitively intact preschool children. A properly trained early interventionist provides an educational setting that facilitates development in all the areas Johnson and Morasky (1980) have identified.

Hare and Hare (1979) have summed up this position as follows:

> During preschool years, when evidence of learning disabilities is generally clouded by unclear criteria and less than satisfactory measurement devices, a positive ap-

proach to preventing school failure is recommended. High priority probably should be given to curricula that include opportunities to learn to attend to critical aspects of the environment, organize information, develop systems to monitor and control one's behavior, and acquire the concepts and language necessary for school success. [pp. 287–288]

In the final analysis, we suggest that to apply this classification of learning disabilities to any child under the age of three is merely an exercise in unfounded speculation.

SUMMARY

This chapter has examined the structures that account for cognitive development during the first six years of life. In addition, it has stressed some of the major qualitative changes in the cognitive abilities of infants and young children and the way these qualitative changes are linked to observable patterns of behavior in children of different ages. The basis of cognitive development is shown to be in the ability of the child to meaningfully relate to her world through perceptual and memory processes. These processes, it is suggested, interact to form the base for the development of all higher cognitive functions. At the same time, deficits in perceptual and/or memory processes, regardless of origin, provide a major basis for more recognizable cognitive deficits during the first six years of life. Finally, the major characteristics of mentally retarded and learning disabled children and the way these characteristics may be manifest during the preschool years are discussed. The suggestion is ultimately made that cognitive problems must be relatively severe in nature to be clearly delineated in young children and that those problems which we associate with learning disabilities may not be differentially identifiable in preschool children at all.

Considerations
for Language
Development

1. What are the major components of language?
2. What is the relationship between language and cognition?
3. What are the major types of language disorders recognizable in children birth to six years of age?

WHAT IS LANGUAGE?

Language is an aspect of human development that has been the subject of lengthy and intensive investigation. Its form and function and the process by which it is acquired have long been of interest to researchers. Perhaps in no other developmental area has research produced more differences of opinion regarding the very nature of the processes under study. This reflects that language is not only extremely complex structurally but is closely related to other equally complex developmental areas, primarily cognition and socialization. Indeed, theorists have not even been able to agree upon just what language is.

Since the 1850s language research has centered on identifying the origins of child language. The basic issue in this research has been the disagreement concerning the nature of these origins. Some researchers have stressed a physiological approach, while others have offered psychological viewpoints.

More recently in the United States the disagreement concerning the nature of

60

language has centered mainly around the ideas of three theorists in psychology. In 1957 B.F. Skinner published a book entitled *Verbal Behavior* in which he postulated that language, like any other behavior, produces a certain pattern which causes changes in the environment. These behaviors, in turn, have consequences that affect the speakers. To Skinner, verbal behavior, like all other behavior, is observable, consisting of complex muscular activities which produce noise. He rejected the association of language with thinking or other internal processes. Noam Chomsky, one of the world's foremost students of language, in 1959 published a critique of *Verbal Behavior* which brought the behavioral model into serious question. Chomsky stated that children must have some innate knowledge about the structures of language since they acquire them so quickly and without perfect grammatical models. The Chomskian view holds that an innate biological/neurological mechanism is responsible for language acquisition. Chomsky's supporters have referred to this mechanism as a language acquisition device, and they have minimized the influence of the environment on language development.

A more recent influence on the theory of language acquisition is the ideas of Piaget, who suggested that language and cognition are two related symbol systems that depend on an underlying *symbolic function*. The symbolic function is defined as the capacity to represent reality symbolically. It develops in children through the interaction between physiological structures and environmental influences. Indeed, any discussion of language must inevitably raise cognitive issues, for the major purpose of language is the coding and expressing of ideas or thoughts. This aspect will be explored in more detail later in the chapter.

Another major area of disagreement among researchers in recent years concerns the relative importance of form, function, and use of language, that is, whether grammar (syntax), content (semantics), or communicative intent (pragmatics) holds the key to unraveling the acquisition mystery.

Syntax

By *syntax* we mean the grammatical forms used by a speaker to express an idea. The same idea may be expressed several ways, as in the following example:

1. (a) The child rides the bicycle.
   (b) The child is riding the bicycle.
   (c) The bicycle is ridden by the child.
   (d) It's the bicycle that the child is riding.

The form the speaker chooses to express his idea is the surface structure; the underlying idea itself is contained in the deep structure and remains unchanged regardless of the form of linguistic expression chosen. In the above example sentences 1(a) and 1(b) are expressed in simple, straightforward syntax: subject-verb-object. The difference between them occurs only in the verb form, 1(a) encoding it in the present tense and 1(b) in the present progressive. Sentence 1(c) represents the passive voice and sentence 1(d) contains the subordinate clause *that the child is riding* which modifies the predicate noun *bicycle.* Despite these differences in surface structure, the deep structure representing the meaning of the sentence is the same in each example.

Conversely, sentences may be expressed in the same grammatical form (surface structure) but represent different meanings. For example:

2. (a) Mary gave John the book.
       Subject—verb—indirect object—direct object
   (b) John gave Mary the book.
       Subject—verb—indirect object—direct object

Thus grammatical structure (syntax) focuses on the forms in which the meaning is expressed, whereas the underlying meaning has to do with semantics.

The process by which children acquire syntax is an interesting one. It is remarkable that children the world over learn the grammatical rules that govern their own languages with little help from adults. It has been determined that each child constructs her own grammar by matching new language information received with previous experiences. This leads to modifications in speech in accordance with the rules she infers. For example, a child who is learning past tense first acquires such irregular forms as *came, did,* and *went.* A few months later he begins using the past tense ending *-ed,* but he uses it with regular and irregular verbs alike, producing such well-known examples of baby talk as *comed, doed,* and *goed.* The new information is overzealously applied to already acquired forms, leading to overgeneralization of rules and production of the many quaint forms that give child language its endearing quality. Acquisition proceeds as the child creates his own grammatical rules by recognizing the patterns inherent in the language he hears and then generalizing these patterns to other situations.

By observing errors in children's early speech, investigators have been able to deduce the process by which syntax is mastered. Dale (1976) has reported that children use the plural *-s* for both count nouns such as *toys* and *spoons* and mass nouns like *milk, sand,* and *sugar* which are not pluralized. They learn that *-s* is added to words to denote more than one, and then overgeneralize the rule resulting in sentences like *Hafta get some sands.* Another example is the inversion of subject and auxiliary verb in a question. When children first learn to ask wh-questions (who, what, where, when, why) they do not invert subject and verb:

What I can do?
Where Daddy's going?

Later they are able to master this inversion but cannot manage when negation is also required in the same sentence:

Why is Daddy going?
Why Daddy isn't going?

These errors demonstrate the independence of children's grammar from rote imitation. As Dale has observed, the child acquires adult grammatical forms, but filters them through his own emerging rule systems, producing ungrammatical forms that help to reveal his level of acquisition. Thus children construct their own systems of grammar as a means for expressing their experiences and ideas.

Brown (1973) has described the child's acquisition of syntax in some detail. He divides early language into five stages, defined by the child's *mean length of utterance* (MLU). We know that chronological age is not a very satisfactory way of grouping children for language development—or for any other developmental area for that matter. In order to more accurately compare children in their acquisition of certain language functions, Brown used MLU as a more suitable index than age. For example, two children with the same MLU will have more similar language than two 3-year-olds or two 8-year-olds. The MLU simply expresses the average number of meaningful elements of language a child uses in an utterance. By meaningful elements we mean words like *dog*, *toy*, or *mama*, or parts of words like the plural marker *-s*, the past tense marker *-ed*, or the progressive *-ing*. These smallest meaningful units of language are called *morphemes*, and children use increasingly more of them per utterance as their speech becomes more complex.

Brown defined Stage I as beginning with the child's first use of multiword sentences and continuing until MLU reaches 2.0. Stages II, III, IV, and V are attained by the child's increasing of MLU by an average of .5 morphemes for each stage. Thus, a Stage II child would demonstrate an MLU of between 2.00 and 2.50; a Stage III child, an MLU of between 2.50 and 3.00; and so on.

This points out an obvious fact about child language: It is simpler than adult language. Sentences are shorter and less complex. (A word of caution: MLU measures only length and not complexity of a sentence.) Children accomplish this by omitting unimportant words from their sentences. For example, instead of the sentence:

I am going bye-bye in the car.

a young child would be more likely to say:

I go bye-bye car.

This omission of prepositions, articles, and auxiliary verbs is called *telegraphic speech* because sentences contain only the necessary words to convey meaning as telegrams do. Early syntax development at Stage I is characterized by this telegraphic form of speech. The omission of these function words is found not only in spontaneous speech but in imitations as well. Brown, Cazden, and Bellugi (1969) provide the following example:

MOTHER	CHILD
I see a seal.	Why you see seal?
I guess I'm not looking in the right place.	Why not looking right place?

As the child moves from two-word to three- and four-word utterances she continues to omit the less necessary function words and retain the content words.

A second syntactic characteristic of early child language is the accurate use of word order. Even at the two-word utterance level a child is able to convey her meaning accurately because she orders the words in a syntactically correct fashion. For example, a child may say, *Daddy cookie*, the meaning of which, with the aid of context, is clearly *Daddy is eating a cookie*. This construction reflects correct English word order, *Agent—object*, which even at this early stage the child uses consistently. *Cookie—Daddy* is not a sentence the Stage I child would use. In fact, it is this correct ordering of words that makes it possible for an adult to accurately interpret many early sentences (although context aids immensely). The classic example widely quoted from the work of Lois Bloom describes two identical utterances of her young subject Kathryn: *Mommy sock*. In the first instance Kathryn used it when she picked up her mother's sock; grammatically the sentence may be coded *possessor—possessed*. Later the same day she said the same sentence when her mother was putting Kathryn's own sock on her; in this case Kathryn was expressing *agent—object*. In both cases correct ordering of *mommy* and *sock* aided in the interpretation of meaning.

Thirdly, Stage I is characterized by the virtual absence of *inflections* or word endings (Dale, 1976). This makes sense when we consider that the use of inflectional endings increases the number of morphemes per utterance thereby increasing MLU. MLU at Stage I is, as we have seen, very low. Children at Stage I talk about what they observe, experience, feel. This means they express simple ideas in the present tense with little need for plurals, past tense endings, and other prefixes or suffixes. As MLU approaches 2.0 (which means the child is using sentences from one to three words in length) the child begins using inflections. The increased use of inflections continues throughout childhood and accounts for both quantitative and qualitative changes in child language.

Brown (1973) has observed that English-speaking children acquire these inflections in surprisingly consistent order. He has identified 14 common morphemes that children begin to use as they enter Stage II and begin using more complex grammatical forms. The first of these grammatical morphemes to be acquired is the present progressive *-ing* form. This is followed in orderly sequence by the prepositions *in* and *on*, the *-s* form to denote plural, the irregular past tense, the *'s* form to denote possession and so on. The complete list of 14 grammatical morphemes and their rank orders of acquisition are summarized in Table 4.1.

TABLE 4.1   The order of acquisition of 14 grammatical morphemes in three children

MORPHEME	AVERAGE RANK
1. Present progressive	2.33
2–3. in, on	2.50
4. Plural	3.00
5. Past irregular	6.00
6. Possessive	6.33
7. Uncontractible copula	6.50
8. Articles	7.00
9. Past regular	9.00
10. Third person regular	9.66
11. Third person irregular	10.83
12. Uncontractible auxiliary	11.66
13. Contractible copula	12.66
14. Contractible auxiliary	14.00

From Brown, R. *A first language.* Cambridge: Harvard University Press, 1973, p. 274. Reprinted with permission.

As the child moves into Stage II he begins to use the full range of sentence types available in English. Declaratives were the first acquired; now the child begins to use questions, negatives, and imperatives. In order to accomplish this he must learn to make certain grammatical transformations. For example, the declarative sentence *John is eating an apple,* becomes *Is John eating an apple?* when converted to a question; the transformation involves moving the auxiliary verb *is* to the beginning of the sentence. Similar transformations are required for negatives:

John eats the apple.

John *does not* eat the apple.

and imperatives:

Don't eat the apple, *John.*

Dale (1976), in reporting the investigations made into child questions by Ursula Bellugi at Harvard, has identified three stages in the development of question-asking.

In the first stage the child makes no transformations but simply uses a declarative sentence with rising intonation at the end of the sentence. Dale reports examples such as *Mommy eggnog? See hole?* and *No more milk?* At this stage *wh-* questions consist primarily of *wh . . . verb* constructions in which the child inserts a noun phrase.

Where Daddy go?

What doggy eat?

The second stage represents an increased use of articles, modifiers, and inflections, but the child has not learned to use auxiliary verbs, so no transformation is yet possible. At this stage typical questions are:

You can't fix it?

See my doggie?

The negatives *can't* and *don't* are interesting at this stage. The first appearance of *can* and *do* in child language is with the negative element and directly preceding the verb. Children use *can't fix, don't like, don't eat,* and so on as if they were single words, similar to the way they use *all gone* early in Stage I.

During this second stage of question-asking, Dale notes that *wh-* words like *what, where,* and *why* appear to serve as markers or introducers of questions rather than as true replacements for a noun phrase, as they are in adult questions. For example, in the adult question, *What are you eating?, what* stands for a noun phrase like *apple.* But in a child's question such as *Where put him on a chair?* the function served by *where* is solely that of a marker. This phenomenon also has produced such examples as:

Why me bent that game?

Why not you looking right place?

Why not me can't dance?

in which *why not* acts as a question marker for a negative declaration and *why* for an affirmative (Dale, 1976, p. 109).

At this stage children are for the first time able to comprehend and respond appropriately to *wh-* questions. Dale (p. 109) has given us some charming examples:

MOTHER	CHILD
What d'you hear?	Hear a duck.
What do you need?	Need some chocolate.
Who do you love?	Mommy, you. I love fishie, too.

The third stage in question-asking finds the child able to use auxiliary verbs. This means that inversions placing the auxiliary at the beginning of the sentence such as *Do you want candy?* and *Is Daddy coming home?* are possible. Negatives are properly attached to the auxiliary verb: *Can't Annie have cookie?* In such yes-no questions the negative is inverted; in *wh-* questions it remains in declarative form: An example from Dale is *Why the kitty can't stand up?* The *wh-* question requires more complex organization than the yes-no question; a young child evidently cannot deal with both the *wh-* word and the inversion aspect simultaneously and so omits the inversion temporarily. Nevertheless, by this stage the child has achieved Brown's Stage V in syntactic development and is well on his way to using language as an adult does.

The preceding discussion points up an important aspect of syntactic development. As children become more adept at using language, their sentences grow longer and more complex. This occurs by means of an orderly, predictable process that is fairly uniform across English-speaking children (and has much in common with that observed among children learning other languages as well, including American Sign Language). It raises the causality question: What factors account for such a well-regulated, predictable process? This question and several possible answers will be explored in Section 4 when we discuss the relationship between language and cognition.

Semantics

The study of semantics focuses on the *meaning* of words in sentences. As we pointed out earlier, language meaning is located in deep structure, then transformed into surface structure by means of syntactical processes. In the study of semantics, then, we must ignore the form sentences take and concentrate on their content.

Linguists who study semantics use such descriptors as *agent, action* or *state, patient,* and *beneficiary* to explain the meaning of the sentence. For example, the sentence:

John gave his bicycle to Harry.

would be coded semantically as follows:

agent—action—patient—beneficiary

In traditional school grammar books we have been taught that *John* is the subject, *gave* the verb, *bicycle* the direct object, and *Harry* the object of a preposition. Semantics labels are different from these "parts of speech" in that they more closely describe the intended meaning of the sentence.

As children acquire language they learn to express their ideas and experiences symbolically. Some of the first experiences they have as infants consist of assuming the role of agent acting upon an object. These experiences are very early coded into language, resulting in many first sentences of young children which consist of the simple semantic relations *agent—action, action—object* or *agent—object*. Bloom and Lahey (1978, p. 134) have noted that children talk about what they are just about to do, what they are doing or trying to do, or what they want to do. They have recorded some first sentences of children which code these early action relations: *Gia ride; Ride bike; Get truck.* Bloom (1970a) has further recorded children's first words at the single-word-utterance level and found that they express what the children are experiencing. Rather than labeling objects, as objects, as so many language development programs emphasize, the child is expressing the following ideas which account for about 75 percent of Stage I utterances:

	SEMANTIC RELATION	EXAMPLE
1.	Nomination	that book
2.	Notice	hi belt
3.	Recurrence	more juice
4.	Nonexistence	allgone cookie
5.	Attribution	big train
6.	Possession	mommy sock
7.	Location (state)	sweater chair
8.	Location (action)	bye bye car
9.	Agent—action	Eve read
10.	Agent—object	mommy sock
11.	Action—object	put book
		see doggie

These relations include action, state (possession and attribution), and location (both action and state). That is, the idea the child is expressing has to do with one of these concepts. An action relation requires an agent to express the doer:

Eve   read
(agent—action)

whereas a state relation requires a patient to express who is experiencing the state:

big   train
(state—patient)

According to Bloom and Lahey (1978, p. 137) children talk more about objects moving in relation to locations (*locative action*) than they do about objects already located at places (*locative state*). They apparently learn to express locative action events before they do locative state events, too. For example, Bloom and Lahey (pp. 137–8) quote a two-year-old child trying to put a barrette in his hair:

Put in my hair my barrette.

which expresses locative action. By contrast, another two-year-old expresses locative state in requesting a book from the shelf:

There's a Humpty Dumpty up there.

These relations represent the earliest events children talk about. The developmental sequence in which these occur in child language at Stage I has been analyzed by Bloom, Lightbown, and Hood (1975) and for the most part confirms the sequence outlined from Brown above. That is, children first use single words to encode existence, non-existence, and recurrence; then they begin using verb relations to encode action and locative events and later to encode state events. Next they begin using attribution and possession. Next in the sequence children learn to specify the beneficiary of an action (for example, "Give book *to Mommy*") and to specify instruments (for example, "with *a fork*"). They also begin to express intention, using the forms like *gonna* and *wanna* with an action verb (for example, "I gonna eat cookie.")

By Stage II sentences are longer and children are combining more than one idea into a sentence. The same semantic relations are used, however; the child simply learns to combine them, sometimes using a conjunction and sometimes embedding the dependent clause.

As children progress through the preschool years, their language development consists of increasing syntactic complexity (greater use of word ending, auxiliary verbs, embedded clauses, *wh-* questions, and so on, in rule-ordered sequences) and increasing variations in content. They learn to talk about increasingly abstract subjects such as feelings, wishes, opinions, or theories. They learn to take the perspective of another person, and this is reflected in their language content. By ages three and four children are no longer tied to their present experiences either cognitively or linguistically; they have learned to express past and future events which concern not only themselves but that increasingly involve other people, objects, animals, and places.

Pragmatics

When we analyze any sentence linguistically, it is necessary to think about not only the form it takes, whether active, passive, interrogative, or imperative, and what meaning it conveys, but it is also essential that we consider the context in which the sentence is spoken. The same sentence may have very different meanings and reflect different intentions on the part of the speaker in different contexts. For example, we can imagine quite different meanings for the sentence, "John loves chocolate cake" in each of these varying contexts:

1. The speaker is someone who knows John. Intended meaning: Chocolate cake is a favorite of John's.
2. The speaker is John's mother. Intended meaning: John had better love the chocolate cake I baked for him.
3. The speaker is a friend of John's who has just learned that John is allergic to chocolate cake.
4. The speaker is John's wife, commenting to their hostess. Intended meaning: John will eat the too-large piece of cake he's been served.

Researchers in language development formerly did not consider context an integral part of the language process. More recently, however, psychologists such as Bates (1976a,b) have maintained that context determines meaning and therefore is an integral part of language. As Bates (1976a, p. 420) puts it, meaning is definable in terms of context in the same way "figure" is definable only in terms of "ground." The study of language in social context is the focus of pragmatics.

Pragmatics includes the nonverbal gestures that accompany (and precede) single-word utterances; thus, it is the earliest form of language to emerge. There is evidence to suggest that semantics emerges developmentally from pragmatics, because pragmatics has to do with the speaker's intention and is thus closely related to cognitive development. Indeed, much of our interpretation of infants' early linguistic efforts depends upon our accurate reading of the context in which these early verbalizations occur.

In fact, a child's first words are not context-free universal *signs* that stand for the same referent wherever they are used, but rather are limited to mean a particular act in a specific context. Piaget (1952, 1962) calls such early communications *signals* because they are a first step in the child's use of symbols and not entirely free of context. A well-known example is his daughter Jacqueline's use of the word *panama* (grandfather) for requesting something. She did not use this word with its generally accepted meaning, but only as a means of requesting something from someone (not necessarily from grandfather). It is not difficult to surmise how such a meaning may have become attached to "panama" given the solicitous nature of a doting grandfather. It illustrates the way children attach meanings to their early words and helps us to understand that early language develops from context.

Bates (1975) states that children's first words derive from action sequences they have learned to perform or have observed. The word often does not extend in reference beyond the particular action the child associates with it. Bates (1975) provides an example from Piaget (1962) in which Jacqueline said "chien" as a dog passed under the balcony on which she was standing. Thereafter, Jacqueline used the word *chien* for anything she observed passing beneath her balcony. From this example, we can see that children arrive at their use of words as referents through their own context-based experiences. It is this aspect of pragmatics that appears to precede the acquisition of semantics in developmental terms.

Pragmatics focuses on the communicative function of language. This means that the speaker must take into consideration whether his message is understood by the listener. Adult speakers unconsciously take into account many non-verbal aspects of a conversation, such as whether the listener is making eye contact, what feedback his body posture and facial expressions give, or whether he has experienced the same event as the speaker and can therefore relate to the speaker's message.

Young children do not attend to these aspects of communication as readily. Their egocentrism (see Chapter 3) prevents them from taking into account the listener's perspective, and makes them much less efficient communicators as a result. For example, a young child talking on the telephone assumes that because he can see an object, so can his listener, and so alludes to it:

CHILD	ADULT
See, Grandma?	
My dolly's sick.	
	What's the matter with your doll?
Well, can't you see?	
Her head's broken!	

Maratsos (1973) conducted a study of the egocentrism of young children's speech. Six groups of three to five-year-old children were shown a set of toys with easily distinguished features (color, size, etc.) They were required to request a specific toy from an adult who sometimes could see the toys and sometimes could not. The children had to decide how much information to provide for the adult in each case in order to receive the toy they were describing. Maratsos found that the children provided more information to the adult who couldn't see the toys, thus demonstrating that they realized the limitation of their listener.

Like other aspects of language development, communication skills develop sequentially. A two-year-old is not aware of the needs of a listener; however, by age four children are able to alter their language according to whether their listener is an adult or a younger child. By age six or seven children are able to use listeners' facial expressions to gauge reactions to their message.

It should be pointed out, however, that many adults are poor communicators. The ability to tune in to another person often requires specific training in group process skills. This aspect of language development needs much further research in order to clarify the acquisition process.

Phonology

Phonology has to do with the sound system of language. Like other aspects of language development it proceeds in a regular step by step fashion. One difference between the acquisition of semantic and syntactic information and the acquisition of phonological competence is that there is a an anatomical aspect to phonology. The sounds of English are made by the muscles in the lips and tongue; the throat plays a part, as do palate, teeth, and vocal cords. Neuromuscular development is, therefore, an important aspect of phonology.

Let us look briefly at the way speech sounds are produced. A good place to start is with breathing patterns. In normal breathing, air is taken in and expelled in a smooth process without interruption. In speaking, air is inhaled in the normal fashion but during the exhalation it is restricted in some way by teeth, tongue, nose, or throat. These restrictions cause different sounds to be made. One of the most dramatic demonstrations of the fact that speech is produced during the exhalation of air and not during inhalation is when we watch a baby cry. Babies take in great gasps of air and produce the noise of crying when they exhale. In adult speech, air flowing from the lungs up through the throat and nasal passages in normal exhalation and then interrupted by the tongue being placed against the teeth produces a consonant sound. This is the way we produce the letter *t*. Conversely, air exhaled through the mouth without a definite restriction but only shaped by pursing the lips produces the vowel sound *o*. This is the basic difference between consonant and vowel sounds. Vowels are produced by the air flowing freely through the mouth cavity once it passes over the vocal cords, and consonants are produced by a definite obstruction in the flow of air through the mouth. The main sources of obstruction are the teeth and tongue.

Phonologists categorize vowels and consonants according to the position of tongue, teeth, and lips during their production. Vowels are categorized according to whether they are produced in the front or the back of the mouth, and whether they are high or low. Thus we might have a high front vowel like short *i* or a low back vowel like the *o* sound in *cod*. Those consonant sounds made by stopping the flow of air completely with the tongue are called *stops*. When the air is almost closed off by the tongue but not completely we have a *fricative*, such as in *f* and *v* or *s* and *z*. Categories have been further broken down to distinguish between stops that are produced with the two lips together and stops that are produced by placing the tongue behind the teeth. The former are called *bilabial stops* and those include *p* and *b*; the latter are known as *alveolars* and include *t* and *d*. Similarly, *s* and *z* are examples of *alveolar fricatives*. Many other such categories exist, but it beyond the scope of our discussion here to describe them. The point is simply that the production of sound by the human voice has been the subject of extensive and detailed study both in English and in other languages, and one of the results of such study has been an increased understanding of the developmental process involved in a child's learning to speak.

Research on early phonological development has focused on the stages through which children go as they acquire the ability to produce more complex sounds and more complex sound combinations. Several authors (Kaplan & Kaplan, 1971; White, 1975; Willis & Ricciuti, 1975) have identified a series of stages that describe the baby's development of sound-producing abilities, without associating this phonological development with progress in other developmental areas. Other authors (Ingram, 1976; Piaget & Inhelder, 1969) have studied phonological development as it relates to cognitive development, and have described stages in the phonological process that correspond to and depend upon the acquisition of certain cognitive skills. Let us look first at the more strictly phonological description.

STAGE ONE   Nearly everybody agrees that the first sound babies make is crying. Most authors put this during the first month of life. Dale (1976) notes that a baby's crying usually has a rising and falling variation in pitch that is sometimes helpful to parents in identifying the baby's needs. The first stage lasts only a month.

STAGE TWO   By the beginning of the second month the baby is able to make vocalizations other than crying. This stage is often called the cooing stage. Cooing consists of sounds resembling back vowels. These are the easiest to produce and thus, not surprisingly, the first to appear in a baby's repertoire. White (1975) describes sounds the baby makes while playing with his saliva. These sounds he calls gurgling, and notes that babies appear to enjoy listening to the sounds they make. Toward the middle of stage two at 3-1/4 to 4 months, White notes that babies increasingly experiment with sounds they make. For example, they may repeat a sound over and over as if they are practicing.

STAGE THREE   At about six months of age this experimental period is followed by a babbling period. By this time vocalizations have become increasingly speech-like and are referred to as babbling. Now consonant sounds are included in the baby's repertoire, and these appear in combination with vowels. Variations in intonation patterns are discernible at this third stage, and these intonation patterns become increasingly similar to adult intonation patterns. Stage three is characterized by the child's production of a wide variety of sounds, both those included in English and many of those which are not. Another characteristic is that many sounds found in English are not heard in the normal babbling of infants. Therefore, the onset of true speech requires the child to both add and subtract sounds that may or may not have been used during the babbling period. Dale (1976) notes that babbled syllables resemble the first meaningful words that the child will later produce. For example, these first words as well as many babbled syllables generally begin with stops rather than fricatives, and end with vowels. He states that both babbling and these first words are independent of the particular language community in which the child lives. Dale reports research that shows that the babbling of infants from different linguistic communities is very similar, as are their first meaningful utterances in terms of phonological makeup. This is evidence that babbling as an aspect of phonological development is independent of the linguistic environment. This information is consistent with the nativistic view of language development, for it implies that there may be an innate mechanism by which the child selects aspects of speech and language to be learned. The process by which this occurs is not fully understood.

STAGE FOUR   Near the end of the first year a baby begins to say her first words. Dale notes that the most striking characteristic of this stage is the transition from babbling to true speech, which entails a sharp decrease in the variety of sounds produced by the child. The first words of a baby are single syllable words consisting of simple consonant-vowel combinations. It is interesting that, whereas they use different intonation patterns during the babbling stage, babies do not differentiate meanings by use of intonations until fairly late in their second year.

Ingram (1976, p. 10) has identified six stages of phonological acquisition that correspond with Piaget's stages of cognitive development. The first two of Ingram's stages correspond to Piaget's sensorimotor period, that is, from birth to about 18 months of age (see Table 4.2). Ingram's first stage spans the first year of life and consists of preverbal vocalizations (babbling) and the development of early perceptual abilities. Ingram notes that infants as young as one month of age have the ability to make fine perceptual distinctions both visually and auditorally. Around the child's first birthday he begins to say his first words and this places him in Ingram's second stage, the phonology of first 50 words. This stage corresponds to the single-word utterance level that is Brown's Stage I of language development and ends when the child's vocabulary reaches about 50 words in size. This six-month period corresponds to the last part of the sensorimotor period identified by Piaget, just before the child acquires the ability to

TABLE 4.2 A comparison of Piaget's stages of cognitive development with six major stages of phonological development

PIAGET'S STAGES	PHONOLOGICAL STAGES
Sensorimotor period (birth–1:6) The child develops his sense and motor ability; he actively explores his environment until the achievement of the notion of object permanence.	1. Preverbal vocalization and perception (birth–1:0) 2. Phonology of first 50 words (1:0–1:6) Child gradually acquires his first words.
Period of concrete operations (1:6–12:0) Preconcept subperiod (1:6–4:0) The onset of symbolic representation. The child can use a system of social signs to refer to the past and future, although he primarily lives in the here and now.	3. Phonology of simple morphemes (1:6–4:0) Vocabulary increases rapidly as child develops a system of speech sounds. The child uses a variety of phonological processes to simplify speech. Most words consist of simple morphemes.
Intuitional subperiod (4:0–7:0) The child's play begins to mirror reality rather than change it to the child's own structures. Child begins to solve tasks such as the conservation of liquids by use of perception.	4. Completion of phonetic inventory (4:0–7:0) Most speech sounds are acquired by the end of this period. Simple words are by and large pronounced correctly. First appearance of more complex words which are poorly pronounced.
Subperiod of concrete operations (7:0–12:0) The ability to solve tasks of conservation is developed as the child can now perform reversible operations. He no longer needs to rely on perception.	5. Morphophonemic development (7:0–12:0) The more complex derivational morphology of language is acquired. Rules such as Vowel Shift become productive.
Period of Formal Operations (12:0–16:0) Appearance of the ability to reflect abstractly. Child can now solve problems through reflection.	6. Acquisition of spelling Child develops the ability to spell the complex words of the language. Development of linguistic intuitions.

Source: Ingram, D. Current issues in child phonology. In Morehead, D. & Morehead, A. (Eds). *Normal and deficient child language*. Baltimore: University Park Press, 1976, p. 10. Reprinted with permission.

represent ideas symbolically. Ingram's research indicates that children do not have the ability to use multiword sentences and engage in syntax until they have achieved Stage VI of the sensorimotor period, when this ability to do representational thinking emerges. For this reason neither Ingram nor Piaget would consider these first 50 words to represent true linguistic development, that is, a child does not use them as context-free socially accepted signs but rather as personal symbols very much tied to and dependent upon the child's direct experience.

It is not until Stage Three, the phonology of simple morphemes, which begins around age 18 months and continues until four years of age, that the child's system of speech sounds are based on true representational behavior. Ingram notes that this stage is initially marked by two abrupt linguistic changes: a rapid increase in vocabulary and the first use of two-word utterances. At this stage most words consist of consonant-vowel or consonant-vowel-consonant syllables. These accomplishments correspond to a similar advancement in cognitive development from sensorimotor to preoperational abilities. A major advancement in cognitive development beginning about two years of age is the ability to understand past and future. Therefore, the child begins to represent these concepts in her language, and we see morphemes to mark past and future tense begin to appear in her speech. During the next two years the child's phonological development concentrates on, first, mastery of vowel sounds and, second, various processes of consonant acquisition. A child's first words during this period have the consonant in the initial position but the child soon learns to use them in the medial and final positions as well. At this stage consonant clusters emerge too, and these are nearly always in the initial position. Early consonant clusters include *st* as in *story* or *stop*, *pl* as in *play*, and *cl* as in *clap*. Initial clusters are used first, followed by clusters at the end of a word as in *apple* or *noodle*.

Ingram (1976, p. 15) has identified some interesting processes young children use at this stage to simplify their phonological productions. Table 4.3 provides a summary of Ingram's data. He identifies three processes that children commonly use. Apparently, young children simplify their speech in very similar ways, and this may be because some sounds are physiologically easier to produce than others. For example, *for* is easier to say than *floor* and so a young child is likely to omit the *l* in the consonant cluster, retreating to a consonant-vowel-consonant pattern. In a similar way *step* becomes *dep*. It is easier to say consonant-vowel-consonant words in which both consonants are made in the same part of the mouth. For example, a child will find *coat* a difficult word to say because the *c* is produced in the back of the mouth and the *t* is produced in the front of the mouth. A common substitution for *coat* is something like *tote*. A similar example is an assimilatory process; the word *top* is pronounced *bop* with a labial initial consonant to match the labial final consonant. Other interesting examples may be gleaned from a perusal of Table 4.3.

It is apparent from Ingram's work and that of other researchers that the period from 18 months to four years, which parallels Piaget's preoperational period, is an important one in children's acquisition of sounds of their language. Although they emerge from this stage with an incomplete phonetic inventory,

TABLE 4.3   Some common phonological processes found in the speech of young children

---

Syllabic structure processes

1. Deletion of final consonant—e.g., out [æw], bike [bay]
2. Reduction of clusters—the reduction of a consonant cluster to a single consonant, e.g. floor [fɔr], step [dɛp]
3. Deletion of unstressed syllables—e.g., banana [nænə]
4. Reduplication—e.g., rabbit [wæwæ], noodle [nunu]

Assimilatory processes

5. Prevocalic voicing of consonants—consonants tend to be voiced when preceding a vowel, e.g., pen [bɛn], tea [di]
6. Devoicing of final consonants—e.g., bed [bɛt], big [bɪk]
7. Nasalization of vowels—vowels tend to take on the nasality of a following nasal consonant, e.g., friend [frẽ]
8. Velar assimilation—apical consonants tend to assimilate to a following velar consonant, e.g., duck [gək], tongue [gəŋ]
9. Labial assimilation—e.g., top [bap]
10. Progressive vowel assimilation—an unstressed vowel will assimilate to a preceding stressed vowel, e.g., apple [ʔaba]

Substitution Processes

11. Stopping—fricatives and occasionally other sounds are replaced with a stop consonant, e.g., seat [tit], soup [dup]
12. Fronting of velars—velar consonants tend to be replaced with alveolar ones, e.g., book [but], coat [towt]
13. Fronting of palatals—similar to above, e.g., shoe [su], juice [dzus]
14. Denasalization—the replacement of a nasal consonant with an oral one, e.g., no [dow], home [hub]
15. Gliding—the substitution of a glide [w] or [y] for a liquid sound, i.e., [l], [r]; e.g., rock [wak], lap [yæp]
16. Vocalization—the replacement of a syllabic consonant with a vowel, e.g., apple [æpo], flower [fawo]
17. Vowel neutralization—the reduction of vowels to a central [a] or [ə], e.g., bath [bat], book [ba]

From Ingram D. Current issues in child phonology. In Morehead, D., & Morehead, A. (Eds.) *Normal and deficient child language*. Baltimore: University Park Press, 1976, p. 15. Reprinted with permission.

they make important progress in their ability to use the more difficult sounds of their language. Meanwhile, their neuro-muscular growth is continuing and they become more efficient in their physiological ability to produce these sounds. Ingram's fourth stage also coincides with Piaget's preoperational or intuitive stage, and is the last of the six stages he outlines to describe the development of the preschool child. This stage marks the completion of children's phonetic inventory, and characterizes the years from four to seven. An important accomplishment of this stage is the mastery of the fricatives s, z, and sh, f and v, and the affricates ch and j.

By age seven children can pronounce most words in their vocabulary correctly. However, during this stage long words continue to be mispronounced. Children seem to be able to pronounce the initial portion of the word correctly, but have difficulty with endings. It is during this stage that children begin to use the correct morphemes –s, –z, and –az for plural, possessive, and to mark the present tense.

A phonological ability which develops quite late is the use of stress to differentiate words. For example, compound words like redhead and highchair are stressed on the initial word, and red head and high chair have their accent on the final word. Ingram states that in order to differentiate words like this, children need to be able to perform a reversible mental operation. For this reason, Ingram believes that this particular phonological ability is not developed until children are well into Piaget's cognitive stage of concrete operations.

Several issues remain unresolved in the study of child phonology. One of the most interesting and most significant has to do with children's use of contrast. In other words, do children consciously use a different sound in a word in their primitive vocabulary in order to differentiate from another similar word? Some linguists (e.g., Jakobson, 1968) believe that children from the earliest stages use contrast in order to clarify their meaning. Two examples provided by Ingram (1976, p. 20) follow:

(a)	plane	me
	plate	pe
(b)	Mark	mɔk
	milk	nɔk

In each of these examples the child has differentiated the initial consonant with a contrasting sound. Jakobson and others who believe in an innate theory of language development would argue that these examples show that children develop their own phonological system independent of adult language. Others would argue that children's use of contrast is taken from and depends upon the adult system. This issue is currently under study by investigators of child phonology. It illustrates that we still know much less than we need to about the acquisition process in language development.

Nevertheless, the evidence presented in the above discussion illustrates that phonological acquisition is similar to the acquisition process involved in semantics and syntax in that children go through an orderly, predictable sequence of development which is common to nearly all language-learning children.

COGNITIVE DEVELOPMENT
AND LANGUAGE DEVELOPMENT

The first studies of child language that adopted Chomsky's linguistic theory (e.g., Brown & Bellugi, 1964; Brown & Frazer, 1963; Miller & Ervin, 1964; Menyuk, 1964) emphasized syntactic structures, with little attention devoted to underlying semantic meanings. The distinction between surface structure and deep structure was not made clearly. Nor was emphasis given to semantics as an important aspect of sentence structure. However, these pioneer studies did contribute tremendously to the knowledge of the way children learn language, the way they create their own grammars with structural rules, and the way they follow an invariant non-age-related order in acquiring these grammars.

In the 1970s, psychologists and psycholinguists began to emphasize the semantic base of deep structure. Language came to be viewed as based on the child's experiences with objects and people, a means of coding these experiences. Language thus depended on the child's level of cognitive development. Schlesinger (1971), for example, stated that the structural relationships in children's utterances are semantic ones (agent, action, patient) which are merely encoded by syntactic devices into surface structure.

Brown (1973, p. 147) summarizes the semantic point of view in his discussion of the work of Bloom (1970b), Schlesinger (1971), and Fillmore (1968):

> Evidence and argument in the past decade have moved us . . . from the earlier nonsemantic characterizations of Stage I speech as telegraphic or as governed by pivot grammar. The direction of the movement is toward a richer interpretation assigning a limited set of semantic relations or roles to the Stage I child's intentions. . . .

Cognitive Bases of Language

The move from syntactic to semantic emphasis in language acquisition theory paved the way for researchers to consider language as a correlate of cognitive development. Much recent evidence suggests that children use language as a means of coding their experiences. This coding ability depends upon prior development of cognitive abilities that make it possible to organize or process information in verbal form.

Bowerman (1973a), for example, notes that children's earliest efforts at word combinations result from their discovery of ways to express various semantic relationships. These relationships are similar across languages because they originate in the way human cognitive abilities process nonlinguistic experiences common to children everywhere. Bowerman proposes that the concept *initiator of action* may be one of the easiest to grasp and so appears early in child language. Less easy to understand is *person affected by stimulus*, and so this appears later. Gradually the child acquires the concepts of *agent* and of *subject*. These steps reflect the increasingly abstract cognitive abilities of the child.

Controversy exists concerning the nature of the relationship between cognitive development and language development. Vygotsky (1962), one of the foremost writers on this topic, believed that preverbal intelligence and preintelligent speech only join when the child's utterances are comprehensible to an adult. He theorized that language stems from totally different roots from those of sensorimotor intelligence. To Sinclair (1969, 1970, 1971, 1973), the primary psycholinguistic interpreter of Piagetian thought, this is an indefensible position. In Piagetian terms, language is a cognitive ability. Sinclair notes that the child's growing awareness of self as agent acting upon the environment is related to his learning of the semantic functions of agent-action and action-object.

In her studies applying Piagetian theory to child language, Sinclair has stated that thought has its roots in action. She traces the infant's progress through the sensorimotor period, noting that his activity is aimed at successful manipulations (cognitive) and personal satisfaction (affective). As the baby overcomes his perceptual and motor egocentrism through decentration, his goals become less immediate and he gains a knowledge of objects and events that he wishes to communicate. Language is thus a means for him to symbolize his activity and to encode his experience.

According to Sinclair, both language and representational thought depend on a more general *symbolic function* which Piaget has defined as the capacity to represent reality symbolically through signifiers that are distant from what they signify (1969, p. 318). She distinguishes among *signals* which are spatially and temporally bound, *symbols* which have personal rather than universal meanings (e.g., a child using a cereal box as a pretend train), and *signs* which are distinct signifiers for objects or events, are abstract, and are socially agreed upon. Adult words fall into the latter category. The first words of children, still context-bound and without universal meaning, qualify as signals or symbols. The general symbolic function emerges at the end of the sensorimotor period and can be observed, for example, in symbolic play, drawing, and language. The first acts that require mental imagery are preverbal acts of imitation. Later, verbal imitations are produced. The roots of the language, therefore, are found in the sensorimotor period.

Sinclair has reported several experiments that show how the child's language is structured by logic. Since this logic is slowly constructed by the child through interactions with objects and people, it follows that language does not depend upon innate structures, but rather depends on the development of universal symbolic structures. These structures are developed during the sensorimotor period, and are also responsible for the development of sensorimotor intelligence. Thus in Piagetian terms, language and cognition are interdependent. Both are based on an underlying symbolic structure that develops through operative knowledge.

Piaget's theory, then, is useful in defining the initial set of linguistic universals used by children. Acting upon the environment is the source of knowledge and language is one way to represent knowledge.

It is only possible for objects and events to be represented when they have acquired an identity of their own and no longer exist for the child only when he is acting upon them. Gradually, the child changes his view of reality so that he is only one agent among many. First other persons and later objects are understood to act upon objects. This experience enables the child to develop the semantic relations necessary to express these concepts in language.

Bloom (1970a) has adapted Piagetian theory to her conceptual framework of language development. She believes that knowledge of the substance and process of language development can be a major source of insight into the development of thought. She theorizes that what a child is able to say is related to what he knows about language. The emergence of syntactic structure in a child's speech therefore depends on the prior development of the ability to organize experience cognitively so that it may be coded into language. This is an important assumption that Bloom makes: Prior cognitive development underlies the emergence of semantic and syntactic structures.

Since the late 1970s, an attempt to relate language development more specifically to Piaget's stages of sensorimotor development has been made. Piaget has identified six stages that the child experiences during the period (see Tables 3.1, 3.2, and 4.2).

Studies linking language development and cognitive development have focused on Stages V and VI of the sensorimotor period. For example, Bloom and Lahey (1978) state that until object permanence is achieved at the end of Stage VI, a child cannot learn the names of many objects. The achievement of object permanence means that the child realizes that objects exist independently of the child's actions upon them and independently of the time and space context in which they appear. Bloom and Lahey thus imply that Stage VI is a prerequisite for language development. Other studies by Edmonds (1976), Bates (1976), and Ingram (1976) indicate that imitation at Stage V and symbolic play and means-end differentiation at Stage VI are prerequisites for the development of language as a context-free sign system.

Support for this point of view comes from Snyder (1975), who examined cognitive development in both normal and language-delayed children and found that only the means-end scale of the Uzgiris-Hunt scales differentiated the two populations. It is interesting that children's first words reflect their own actions in the events in which they are participating, and are strongly context-bound. For example, *ball, no, more,* and *all gone* are among the first words of many children (Bloom & Lahey, 1978). Such words express the conditions of existence, non-existence, recurrence, and disappearance as noted above in the discussion of semantic development. Children are able to express these concepts with one-word phrases. Earliest words record a child's actions. For example, Edmonds (1976) reports a child saying "Going" as he walked out of the room, or "Fall" as he fell down. Bloom and Lahey (1978) have noted that a child's success in learning to talk depends on his ability to perceive and organize his environment. This is consistent with the cognitivist view of language development discussed above.

The Child's Linguistic Environment

In tracing the roots of language acquisition, it is important not to place too much emphasis on cognitive prerequisites at the expense of consideration of linguistic input. It is certainly true that the child's environment, and particularly the adults in that environment, has a great impact on the child's language-learning ability.

Early in the first year of life, mother-infant interactions prepare the baby for later language learning. The most interesting aspect of this early communication between infant and caregiver is the ritualized turn-taking that characterizes it. Like a true conversation, the interactions between mother and baby consist of a series of activities in which first the mother and then the baby takes the initiative. These interactions appear to be rule-governed, sequential, and orderly. Even though the infant cannot speak, the mother interprets his nonverbal behavior (smiles, cries, coos, and gestures) as attempts to communicate, and she comments upon them as if the baby were engaging in a true conversation. The following example of a mother talking to her six-month-old infant (Widerstrom, 1982) illustrates the conversational nature of the interchange.

MOTHER	INFANT
Oh, sucking your thumb in the bath tub.	(Lying in tub with thumb in mouth)
My goodness, you *are* comfortable.	
You are comfortable, aren't ya?	
Yeah.	
Yeah.	
Hey! What are ya doin' with that washcloth?	(Reaches for washcloth)
We'll have to get you some more soap.	
We'll have to get you some more soap.	
Right?	
Ah ah ah!	
Talk to me.	
Talk to me.	
What are ya doin' with your thumb in your mouth all the time?	
Huh?	
Kinda hard to talk with your	

thumb in your mouth all the
time?

Don't talk with your thumb in
your mouth.

Oh what?

Oh what?

Want that finger or do you want   (Puts washcloth in mouth)
the washcloth?

Bruner (1975) believes that this dialogue between infant and mother is crucial for the development of later language. He has identified certain rituals which mother and child carry on during play that teach the child that conversation requires reciprocal responses. Such activities as playing peek-a-boo or reading picture books together are examples. According to Bruner, the dialogue also teaches the child early semantic relations. He suggests that the child learns role-shifting from *agent of action* to *recipient of action,* when the mother gives the baby an object or holds out her hand in order for the baby to give her an object.

These early interactions are basically pragmatic in nature, for they rely heavily on contextual information provided by means of gestures, smiles, and physical contact as well as words. At this early pragmatic level communication consists of perceptual information provided to the infant. These interactions appear to pave the way for the development of semantic and later syntactic knowledge on the part of the infant.

One area of interest to researchers that has generated much controversy concerns the role imitation plays in the child's learning of language. The behavioral viewpoint has placed a heavy emphasis on imitation, going so far as to maintain that children learn all of their language by imitating adults. This point of view has been refuted by evidence that parents do not provide correct and complete language samples to their young children, nor do they correct errors in grammar when they talk to their young children (Chomsky, 1965; Moerk, 1975). Rather, adults appear to monitor the content of their children's language, but ignore grammatical errors or idiosyncracies. An example of this process comes from the research of Lois Bloom (Bloom & Lahey, 1978, p. 281):

MOMMY	GIA
(Mommy gave Gia a bottle of milk for lunch; milk was fresh; Gia pushing bottle away)	
	it old
It's old?	
	yes
It's not old	
	it old

It's not old
(Mommy picks up Gia's bib; starts to put it on her; bib is
soiled)

                                                                    that old

It's not old/Well if you didn't spill all your food over it it
wouldn't be old.

Nevertheless, it is obvious that imitation must play some role in child language acquisition, for the nativist position that the language acquisition device
accounts for nearly all language learning does not account for all the facts either.
Let us look for a moment at the research on mothers' speech to young children.
Some characteristics that aid the child's developing language have been identified. The following features are of interest. Ferguson (1977), Gleason (1973),
Sachs (1977), and Garnica (1977) have noted that mothers use higher pitch when
talking to their infants than they do in normal speech. They use special intonation patterns (Sachs) and prolong the duration of stressed words (Garnica). The
vocabulary of mothers is less varied and more concrete than that of nonmothers
and sentences are syntactically less complex (Phillips, 1973; Ringler, 1975).
Snow (1972) found many questions in mothers' speech and much redundancy,
and Phillips noticed many affirmatives, all of which would encourage communication. Both Phillips and Snow found that mothers limit the semantic content of
their speech to the constructions the child has mastered, talking about the here
and now rather than past or future and limiting conversation to what the child is
experiencing. Thus it appears that linguistic input to children learning language
is neither too complex nor confusing. Nevertheless, Dale (1976) has noted that
the mother's speech is always found to be more complex than the child's. He
believes that imitation aids the child in extracting what he is developmentally
capable of processing. Bloom (1970b) concurs with this analysis, for she found
significant differences in the way children use imitation. Her research confirmed
that children imitate the words and grammatical structures they are in process of
mastering. If Dale and Bloom are correct, children use imitation selectively to
help them in mastering new grammatical forms, new semantic relations, and
new vocabulary. Such a point of view is compatible with the Piagetian perspective on cognition and language development.

PROBLEMS IN LANGUAGE DEVELOPMENT

To intervene successfully with children who are not developing adequate language spontaneously, it is necessary to answer some questions about language
disorders. Are language-disordered children *delayed* in their acquisition of normal forms or are they *deviant?* Do they learn best through *imitation* or do they
need to base language on their own experiences? For what purposes do they need

language skills? Answers to these questions will help us to develop a sound intervention program based on a consistent theory.

Research indicates that children who have language disorders learn language the same way that normally developing children do, but at a slower pace. They are not *deviant* in their acquisition, merely delayed (Johnston & Schery, 1976; Lackner, 1968; Leonard, Bolders, & Miller, 1976; Menyuk & Looney, 1972; Morehead & Ingram, 1973).

Evidence from normal acqustion research also tells us that while children do imitate adult language, they are very selective about what they imitate, choosing only those aspects that they are in the process of acquiring (Bloom, 1973). They do not imitate forms that are either too easy (already acquired) or too difficult (beyond their competence). More importantly, their acquisition of new forms is based on their current experiences rather than on what they hear adults talking about (Bryen, 1980). This would favor an experiential approach to intervention, with major importance given to developing the cognitive concepts and social interactions underlying the language expression.

Finally, language acquisition studies have determined that children use language to express their experiences and their understanding of the world (Bates, 1976; Bloom & Lahey, 1978) and this is also true of children with language disorders (Bricker, Dennison, & Bricker, 1976; Widerstrom, 1979).

We may assume, then, that a language intervention model based on normal development and providing an experiential approach makes the most sense. The following discussion is based on the work of Bloom and Lahey (1978) for the developmental approach and on that of McLean and Snyder-McLean (1978) for the experiential basis. This is not to say that other authors have not developed useful intervention approaches for language-disordered children. On the contrary, the field is expanding rapidly, making many program alternatives available. Among those recommended for their sound theoretical base are the developmental/interaction approach of Bricker, Dennison, and Bricker (1976), the developmental approach of Miller and Yoder (1974), and the cognitive/linguistic approach of Muma (1978). For those who favor a behavioral approach to intervention, the behavioral psycholinguistic models developed by Ruder and Smith (1974) or Stremel and Wargas (1978) are quite comprehensive.

According to Bloom and Lahey (1978, p. 290), a language disorder may involve difficulty in conceptualizing ideas about the world, coding those ideas into language, or using the code for speaking or understanding.

Form, Content, and Use

In the developmental-cognitive approach, language skills are divided into three areas in order to assess delays and plan interventions. Traditionally speech therapists have focused their remedial programs on disorders of form or syntax. We now realize that disorders of content (semantics) and use (pragmatics) are more serious and demand at least equal attention. Let us examine each area in order to provide background for planning intervention.

Disorders of form include problems with lexicon (vocabulary) and grammar. The most common problem young children exhibit in this area is the substitution of earlier, simpler forms for more advanced, complex ones. These are usually representative of the child's developmental level. For example, an older child with language delays might use such younger forms as:

I falled down and hurted myself.

I going school now.

Please more milk.

The omission of auxiliary verbs and prepositions and the substitution of improper past tense forms are normal for the three or four-year-old, but not for the five or six-year-old. An analysis of the grammatical forms a child uses is a first step in diagnosing language disorders.

Disorders of content or meaning are generally more serious than disorders of form, since they usually indicate a lack of concept development. To remediate content disorders, it is necessary to teach the concepts underlying the linguistic expression. An example of disordered content from Schwartz (1974) appears in Figure 4.1. The speaker is a six-year-old hydrocephalic child. He obviously does not understand the concept button and its use. In planning an effective intervention for this child we must consider his cognitive deficits. Before we can expect the child to code ideas into correct language we must help him to become familiar with many objects and understand that different objects have different uses.

| (Shown a button and asked to tell about it) | this is a button/it has two holes in it/it's like a lady has/it has a shape/it is round/ this is a button/you put it on your blouse or an apron in case an apron has a button/that's big like this/you can roll it and throw it but you never smash a window/ because if you have a button or a shape that goes on the wall or if you take it and hang it on the dress that would be very nice/would you do that for me?/if you have a dress or a coat you can hang it on or you can keep it out to take it to the store. |

FIGURE 4.1   An Example of a Disorder in Content from a 6-Year-Old Hydrocephalic Child. From E. Schwartz, Characteristics of speech and language development in the child with myelomeningecele and hydrocephalus. *Journal of Speech and Hearing Disorders.* 1974.

Disorders of use also depend on the child's level of cognitive development. We use language to communicate, and if this is not possible for a child, as in Figure 4.2, it represents a serious problem. The child in this example shows an inability to process prior utterances, to focus on a relevant subject, and to take into account the needs of his listener. These represent cognitive accomplishments rather than linguistic ones. Communication is a thinking process as well as a linguistic one, and so intervention must be designed to develop such cognitive concepts as decentration, representational thinking, and memory.

Studies of child language have revealed that children talk better in context than when they are imitating adults and that they use more advanced forms when they talk about what they are doing. Intervention in disorders of language use should be experientially based to allow the child to develop the concepts necessary for accurate communication of his ideas.

(Mark and his teacher are talking)	
	Mom used to take me to McDonalds February 1974/she used to put me up in the --- at 1:30/and I went to the doctors' office at 2:45
What kind of things do you eat when you go to McDonalds?	
	a hamburger/a Big Mac quarter pounder/soft drinks/and french fries/I never go to McDonalds for breakfast you know
Why not?	
	why well you know/I used to sleep in New York/in the Catskill Mountain/I used to go to a motel/I don't know where I ate breakfast/you know RD's roast beef sandwich/that restaurant was in Pennsylvania but it's in New Jersey/It's now in New York on the way to New York City/ Manhattan

FIGURE 4.2 Dialogue with Mark, 10 years old. An Example of a Disorder in the Use of Language. From Bloom, L. and Lahey, M. *Language Development and Language Disorders*. New York: Wiley, 1978, p. 299. Reprinted with permission.

We now turn our attention to several specific disorders that may affect the development of language in preschool-age children. These include: hearing impairment, aphasia, and speech problems.

Hearing Impairment

Hearing impariment according to Moores (1982, p. 5) "covers the entire range of auditory impairment, encompassing not only the deaf child but also the one with very mild loss who may understand speech without difficulty." Children considered deaf usually have hearing losses in 70–75 dB within the frequency range critical for comprehension of speech sounds. Hearing impairment obviously interferes with the young child's ability to communicate using spoken words. Hallahan and Kauffman (1982) suggest that hearing impaired children have three obvious disadvantages in learning to speak. First, they receive inadequate auditory feedback when they make sounds. Second, they do not receive adequate verbal reinforcement from adults. Third, they are unable to adequately hear adult speech and thus cannot use it as a model.

While they are clearly at a disadvantage in learning to speak, deaf children are capable of learning language and communication skills. In fact, most deaf children become proficient at the use of American Sign Language (ASL). The linguistic structure of ASL is as complex as that of spoken English and, in fact, is able to show some relationships that spoken English is not (Moores, 1982, p. 218). In short it is important to recognize that preschool-age, hearing impaired children can and do learn language. They are, however, not particularly well equipped to communicate in the oral-aural modes of English.

Preschool education of hearing impaired children has become more and more commonplace. These programs have been developed and housed most often outside of the public schools, and have been affiliated with private schools, universities, or speech and hearing centers. Early intervention programs for hearing impaired children have sparked debate about the most effective type of communication system to use to educate them. As Moores (1982, p. 240) suggests, "some educators firmly believe that the use of any kind of manual communication will prevent children from developing speech and language and doom them to lifelong existence in a mute subculture. Others just as firmly believe that depriving children of such a system will cause them irreparable linguistic, educational, and emotional damage." In an attempt to resolve these dichotomous positions Moores concludes that "if there is any chance that a child will have difficulty through sole reliance on auditory-vocal communication, oral-manual communication should be initiated immediately. The use of oral and manual communication can facilitate development" (p. 252). This type of approach, called total communication and combining oral and manual approaches, was provided impetus in the late 1960s when studies began to reveal that manual communication facilitated language development and academic achievement in deaf children (see Stuckless & Birch, 1966; Vernon & Koh, 1970). Moores, Weiss, and Goodwin (1976) have further suggested that preschool programs for hearing impaired children should put strong emphasis on cognitive-academic activities and that math should receive equal attention to reading and language from the beginning of instruction. In the final analysis, early interventionists must provide young, hearing impaired children with opportunities to develop language, communication, academic, and social skills. Because of the relatively low incidence of deafness, this has not always been the case for hearing impaired children in infancy and early childhood years.

Aphasia

Aphasia is the inability to use or understand spoken language in the absence of hearing impairment or mental retardation. Thus, aphasia is solely a language disorder. Generally, two forms of aphasia are recognized. One is *expressive* or *motor* aphasia in which the child has difficulty in using words. For example, the child may be able to show or even tell how a common object is used, but may not be able to name it. The other type of asphasia is *receptive* or *sensory* aphasia. Children with this type of aphasia appear to hear what is being said to them, but are unable to meaningfully process it. As Culatta and Culatta (1981, pp. 125–126) have suggested, children with receptive aphasia are in a situation that "is somewhat analogous to what yours would be if you had to communicate using a foreign language you understood very poorly. This analogy is not completely appropriate, however, because you would be able to trust your understanding of the words you could communicate with, whereas an aphasic . . . cannot." Both expressive and receptive aphasia may occur in the same individual simultaneously.

In a sense, aphasia is analogous to a learning disability of language function. It is linked to central nervous system dysfunction that can either be congenitally based or result from later central nervous system damage. Young, aphasic children can manifest characteristics like those of hearing impaired children and careful assessment is often necessary to distinguish them. Fortunately, aphasia occurs only rarely in children. However, aphasia presents a particular challenge for early interventionists since it can so significantly interfere with the early development of language and related cognitive abilities when it does occur in young children.

Speech Disorders

Speech disorders interfere with a child's ability to speak clearly. Speech disorders may cause social problems if children are teased and ridiculed, but these disorders only cause language problems when they interfere with effective communication. It is difficult to classify chldren under the age of five or six as speech disordered, since many speech characteristics of very young children mimic those of older speech disordered children. But early interventionists should keep these problems in mind so that facilitation and remediation programs can be designed for children whose difficulties do not improve as they reach kindergarten or first grade. Three basic types of speech problems can be seen in children. These are problems of articulation and voice and stuttering.

Articulation problems are characterized by imperfect sound production. These imperfections can be in the form of sound *distortions*, sound *substitutions*, or sound *omissions*. Again, remember that within the normal speech development of two to six-year-old children these imperfections occur naturally. If, however, they persist to any degree into the first grade, more vigorous interventions should be designed and speech and language therapists should be consulted. Correct speech models should be provided for young children. However, caution should be used in directly calling attention to a child's errors. Attention may increase the child's anxiety about speaking and thus reduce his verbal output.

Voice disorders include excessively loud, soft, and hoarse voices and are usually associated with imperfect vocal cord structures. Preschool children need to learn to control their voices in an acceptable fashion. Constant yelling and screaming, for example, can lead to vocal cord strain and eventual damage. Remember, too, that loud speaking may be a sign of hearing loss in young children. Excessive hoarseness in a child's voice should be thoroughly investigated if it is persistent, since hoarseness is often related to nodules on the vocal cords which often require surgical removal. As with articulation disorders, speech and language therapists often are the best resources for remediating these problems.

Stuttering is defined as excessive disfluency in speech and is characterized by no meaningful repetition of sounds, words, or phrases while speaking. It may also be characterized by repeated and frequent hesitation during speech. The causes of stuttering have not clearly been established and theories suggest both biological and psycho/emotional causation. Everyone, especially young children whose speech is emerging, has disfluencies when speaking. Like articulation errors, disfluencies are a natural part of speech development and only become a problem when they persist after age five or six and are of a severe enough nature to interfere with the child's effective communication.

Parents and early interventionists should be patient with their preschoolers when they experience disfluencies. Urging a child to slow down or start again just calls attention to the disfluency and may result in anxiety. This anxiety can provide the basis for a child becoming a stutterer and actually may cause an increase in anxiety. Stuttering can be difficult to remediate in older children and adults, so early intervention is important. The early interventionists must strike a careful balance between producing anxiety in a child by calling undue attention to her disfluencies and ignoring to the point that the child's disfluencies which are not being corrected through natural maturation and development.

CONCLUSION

Language development is much too broad a subject to treat with very much depth in a single chapter of this textbook. Nevertheless, it is hoped that the information in the present chapter will encourage the reader to explore this fascinating subject at greater length elsewhere. Certainly the research into how children learn language is expanding at a rapid rate, making it highly probable that ever better language intervention programs will become available as our knowledge base expands. Meanwhile, language intervention based on sound concepts of development and interaction should yield satisfactory results for classroom teacher and clinician alike. Although such procedures require more initiative and effort than are required in using a prepackaged language development kit, the results in most cases are correspondingly more satisfactory.

This chapter also should have provided the reader with some basic understanding of different language disorders. Early intervention is often the key to successful remediation and more importantly prevention of long-term language problems.

Considerations for Social Development

1. In what ways are temperament and play influential in social development?
2. How can the development of self be influenced by a disability in a young child?
3. How can social development be distinguished from cognitive development?
4. What may be the relationship between deviance and problems in social development?

DEFINING SOCIAL DEVELOPMENT

Any behavior of any individual that takes place in the presence of another individual may be considered social behavior if that behavior is in some way reacted to by the second individual. The interaction between parent and infant is therefore a social interaction. Data presented by Brazelton, Kowslowski, and Main (1974), for example, suggest that infants have a repertoire of social behavior at birth. Their definition of social behavior is over-simplified, since it is through social behavior that the young child achieves her awareness of self, feelings of emotion, feelings of trust and security, and social role identification. In essence as Anastasiow (1981) has suggested

socioemotional development seems to mean a lot of different things to different people. . . . [It] means the development of emotions, the ability to get along with peers, the development of ego and superego, the ability to control emotions, the ability to work and love, the ability to form attachments and affiliations with

91

caregivers and peers, and the ability to grow and develop as a person—in other words it is a confusing puzzle. [p. 2]

In this chapter we discuss social and emotional development in young children and then address some of the specific social development problems children can have. As the statement from Anastasiow suggests, social and emotional development covers an entire spectrum of behavioral and intrapsychic states. We only have space to discuss here those areas of social-emotional development judged to be most important in the lives of young, handicapped children. These areas are: (1) the role of temperament and play in social development, (2) attachment, and (3) development of self. Problems of social and emotional development including autism, childhood psychosis, oppositional behavior, hostile and aggressive behavior, shyness, and fears are also discussed.

Social and emotional development progresses through the first three years of life in a series of relatively discrete and identifiable steps. Sroufe (1979) calls these steps "stages" although he adds the proviso that "these 'stages' are not proposed as a necessary, invariant sequence, but rather as normatively descriptive." In fact he suggests that "whether they are true 'stages' . . . is an empirical question" (p. 475). Nonetheless, these "stages" are of heuristic value in helping to understand the unfolding of social and emotional behavior during the first three years of life. Table 5.1 outlines the stages of social and affective development. A relationship between cognitive and social development stages is apparent in the table. The cognitive and social domains feed and facilitate each other. In essence, while we can and do study the various domains of development separately, they are clearly interrelated. What a child is doing in one developmental domain (e.g., cognition) affects what he is doing in another developmental domain (e.g., social) and vice versa.

In the preschool years children begin to develop additional awareness of sex roles. Sex roles are learned through identification with and imitation of parents and other primary adults in the environment. As Lewis and Feiring (1979) have noted, it is also during this period of time that children learn to seek what these authors term social functions from appropriate social agents in the environment. For example, a child would learn during this period to turn to a parent for caretaking rather than to a sibling. On the other hand, the child might learn to turn more readily to a sibling for various play activities. Edwards and Lewis (1979) present data that underscore this notion. They suggest

a strong social object-social function interaction with some functions more relevant for some objects. In particular, older people are preferred for dependency functions centering around help-giving. . . . In terms of play . . . peers, either older or same age, are preferred, certainly over adults and younger children. [p. 258]

Two important factors that play a role in the social and emotional development of children are temperament and play. Temperament is measurable in the

TABLE 5.1   The Relationship of Cognitive, Social, and Affective Development
During the First 36 Months of Life

COGNITIVE DEVELOPMENT	AFFECTIVE DEVELOPMENT	SOCIAL DEVELOPMENT
0–1 Use of Reflexes Minimal generalization/ accommodation of in-born behaviors	*Absolute Stimulus Barrier* Built-in protection	*Initial Regulation—* Sleeping, feeding, quieting arousal Beginning preferential responsiveness to caregiver
1–4 Primary Circular Reaction First acquired adaptations (centered on body) Anticipation based on visual cues Beginning coordination of schemes	*1–3 Turning Toward* Orientation to external world Relative vulnerability to stimulation Exogenous (social) smile	
4–8 Secondary Circular Reaction Behavior directed toward external world (sensorimotor "classes" and recognition) Beginning goal orientation (procedures for making interest sights last; deferred circular reactions)	*3–6 Positive Affect* Content-mediated affect (pleasurable assimilation, failure to assimilate, disappointment frustration) Pleasure as an excitatory process (laughter, social responsivity) Active stimulus barrier (investment and divestment of effort)	*4–6 Reciprocal Exchange* Mother and child coordinate feeding; caretaking activities Affective, vocal, and motor play
	7–9 Active Participation Joy at being a cause (mastery initiation of social games) Failure of intended acts (experience of interruption) Differentiation of emotional reactions (initial hesitancy, positive and negative social responses, and categories)	*7–9 Initiative* Early directed activity (infant initiates social exchange, preferred activities) Experience of success or interference in achieving goals
8–12 Coordination of Secondary Schemes & Application to New Situations Objectification of the world (interest in object qualities and relations;	*9–12 Attachment* Affectively toned schemes (specific affective bond, categorical reactions) Integration and coordination of emotional reac-	*10–13 Focalization* Mother's availability and responsivity tested (demands focused on mother) Exploration from secure base

(continued)

TABLE 5.1   continued

COGNITIVE DEVELOPMENT	AFFECTIVE DEVELOPMENT	SOCIAL DEVELOPMENT
search for hidden objects) True intentionality (means-end differentiation, tool using) Imitation of novel responses Beginning appreciation of caused relations (others seen as agents, anticipation of consequences)	tions (context-mediated responses, including evaluation and beginning coping functions)	Reciprocity dependent on contextual information
12–18 Tertiary Circular Reaction Pursuit of novelty (active experimentation to produce new effects) Trial and error problem-solving (invention of new means) Physical causality spatialized and detached from child's actions	*12–18 Practicing* Mother the secure base for exploration Elation in mastery Affect as part of context (moods, stored or delayed feelings) Control of emotional expression	*14–20 Self-Assertion* Broadened initiative Success and gratification achieved apart from other
18–24 Invention of New Means through Mental Combination Symbolic representation (language, deferred imitation, symbolic play) Problem-solving without overt action (novel combinations of schemes)	*18–36 Emergence of Self-Concept* Sense of self as actor (active coping, positive self-evaluation, shame) Sense of separateness (affection, ambivalence, conflict of wills, defiance)	

From L. A. Sroufe. Socioemotional development. In J. D. Osofsky (Ed.), *Handbook of infant development*. New York: John Wiley, 1979. Reprinted with permission.

infant at birth and throughout early childhood. Play is a social function that is critical in the development of social and affective behavior. While they are clearly not the only two that mediate the social development of young children, these factors are typical of others that lead to social development. Furthermore, a good deal of attention has been given to both temperament and play in the literature concerning social development.

Temperament

The pioneering work on temperament was conducted by Thomas, Chess, Birch, Hertzig, and Korn (1963) as part of the New York Longitudinal Study (Beckwith, 1979). These researchers were concerned with the "how" of behavior—the non-motivational and stylistic ways in which infants and young children behave. From this interest the construct of temperament emerged. *Temperament* can be defined as the underlying style or pattern of a person's behavior which sets the stage for his reactions to the world. Thomas, Chess, and Birch (1968) identified ten categories that can be used in assessing the temperament of infants and young children. These categories are activity level, rhythmicity, approach/withdrawal, adaptability, intensity of reaction, threshold of responsiveness, quality of mood, distractability, attention span, and persistence. *Activity level* refers to the degree of activity a child displays. Essentially a child can be rated as active or passive. *Rhythmicity* refers to the regularity of behavioral patterns. For example, the infant who has bowel movements at about the same time each day and takes naps during the same periods daily would be judged to be higher in rhythmicity than an infant who were less predictable in those functions. *Approach/withdrawal* refers to the child's tendency to approach or withdraw from a new situation or person. In a sense it represents a child's outgoingness. *Adaptability* is related to the child's ability to adjust to a new situation. *Intensity of reaction* refers to the degree or level of reaction a child has to different environmental situations. This category measures the child's degree of vigor or emotional furor. *Threshold of responsiveness* deals with the degree of stimulation necessary to evoke a response on the part of the child. The lower a child's threshold the more quickly she responds to environmental stimuli. *Quality of mood* refers to the child's general disposition and measures the degree to which she is "up" or "down." *Distractability* is a measure of the degree to which environmental stimuli can divert the child's attention. *Attention span* relates to the child's ability to keep his attention focused on a particular task. *Persistence* is related in a sense to attention span but deals more directly with the child's tendency to stick with a task despite obstacles to the completion of the task. Carey (1970) and Buss and Plomin (1975) have used similar categories to codify infant temperament.

Temperament is important in the social and affective development of the child because it is responsible, in part, for how others in the environment react to the child. This issue is particularly important in dyadic interaction between infant/child and primary caregivers. A mother responds differently to children of different temperaments, and these responses may lead to different social developmental outcomes. Furthermore, some evidence suggests that infants and children with certain temperamental patterns are more likely to display behavior disorders later in childhood (Thomas, Chess, & Birch, 1968). But, as was discussed in Chapter 2, the probability of exhibiting a particular characteristic in the future is based on a multitude of risk factors. Thus, while the premise of Thomas, Chess, and Birch has some validity, it is also important to note that what may be considered a difficult temperament by one caretaker would not necessarily be considered a difficult temperament by another caretaker. The prediction of behavior disorders is probably more closely associated with the interaction of the temperaments of caretakers and their children than it is a function of the individual temperamental characteristics of one or the other (cf. Sameroff & Chandler, 1975). Cameron (1977, 1978) has made this point explicitly in studying the relationship between parental characteristics and children's temperament. Simply, then, the goodness of fit between the caretaker and the child is probably more important in determining the ultimate outcomes of social and affective development than are the characteristics of the individual interactants.

Play

Play is one of the important functions of childhood and is essential in facilitating a child's development. Bruner (Bruner, 1972; Bruner, Jolly, & Sylva, 1976) has suggested that play is particularly important as means for a child to learn the social function of her behavior in a safe and non-threatening situation. Piaget (1951), in discussing the role of play in the development of symbolic processes, suggests "that play emphasizes assimilation rather than accommodation [because] play need not fit the demands of reality" (Baldwin, 1968, p. 232). This suggestion underscores Bruner's point that play provides a safe situation in which to explore social as well as cognitive schema.

Play has traditionally been considered an important part of the curriculum in preschool programs. This is because play was thought to promote development in all the growth areas—intellectual, social, language, and motor skills. Spontaneous play was encouraged in traditional nursery school programs, for example, simply by allowing some time in the schedule each day for "free play." Teachers generally did not believe that they had to teach children to play, but rather thought that the learnings to be gained from play would accrue indirectly from the experience.

As programs for handicapped children became more numerous at the preschool level due to the increasingly widespread philosophy of early intervention, emphasis came to be placed on the direct teaching of skills to the young child, and teachers were less willing to trust in the seemingly haphazard benefits of play to promote learning. The purpose of such programs was to help the at-risk or handicapped child to "catch up" with his peers, and direct instruction seemed a faster method of insuring progress. In addition, early intervention programs were generally funded through federal grants and many were experimental in nature, so a strong emphasis was placed on testable results. Teaching of specific skills, therefore, was and continues to be the major focus of most preschool programs for the handicapped. The traditional nursery school emphasis on play has been rejected as too non-directive and too haphazard an approach.

As a result of this directive teaching trend, the benefits of spontaneous play as a means for cognitive, social, language, and motor development have been temporarily lost or at least underemphasized. There is nevertheless a strong case to be made for the inclusion of play in the curriculum of the handicapped child for there is compelling evidence that play is necessary for a child's optimum development.

In the following discussion we will examine some issues related to play and learning in general, including the implications of research in this area, and then relate these to what we know about the play of handicapped children. Finally, we will discuss the role of parents in helping handicapped children to optimal development through play.

Let us begin with a definition of play. Sylva (1977, p. 62), drawing on several other writers, defines it as active, persistent manipulative or locomotor experimentation with objects, with the environment, with one's own body and/or with other organisms. It is self-initiated and apparently lacks immediate survival purpose. Bower, Bersamin, Fine, and Carlson (1974) add that it is enjoyable, serious, and voluntary. According to Tizard and Harvey (1977), it is orderly and not goal-oriented. The lack of a goal in play distinguishes it from problem-solving (Sylva, 1977).

In summary, we may say: (1) that play is an enjoyable activity that the child engages in voluntarily for the fun of it, (2) that the child has no particular goal in mind but nevertheless pursues the activity in an orderly fashion, and (3) that the child is quite serious about the activity. And there seem to be quite serious consequences of a child's play experiences, as we shall see in the following section.

PLAY AND LEARNING   In studies of animals other than humans, play has been found to be biologically useful (Lorenz, 1972). Many animals have an inborn curiosity that encourages them to explore their environment. Through play, they learn about new objects, experience a greater variety of events, and become more adaptable to new situations. They are at home in a variety of environments as a result and are therefore better survivors.

Through play, animals also learn flexibility (Sylva, 1977). The playing animal uses behaviors from survival patterns such as feeding or fleeing and combines them into novel approaches. This combinatorial aspect is considered by some researchers to be the very essence of play; it trains the animals to string together bits of previously acquired behavior to form novel solutions to problems. In this sense playing is important training for problem-solving.

In a similar fashion, play emerges in children as a result of curiosity about their environment. Because it is self-initiated and because it is relatively tension-free (one can't "fail" in play because there really isn't any goal), it is an excellent means for a child to practice problem-solving.

Studies of children's play and its effect on learning have demonstrated that there is indeed a close relationship between the two. A classic study by Smilansky (1968) associated deficits in dramatic play with cognitive deficiencies in disadvantaged preschoolers. Smilansky's definitions of cognitive play follow.

1. *Functional play* involves simple, repetitive muscle movements with or without objects.
2. *Constructive play* is goal-directed and consists of educational activities like building with blocks or tinker toys and working with puzzles. Objects are necessary.

3. *Dramatic play* involves make-believe activities, role playing, and symbolic play. Dressing up, dramatizing stories, and playing house are examples.
4. *Games* are formal, usually highly organized and rule-bound. They vary from simple circle games or chase games to more complex team games.

In an experiment with three, four, and five-year-old nonhandicapped children involving a problem-solving task, Sylva (1977) found that children who played with test materials solved the problem as well as those who observed an adult solve the problem and then attempted it themselves. The "play" group progressed from simple to complex means in completing the task, showing they learned as they progressed. By contrast, the "observer" group immediately used the most complex means, demonstrated by the adult, to solve the problem. These children did not try to work the problem out gradually and so less learning took place. In another study, Feitelson and Ross (1973) reported increases in originality and exploration as measured by a test of creativity for five-year-olds who were trained in symbolic play.

Another study of the relationship between play and problem-solving involved groups of disadvantaged children who were taught to expand their play into more symbolic activities through adult modeling (Rosen, 1974). These children showed significant improvement in post-test problem-solving behavior. In a similar experiment Dansky (1980) examined three groups of low SES children on their performance on cognitive tasks following experiences in (1) sociodramatic play, (2) exploration, and (3) free play. The first two groups received training; the third acted as controls. Only those trained in sociodramatic (symbolic) play demonstrated improvement in cognitive performance. Finally, Saltz, Dixon, and Johnson (1977) found that fantasy play (e.g., acting out fairy tales) increased the cognitive performance of disadvantaged preschoolers, whereas activities such as cutting, pasting, and listening to stories had no such measurable effect.

Studies with young, handicapped children yield similar results. Newcomer and Morrison (1974) used play therapy with institutionalized, mentally retarded children and found increases in their scores on the Denver Developmental Screening Test. Both group and individual play therapy seemed to promote cognitive and social development. Fraiberg and Adelson (1973) found that play helps the blind child develop the capacity for symbolic representation as evidenced, for example, in use of pronouns "me" and "I."

In summary, there indeed appears to be a strong link between the type of play variously described as symbolic, sociodramatic, or fantasy and the development of cognitive abilities.

PLAY AND SOCIAL DEVELOPMENT   Although it depends upon cognitive structures, play can also be viewed as a social phenomenon, since it also depends to a large degree on a child's interaction with other people. Early forms of play are solitary and may be based on the child making variations on a theme in a similar manner to tertiary circular responses (see Chapter 3). Vocal play may not even depend upon a social object but may result from the child making adaptations with the voice. These early solitary play behaviors are important in social development in that they help the child to establish and differentiate self from other. It is only as the child's cognitive development becomes less egocentric that he can begin to play cooperatively with others. Cooperative play relies upon a child's ability to take the perspective of the playmate, setting the stage for the development of prosocial behaviors like sharing, helping, and cooperation.

It should not be inferred, however, that solitary play is by definition a lower level of play than cooperative play. Rubin, Maioni and Hornung (1976) suggest that parallel, not solitary, play is indicative of the least mature level of a social play hierarchy for three and four-year-olds. Children who play by themselves may simply wish to "get away from it all," they suggest, and the children's activities—such as painting, clay modeling, or writing a story—may be at a very high level indeed. On the other hand, children who exhibit parallel play, that is, playing beside other children rather than with them, may actually want to play with the other children but lack the ability to do so.

Researchers have identified several types of play, some focused on interactions with people and others concerned with exploration or use of objects. The best known and most widely used category system for social play is probably that of Parten (1932). By observing normal nursery school children during free play, she identified six categories of play in which children typically engage. These are summarized below.

1. *Unoccupied behavior.* Child engages in random behavior such as watching something of momentary interest, following the teacher, or engaging in play limited to her own body.
2. *Onlooker.* Child spends most of his time watching others play. He often talks to the children he's watching, making suggestions or asking questions, but doesn't enter into play himself.
3. *Solitary independent play.* Child plays alone and independently with toys different from those used by children within speaking distance and makes no effort to get close to other children.
4. *Parallel activity.* Child plays independently but the activity she chooses naturally brings her among other children. She is *beside* rather than *with* other children; uses toys similar to those of children nearby, however.
5. *Associative play.* Child plays with other children in a common activity forming a group which excludes other children. Each child acts as he wishes; there is no subordination to the needs of the group. All children engage in similar if not identical activity; there is no division of labor.
6. *Cooperative or organized supplementary play.* Child plays in a group

organized for some play purpose (product, drama, competition, or game.) There is division of labor, with children taking different roles. One or two children dominate, become leaders, and exclude some other children from the group.

Parten found that all the children she observed, who ranged in age from two to five years, participated in all the types of play described except *onlooker behavior*, which was observed only in children younger than three years, and *cooperative play*, which was not seen in the youngest children. She noted that onlookers were most common at 2 1/2 to 3 1/2, solitary play was most common at 2 1/2, parallel play was most common at 2 years, associative play was observed mostly among the 4 and 5-year-olds, and cooperative play was most common among older children who had the highest I.Q. levels. There was also a positive correlation found between group play and I.Q. level in three-year-olds. That is, only the three-year-olds with higher I.Q. levels engaged in group play. By four years, all the children engaged in associative or cooperative play. Parten speculated that language development facilitated group play.

Parten considered solitary play a lower or younger form of play, but it should be noted that her purpose was to measure social (group) participation. This would automatically relegate solitary play to a less favored position. As we have noted above, her evaluation may not be accurate. Capobianco and Cole (1960), in their study of the play of educable and trainable mentally retarded children based on Parten's categories, felt that those children assigned to Parten's *solitary* category had their play ability underestimated.

PLAY OF HANDICAPPED CHILDREN   How does the play of handicapped children differ from the way nonhandicapped children play? Or does it? Do handicapped children play in a manner expected for their mental age? Or are their play habits qualitatively different from those of other children? The answers to these questions are important in helping us to understand the educational needs of handicapped children. In addition, we need to know whether handicapped children play spontaneously or whether they need to be taught to do so. Can or should they be taught to play at higher levels than they play spontaneously?

Fortunately a great deal of research has been done to attempt to answer these questions. Although the results are mixed, there are some definite trends. Let us examine the evidence.

As Rogers (1982 and Li (1981) pointed out, many studies of handicapped children's play involve institutionalized children. The effects of institutional life are difficult to separate from the effects of the handicapping condition on the children's play abilities. Another confounding variable is socioeconomic status, and a third is the subject's degree of emotional adjustment. These three variables sometimes affect the child's play more than does the handicapping condition. Taking these variables into consideration, we find few differences between handicapped children's play and the play of nonhandicapped children.

For example, Tizard (1964) found that mentally retarded children play at a level commensurate with mental age, and that they engage in spontaneous free play. In a study involving relatively well-adjusted, non-institutionalized, mentally retarded children Hulme and Lunzer (1966) found that the play behavior of these children was not easily distinguishable from that of normal children of comparable mental age. In a similar study, Weiner and Weiner (1974) analyzed the toy-play behavior of mentally retarded, non-institutionalized children and compared it to that of normal children. They found that some types of play are primarily related to chronological age, and other types to mental age. Only a few play behaviors seemed to be found exclusively in normal children. Throwing and pounding of toys, for example, were observed only in a group of three-year-old, normal children but not in six-year-old, mentally retarded children whose mental age was three years. Using push-pull toys, manipulating toy parts, and oral exploration of toys, on the other hand, are associated with mental age, for both normal three-year-olds and mentally retarded six-year-olds (MA of three years) demonstrated these. And only the normal three-year-olds and six-year-olds combined toys into more complex forms. The mentally retarded children, even those of similar mental age, did not do this.

All the studies reported here involving institutionalized children suffer from the problem described above. Nevertheless, they provide evidence that young, handicapped children can be taught to play in more symbolic and/or cooperative ways. Strain's (1975) study is an example. In this project, severely retarded four-year-olds were involved in sociodramatic activities such as listening to a story and taking roles of the story's characters. Their subsequent free play was found to be more social and less solitary than previously. Similarly, Knapczyk and Yoppi (1975) successfully trained young, mentally retarded children with behavior and communication disorders, using behavior modification techniques, in cooperative and competitive social play.

In a study of the symbolic play of severely retarded and autistic children, Wing, Gould, Yeates, and Brierley (1977) found that both the type of handicap and the environmental setting (home, school, residential care) affected the child's level of play. Autistic children were not observed to engage in symbolic play, even when their mental ages were greater than two years, the time when normal children emerge from the sensorimotor period. Wing and her colleagues (1977) further noted that children without any symbolic play were more likely to be in residential care than living at home. Many of these children, too, had mental ages above two years. On the other hand, children with Down's syndrome tended to play symbolically most often.

Not all studies of young, handicapped children have been limited to the mentally retarded. Mogford (1977) examined the play of children with other handicapping conditions. She reports that deaf children engage in imaginative play and play involving representation as much as do hearing children. Mogford reports that deaf children, even though they experienced serious expressive and receptive language deficits, have been observed to have imaginary playmates.

The play of these children was less social and more solitary in nature than that of hearing children. Aphasic children engaged in make-believe play and produced symbolic drawings, according to Mogford, whereas autistic children did not.

Mogford also reports that children with cerebral palsy do not play as spontaneously as nonhandicapped children and need both encouragement and some assistance with toys. This is true of blind children as well (Fraiberg & Adelson, 1973).

In summary, research shows that although some handicapped children are very much like other children in the quality and spontaneity of their play, others need encouragement, assistance, or training. Sheridan (1975) expresses the consensus of several authors (Li, 1981; Mogford, 1977; Wehman, 1977) when she states that some disabled children learn slowly and sometimes lack drive and powers of concentration. Having once achieved a basic skill, these children may not elaborate on it but become stuck at an elementary level. To progress they need "prolonged patient individual step-by-step instruction and must be stimulated to constant practice" (p. 118).

As will be discussed in Chapter 11, some models of preschool education rely heavily on the child's basic ability to play and her natural curiosity to explore the environment. Unfortunately, as Lerner, Mardell-Czudnowski, and Goldenberg (1981) point out, handicapped children, especially the severely handicapped, tend not to engage in spontaneous play. As a result, it is often necessary to provide these children an opportunity to learn to play and/or to arrange their learning environments to maximize their ability to interact with adults and other children. In addition, as Lerner and her colleagues further suggest, it is necessary to provide children with directed play experiences in which certain aspects of the play situation are emphasized so that the children are more likely to acquire certain desired outcomes (e.g., cooperation, helping, etc.) from a particular play experience.

Childen try out new roles, experiment with their environment, and test their limits in physical and mental activity through play. Play also provides a safe forum in which to experiment with aggression and sexual arousal as a means of learning how to handle these feelings, without fear of adult antagonism. Hartup (1978) points out that play is a uniquely child-child activity and that peer interaction is therefore a better means of eliciting play behavior than adult-child interaction. In play activity with peers, children encounter an equalitarian environment with fewer constraints than adult-child relationships typically encompass, and this environment facilitates many kinds of learning: social, cognitive, moral, language, and motor. Indeed, inadequate peer relations are prognostic indicators of social and emotional trouble in young children, for loners more often end up as delinquents or develop adjustment difficulties in adulthood.

In the final analysis, play is important in the development of social and affective behavior. Play facilitates both the adequate development of self and of interpersonal social behavior. Play should be an integral part of any program designed to maximize the development of handicapped, preschool age children.

Attachment

Members of a species tend to affiliate or attach themselves to each other. Lorenz (1957) described an early form of attachment when he identified imprinting. This phenomenon, which is most notable in birds, is characterized by what appears to be an automatic attachment between newly hatched birds and their mothers. Phenomena like imprinting support the supposition that attachment within a species is an innate function. However, Lorenz (1957) also demonstrated that young birds tend to imprint not only to their mothers but also to the first, large, seemingly animate object in their environment. Lorenz, in fact, successfully demonstrated that these young birds would imprint to him. Research by Gottlieb (1965) indicates that imprinting may be affected by auditory stimulation during the prenatal period. Gottlieb demonstrated that birds of one species are more likely to imprint to birds of another species than their own if the singing of the latter species is predominant in the environment during the gestation period. This work on the basic animal process of imprinting led to the development of an ethologically based theory of attachment as suggested by Bowlby (1969).

Bowlby suggests that attachment begins with an instinctual tie of the infant to her mother but "he also [suggests] that maternal responsiveness is important in augmenting and maintaining the instinctive social responses" (Corter, 1974, p. 179). Bowlby posits that attachment had adapative function for species in earlier evolution by providing a basis for protecting young from predators. Bowlby's theory of attachment, in a sense, grows from that of Freud (1915, 1926) who suggested that the mother provides the source of all pleasure for the infant by satisfying his instinctual needs (e.g., eating). Attachment results as the mother becomes a greater and greater source of infant satisfaction.

Freud's theory is also related to that of Sears, Maccoby, and Levin (1957) who suggest a drive-reduction model of attachment. Corter summarizes the drive reduction theory of attachment thusly:

> Drive reduction theory [places] emphasis on the feeling situation as a wellspring for attachment; the infant's responses to the mother, such as crying, are reinforced by her drive reducing caretaking activities. Gradually the mother comes to be valued and sought in her own light, as well as for the caretaking she provides, and a dependency drive is established. [1974, p. 175]

While these three theories provided the basis for studying attachment in the 70s, more emphasis is now being given to attachment as an interactive and reciprocal process. Operant conceptualizations like those of Bijou and Baer (1965) stimulated this shift in thinking. Bijou and Baer view attachment as resulting from the mutual reinforcement exchanged by mother and child. Bell's (1968) recognition of reciprocity between mother and infant also contributed to a reconceptualization of attachment. Bell's work brought out the somewhat obvious but previously overlooked realization that the mother and child are a dyadic and interactive system. Infants are not attached to their mothers; rather infants and their mothers are attached to *each other*. Both mother and child bring responses to the interaction that lead to the development of attachment between them.

Development of Self

Self may be defined as the set of ideas, values, attitudes, and feelings that make up a person's internal state. Lewis and Brooks (1978, p. 211) have called this notion of self "self as an object." On the other hand, we have self as a subject or what "James termed . . . the *I* [and] Freud termed the *ego.*" *Self-awareness* develops with the child's recognition of this internal state and of his effectiveness on the world about him.

The development of self begins with the child's recognition that she is separate from other; that is, realization of the self/other dichotomy. This recognition starts with the infant's action on the world and has its basis in the initial contingency experiences which the infant has (Lewis & Goldberg, 1969a, 1969b; Thurman, 1978). As Lewis and Brooks have stated:

> the basic notion of existence separate from other (both animate and inanimate) is developed from the interaction of the infant with its environment and is developed from the regularity and interaction of the infant's action and its outcome. The mechanism of feedback provides the basic contingency information for the child; kinesthetic feedback produced by the infant's own actions forms the basis for the development of self. [1978, p. 212]

In infancy, circular responses as discussed in Chapter 3 provide a major avenue for the child to "test" his effectiveness on the inanimate world. Interactions with parents and other social beings provide the young child another major means of developing self. This human interaction can be critical in determining the types of perceptions and feelings the young child has about himself. These early feelings and perceptions of self form the basis of the way an individual will feel about himself later in life. For example, in discussing the vivid case of John Merrick, the Elephant Man, who was horribly disfigured by neurofibromatosis, Montagu (1971, p. 7) speculates that Merrick must have received "a great deal of love from his mother [during his early childhood and that] . . . on any other assumption it would be difficult . . . to account for the strength, health, integrity and amiability of John Merrick's personality." Each of these traits were developed by Merrick in spite of the mistreatment and exploitation he underwent during his later childhood, adolescence, and young adult years.

The development of a positive self-image is largely dependent on the child's feeling that her primary caregivers are trusting and acceptant. A feeling of trust provides the infant with a general sense of well-being and sets the stage for the infant to take the risks necessary to try out new forms of behavior. Testing new forms of behavior not only is necessary for the development of cognitive abilities as was seen in Chapter 3, but it is also important for the child's development of self. It is through these new behavior patterns that the child learns to behave autonomously and to exert self-control. Commenting on Erikson's (1963) second stage of psycho-social development, Suran and Rizzo (1979, p. 33) suggest that when the child is 18 to 36 months old, "the main focus is on the integration of self as an autonomous unit able to exist in an independent fashion."

Unfortunately, it is difficult for some parents to provide trust and acceptance to a child who is developmentally delayed. A parent's acceptance is often based on the child's ability to meet the parent's expectations. When the child is unable to meet parental expectations because of developmental problems, deficits in the child's self-concept and overall social and emotional development can occur. Thus, a child who is experiencing a physical or cognitive problem may develop a concomitant problem in the social and emotional area. Professionals providing services to young, developmentally disabled children must be concerned with both the needs of the child and the needs of the family in dealing with the child. It is often necessary to make a difficult decision about whether the child or the family should come first. It is possible that the trust and acceptance necessary for the child's ultimate development of self and general well-being may only be created by shifts in and even dissolution of existing family units. Chapter 10 provides a more complete discussion of families with disabled, young children and how to deal effectively with them.

PROBLEMS OF SOCIAL AND EMOTIONAL DEVELOPMENT

Having addressed some major points about social and emotional development in infants and young children, we can now turn our attention to some of the problems that arise in social and emotional development. As Samuels (1981, p. 153) has pointed out, "there is no question that children with exceptionalities are at a greater risk of developing maladaptive behavior [i.e., social and emotional problems]." It follows from Samuels' statement that there are two classes of emotionally disturbed or behavior disordered children. One class consists of those children who have as their only disability some impairment in social and/or emotional development. The other class of children are those to whom Samuels is alluding, viz., those who because of other disabling conditions like cerebral palsy, mental retardation, or chronic illness also develop problems in social and emotional development. As was suggested in Chapter 2, one of the primary purposes of early intervention programs for developmentally disabled children is to reduce the degree of risk they experience during their development. Early interventionists must strive to create environments that minimize the development of concomitant problems in the social and emotional domains. The remainder of this chapter is devoted to the various types of social and emotional disabilities present in preschool age children. Our emphasis is on preschool age children because only rarely, and in the most severe case, do social and emotional disabilities manifest themselves prior to the age of three years.

Social Deviance

It is difficult to begin any discussion of problems in social-emotional development without talking first about social deviancy. *Deviance* can be defined as difference with a negative connotation. In a sense, deviancy is inherent in the label.
Simmons (1969) suggested, for example, that no human behavior is inherently
deviant. According to his reasoning only those behaviors labeled as such are deviant. While Simmons' notion can be applied to the labeling of any disabling
condition, it is particularly relevant to social and emotional disabilities. These
disabilities more than others are defined in terms of adherence to social norms.
As a matter of fact, most young children engage in some behavior patterns that
could be labeled socially deviant. Almost all young children, for example, express fears, are oppositional, and even display autistic-like behavior. But it is
only when these behavior patterns are seen as being outside of the accepted
norm that children are labeled phobic, oppositional, or autistic. It is often possible to reduce the degree and severity of these behavior patterns, concomitantly
reducing the probability of the child being labeled in the future. Here again we
see an avenue by which early intervention can decrease risk to the child.

The concept of deviance is discussed more fully in the context of intervention
in Chapters 8 and 9. It is mentioned here so that the reader will be mindful of its
implications in the definition and labeling of problems in social-emotional development. Having said this we are now ready to discuss some of the specific problems of social and emotional development.

Autism

Perhaps the most severe type of social and emotional disorder of early childhood
is autism. In its classic form, early infantile autism, the child begins to show
symptoms of the condition prior to the second year of life. Kanner (1943), who
first identified the parameters of infantile autism, suggested that autistic infants
felt strange in their mothers' arms, would not mold to their mothers' bodies
when held, and would not anticipate or seek human contact. Fallen and
McGovern (1978) report that the incidence of autism ranges from 2 to 4.5 cases
per 10,000 population. These incidence estimates vary depending on the nar-
rowness of the definition used. Classic cases of autism as defined by Kanner are
at the lower end of the incidence figures. Higher incidence figures reflect more
broadly based definitions which include children with severe communication
and affective disorders.

According to Fallen and McGovern (1978, p. 16), autism's specific characteristics, attributable to Kanner, are as follows:

1. Onset of condition at birth or at about two years of age after apparently normal development.
2. Impaired or complete lack of appropriate social interactions with
   parents, other adults, and children.

3. Severely impaired or complete lack of language ability.
4. Lack of intellectual development, or retardation in certain areas accompanied by normal or superior abilities in other areas.
5. Self-stimulating behavior, for example, repetitive and peculiar use of objects and toys or repetitive and peculiar body motions such as rocking or spinning.
6. Little or no eye contact with others.
7. Compulsive behaviors and extremely negative reactions to changes in the environment.
8. Extreme distress for no discernible reasons.
9. Hyperactivity (excessively active) or hypoactivity (inactive) often accompanied by erratic sleep patterns.
10. Inability to perform certain gross and fine motor activities, for example walking with a peculiar gait and having limpness in fingers.
11. Unusual reaction to sights and sounds, for example, seeming not to hear certain sounds and overreacting to others by holding hands over ears.
12. Apparent insensitivity to pain, frequently resulting in self-abusive behaviors.

The etiology of autism is not precisely known. Some have theorized that mothers who are cold and aloof are responsible for autism in their children (e.g., Mahler, 1952). Others have attributed it to arousal states (e.g., Hutt & Ounsted, 1970) or to perceptual difficulties (e.g., Ornitz & Ritvo, 1977). Ornitz and Ritvo (1977) have also related autism to increased levels of the neurotransmitter serotonin in the blood, thus suggesting a biochemical basis for the condition. The actual development of the autistic state is undoubtedly a function of multiple factors some of which are biologically determined factors and others which are inherent in the child's environment. It will be some time before all the factors accounting for autism are fully delineated and understood.

Effective interventions with autistic children have been limited, especially those employing psychotherapeutic models. Therapies based on operant conditioning have met with relatively more success. Lovaas (1973), in particular, has demonstrated a good deal of success with the use of behavioral methods with these children. The aversive nature of some of his techniques, however, has made them unacceptable to many interventionists. Regardless of the intervention methods employed, the prognosis for autistic children is far from optimistic. And, in almost all instances, symptoms persist to some degree throughout an affected child's life. Autism remains one of the least understood and hardest conditions to intervene upon effectively of any disability of childhood.

Childhood Psychosis

Unlike autism, childhood psychosis first manifests itself in preschool age children. These children often have shown patterns of development within the normal range prior to the time when psychotic symptoms first appear. The onset of symptoms is usually gradual, and, as a result, symptoms often go unnoticed for a period of time. Childhood schizophrenia is the most widely recognized form of childhood psychosis. Treffert (1970) found 3.3 cases of childhood psychosis per 10,000 population in the state of Wisconsin. About 56 percent of those identified had childhood schizophrenia while only about 20 percent suffered from infantile autism (Samuels, 1981, p. 39).

Childhood psychosis is characterized by the same types of symptoms associated with adult psychosis. Children with childhood psychosis may exhibit disturbed patterns of thought. They may become withdrawn or disoriented. There may be a decrease in their language ability. They may also exhibit inappropriate mood shifts and affective states. The incidence and severity of symptoms varies greatly from case to case. Rimland (1964) has suggested that children with childhood schizophrenia have more varied symptoms than those with autism and that the former are more likely to have contact with other people than are children who are autistic.

While the factors generally accounting for childhood psychosis and schizophrenia appear to be as varied as those associated with autism, there is notable difference. There is a clear family relationship in childhood schizophrenia. Gianascol (1973), for example, disclosed that 16 percent of families with one schizophrenic parent also had schizophrenic children. When both parents were schizophrenic the same percentage jumps to about 40 (Erlenmeyer-Kimling, 1968). Although these authors have tended to make a case for genetic causation of schizophrenia, it must be pointed out that children may just as likely exhibit schizophrenic patterns of behavior because of the models provided and the child-rearing practices used by their schizophrenic parents. Sameroff and Zax (1978), in their study of children of schizophrenic mothers, suggested just such a transactional model and were unwilling to link schizophrenia in these children solely to genetic mechanisms.

The same models of intervention that have been employed with autistic children have been used with those displaying childhood psychosis. As with autism, operant behavioral methods have been among the most successful in bringing about improvement in these children (cf. Lovaas & Bucher, 1974).

Phobias

Another problem in social-emotional development that sometimes manifests itself in children is fears or phobias. A *fear* may be defined as a persistent behavioral overreaction to some aspect of the environment, the result of which is often anxiety and withdrawal. Generally, the fearful individual will make every attempt to avoid the fear-inducing situation.

As work presented by Lewis and Rosenblum (1974) suggests, infants and young children display fear and wariness in certain situations (e.g., an eight or nine month infant will usually show wariness of an unfamiliar adult). It is important to recognize that such fear responses may be appropriate and adaptive for the young child and that these responses should not be discouraged. On the other hand, these fear responses, most of which have a physiological basis, are the basis for the development of fears. Thus, while fear responses are important and necessary for the individual survival and developmental progress, when these same responses are converted into generalized fears they can become a major hindrance to maximum social and emotional development.

Bijou and Baer (1961) suggest that fears develop when naturally occurring fear responses are classically conditioned to other stimuli and then brought under operant control. Classical conditioning derives from Pavlov's (1927) early work with dogs. His paradigm suggests that certain stimuli will bring about certain physiological responses. The link between a particular stimulus and the subsequent response which occurs is an unlearned or unconditioned stimulus (UCS) and elicits or brings about an unconditioned response (UCR). Pavlov demonstrated that if a UCS was presented simultaneously with a neutral stimulus (i.e., one that does not automatically elicit a certain physiological response), after a number of trials of simultaneous presentation the neutral stimulus when presented singly would also elicit a response of the type elicited by the UCS. At this point the neutral stimulus becomes a conditioned stimulus (CS) and the response to it a conditioned response (CR). In Pavlov's experiments with dogs he used meat powder as a UCS which was followed by salivation as a UCR. After pairing meat powder with a buzzer (neutral stimulus) for a number of trials, the buzzer became a conditioned stimulus which elicited salivation. Figure 5.1 shows schematically Pavlov's experiment.

Fears, according to Bijou and Baer, can originate in a similar manner. Suppose, for example, that a three-year-old child is sleeping in a dark room and is suddenly awakened by a clap of thunder. This loud noise acts as a UCS for fear responses. This UCS is paired with the neutral stimulus of darkness. If this experience is frightening enough or if it occurs several times in rather close succes-

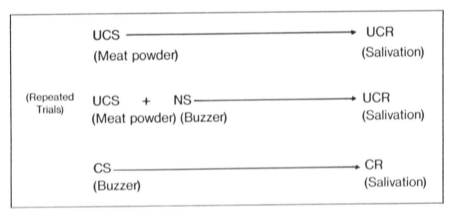

FIGURE 5.1   A Schematic Representation of Classical (Pavlovian) Conditioning

sion, then darkness can become a CS for the same types of fear responses which are automatically elicited by the loud sound of the thunder. Herein would lie the basis of a child's fear of the dark.

This fear could become even more firmly established if the child's parents became overly attentive to her fearful responses, thus providing her with positive reinforcement. Bijou and Baer have suggested that fear responses come under operant control in this way. That is, the responses become, in part, a function of their reinforcing consequences. It is often difficult for parents and other caregivers to know how much attention to provide to children when they are exhibiting fear. Too much attention can contribute to a maladaptive, long-standing fear, while not enough attention may make the child feel isolated and insecure.

Oppositional Behavior

The adaptive social and emotional development of a group of children are interfered with because of a pattern of oppositional behavior. *Oppositional behavior* can be characterized as negative and uncooperative. Affected children may also exhibit temper tantrums. Oppositional children often refuse to obey requests by caretakers and have violent and prolonged temper tantrums when made to do something they do not want to do.

The basis for oppositional behavior in preschool age children often resides in the pattern of interaction between the child and his parent(s). Typically, oppositional children receive a good deal of parental attention when they behave in undesirable ways. On the other hand, parents of these children will seldom, if ever, attend to them when they are behaving in more appropriate ways. Thus, the child learns that she can receive the attention of parents by being negative and uncooperative. Since parental attention is so important to young children, they will continue to behave in inappropriate ways *even when the attention they receive from their parents is of a negative variety.* The negative attention they receive becomes even more rewarding to them because their parents are simultaneously giving them no attention for desired behavior.

As long as the same pattern of interaction is maintained the oppositional behavior will continue. This builds up feelings of frustration in the parents and often causes them to have negative feelings toward their child. These feelings may affect the parents' ability to make the child feel wanted and secure and thus further impede the child's social and emotional development.

The most effective means to change an oppositional child is to modify the pattern of interaction between the child and his parents. The parent can be taught to direct more positive attention to the child when he is behaving in an appropriate or cooperative way and to pay no attention to the child's inappropriate behavior (unless of course a dangerous situation exists). In this way the pattern of interaction between the parent and the child is reversed. What had been attended to is now ignored and what had been ignored is now attended to. Some of the means by which parents can be effectively trained are discussed later in Chapter 10.

Aggression

Aggressive behavior is any behavior designed to hurt property or people in the environment. Aggression or hostility, if prevalent in a child's behavior, can interfere significantly with her social acceptance both by adults and peers. This often leads to further aggressive behavior as the child attempts to gain attention and recognition from others. It is important to deal effectively with aggressive behavior in children at its onset, since it not only can hinder the child's social development but it can also cause injury to others in the environment.

There are several potential bases for aggressive behavior. Some authors (e.g., Rutter, 1975) have suggested that brain damage brings about increases in aggressive behavior. While this may be true, it is often difficult to demonstrate, since aggression itself may be used by clinicians as a means of suggesting that brain damage exists in a child. Thus, a circularity is evident. Children are defined as brain damaged because they are aggressive. Their presumed brain damage is then used as a basis for explaining their aggressive behavior.

Aggression has also been relaed to frustration. This point of view suggests that children work through their frustration by being aggressive towards others.

Children may also become aggressive because of aggressive models in their environments. Parents who use physical punishment as a primary means of child management are providing aggressive models to their children. Kazdin (1975) has suggested that punishment leads to aggression in children precisely for this reason. Of course television also provides a myriad of aggressive models for children to imitate. Even the typical Bugs Bunny or Roadrunner cartoon is full of aggressive models. Oftentimes, as do oppositional children, aggressive children gain parental attention through their aggressive behavior and only through it. It is therefore not uncommon to find children who are simultaneously aggressive and oppositional.

Like oppositional children, aggressive children must be given large amounts of attention and social praise for acting in appropriate ways. At the same time, they must be taught more adaptive ways of behaving, since they have learned that their main means of getting what they want is through hostile and aggressive acts. This aggressive form of interaction often becomes so firmly established that these children never engage in more prosocial behavior like helping, sharing, and cooperating. To lessen their aggressive tendencies takes from them their primary means of social interaction unless these other more desirable patterns of behavior are specifically taught to them.

Isolation

Some children tend to isolate themselves from others. This isolation may be due to shyness or it may be related to patterns of withdrawal that are associated with the more severe forms of impairment in social and emotional development (e.g., autism and childhood schizophrenia).

SHYNESS   Shyness is a function of the child's temperamental makeup and is characterized by the child's hesitancy and/or lack of ability to socially interact with others. Because of the highly competitive nature of our society and our basic belief that human interaction is necessary, shy children are often viewed by parents and teachers as having a social problem. The assumption is that if the child is shy his social development will be impeded. These attitudes often make the shy child feel unaccepted and may even promote a tendency to further withdraw from others. The child gets the message that it is not all right to be shy. It then becomes more difficult for the child to become assertive because his self-concept becomes negative as he is pushed to become more assertive or outgoing.

Interventions designed to help children overcome shyness should be implemented in a way to keep the child from feeling strange because of shyness. It is important to keep in mind that there is nothing inherently wrong with being shy, but rather that our cultural norms are such that shyness in other people is not well tolerated. Perhaps if early interventionists were more concerned with the development of good self-feelings and less concerned with shyness *per se*, this norm might begin to reverse itself. Self-acceptance, after all, ought to be one of the major objectives of activities designed to facilitate social and emotional development.

WITHDRAWAL   Withdrawal is distinct from shyness in that withdrawn children not only fail to make and maintain social contact with others, but they also withdraw when others make social contact with them. While the shy child may avoid social contact, she will not usually withdraw from it. The withdrawn child neither seeks nor wants social contact and behaves as if she abhors such contact.

Withdrawal is often one of several "symptoms" of severe social or emotional disability. As was suggested above, it is one of the characteristics noted in both autistic children and in those classified as having childhood schizophrenia. Strain and his associates (e.g., Strain, Kerr, & Ragland, 1981; Strain & Timm, 1974) have demonstrated and discussed methods for dealing with socially withdrawn children. These methods depend generally on the use of peer models and reinforcement techniques. However, interventionists of a more psychodynamic orientation question whether such techniques are treating a symptom of a more deep-seated emotional disability rather than the disability itself. Be this as it may, Strain's techniques can reduce the amount of social withdrawal exhibited by preschool children. Whether this decrease in social withdrawal then makes these children less autistic or schizophrenic depends on how one views the problem (i.e., whether one is of psychodynamic or a behavioral persuasion).

SUMMARY

This chapter has discussed some of the major features of the social and emotional development of young children. Specifically, it has looked at temperamental characteristics, attachment, and play and the role each plays in the social and emotional development of a child. The development of self and self-concept were also discussed. Finally, attention was given to various problems in social-emotional development as well as some of the means by which these problems are thought to develop.

Considerations for Motor Development

1. What is the role of reflexes in the motor development of infants?
2. What are the major features of motor development during the first five years of life?
3. What are the major characteristics of children who have cerebral palsy?

Of the main areas of development—motor, cognitive, social, and language—motor development is the least influenced by environmental factors. It progresses in more predictable stages than do the other areas, and so we tend to pay less attention to it in educational programs than we do the other developmental areas. Normal children generally attain the milestones of physical development with minimal assistance from teachers, parents, or specialists. This fact is probably more descriptive of educational programs in the United States than it is for some other countries that place greater emphasis on physical fitness and prowess. Our culture values cognitive and social skills more highly, and therefore gives these greater emphasis in school programs.

Physical development is nevertheless an important area of consideration for many disabled children. Goals for improving gross and fine motor functioning are often the primary focus of the disabled child's individualized education plan (IEP). This would be true for example, for a child with spina bifida or cerebral palsy. In addition, many children with multiple disabilities have educational goals established in all areas, and goals for motor functioning share equal impor-tance with cognitive, social, or language goals. The special knowledge of the physical or occupational therapist is often sought for designing strategies to pro-mote motor development.

In this chapter we will first discuss gross and fine motor functioning and the difference between them. Next we will look at normal neurophysiological devel-opment in order to gain an understanding of the neuromotor functions underly-ing motor development. We will pay special attention to the nervous system and its importance in achieving adequate motor functioning. Then will follow a brief discussion of early reflexes and their role in motor development and an examina-tion of the normal developmental milestones in gross and fine motor from birth to five years. The major portion of the chapter will then be given over to a review of problems in motor development that may be encountered in young children.

GROSS AND FINE MOTOR DEVELOPMENT

Gross motor development refers to the large muscle groups of the arms and legs, whereas *fine motor skills* are those involving the small muscles of the hands. Because motor development is a *proximodistal* process, with growth occurring from the trunk to the extremities, children gain control of the large arm and leg muscles before they achieve good coordination of the hands and fingers. Motor development is also *cephalocaudal*, progressing from head downward, which ex-plains why infants achieve head control and sitting before they can walk.

These facts illustrate that motor development is primarily a maturational process. According to Zaichkowsky, Zaichkowsky, and Martinek (1980), motor development is the product of growth, maturation, heredity, and learning. Growth refers to increases in size, while maturation includes qualitative changes: increases in complexity, organization, or control. In its pure form, mat-uration determines development without any external influences, but in reality environment always has an effect on development. Although motor development is probably less affected by environmental factors than is intellectual or language development, and as previously noted, strongly influenced by maturational fac-tors, such aspects of the environment as nutrition, physical activity, and illness obviously can cause differences in rate and quality of motor development. Per-haps it would be most accurate to state that given an adequate environment, physical development is primarily a maturational process.

Neurophysiological Processes

Motor functioning depends on bones, muscles, and nerves working together. The bones of the body originate as soft cartilage tissue and then ossify or harden. The ossification process begins during the prenatal period and continues until late adolescence. Girls generally have a more fully developed skeleton at birth than do boys (Zaichkowsky, Zaichkowsky, & Martinek, 1980), a difference that increases with age. Girls appear to be more stable in skeletal development than boys: for example, the rate of bone ossification is less variable in girls than in boys.

Muscles are attached to bones at the joints and work in pairs. If you bend your arm at the elbow, for example, the muscles in your inner arm flex and the muscles along your outer arm extend. This complementary process of flexion and extension is the basis for all muscle movement. A newborn baby is normally in a state of flexion, with arms, legs, and head drawn in toward the body. As the infant grows, muscles learn to extend for reaching, bending, and then to alternate flexion and extension for crawling, walking, and running.

The ability to flex or extend a muscle smoothly depends partly on the tone of the muscle. It is important that muscle tone not be too high (hypertonicity) or too low (hypotonicity) in order that muscles perform smoothly. Hypertonic muscles are tense, rigid, and resistant to movement. Hypotonic muscles are lacking in tone, appear limp and weak, and do not provide adequate support. Hypertonicity and hypotonicity are seen in cerebral palsied children, for example.

Two other characteristics of good muscles should be mentioned here: strength and control. The level of motor functioning a child is able to achieve depends to a great extent on the strength, control, and tone of her muscles (Johnston & Magrab, 1976). We will discuss these in more detail in a moment.

Muscles and bones work only when they are connected to the central nervous system by means of nerves. In fact, the nervous system is basic to all physical activity; nearly all problems in motor functioning in young children involve some dysfunction of the nervous system. Therefore, it is appropriate to briefly describe its functioning.

The brain controls all bodily activity through the nerves of the peripheral nervous system, that is, the spinal cord and the networks of nerves that reach to every part of the body. Muscle activity depends on electrical impulses that originate in the brain and travel from the spinal cord through peripheral nerves to specific muscle groups (Johnston & Magrab, 1976). Muscle control is the result of electrical impulses traveling back and forth between the brain and the muscles. When the brain or some part of the peripheral nervous system is damaged, the messages are incomplete and poor muscle tone, control, or strength result. Cerebral palsy, for example, stems from the motor area of the brain rather than from the muscles of the arms and legs, where the dysfunction is most apparent. Spina bifida is caused by a damaged spinal cord and results in the inability to use the lower parts of the body.

Changes in the muscle tone cause movement (see Figure 6.1). These changes in tone are dictated by the nervous system stimulating or inhibiting through impulses. The former cause the muscle to contract while the latter cause it to relax. Muscle control is centered in several areas of the brain. Voluntary motor activity is controlled by upper brain centers located in the cerebral cortex (see Figure 3.3). Involuntary or unconscious muscle movement (e.g., digestion of food, eye blinking, reflex movements) is controlled by lower brain centers, that is, the cerebellum and parts of the brain stem.

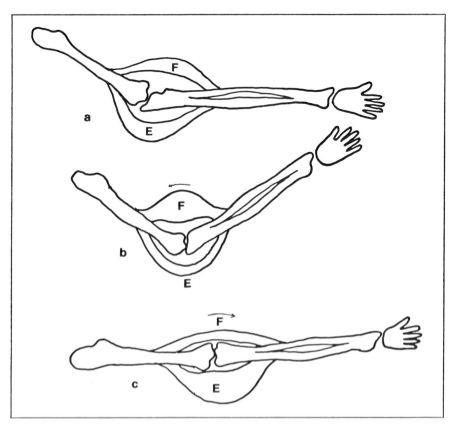

FIGURE 6.1   Musculoskeletal Interaction. From Johnston, R. & Magrab, P. *Developmental Disorders*. Baltimore: University Park Press, 1976. Reprinted with permission.

Although muscle strength has something to do with muscle size, it is more dependent on coordination of muscles or how well muscles in a group work together. This in turn is determined by the quality of the signals the muscles receive from the brain. Proper stimulation is necessary for a muscle to work effectively, no matter how large it is.

It is thus apparent that muscle tone, control, and strength depend on a well functioning brain and peripheral nervous system. The previous discussion has been necessarily short and lacking in detail. For a more complete but highly readable description of the muscular, skeletal, and neuromotor systems, the reader is referred to Johnston and Magrab (1976).

Perceptual-Motor Function

Consider for a moment a young child's everyday motor activity. The muscles move to reach, grasp, run, stoop, or stretch in response to a stimulus of some sort: a desired toy, teacher's voice calling to come eat lunch, Daddy appearing in the doorway. Motor responses are closely tied to the sensory stimulation that triggers them. These stimuli are received by the brain, which coordinates the sensory information it receives and the appropriate motor responses. Motor development, therefore, is one part of sensorimotor activity.

For optimal motor functioning to occur, the sensory systems which supply information to the brain must be well functioning. Ayres (1972) has identified six sensory systems: visual, auditory, tactile, vestibular (balance), proprioceptive, and olfactory (smell). While all six provide the brain with environmental information, vestibular and tactile systems are of particular interest to teachers and specialists working with motor impaired children.

The vestibular system controls balance and is centered in the inner ear. Other lower brain functions are influenced by vestibular input. Reduced input can be dangerous to a child, causing decreased respiration and heart rate, nausea, or perspiration (Lerner, Mardell-Czudnowski, & Goldenberg, 1981).

Touch is important to infants as a communication system. A major reason for defective development in institutional babies is infrequent handling. Babies seem to respond best to a quiet, soothing touch administered with a firm, steady pressure as in swaddling, the age-old remedy for a fussing baby. The young infant's crying is often triggered by the Moro reflex. A sudden change in position will cause his head to go back and he will start to cry. Crying causes him to throw his head back, triggering a second Moro response followed by more crying. In this way a circle of behaviors is established unless the Moro reflex is inhibited by touching the baby. Firm, steady restraint soothes him by interfering with the circle of responses (Brazelton, 1969, p. 28).

Tactile stimulation is thus basic to a child's early development, creating a sense of comfort and well-being or contrarily discomfort, aversion, or fear. The tactile system, like the vestibular, functions prenatally. Much of the intervention for children who have problems in motor development is concerned with proper tactile stimulation. Many multiply handicapped children who function at retarded levels have an aversion to being touched or touching other people and objects. Occupational therapists must spend a good deal of time helping such children adapt to tactile stimulation in order to promote normal sensorimotor integration.

Primitive and Automatic Reflexes

Early motor activity is primarily involuntary and is expressed through primitive reflexes. Some of these, such as the sucking and grasp reflexes, are present in the fetus, and continue after birth. Others appear at or soon after birth and prepare the infant for later, more complex movement. They are centered in the lower parts of the brain (midbrain, brain stem) and are gradually suppressed as higher control centers mature and more voluntary movement emerges.

Automatic reflexes, by contrast, are not present at birth but develop during the first two years of life. They remain an important part of our involuntary and largely unconscious nervous system that monitors our daily functioning. An example is the reflexive thrusting out of arms to protect one from a fall when one trips. These reflexes too, are located in the lower brain.

All reflexes are elicited by a stimulus of some sort. When the proper stimulus is present, the reflex is enacted independent of any conscious decision on the part of the child. Because of this fact and because the primitive reflexes normally disappear at about six months of age when the cerebral cortex matures enough to take over voluntary control of movement, these reflexes are used as the basis for diagnosing neurological dysfunction in infants.

Because thorough discussions of this procedure are available elsewhere (Brazelton, 1969; Cratty, 1970; Fiorentino, 1972; Johnston & Magrab, 1976; McGraw, 1966), we will limit ours to a brief summary of some of the major primitive and automatic reflexes, their purposes, and their significance in children who lack voluntary control of body movement.

Primitive Reflexes

The *Moro reflex* is present at birth and prenatally. In a normal infant, it disappears at approximately three to five months of age. Its absence at birth or its presence beyond five months is indicative of neurological dysfunction.

The Moro reflex is elicited by striking the surface on which the baby is lying or by shaking its head quickly. The baby first extends arms in an "embracing" position, then returns arms and legs to a flexed position close to the body. Unlike the startle response, the Moro is not an auditory reflex. It has two stages, extension followed by flexion, whereas the startle response is simply a flexion movement. The Moro reflex is not only diagnostically important, but it can interfere with normal motor functioning if it does not disappear on schedule. The protective extensor reaction that normally replaces the Moro response at about six months of age is suppressed if the Moro is too strong. If the Moro is too strong the baby's arms extend to either side rather than downward, a movement that is not useful in preventing a fall. In addition, a sudden change of position continues to elicit the response, upsetting balance and interfering with voluntary movement.

The *asymmetrical tonic neck reflex* (ATNR) is evident when the infant's head is turned to one side. If the infant's head is turned, the stretch of the neck muscles causes an extension of the arm and leg on the side of the body toward which the head is facing. The opposite arm and leg remain in a flexed position.

This reflex is seen in nearly all premature infants and in about half of all normal infants during the first week of life (Cratty, 1970). It normally disappears by the fifth month, although it may last until the ninth month during sleep. Maintenance of this reflex beyond the normal limit interferes with voluntary reaching and self-feeding. The teaching of feeding skills to severely retarded or cerebral palsied children can be a frustrating experience if the ATNR is not sufficiently suppressed to allow voluntary bringing of the hand to the mouth. When it is not suppressed, the ATNR also prevents the learning of many important gross motor movements such as turning from back to stomach, crossing the midline, and crawling on hands and knees. On the other hand, in the very young infant this reflex encourages extension of the arms to prepare for reaching and grasping.

The *Landau reflex* does not appear at birth, but is usually present by six months of age and lasts until the second year of life. In a prone (on stomach) position the infant extends arms and legs when the head is raised, and flexes these limbs when the head is lowered. It therefore encourages extension of hips and legs that is necessary for crawling and standing.

The *crossed extension reflex* is present at birth and normally disappears at three to four months of age. When stimulated on the sole of the foot the infant extends that leg; the opposite leg remains in flexion. This reflex interferes with crawling if it is not suppressed at the proper time, since the baby cannot make reciprocal movements, extending one leg after the other.

The *positive supporting reflex* is present at birth and lasts until six to eight weeks of age. It then reappears as early as three months of age and finally is suppressed at about ten months in normal babies. The reflex is elicited by touching the soles of the feet on a hard surface, causing extensor tone in the hips and knees so that the legs straighten and support the body's weight. The child has the tendency to stand on the toes, bringing the legs together. While this reflex encourages extension patterns in the young infant to prepare for standing, it interferes with learning to walk if it continues after ten months of age, for reciprocal movement of the legs is blocked. Balance and coordinated bending of the knee and ankle joints are also inhibited by the increased tone in the leg muscles.

By six months of age a normal infant has broken the early patterns of total extension or flexion as seen in the Moro or Landau responses and has learned to extend some muscles while flexing others. For example, she will be able to extend head and trunk muscles while flexing the hips, a necessary combination for sitting.

Automatic Reflexes

Three major categories of reflexes are not present at birth but develop during the first two years of life. They maintain the child in an upright position (righting reflexes), maintain equilibrium, and protect the child during a fall (protective reflexes) (Johnston & Magrab, 1976). We will briefly examine two examples of these reflexes.

The *labyrinthine righting of the head* is an important reflex for the promotion of head control. Seldom present at birth, it is first seen at about two months of age, and is a strong influence on the child at six to eight months of age, when sitting and crawling are first learned. The reflex is evident when the child is tipped downward, to one side, or backward. The tendency is for the head to maintain an upright position. This reflex does not disappear but continues to offer protection throughout life by maintaining the head in an upright position.

The *protective extensor reaction* (parachute) emerges at about six months of age and replaces the Moro response. Whereas the Moro response causes the child to throw her arms out to the sides, a useless movement for protecting the head during a fall, the parachute reaction causes the arms to extend above the head so that the hands, not the head, bear the brunt of the fall. This is an excellent example of an automatic reflex taking over or suppressing a primitive one as the child's needs change, for while the Moro response is useful to the very young child in developing extensor muscles, the parachute reaction better meets the needs of the more active older infant who needs protection from falls.

It is thus apparent that the primitive reflexes serve a useful purpose in the very young infant, and that their maintenance beyond the first year of life interferes with higher development. This is not true of the automatic reflexes, which emerge as the baby begins to crawl, stand, and walk, for they complement rather than inhibit voluntary movement.

In children with motor delays, these automatic responses do not develop at the normal rate and so are not available to the child for facilitating motor development.

The Developmental Milestones

THE FIRST YEAR (0–12 months)   In a normal infant, the first year of life is a period of amazing growth and development, as anyone realizes who has had the opportunity to be either participant or observer in the upbringing of such a creature. Although rapid progress is apparent in developmental areas other than motor, as demonstrated by recent research in cognitive development, for example, motor growth from birth to twelve months is truly remarkable and probably the most striking area of change. From a helpless infant who cannot hold his head up to a child who can walk without support, arise from a back-lying position to standing without assistance, and stack one block atop another with precision, the first twelve months represent the most rapid period of motor development in the young child's experience.

What are the specific events that take place during the first year of motor development? Cratty's (1970) summary chart of motor behaviors is useful for outlining these events (see Table 6.1).

During the first four months or so the baby concentrates on development of head control: raising, turning, and maintaining an upright position. The Landeau and Moro reflexes and the emerging righting reflexes promote the extension of arm and neck muscles to aid in this process. At the same time, the baby begins to use his forearms to help lift his head while in a prone position. Arms and legs extend, at first unilaterally and by six months bilaterally, that is, both arms and both legs extending at the same time.

During the next two months the baby learns to reach for objects, bring objects to her mouth, bring her hands together, and bring her foot to her mouth. By six months she can roll over from her back to her stomach and crawl forward and backward on her abdomen. She can sit up with minimal support, which puts her in a better position to examine objects she finds. She does this by grasping them

TABLE 6.1   Motor Development Milestones in the First Year of Life

APPROXIMATE TIME BEHAVIOR OCCURS	BEHAVIOR INDICATIVE OF THE ORIGINS OF MOVEMENT IN INFANTS
Gestation	Moro reflex appears
	Fetal activity prior to birth indicative of later motor competency and vigor
Birth	Birth reflexes including Moro, startle, palmar grasp, rooting, sucking, crawling reflex, etc.
	Seeks novel stimuli, variable activity levels evidenced
	Walking reflex seen
1 Month	Arm-supporting reflex seen
2 Months	Labyrinthine righting reflex appears
	Separate perceptual-motor and cognitive traits identifiable
3 Months	Pull-up reactions in the arm (reflex)
	Walking reflex terminates
	Infant can turn over from back to stomach
6 Months	Moro reflex terminates
	Voluntary creeping appears
	Swimming reflex disappears
	Voluntary crawling appears
	Crawling reflex disappears
9 Months	Supporting reflex in the legs seen
	Palmar and plantar grasp reflexes disappear
	Righting reflexes of the head and body disappear
12 Months	Supported walking
	Can arise from a back-lying position to a standing position, independent locomotion

Adapted from Cratty, B. J. *Perceptual and motor development in infants and children.* New York: Macmillan, 1970, pp. 28–29. Reprinted with permission.

with a radial grasp and then shaking or mouthing them. The radial grasp uses primarily the thumb, index, and second fingers, an improvement over the earlier palmar grasp in which the object is grasped by the middle fingers and palm of the hand (Johnston & Magrab, 1976).

From eight to twelve months the child continues to gain increased control over movements. Arms and legs move independently (one at a time) or reciprocally, as for crawling. The child can rotate his trunk, moving from a supine (lying on back) position to sitting upright, and can then pull himself to a standing position without assistance. He can often walk with support (cruising). In hand movement, he has developed the pincer grasp as well as the ability to voluntarily release an object he has picked up. This important new skill allows him to stack one block atop another when he is about a year old. The ability to release with precision develops rather slowly, so that one year later at two years of age, a child can stack only six or seven blocks.

THE SECOND YEAR (12–24 months)   Walking and its various refinements represent the major accomplishments of the two-year-old in gross motor. Walking forward without support is generally accomplished by eighteen months. The second half of the year is devoted to walking up and down stairs with assistance, one step at a time, standing up from a sitting position, and rolling over. Fine motor development progresses to the greater control needed for such activities as throwing a ball overhand (using both hands), pouring objects from a container, or finger feeding.

THE THIRD YEAR (24–36 months)   As the child approaches her third birthday she has learned to walk up and down stairs by herself, although she still cannot alternate her feet and still needs to hold on some of the time (Bayley, 1935). She can pedal a tricycle, run, jump holding on, and hop on one foot. When she walks she swings her arms alternately with her feet. She is learning to button her dress, do zippers and buckles, and can generally dress herself quite independently. She has begun to use tools such as pencils, paste applicators, and scissors. She can string beads, place puzzle pieces, and do other similar preschool tasks with ease and apparent pleasure. She can throw a ball four to five feet. She can build a tower of ten cubes and copy a circle (Gesell, 1940).

THE FOURTH YEAR (36–48 months)   During the fourth year a child refines those skills learned at two such as running, jumping, and hopping. He improves in balance and coordination so that he can walk a balance beam, jump down from a step, hop from foot to foot, and walk downstairs using alternate feet.

It is interesting to note that in learning to use stairs a child follows a predetermined sequence based on increasing demands for balance and coordination. Just as a young puppy who crawls upstairs is unable to descend again, setting up a wail at the top of the landing, a very young child can creep upstairs before he learns to creep down because less balance and coordination are required to perform the former. At each level of difficulty—walking with support, walking without support, and alternating feet—the child masters the skill while ascending before he demonstrates it while descending.

In fine motor coordination the nearly four-year-old refines the eye-hand coordination skills mentioned above, such as ball-throwing, buttoning, drawing, and so on. He is not ready to catch a ball or tie his shoes with much success.

THE FIFTH YEAR (48–60 months)   During this final year before kindergarten the child learns to skip (this task has been used as an indicator of readiness for kindergarten), to improve ball skills and generally to continue improvement of balance, coordination, and strengths, a process that continues throughout the childhood years and into early adulthood. By age five most children can dance to music, climb ladders and trees (Sheridan, 1968), and walk backward (Frankenburg & Dodds, 1969) and are learning to jump rope and even to roller skate (Sanford, 1974).

In fine motor skills, the child can draw a simple house, print the capital initials of her name, copy a circle, square, and cross (Gesell, 1940), dress and undress herself, lace her shoes, do her own buttons, and cut with a knife (Sanford, 1974).

In summary, although there is wide variance in individual motor accomplishments, the average child entering kindergarten is very competent in physical activities and able to perform most motor acts quite independently. Table 6.2 from Cratty (1970) provides a concise summary of the normal progression.

PROBLEMS IN MOTOR DEVELOPMENT

In order to function optimally, the entire motor system must be intact. Problems occur when any part—bones, muscles, joints, or nerves—is malfunctioning. Motor delays may be the primary developmental problem in certain conditions, such as cerebral palsy, or they may be one problem among several, as in severe mental retardation where serious delays in cognition and language are of equal concern. In this section we will review the most commonly seen problems in motor development in children from birth to five years. For purposes of this discussion we will divide the problems into three groups: Those caused by lesions of the brain, those due to abnormalities outside the brain in the peripheral nervous system, the muscular system, or skeletal system, and those involving other physical impairments.

Motor Problems Due to Brain Damage

The most commonly occurring problem of this kind is *cerebral palsy*. According to Johnston and Magrab (1976) there is usually one prominent dysfunctioning element which affects the cerebral palsied child more than others, and this element gives its name to the type of cerebral palsy the child suffers. The elements that may be dysfunctioning are tone and control, and these, in turn, affect muscle strength. When the primary deficit is too much muscle tone, the child is labeled *rigid* or *spastic*; if there is too little tone, the label is *atonic*. Defects in control are labeled *choreoathetoid*, *tremor*, or, when poor balance results, *ataxic*. Defects in strength do not generally occur in isolation, but they are labeled *paresis* (weakness) or *plegia* (paralysis). A number of prefixes are used with the term *plegia* to describe the parts of the body that are paralyzed. Paraplegia, for example, means paralysis of the legs, quadraplegia refers to paralysis of both arms and legs; and hemiplegia to paralysis on one side of the body.

TABLE 6.2   Gross Motor Attributes in Early Childhood

APPROXIMATE TIME OF APPEARANCE	SELECTED BEHAVIORS
1 year	Walking unaided
	A rapid "running-like" walk
	Will step off low objects
2 years	Walking rhythm stabilizes and becomes even
	Jumps crudely with two-foot take-off
	Will throw small ball 4-5 ft.
	True running appears
	Can walk sideward and backward
3 years	Can walk a line, heel to toe, 10 ft. long
	Can hop from two to three steps, on preferred foot
	Will walk balance beam for short distances
	Can throw a ball about 10 ft.
4 years	Running with good form, leg-arm coordination apparent, can walk a line around periphery of a circle
	Skillful jumping is apparent
	Can walk balance beam
5 years	Can broad-jump from 2-3 ft.
	Can hop 50 ft. in about 11 seconds
	Can balance on one foot for 4-6 seconds
	Can catch large playground ball bounced to him

Cratty, B. J. *Perceptual and motor development in infants and children.* New York: Macmillan, 1970, p. 61. Reprinted with permission.

As noted previously, hypertonicity results in either spasticity or rigidity. A spastic muscle is initially very resistant to movement but then quickly collapses; a rigid muscle maintains a strong resistance to change of position throughout the movement.

Problems with control of movement usually manifest themselves as involuntary movement disorders. When any of the major cortical motor areas of the brain are damaged, there is a lack of inhibition of involuntary movements originating in the lower brain. This causes the child to become dominated by movements over which she has no control. *Chorea* involves rapid, jerky movements of the arms and legs, while athetosis involves slower, more writhing movements of the hands, feet, or face (Johnston & Magrab, 1976). *Choreoathetosis* describes the condition when both types of movement are present.

Problems with balance characterize the child with ataxic cerebral palsy. Such a child has difficulty with all gross motor tasks, including walking. Fine motor tasks are more readily mastered unless there are serious problems with muscle tone.

Cerebral palsy is caused by injury to the brain before, during, or after birth. According to Hart (1979) conditions that may cause a brain lesion include:

1. anoxia (lack of oxygen) during prenatal development or the birth process
2. birth trauma
3. heavy use of alcohol by the mother during pregnancy
4. hyperbilirubinemia, a condition involving excessive destruction of red blood cells or an interference with bile excretion
5. chromosomal abnormalities
6. Rh blood incompatibilities
7. complications of twin pregnancy delivery
8. prenatal conditions such as rubella
9. complications of the placenta
10. thyroid disease
11. kidney infection or diabetes in the mother

Because cerebral palsy is caused by a nonprogressive brain lesion, the motor performance of an affected child does not deteriorate, and the child is often able to improve her condition through physical or occupational therapy.

It is now the practice to begin working with cerebral palsied babies from birth onward, since methods for diagnosing the condition at birth are now available. The therapist works to encourage voluntary movement, to minimize the effect of involuntary reflexes, and to encourage spastic or rigid muscles to work smoothly.

Children who are born prematurely are at the greatest risk for cerebral palsy, because they have less resistance to problems that may occur during and after birth. The prematurity may be an indication, too, of problems that occurred prenatally. At any rate, the premature infant is generally weaker and more susceptible to brain injury than is the full-term baby.

The incidence of cerebral palsy is directly related to low birth weight, a condition usually accompanying prematurity. About 15 percent of infants who weigh between 1000 and 1500 grams at birth have damaged nervous systems; for those weighing less than 1000 grams the rate is 33 percent (Hart, 1979). Thus, the more premature the child the greater the risk of cerebral palsy (Hart, 1979). Due to better care of premature newborns during the past twenty years, the incidence of cerebral palsy has declined by about one-half (Hart, 1979).

Although many children with cerebral palsy are of normal intelligence, about one-third are mentally retarded, and a substantial number have seizure disorders, hearing and vision problems, and language problems. These problems vary with the severity of the cerebral palsy. About 35 percent of severely impaired cerebral palsied children die before their fifth birthday. The life expectancy for those who live past age five is 40 to 45 years.

Muscular dystrophy is another condition of early childhood due to brain lesion. However, in muscular dystrophy the lesion is progressive, that is, the child's condition deteriorates over time and death is often the result, usually before the teen years. The cause of muscular dystrophy is unknown, but the disease is thought to be an inherited, recessive, metabolic disorder. It affects three times as many males as females.

The most common form of this disease is Duchenne, juvenile muscular dystrophy, which is usually diagnosed at the time the child should normally begin to walk. Because the disease gradually destroys the voluntary muscles of the body and replaces them with fatty tissue, the child loses the ability to walk, appears to gain weight, and becomes increasingly weak and immobilized, finally being confined to bed. Death usually follows an attack of infection.

There is no cure at present for muscular dystrophy. Treatment focuses on the symptoms: postural drainage, treatment of contracted muscles, and administration of antibiotics to combat infections.

Motor Disorders Due to Other Causes

Osteogenesis imperfecta is a congenital condition involving fragile bones that break easily, causing abnormal skeletal development and sometimes shortened height. Deafness may also result from this condition.

Osteomyelitis is an infection of the bones which causes crippling. Treatment with antibiotics and sometimes surgery have proven successful in reducing the incidence of this condition.

It has been estimated that nearly 175,000 children suffer from rheumatoid arthritis (Calabro, 1970). This disease involves deterioration of the linings of the body's joints, which causes painful swelling and deformity in hands, arms, or legs. The cause of *childhood arthritis* is unknown and so treatment must focus on the symptoms: relief from pain, infection, and swelling (Wyne & O'Connor, 1979).

Hip Dysplasia is a congenital condition involving dislocation of the hip and can be diagnosed soon after birth. It is more commonly found in girls than boys. Treatment may involve braces or surgery; if untreated, the child is unable to walk normally. Early treatment is usually very successful.

Scoliosis is a spinal malformation, specifically lateral curvature. It is currently being successfully treated orthopedically, so that children with the condition do not require special educational programming.

Spina bifida is a congenital condition that develops prenatally while the spinal cord is being formed. A normal spinal column consists of the spinal cord and its protective covering, the meninges, completely surrounded by bone. In spina bifida there is an opening in the bones of the lower spinal column, exposing the spinal cord and meninges. Sometimes part of the meninges will protrude through the opening and form a sac on the child's back. This sac, known as a *meningocele*, is filled with cerebrospinal fluid and covered with skin so that it appears as a bulge on the child's back. A more serious form of spina bifida, *myelomeningocele*, occurs when a portion of the spinal cord itself protrudes through the opening and is not completely covered with skin, thus exposing the child to loss of cerebrospinal fluid as well as to bacterial infection.

If there is no protrusion, treatment is usually not required. For myelo-meningocele surgery is required, and this is usually done a few hours after birth. Since the condition can be identified prenatally through amniocentesis (Hart, 1979), treatment can begin very early. The surgery consists of replacing the protruding cord and membrane within the spinal column. Some damage to nerves usually remains, however, and so the child usually has problems with walking, bladder and bowel control, sitting, and standing. Because spina bifida only affects the lower part of the body, children with the condition are of normal intelligence. If their physical problems can be managed, they perform very well in regular classrooms.

Educational programming for spina bifida children is usually limited to providing training by the physical therapist to improve muscle tone in lower extremities and to use artificial aids for ambulation, i.e., wheelchair, braces, or canes.

Hydrocephalus is a condition encountered in spina bifida children that results from an accumulation in the brain of cerebrospinal fluid, the fluid normally found circulating through the brain and spinal cord. The fluid is prevented from normal circulation by the meningocele. A buildup of fluid in the brain causes swelling and enlarging of the head that may result in damage to the brain and the optic and auditory nerves. Present surgical techniques make it possible to prevent this condition by shunting the excess fluid from the skull to another body cavity (Hart, 1979). It was formerly necessary to replace these shunts frequently as the child increased in size; recent advances in technique have produced shunts that expand as the child grows.

OTHER PHYSICAL IMPAIRMENTS

Congenital Conditions

Sickle cell anemia is carried by a recessive gene and is found almost exclusively in black children. In this disease the red blood cells change shape (to look like sickles) and cannot carry their normal supply of oxygen. When this oxygen deprivation occurs, the child is subject to extreme pain, dizziness, and weakness. Swelling of fingers and toes is noticeable. These bouts of severe pain, known as sickle cell crises, usually begin in children before the age of two and are common during the preschool years. They decrease in frequency as the child approaches adulthood.

Like those of muscular dystrophy, carriers of sickle cell anemia can be detected through laboratory tests. There is at present no cure for the disease, and treatment consists of blood transfusions, pain relievers, and bed rest.

Cystic fibrosis is a metabolic disorder that results in the lack of an enzyme necessary for production of saliva, sweat, and mucus. The result is production of a sticky mucus that interferes with normal digestive and respiratory processes.

The disease is inherited through a recessive gene. Infants can be identified earlier than previously, which has resulted in more children surviving the disease. However, most do not live beyond age twenty, even with the more intensive care available in recent years. There is not at the present time a known cure.

Infections

Meningitis and encephalitis are the result of damage to the brain or spinal cord from infection. If the meninges is infected it is known as meningitis; if the brain itself is infected, the result is encephalitis. These conditions previously were fatal but are now controlled quite well by antibiotics. Some children suffer brain damage which remains after the infection has been treated.

Seizure Disorders

The most commonly encountered seizure disorder (epilepsy) in young children is the *akinetic* or *minor motor* seizure. During an akinetic seizure the child may fall forward or backward, resulting in head injuries unless the child wears a helmet for protection. Akinetic seizures may occur hundreds of times a day and they are less responsive to drugs than are other types of epilepsy. Many infants and children with minor motor seizures must be institutionalized.

There are three other types of seizures that are rarely seen in children younger than age two: psychomotor seizures and petit mal and grand mal seizures.

Psychomotor seizures may occur as early as two years of age. They are manifested by high pulse rate, perspiration, salivation, repetitive motor behavior, and sometimes visual or auditory hallucinations. Momentary loss of consciousness may occur.

Petit mal and *grand mal* seizures rarely occur below age five. Petit mal seizures are most common between the ages of five and eighteen; grand mal seizures are commonly found in adults. Both involve loss of consciousness and various other symptoms.

About 85 percent of seizure disorders are controllable by means of medication, so that the child or adult may lead a normal life (Hart, 1979). The remaining 15 percent are less responsive. Included in the latter group are many young children with minor motor epilepsy.

The causes of epilepsy are not well understood, but a few facts are of interest. Heredity appears to play a role in some cases, although 65 percent of those with seizures have no family history of epilepsy. Some seizure disorders are related to other disabling conditions such as cerebral palsy; others are related to high fevers in infancy. These latter, known as febrile seizures, may lead to epilepsy if not treated. Continuing the child on anticonvulsant drugs over a long period of time is effective in preventing febrile seizures (Carter, 1975).

VISUAL IMPAIRMENTS

Since the development of the visual system is presented in detail by numerous authors of standard texts on disabled children (e.g., Kirk & Gallagher, 1983;

Safford, 1978), the present discussion is limited to a brief overview. The primary focus of this section is a description of congenital and other visual impairments which are generally diagnosed in early infancy and which affect the development of children during the preschool years. Some attention is also given to identification procedures and to intervention techniques.

Visual impairments are not generally considered to be a disability of motor development, but we include them here because, although the infant or young child with serious vision problems most certainly suffers delays in language, cognition, and social development, these are in large part related to the visually impaired infants' limited ability to move, explore the environment, and interact with others (Adelson & Frailberg, 1975; Fraiberg, 1975).

Normal Visual Development

The eyes develop from outgrowths of the forebrain, differentiating prenatally into very specialized sensory organs which in the normal full-term infant are almost fully developed at the time of birth. Nevertheless, because the eyes develop originally from the brain, their further growth and development in early childhood parallel that of the brain, resulting in an enormous increase in size during the first three years of life (Buncic, 1980). By age 15, the child's eyes have tripled in size from birth, and three-fourths of this growth occurs in those first three years.

By six weeks of age, an infant's eyes are able to move in unison or symmetrically, whereas at birth they move somewhat independently. By two months of age the infant can fixate and follow a bright light. Although the optic nerve is fully myelinated at term, it is not until four months of age that the eyes have anatomically reached a reasonable state for function, with full differentiation of the visual cortex and complete myelination of the rest of the neural optic system.

By six months of age the development of stereoscopic binocular (three-dimensional) vision has begun. The cerebral reflexes that control three-dimensional vision continue maturing until the child is about eight years of age. Straightness of the eyes during the act of vision is maintained by the binocular reflex which must be strong enough to prevent involuntary movement (nystagmus).

Recent research on infants' visual abilities (Schwartz & Day, 1979) has found infants to be more adept at visual discrimination and visual/motor coordination than was once thought.

Vision Testing

According to Buncic (1980), the clinical assessment of visual acuity in infants is indirect at best, consisting as it does of observation by the physician of constrictions of the baby's pupils to direct light and observation of whether the infant fixates on the light. Nevertheless, using such optokinetic techniques, researchers have been able to measure the visual acuity of infants soon after birth (Gorman, Cogan, & Gellis, 1957; Kiff & Lepard, 1966).

In older children, visual acuity is usually screened initially by means of the Snellen chart, which consists of rows of letters descending in size or, alternatively, rows of capital Es pointing in various directions. The child, standing at a distance of 20 feet, identifies the letters or their direction. A reading of 20/50 Snellen means that the child can see at 20 feet what a person with normal vision can see at 50 feet. Although Snellen charts are merely screening instruments, the Snellen method of indicating acuity (20/x) is widely used by those involved in vision testing. For example, the research on infant vision referred to above reported acuity of 20/280 Snellen in a group of premature infants and of 20/670 Snellen in a group of babies less than five days old. The average two-month-old is thought to have visual acuity of about 20/200.

For testing near point and far point vision and for assessing other aspects of vision such as muscle balance and fusion, more elaborate equipment is required. The Keystone Telebinocular or the Bausch and Lomb Orthorater are examples of instruments used for these purposes. For further information the reader is referred to Warren (1977), Lowenfeld (1973), or Harley (1975).

Definitions of Normal Visual Acuity

Visual acuity is defined in terms of the better performing eye and is measured with corrective glasses or lenses. According to the National Society for the Prevention of Blindness, a person with visual acuity of 20/70 or better in the better eye after correction is considered to be within the average range. The two legally recognized categories for visual impairment in the United States are *blind* and *partially sighted*. They are defined as follows:

> Blindness is visual acuity for distance vision of 20/200 or less in the better eye after correction; or visual acuity of more than 20/200 if the widest diameter of field vision substends an angle no greater than 20 degrees. The partially seeing are defined as having a visual acuity greater than 20/200 but no greater than 20/70 in the better eye with correction. [National Society for the Prevention of Blindness, 1966, p. 10.]

Partially seeing children have sufficient vision to allow it to be used as the primary modality for their education.

Disorders of Vision

Several conditions may cause visual problems for the infant or preschool child. The following summary is based primarily on Buncic's (1980) excellent chapter in Gabel and Erickson, *Child Development and Developmental Disabilities*.

REFRACTIVE ERRORS   Most infants and young children are mildly *hyperopic* (far-sighted), a condition that increases to about age three and then gradually decreases after age seven. However, about 25 percent of infants are *myopic* (near-sighted); these infants' visual acuity must be monitored for possible fitting of glasses or contact lenses. Contact lenses, by the way, can be fitted reasonably successfully in early childhood. The initial fitting is often done under general anesthetic, and parents must be ready to cope with the stress of the child's adjustment period.

The other refractive error commonly seen in young children is *astigmatism* which prevents the accurate focusing of the retinal image. Astigmatism may be either hyperopic or myopic.

AMBLYOPIA   Amblyopia may be defined as a significant reduction in visual acuity, at least by two lines on the Snellen chart. It is commonly referred to as a "lazy eye," because the amblyopia interferes with the eye's fusional reflexes, causing that eye to turn or "cross," so that the child's eyes no longer focus together. The condition is usually corrected by patching the good eye, forcing the amblyopic eye into use.

STRABISMUS   This condition, caused by imbalance of the eye muscles, results in the eyes not focusing together. There are many forms of childhood strabismus, including *pseudostrabismus*, an apparent crossing of the eyes in infancy which disappears with age. *Manifest strabismus*, the condition in which the eyes are misaligned, results in either estropia (cross-eye or turning in of the eyes) or exotropia (wall-eye or turning out of the eyes). This most common type of childhood strabismus should be identified by age six months so that corrective lens or in some cases surgery may be prescribed as early as possible. Sometimes strabismus is associated with conditions such as Down's or Turner's syndrome. In such cases, the eyes are often severely crossed, do not respond well to glasses, and require early surgery. Strabismus and amblyopia often occur together and one often causes the other.

LEUKOKORIA   Leukokoria refers to the presence of a white pupil in the child's eye. It can be caused by several factors, including cataracts and retrolental fibroplasia (see below) or, more seriously, it can indicate the presence of a malignant retinal tumor known as retinoblastoma.

Retinoblastomas usually occur in only one eye. A small number of them are genetic in origin, having the autosomal, dominant mode of inheritance. Treatment consists of removal of the tumor followed by radiation or chemotherapy. With early detection, the prognosis for unilateral cases is good.

RETROLENTAL FIBROPLASIA   Oxygen administration to premature infants has in the past resulted in these babies going blind. In recent years, the incidence of retrolental fibroplasia, or blindness due to oxygen toxicity, has greatly decreased as hospital staff have learned to carefully monitor the amounts of oxygen administered to high-risk infants. Sometimes the physician must choose, however, between the baby's life and his possible blindness, since in such cases the oxygen is necessary to save the baby's life. The physician then tries to administer the least amount of oxygen possible in the hope of preventing total blindness in the infant.

GLAUCOMA   Like strabismus, glaucoma occurs in many forms in young children. The most serious is a congenital form, autosomal recessive, which causes blindness through overaccumulations of intraocular fluid, resulting in pressure on the eyeball. This form, known as primary congenital glaucoma, responds well to treatment in which the excess fluid is drained from the eye by means of a surgically created drainage channel. It is usually diagnosed early in infancy.

Other forms of glaucoma in childhood, also due to increased intraocular pressure, are found in association with such conditions as neurofibromatosis, juvenile rheumatoid arthritis, and retrolental fibroplasia.

CATARACTS   A cataract is, by definition, any opacity in the lens. It may or may not lower visual acuity, depending on its size and location. Several types of cataracts are hereditary, usually autosomal dominant. In addition, cataracts may be associated with other medical problems, such as maternal rubella, glactosemia, diabetes mellitus, and Down's syndrome. They may also be acquired through trauma to the lens due to factors such as radiation, inflammation, or long-term drug use.

Recent improvements in surgical techniques have made possible early removal of cataracts in children, as early as four to six months of age. The infant is then fitted with contact lenses. Some physicians favor waiting until later childhood for the surgery, when visual disability requires it.

An important point to be made concerning visual disorders is that they rarely cause serious enough delays in cognitive or language development to warrant the child's isolation from the educational mainstream. While infants blind from birth experience significant developmental delays (Fraiberg, 1975), children whose visual impairment occurs later in childhood generally experience less serious, if any, delays. Both groups can profit from association with seeing children. The primary educational needs of blind and visually impaired children center around gross motor training in infancy (Adelson & Fraiberg, 1975) and orientation and mobility training in early childhood (Kirk & Gallagher, 1983). Educational programming for the visually impaired is beyond the scope of this chapter. The reader is referred to the many excellent materials available on the topic from the American Foundation for the Blind, the National Society for the Prevention of Blindness, and National Aid to the Visually Handicapped.

CONCLUSIONS

Many types of neurological dysfunction, stemming from a variety of causes, can affect a young child's motor development. Central nervous system damage is a major factor, but other factors, such as metabolic disorders or infection, may also play a part.

In planning educational programs for young children, the development of motor skills is an area to which much attention must be paid. Optimum growth cannot be taken for granted, either for disabled or nondisabled children, but rather must be promoted through an organized series of activities based on normal developmental sequences. For this process, the consultation of an occupational or physical therapist is often necessary and always helpful.

IDENTIFICATION
AND EVALUATION

Screening and Assessment

1. How are screening and assessment used in identifying young children with special needs?
2. Is it possible to develop tests that are not culturally biased?
3. What are the advantages to using standardized tests?
4. What are the advantages to using informal assessment methods?
5. What is the importance of reliability and validity?

7

two

INTRODUCTION

During the past two decades interest in identifying disabled, young children in educational settings has been growing. A major impetus for this trend was the Education for All Handicapped Children Act (P.L. 94–142) of 1975, which provided for a diagnostic/prescriptive approach to service delivery for handicapped children 3 to 21 years of age. The individual educational program (IEP) prescribed for each handicapped child by that law forced all professionals working with handicapped children to become involved in some way in the diagnostic process. As a result, the demand for diagnostic instruments useful for educational program planning as well as for intelligence tests and other standardized instruments designed for preschool children has grown.

Identification of young, handicapped children begins with screening, followed, when appropriate, by more comprehensive assessment. The purpose of this chapter is to discuss screening, assessment, and identification of young, de-

Terry D. Meddock contributed to the writing of this chapter.

velopmentally disabled children and some of the issues related to these processes. Table 7.1 defines some of the basic terms used in this chapter. The reader

TABLE 7.1   Definitions of Terms Used in Chapter 7

Screening involves a large-scale, one-time procedure which is usually quick and inexpensive and designed to determine the presence or absence of developmental problems. Screening is done to identify those infants or children considered at risk, who will probably need special services to aid their normal development.

Assessment is the process by which children are identified as handicapped and in need of special educational services. Testing is not synonymous with assessment, for a test may yield only a score whereas a good assessment will yield much information useful for educational programming. Assessment is not so much a process as *part* of a process; the other part is intervention, without which the assessment is useless.

Standardized tests contain fixed administration and scoring procedures, empirical testing of items, standard apparatuses or format, and tables of norms. They most often yield a score or set of scores which may be used to compare the child's performance with those of others in his age group. Standardized tests may be either *norm-referenced* or *criterion-referenced*. Most often however they are norm-referenced.

Norm-referenced tests provide tables of scores describing the performance on the test of a reference group of children, usually from various parts of the country and from different socio-economic backgrounds, against which a particular child's score may be compared. The tabled scores are usually expressed as grade or age-equivalents, standard scores or percentile equivalents.

Criterion-referenced tests consist of series of skills in academic or developmental areas grouped by age level. They compare the child's performance on each test item against a standard or criterion which must be met if the child is to receive credit for that item. The child is measured against the criterion rather than against norms established by other children's performance. Often informal teacher assessments are based on criterion-referenched techniques. There are some standardized tests, nonetheless, that are criterion referenced.

Ordinal scales contain items arranged in the order in which they emerge developmentally. Many standardized tests use a cluster of items at each level which are typical of development at that level and which are arranged in order of increasing difficulty. However, within each age level, the items simply represent development at that level and do not emerge sequentially as items in ordinal scales do. For example, on the Uzgiris-Hunt ordinal scales a baby must have mastered reaching before gasping, whereas on the Binet standardized scale a child may pass some items at the four-year-old level before mastering all three-year-old items.

Validity has to do with whether a test measures what it purports to. This may be assessed by investigating its content validity (the actual items on the test), construct validity (the underlying construct such as intelligence or creativity that is being tested), or predictive validity (how well the test predicts future performance in the same or a related area).

Reliability measures how accurate and consistent the test is. This is usually ascertained by administering the test to the same person more than once and comparing scores (test-retest reliability) or by administering first the odd items and then the even items on the test to the same person and comparing the two resulting scores (split-half reliability). Standardized norm-referenced tests usually have more extensive information available concerning their validity and reliability than do criterion-referenced tests. However, this does not necessarily mean that the former are superior or are more useful.

is urged to become familiar with these terms before reading the rest of this chapter.

SCREENING

Screening involves examining the population at large to determine which individuals are most likely to manifest a specific condition. Screening is not a positive identification procedure, and further assessment is typically necessary to determine with any certainty that a problem indeed exists.

Infants and young children may be screened for developmental delays or abnormalities, for emotional problems, for hearing and vision difficulties, for learning problems, and for specific medical problems. Screening ranges from inexpensive procedures like routine tests for phenylketonuria or pediatrician-administered developmental checklists to complex tissue examination of fetal development. Given this scope of possible medical and developmental screening efforts, several authors have identified guidelines or criteria for developmental screening procedures (Frankenburg & Camp, 1975; Lillie, 1977). These criteria include:

1. Screening for a particular disorder (e.g., retardation, hearing impairment, visual impairment, emotional problems, motor delay) assumes that the problem is treatable, and that intervention of some nature will improve the condition of or outcome for the child.
2. Early intervention or treatment (due to screening efforts) is superior to intervention if the condition was identified at a later date.
3. The condition being screened for can be specifically diagnosed through further assessment procedures. As Lillie (1977) notes, this criterion is more important in medical screening than in educational and developmental screening. Educational screening is a first step in information gathering prior to decision making in preschool or early childhood intervention. The nature and severity of the problem is much more important than often unknown causes or etiology.
4. Services exist to provide the necessary diagnosis and treatment for problems identified by screening. As the work of Kearsley (1979), Hobbs (1975), and others suggests, identification alone may set up reduced expectations for development among those aware of the screening results and operate to produce a self-fulfilling prophecy of developmental delay.
5. The disorder or condition being screened for is relatively prevalent or, if not relatively prevalent, the consequences of not discovering the rare problem are quite severe. This issue is essentially one of cost versus benefit. Screening an entire population may be costly and time consuming. Are the benefits to a few gained by screening worth the expenditure of time and money? The effectiveness of intervention in

mitigating the identified condition would enter into a decision of this
kind.

6. Accurate screening services for the problems should be readily available. Since screening involves administration of procedures to large
numbers of individuals, screening devices should be accurate in identifying most individuals with a problem without overreferrals and
should overlook few individuals who have the problem. Additionally,
screening devices should be rapid to administer, have a low cost-bene-
fit ratio, require a minimum of professional time, and be acceptable to
the population being screened.

The need for systematic screening increases with the mildness of the disorder
regardless of age. The child with a severe handicap is more readily identifiable
and more quickly receives services. The child with a mild but significant handicap more likely may go undetected.

Prenatal and Perinatal Screening

The screening of children for potential problems begins before birth. Routine
physician examinations during pregnancy check for the growth of the developing fetus. Special procedures such as sonography, ultrasound, fetal biopsy, and
amniocentesis are available to detect deficits in the fetus if difficulties are suspected. There are 27 or more neurological disorders involving severe mental retardation that can now be identified and diagnosed during the fourth and fifth
months of pregnancy (O'Brien, 1971). *Amniocentesis,* which has become quite
common in the past decade, plays a major role in this identification process. In
amniocentesis, a small amount of amniotic fluid is drawn out of the embryonic
sac for biochemical analysis. The fluid contains fetal cells that can be analyzed
to determine chromosomal or other genetic abnormalities. The procedure is usually performed during the fourteenth to sixteenth week of pregnancy. A major
screening use of amniocentesis is for the detection of Down's syndrome, a chromosomal disorder whose risk increases with increasing parental age. Other problems identifiable through amniocentesis include Tay Sachs disease, PKU, and
spina bifida. Regardless of the disorder being screened for, prenatal detection
procedures should be combined with genetic counseling which presents the pro-
spective parents with the necessary background in (1) the risks of the procedure
to the developing fetus, (2) the mathematical probability of the risk of occurrence or recurrence, (3) exposure to possible options available, and (4) support in
the decision-making process involved in continuation or termination of the pregnancy. Follow-up support should be available once the parents have made their
decision. Prenatal screening of high risk pregnancies may serve three major
functions:

1. If the results are negative, it relieves parental anxiety and concern over
possible difficulties.

SCREENING AND ASSESSMENT   **141**

2. Screening procedures may confirm difficulties and allow the parents to prepare for dealing with the difficulties the infant may present.
3. Screening procedures may provide parents with the necessary information to decide to terminate the pregnancy.

Hansen (1978) reported that abortion reform in New York state has been associated with a decline in the number of children born with Down's syndrome. Abortion is controversial, but screening procedures at the prenatal level can provide parents with the necessary knowledge to make their own choice.

More common screening procedures begin at birth. The Apgar test of vital signs (Apgar, 1953) is perhaps the most commonly used screening technique with young infants. It is routinely used throughout the United States and other countries. Developed by Dr. Virginia Apgar, the procedure consists of measuring the physiological functioning of the newborn infant in five areas immediately at birth and then five minutes later (see Table 7.2). Each area of functioning—respiration, circulation, color, tone, reflex response—is evaluated on a scale of 0, 1, or 2, making a total of 10 points possible. A normal infant scores at 8, 9, or 10

TABLE 7.2   Apgar Evaluation Score

			60 sec.	5 min.
Heart rate				
	Absent	(0)		
	Less than 100	(1)		
	100 to 140	(2)		
Respiratory effort				
	Apneic	(0)		
	Shallow, irregular	(1)		
	Lusty cry and breathing	(2)		
Response to catheter stimulation				
	No response	(0)		
	Grimace	(1)		
	Cough or sneeze	(2)		
Muscle tone				
	Flaccid	(0)		
	Some flexion of extremities	(1)		
	Flexion resisting extension	(2)		
Color				
	Pale, blue	(0)		
	Body pink, extremities blue	(1)		
	Pink all over	(2)		

Total _____

Signature of Person Rating _____

on one or both evaluations. An infant who earns a score of 6 points or less is considered to be at risk.

Another routine screening procedure undertaken at birth is the analysis of newborn blood and urine samples to detect phenylketonuria (PKU). While this procedure is widely practiced in the United States (48 of 50 states required it in 1975), only 8 states routinely screen for six other metabolic disorders that also cause retardation (Heward & Orlansky, 1980). Although the incidence of these disorders is low, it would seem that such procedures are well worth the expenditure of time and money and that they should be expanded.

Postnatal Screening

No nationally coordinated effort to screen all children in infancy for developmental delays currently exists. One such effort that has met with limited success is the Early and Periodic Screening, Diagnosis and Treatment (EPSDT) program required by the Social Security Amendments of 1967. This program is required by law for the purpose of identifying child health problems and developmental disabilities in preschool children. Nevertheless, the screening effort is far from universal, for until 1981 it involved only those children receiving AFDC (Aid to Families with Dependent Children) who were eligible for Medicaid. The guidelines have now been expanded to include all children eligible for Medicaid, but the program still cannot be considered a national screening effort involving all young children, nor is any such program even recommended by federal or state governments at the present time (Heward & Orlansky, 1980). Given the present trend toward cutting back social services in this country, it is unlikely that such an effort will be undertaken in the foreseeable future, however cost effective it might prove to be.

One limitation of EPSDT and other screening efforts has been the lack of available tests for predicting developmental disabilities in low income children from minority backgrounds (Warren, 1977). *The Denver Developmental Screening Test* (Frankenburg & Dodds, 1969), for example, was normed on middle-class, Anglo children in Denver. Although widely used to screen children from urban minority backgrounds, its validity for such purposes is open to question.

Several screening tests for young preschool children are based on the *Gesell Developmental Schedules*, first used in the 1930s to identify developmentally delayed infants (Knoblock & Passamanick, 1974). These schedules include tasks designed by Gesell for his study of normal development and have been adapted for use in many recent tests, both standardized formal tests like the Bayley (1969) and McCarthy (1972) scales and more informal procedures like the *Brigance Diagnostic Inventory of Early Development* (1978), the *Learning Accomplishment Profile* (1974), and the *Portage Guide to Early Education* (1976). A number of assessment instruments are more fully described in the appendix.

An interesting approach to screening is the *Developmental Indicators for the*

Assessment of Learning (DIAL, 1975), an interdisciplinary approach in kit form which makes it possible for a group of children to be evaluated simultaneously in several developmental areas: gross and fine motor development, concepts, and communication. The classroom teacher plays a major role in the DIAL screening process, thus eliminating one problem involving interdisciplinary teams, that of the assessment specialist too far removed from the every day intervention process in the home or classroom.

ASSESSMENT

As noted, screening infants and young children for developmental delays is an attempt to identify those children that we *suspect* have a problem serious enough to require intervention. Assessment is typically a process to *confirm* or *deny* the existence of a problem and locate its etiology. In a medical context, assessment often leads to diagnosis—the process that determines the specific cause or etiology of the disorder and delay. By contrast, in special education assessment generally refers to the use of medical, psychometric, educational, and clinical techniques to place a child in one or more classification categories (e.g., retarded).

The assessment process is an attempt to determine the strengths and weaknesses of the child so that a specific program of intervention can be planned and implemented. Harbin (1977) views assessment as a systematic process of (1) collecting information both on a child's level of functioning in specific areas of development and on his learning characteristics and (2) carefully interpreting the collected information to provide direction in the day-to-day management of the child.

Current Issues in Assessment of Young Children

In this section we will examine certain issues that currently affect the assessment of young, handicapped children. We have identified four issues that have major impact on intervention programs for preschool, disabled children today. These include (1) cultural bias and educational testing, (2) standardized testing versus other alternatives, (3) early intervention and implications for assessment, and (4) predictive validity and reliability of early childhood assessment instruments.

CULTURAL BIAS AND EDUCATIONAL TESTING   The Education for All Handicapped Children Act (P.L. 94–142) established the principle of non-discriminatory testing to determine the existence and extent of handicapping conditions in children. The principle has not been put into practice effectively, however, for several reasons. Attitudes of psychometricians have been difficult to change; traditional methods of standardized testing have proven hard to replace. Additionally, few available assessment instruments attempt to avoid cultural bias; the available instruments have not proven successful in this regard. (For an excellent discussion of this issue, see Goodwin & Driscoll, 1980, pp. 14–15). It is probably true that no instrument can ever be culturally unbiased, since every test tends to favor the cultural group used in its development (Anastasi, 1976). Nevertheless, there is a great difference between mere compliance with law to avoid federal scrutiny and active interest in improving educational services to minority children. Evidence suggests that in many school districts it is the former motive which gives impetus to testing programs and thus a commitment is lacking to make testing truly nondiscriminatory (Bernal, 1977).

Cultural bias in testing has come to mean the use of standardized tests. P.L 94–142 specifically prohibits the classification of a child as handicapped on the basis of one criterion or test score. Impetus for this stipulation came from the work of several people interested in the education of handicapped children, notably Jane Mercer and Nicholas Hobbs. Mercer's (1973) study of mentally retarded children in Riverside, California, revealed that a disproportionate number of black and Hispanic children were labeled mentally retarded on the basis of standardized tests and placed in segregated classes. Mercer concluded that such tests as the Stanford-Binet Intelligence Scales are culturally biased and, therefore, underestimate the potential ability of children who are not from white, English-speaking (Anglo), middle-class families. Her response to the problem is the System of Multicultural and Pluralistic Assessment (SOMPA) which is based on the assumption that multiple criteria give a more accurate estimate of potential ability.

The SOMPA consists of a series of assessment instruments, both norm-referenced and criterion-referenced, and is intended for children from 5 to 11 years of age. The instruments include identification of the socialization milieu in which the child is being reared, evaluation of the child's general academic readiness, assessment of the child's adaptive behavior in nonacademic activities, an inventory of the child's health history, and screening for physical impairments (Mercer, 1973). Academic readiness is measured by the Wechsler Intelligence Scale for Children-Revised (WISC–R) or the Wechsler Preschool and Primary Scale of Intelligence (WPPSI) and the Bender Visual-Motor Gestalt Test. Except for the physical screening, all assessment data are secured in interviews with the child's primary caregiver. These include the Sociocultural Scales, which identify the social, cultural, and economic characteristics of the child's home environment and compare them with the predominant school culture; the Adaptive Behavior Inventory for Children (ABIC); and the Health History Inventory. The assessment system yields an Estimated Learning Potential instead of an IQ score; this is derived from the WISC-R score adjusted for the child's sociocultural background.

In arguing for pluralistic assessment, Mercer states:

> By developing multiple normative frameworks to describe children from different sociocultural settings, pluralistic assessment will recognize the child's right to be evaluated within an appropriate sociocultural framework. Assessing a child's per-

formance in relation to that of other children from similar backgrounds will free
evaluation from the single normal curve, adjust definitions of "normal-abnormal"
for differences in sociocultural background and take into account sociocultural
differences within ethnic/racial groups. [1973, p. 155]

The standardized testing movement in the United States was accompanied by
the melting pot theory with its assumption that all culturally different people
should adapt to the majority culture. Cultural pluralism challenges this assumption and promotes a recognition and appreciation of difference. While it is true
that standardized tests do measure accurately how well a minority child will perform in a white, Anglo, middle-class educational setting, and while this information may be important and necessary, it nevertheless also remains true that
cultural *difference* is often translated by these tests into *deficit* (Cole & Bruner,
1971) which results in the minority child being erroneously diagnosed as needing
special services to overcome her "handicap."

Some proposed solutions for avoiding culturally biased evaluation will be discussed in the following section, since avoiding cultural bias has been interpreted
to mean avoiding standardized testing.

STANDARDIZED TESTING VS. OTHER ALTERNATIVES   With the increasing criticism of standardized tests voiced by the courts and by children's advocacy
groups, as well as by parents of handicapped children and by professional educators, an interest in identifying alternative procedures has developed.

A second concern with standardized testing is that it is often substituted for a
complete program of assessment. Such a program should include the following
four functions (Bernal, 1977):

1. Classification as handicapped
2. Education programming
3. Decision-making regarding provision of services
4. Intervention planning and evaluation

The score yielded by the standardized test is not useful information for any of
these functions. The score might be included as part of the information on which
classification decisions are based, but since P.L. 94–142 specifically forbids labeling children as handicapped on the basis of a single test score, it cannot sub-
stitute for a broader, more comprehensive assessment.

Laosa (1977) offered four alternatives to standardized testing. First, criterion-referenced tests that measure the child against her own previous performance rather than against the majority may be less biased. However, Laosa
cautions that criterion-referenced tests must be evaluated in terms of who determines what the objective will be and who establishes the criterion. This type of
test may also be culturally biased if the objectives and criteria reflect majority
standards or values. One advantage of the criterion-referenced test is that it
yields specific information regarding skills the child can or cannot perform. This

information is more useful for educational programming than is the numerical score yielded by the standardized test.

A second alternative is to test the child's ability to perform Piagetian tasks. Stages associated with these tasks occur across cultures and, therefore, tests associated with them are less likely to contain bias. Although several of them have been developed, these tests have not achieved wide acceptance among psychometricians and are mainly used for research at the present time (Keogh & Kopp, 1978). The best known of these, and the most appropriate for preschool children, are the Ordinal Scales of Psychological Development developed by Uzgiris and Hunt (1975). Another assessment of Piagetian task performance is the Concept Assessment Kit-Conservation (Goldschmid & Beatler, 1968).

The Concept Assessment Kit is intended for children four to seven years of age. It tests their ability to conserve. This test is individually administered and uses Piaget's research technique, that is, the examiner demonstrates a phenomenon that the child is then asked to explain. The test is normed and provides validity and reliability data. Studies have revealed some positive correlation between performance on these Piagetian-based scales and more traditional tests of intelligence (Goodwin & Driscoll, 1980).

As a third alternative, Laosa suggests using diagnostic tests. While many of these are standardized, they test specific areas such as visual-motor coordination rather than general ability. The information they yield is therefore less likely to be culturally biased and less likely to be used to label children. However, few standardized diagnostic tests are available for use with children below four years of age; more commonly, instruments designed for very young children are criterion-referenced skill assessments.

Finally, Laosa (1977) recommends using informal observational techniques to assess the child's behavior. This approach is very appropriate for preschool children, since they are less inhibited by adult observers than older children, and thus can provide much valuable information to the trained observer. This approach, discussed in greater detail later, is gaining wide acceptance among preschool educators of both handicapped and nonhandicapped children. Of course, the information gleaned from informal observation is only as biased as the observer who records it. Perhaps there is no assessment method that is entirely free of bias.

EARLY INTERVENTION AND EDUCATIONAL ASSESSMENT   In their review of factors contributing to good early intervention programs, Keogh and Kopp (1978) note the general lack of assessment procedures designed to provide information for differentiated program planning. As a result, most programs for handicapped infants and preschoolers are broad-based and non-specific, providing enrichment activities that may or may not address the child's deficits. The research data on most of these programs (see Karnes & Teska, 1975; Levitt & Cohen, 1975; Parker and Day, 1972) indicate that these programs are not very effective in the long term.

When we review the factors contributing to the development of the early intervention movement, it becomes easier to understand why assessment at this level has been for the purpose of identifying a general "at risk" category rather than for providing specific educational information.

According to Keogh and Kopp (1978), early intervention programs for both handicapped and disadvantaged (potentially handicapped) preschoolers reflect the present lack of assessment instruments that are specific enough in the information they provide to identify fundamental developmental processes. Weak assessment procedures at entry into these programs, designed primarily to label the handicapping condition, result in all children receiving similar interventions regardless of symptoms. This produces inconclusive outcomes, reflected in data that do not show rehabilitative results. Keogh and Kopp summarize their position:

> Where assessment provides description and delineation of the developmental sequence of behaviors, and when antecedent and outcome developmental events are identified, there is an increased probability that assessment data will lead to appropriate and selective interventions and that program outcomes can be objectively evaluated [p. 537].

Keogh and Kopp maintain that a good assessment instrument will not only describe the developmental sequence and specify where the child is functioning within the sequence, but also will identify desired developmental outcomes for an individual child. Antecedent experiences that underlie a particular skill should be identified also, so that these may be taught as prerequisites for the developmental skill to be learned. This process requires very specific task analysis and is evident in few assessment instruments currently in use. Exceptions are the ordinal scales of sensorimotor development (Escalona & Corman, 1969; Honig & Lally, 1970; Uzgiris & Hunt, 1975), which require extensive training to administer.

An alternative to commercial instruments is to develop informal procedures for use with children in a specific program. An example of this process is the early intervention program for blind infants developed by Fraiberg (1971) and her colleagues (Fraiberg, Smith, & Adelson, 1969), in which a thorough developmental sequence of sensorimotor skills was constructed through observation of the infants. The researchers noted, for example, that because blind babies fail to develop midline hand play at four to five months, they experience delays in developing object permanence and sensorimotor schemes. Object permanence is not achieved by blind infants until three years of age or later (Fraiberg, Smith, & Adelson, 1969). Further observation of the development of hand play in blind infants revealed that delays in reaching for objects on sound cue interfered with the infant's progress in learning to creep. The importance of adaptive hand behavior to later locomotive and cognitive learnings thus became apparent; without such careful observation the existence of such links might not have been discovered. The result was a sequence of components and antecedent experiences that underlie such developmental accomplishments as head and trunk control, reaching and grasping, crawling, and object permanence. These sequences then became the basis for definitive, specific assessment procedures that led to meaningful intervention programming for the infants.

It would appear, then, that there is a strong intuitive feeling among educators and psychologists today that early interventions of any type will aid development and lead to positive outcomes, that stimulation should concentrate on cognitive and language abilities, and that children at risk for a variety of conditions, both medical and socioeconomic, will benefit from global "enrichment" activities. This point of view lacks a strong theoretical base as well as research data to justify it, as will be seen in the next section.

RELIABILITY AND PREDICTIVE VALIDITY OF EARLY CHILDHOOD ASSESSMENT INSTRUMENTS   When assessment is conducted for the purpose of planning efficacious intervention, as it should be, the most useful procedures are behavioral observation and criterion-referenced skills inventories. However, a second purpose of assessment, to identify potentially handicapped children, requires instruments that predict well which children are at developmental risk. For this purpose, the validity and reliability of the assessment instruments are crucial.

Unfortunately, evaluation of the predictive validity of infant assessment instruments indicates that the most commonly used instruments are not very good predictors. Perhaps the best known summary of these studies is by Bayley (1970), who concluded that her scales of infant intelligence are not predictive of later IQ. Holden (1972 also used the Bayley scales and found that they did not predict mental retardation.

Even the Apgar rating of neonatal physiological functioning has not been found to predict later neurological dysfunction (Drage et al., 1966). Infants who had low (0–5) Apgars at birth had significantly more indicators of neurological dysfunction at one year than did infants whose Apgars at birth fell from 7 to 10, but by age seven these differences in central nervous system functioning had disappeared.

Lewis (1976) in reviewing the predictive validity research, states that little predictive validity has been reported between early infant IQ scores and later measures of intelligence, and indeed that even within the first two years of life there has been demonstrated little consistency in IQ performance. In a longitudinal study involving retarded and non-retarded infants, Werner, Honzik, and Smith (1968) found the correlation between IQ at 20 months measured on the Cattell Infant Intelligence Scale (Cattell, 1960) and IQ at 10 years measured on the SRA Primary Mental Ability Test (Thurstone & Thurstone, 1954) to be 49; if only those children who scored below 80 at 20 months were included in the correlation, it rose to 72. Similarly, Share, Koch, Webb, and Graliker (1964) found significant correlations between Gesell scores at infancy and IQ scores (Stanford-Binet) at 5 years for children with Down's syndrome. It appears that predictive validity for standardized infant tests is only adequate when the instruments are used with children at the low end of the normal distribution.

According to Parmalee, Kopp, and Sigman (1976), identifying infants at developmental risk by using only one factor (e.g. test score, prematurity, low SES) is not very accurate. They recommend instead a cumulative risk score (see Chapter 2) that takes into account biological, behavioral, and sociological factors such as nutrition, quality of caregiving, and the cognitive environment of the home. This approach is an attractive alternative to the present practice of identifying infants at risk on the basis of a Bayley or Gesell score.

The reliability of standardized early assessment instruments is generally considered to be adequate (Goodwin & Driscoll, 1980). Lewis (1976) points out that such tests have good validity in part because test constructors have borrowed items from each other, giving those items a high validity. Sigel (1979) has cautioned that using standardized tests with high-risk children may not yield the same level of reliability as that obtained on administrations to average children. He attributes this to the fact that high-risk children tend to be moodier and more easily fatigued and to have higher activity levels and lower attention levels than normal. All of these factors adversely influence their test performance. Sigel also criticizes the use of norm-referenced tests to identify high-risk children from minority populations, since their ethnic group may not be adequately represented in the standardization sample.

Thus, although it is generally agreed that instruments used to predict risk must be both valid and reliable, there is question as to whether those currently in use can be so considered. Most current tests are reliable. Reliability, however, does not mean a test is valid.

AN ECOLOGICAL PROGRAM OF ASSESSMENT

No topic in the field of educating young exceptional children is so fraught with criticism and controversy as that of screening and assessment. Students are likely to question whether a fair and effective program of assessment that avoids all of the problems we have discussed thus far is possible at all. While it may not be possible to develop an ideal assessment program, it is not possible to do without assessment either, since assessment is the vital prerequisite for meaningful educational intervention with disabled, young children. Therefore, we will attempt to outline a program of assessment that will meet the following objectives:

1. The assessment program will be fair to children from diverse cultural backgrounds by accurately identifying their relative strengths and deficits and by taking into account the environment in which they function.
2. It will provide data that are useful for planning a meaningful and realistic intervention program.
3. Both assessment and the resulting intervention will be specifically designed for each child so that learning may be individualized.
4. The assessment program will be on-going so that teaching strategies can be adjusted daily if necessary to provide effective intervention.

Assessment will be carefully matched to what is taught so that it accurately evaluates a child's progress in the intervention program.

An important characteristic of a good assessment program is an ecological approach to evaluation. By this we mean that the assessment data accurately describe as many aspects of the child's functioning as possible (physical, intellectual, social) in as many settings as possible (home, school, community) so that we have the information necessary to plan an intervention program that will affect as much of the child's life as possible.

To meet these objectives, an assessment program must be broad enough to include a fair sampling of the child's abilities yet specific enough to provide useful information. It must include several instruments administered by specialists in various areas of development (e.g., language, motor development, cognition), as well as observational data and data concerning the child's daily environment. Concerning the latter, the parent/child interaction is of primary concern. We will outline these various aspects below. Together, they constitute an ecological approach to educational assessment.

Information from Observation

As sole reliance on standardized tests for assessment information decreases, observation of the young child becomes more important as a source of such information. Observation can take place in the home or center (naturalistic) or in a more controlled laboratory-like setting (clinical). The nature of the setting is determined by the type of information needed. A language specialist may wish to observe a child individually in conversation with her mother; this session could satisfactorily take place in a clinic or office. However, to obtain information regarding the child's social interactions with peers and adults, informal language with peers, or interactions with other family members, a naturalistic observation in the home or preschool center is called for.

Several strategies for observing children have been developed during the past 50 years. Some of these techniques come to preschool education from the field of ethology, the study of animals in their natural environment. Others, such as the keeping of anecdotal records, have been tools of the preschool teacher for many years. This section will be divided into three parts: first, a look at narrative descriptions (anecdotal records, running records, specimen descriptions), second, sampling techniques (specifically time sampling and event sampling) and third, checklists and rating scales. This organization is taken from Irwin and Bushnell, *Observational Strategies for Child Study* (1980).

NARRATIVE DESCRIPTIONS   Perhaps the easiest and least structured form of informal observation, anecdotal records have been used by classroom teachers for years to record the behavior of children about whom they were especially concerned. The anecdotal record requires no particular length, time, or structure of recording. It is simply a collection of descriptions about one child gathered whenever there is something of interest or importance to record. It is usually hand-written and varies in length and style. It usually reflects the writer's biases because there are no built-in protections against them. Nevertheless, anecdotal records can help teachers gain specific information concerning a child's behavior patterns and what conditions might be reinforcing them. For example, a child considered to be aggressive may react to provocation by certain other children, a fact which may not become apparent until a series of provocative episodes have been recorded and analyzed.

Anecdotal records may also be used to find out what children have learned from a particular curriculum unit or presentation (Irwin & Bushnell, 1980). This is especially true for younger children whose informal play is very spontaneous and who readily incorporate new experiences into play situations.

It is useful to reproduce here some guidelines developed by Brandt (1972) for researchers using anecdotal records. As Irwin and Bushnell note, these guidelines are also useful for teachers. They have been adapted from the original.

1. *Write down the anecdote as soon as possible after it occurs.* This is sometimes difficult, since teachers are busy people with many demands on their time from the children in their charge. Nevertheless, it is important to have as accurate information as possible. and fresh information tends to be more accurate than stale.
2. *Identify the basic action of the key person and what was said.* It's important to try to record word for word what was said by the child in question and response. It may be necessary to paraphrase what was said by other involved people. Brandt stresses preserving the *flavor* of the conversation.
3. *Include a statement that identifies the setting, time of day, and basic activity.* This statement should be recorded at the beginning of each anecdote. Brandt suggests also including what was *supposed* to be happening if the child is doing something different from what he is expected to do.
4. Preserve the sequence of the episode. The anecdote should have a beginning, middle, and conclusion.
5. Three levels of actions should be included in the anecdote. (1) *Molar.* This level describes the main activity of the anecdote: Jack was playing the piano. (2) *Subordinate molar.* At this level is recorded more specific information about the main activity: Jack was playing the same four notes over and over again on the piano. (3) *Molecular.* The molecular level gives a qualitative description of the activity: Jack smiled and hummed to himself as he noisily banged away on the piano.

The running record provides more complete information than does the anecdotal record because it continues over an extended period of time. Whereas the anecdotal record is kept intermittently, the writer of the running record must be on the job at scheduled times: every hour or every day at predetermined intervals. The more detail included, the more useful is the record for understanding the child's behavior. The following excerpts from a running record written in 1941 (Woodcock, 1941, pp. 186, 191) give an idea of what kind of information this type of observation can provide.

> Frances slid, bumped herself, and cried. Mary, watching, said, "What did Frances doing? What did Frances do?" to recorder, who explained.
> Mary: "Frances broke that hand," holding up her own right hand. Recorder repeated the remark to make sure she had heard correctly and Mary answered, "Yeh."
> (Ten minutes later) Mary: "I didn't bump my finger," holding up her hand with fingers spread.
> Adult: "You *did?*"
> Mary said, "I didn'. Frances bumped it."
> Polly, coming out into the hall and finding Mary there, said, "Oh, here's two Barb'ras. 'Is is a Barb'ra," touching Mary, "an' *is* is a Barb'ra," indicating herself.
> Mary looked at her solemnly and replied, " *'Is* me."
> Polly, smiling and affable, repeated, "Here's two Barb'ras. Here's a Barb'ra and here's udder Barb'ra," touching each of them as before.
> Mary let her finish her sentence, then repeated stoutly without a smile, " 'Is *me.*"
> Polly started to repeat her story, but may have sensed Mary's disapproval, for this time she called herself a "Barb'ra," then said, "An' 'is is Ma'y."
> Mary looked mollified and nodded saying again, " 'Is is *me.*"

Running records are generally more complete than anecdotal records, but both forms of recording are easy to do and require little preparation or training. They are time consuming if done effectively, and this is one of their drawbacks.

Specimen descriptions were first used by researchers in the field of ecological psychology to record behavior of children or animals in their natural environment. Barker (1955) first used them in his study of midwestern children. The specimen description is different from the anecdotal and running records in the following ways:

1. It is more formal, requiring that subject, setting, time, and episode be identified at the beginning of each narrative.
2. It is limited to a series of *episodes*. Each description must contain only one episode or event.
3. The observer must be able to sit uninterrupted and record events during an entire episode. This is not difficult for someone engaged in research, but it is impossible for a classroom teacher working with a group of children.
4. The specimen description contains more objective reporting. The observer is supposedly less involved with the subject(s) and makes fewer inferences regarding their feelings, thoughts, and intentions than do writers of anecdotal or running records.

Irwin and Bushnell (1980) have include in their excellent review of running records and specimen descriptions guidelines developed by Barker's associate, Herbert Wright. These are summarized in Table 7.3.

As stated above, the major advantage of the narrative description techniques discussed here is the ease with which they can be carried out. For this reason, they are widely used by classroom teachers and researchers interested in obtaining information informally about children as they go about their daily business of exploring and learning. These techniques can provide the teacher with information for program planning that cannot be gleaned from other sources such as

TABLE 7.3   Guidelines for Recording Running Records and Specimen Descriptions

1. Describe the scene as it is when the observer begins the description.
2. Focus on the subject's behavior and whatever in the situation itself affects this behavior. Wright defines two cases in which events or conditions removed from the subject need to be considered:
   a. an action or circumstance that would normally impinge on the subject but does not do so in this case.
   b. an action or circumstance that leads to a change in the subject's situation, even though the subject is not initially aware of the change.
3. Be as accurate and complete as you can about what the subject says, does, and responds to within the situation.
4. Put brackets around all interpretive material generated by the observer so that the description itself stands out clearly and completely.
5. Include the "how" for whatever the subject does.
6. Give the "how" for everything done by anyone interacting with the subject.
7. For every action report all the main steps in their proper order.
8. Describe behavior positively, rather than in terms of what was NOT done.
9. Put no more than one unit of molar behavior in one sentence.
10. Put no more than one thing done by a person other than the subject into a single sentence.
11. Do not report observations in terms of the time an event happened, but do mark off predetermined time intervals (one-minute intervals, for example).
12. Write in everyday language.
13. Use observational tools whenever possible (tape recorders, cameras, or video tape) and transcribe notes on the typewriter. Barker and Wright (1955) used a system of observe-dictate-interrogate-revise in making their observations for *Midwest and Its Children*. This procedure calls for an initial observation period followed by dictation of the observation. A colleague then listens to the dictated narration of the observation and asks questions or interrogates the observer to correct inconsistencies, ambiguities, unclear or incomplete information, and so on. The observer then transcribes the dictation and revises the observation. Barker and Wright find it helpful to have the interrogator look at the revised transcription once more before it is submitted for final typing. Time, purpose, and budget will determine what, if any, observational tools you will be able to use and what steps you will take in preparing a final copy of your anecdotal observations.

From Irwin, D. M. & Bushnell, M. M. *Observational Strategies for Child Study*. New York: Holt, Rinehart & Winston, 1980, p. 106. Reprinted with permission.

testing or parent interview. For this reason, they remain an essential ingredient in a good assessment program.

Nevertheless, narrative descriptions have a major flaw, namely that of observer bias. Since only one person is observing the child and interactions, the record inevitably contains the interpretations, perceptions, and inferences of this one recorder. In addition, the very nature of the narrative style encourages the imputing of intentions, feelings, and thoughts to the subject which may not actually exist (Thurman & Widerstrom, 1979). An example of this taken from one of our students' classroom observations makes the point clearer.

> Michael eyed the plate of cookies *as if he wanted to take one.* He looked around *to make sure no one was looking at him.*

Note the inferences contained in the italicized portions. These impart quite negative conclusions about Michael's intentions. Since the observer cannot read Michael's mind, however, there is no evidence that the inference is correct. This kind of interpretation of a child's intentions or feelings is very common to classroom teachers and may be very destructive to a child. It subverts the purpose of informal observation and may result in the child being inaccurately and unfairly labeled. In its way, the narrative description may be just as biased as the standardized test. It is important for this aspect of the assessment program to be as fair and objective as possible, and so teachers have a responsibility to obtain narrative, observational data that are not reflective of their own culture, their own values, and their own expectations for the children they teach.

SAMPLING TECHNIQUES   One major disadvantage of narrative recording procedures is the large amounts of time required to carry them out effectively. By contrast, sampling techniques offer a means of obtaining information about a child by concentrating only on certain behaviors or on specific time periods for observation. For example, we may be interested only in the problem-solving ability of a child and so need only record instances relating to that ability. Or we may wish to learn more about how a child conducts herself in a free play situation; only that time period needs to be observed. Although the information gathered using sampling techniques is not as comprehensive as that from anecdotal records, it is less demanding for a busy classroom teacher to obtain. Sampling techniques are most appropriate for center-based classrooms, but may also be adapted for home-based program use. Although they have been most widely used in child development research to date (Irwin & Bushnell, 1980), they offer much to teachers as an assessment tool to aid in program planning.

In time sampling the observer chooses specific behaviors that are easily observable and occur with some frequency. These might be negative behaviors like spitting or hitting or positive ones like sharing a toy or showing affection. A small number of behaviors are chosen and their occurrence is recorded during regularly scheduled, short observation periods. A behavior (e.g., hitting) is operationally defined and then recorded each time it occurs during the observation period (frequency). Some behaviors, such as crying, are more appropriately measured by the length of time they occur (duration). The short time periods are assumed to provide accurate samples of the child's ordinary behavior.

The behaviors in question are generally recorded on a special recording sheet that considerably simplifies the process. A sample form for frequency recording is provided in Figure 7.1. Note that the observer may simply check the presence or absence of the behavior during the observation interval, tally its frequency of occurrence, or record its duration. An alternative to the recording sheet is the wrist counter, on which the wearer pushes a button to record instances of the behavior observed during a given time period.

Unlike time sampling, event sampling is not restricted to specific preplanned time intervals but takes place whenever the targeted behavior occurs. An observer who is studying a child's temper tantrums, for example, records information whenever a tantrum occurs. There may be many hours or days in between recording periods. Thus, event sampling is more appropriate for infrequently occurring behaviors and the behaviors of one or several children may be recorded at once.

Event sampling is very time-consuming for researchers who may be forced to spend hours waiting for a behavior to occur, but it is well suited for classroom teachers who can simply go about their daily business between recording sessions. Event sampling has the advantage of not isolating the target behaviors and interrupting the sequence in which they occur as does time sampling. It preserves the context in which the behaviors occur, making it possible to analyze causal relationships, getting at the *why* as well as the *what* of the behavior (Wright, 1960). Whereas time sampling is a method for quantifying behavior, event sampling allows us to examine it in qualitative terms as well. The sample recording sheet in Figure 7.2 helps to illustrate the difference between the two methods. Which method to use in a given situation depends on the kind of information desired and the amount of time available for obtaining it.

CHECKLISTS AND RATING SCALES   A more structured form of observational data is provided by checklists. These are useful for gathering information concerning development of specific skill areas. While narrative and sampling techniques seem best suited for assessing a child's social or emotional development, the checklist is useful for assessing academic needs. There are good commercial checklists available, but checklists are also quite simple to construct.

If we placed all of our assessment techniques on a continuum from informal and unstructured to formal and structured, the checklist would fall somewhere in the middle. Anecdotal and specimen records would fall at the informal, unstructured end of the continuum and standardized tests would be placed at the structured and formal end. The checklist moves us down the continuum toward formal testing, because it requires the observer to participate in the assessment process by presenting specific tasks to the child to perform, rather than merely recording whatever the child happens to do. The checklist remains informal, however, in that there is not a prescribed way in which tasks must be presented.

	TUGS	CALLS	OBJECTS	STANDS	"ME"	ASKS	CRIES	YELLS	TEASES	HUGS	COMMENTS
Observer_____ Setting_____Date_____Time_____ Adult_____Age of Children_____Size of Group_____											
1. _____											
2. _____											
3. _____											
4. _____											
5. _____											
6. _____											
7. _____											
8. _____											
9. _____											
10. _____											
11. _____											
12. _____											
13. _____											
14. _____											
15. _____											
16. _____											
17. _____											
18. _____											
19. _____											
20. _____											
21. _____											
22. _____											
23. _____											
24. _____											
25. _____											
26. _____											
27. _____											
28. _____											
29. _____											
30. _____											
GROUP TOTALS											

FIGURE 7.1   Recording Sheet for Time-Sampling (Frequency)

Observer _____

OUTCOME BEHAVIORS

IA: *Immediate Attention:* Adult focuses on child within two seconds of attention bid.

DA: *Delayed Attention:* Adult focuses on child within 5 seconds of attention, but with a delay of at least 2 seconds.

I: *Ignores Bid:* Adult does not respond to attention bid.

Adult Affect

+A: *Positive Affect:* The adult's affect (the emotional tone of his or her response) is positive.

–A: *Negative Affect:* The adults' affect is negative.

Setting _____ Date _____ Time _____

Adult _____ Age of Children _____ Size of Group _____

EVENT	CHILD	SEX	AGE	ATTENTION BID(S)	DURATION	OUTCOME BEHAVIORS	AFFECT	COMMENTS
1.								
2.								
3.								

FIGURE 7.2   Recording Sheet for Event Sampling with Codes for Outcome Behaviors and Adult Affect in Children's Bids for Attention. Adapted from Irwin, D. M., and Bushnell, M. M. *Observational Strategies for Child Study.* New York: Holt, Rinehart & Winston, 1980.

Additionally, many items on checklists may be assessed by observing the child during his daily routine. Using a pincer grasp, speaking in complete sentences, and sharing toys with others are examples of this.

A checklist is simply a list of skills, usually arranged in developmental sequence and sometimes with normative age levels noted for each skill, which are presented to the child in sequence and graded on a pass/fail basis. The checklist may be either criterion or norm-referenced. Sometimes it is both. In the sense that it measures the child's performance against a written criterion it is criterion-referenced; in the sense that it provides normative age levels against which to measure the child's performance it is norm-referenced.

Generally the child either passes or fails an item without consideration for the quality of his performance. However a good checklist provides a clear criterion for each task so that the observer can decide on an objective basis whether or not the child can perform the task in question. This is the most important requirement for a good checklist, for clearly spelled out mastery criteria increase the reliability of the instrument and make it easier to administer.

Two well known and commonly used skills checklists are the *Learning Accomplishment Profile* (Sanford, 1974) and the *Portage Guide to Early Education* (Bluma et al., 1976). These instruments list tasks in each developmental area—cognitive, language, motor, and social development and self-help skills— and provide a column for recording pass/fail. A second column is used for recording the date at which mastery was achieved. The checklist thus shares another characteristic with the informal narrative description: It is meant to be part of an on-going process rather than to be administered only once or twice as are formal tests. This greatly increases its usefulness as a tool for program planning, since new information regarding the child's skill levels is constantly available for incorporating into individualized plans.

Many early childhood educators feel that commercially available checklists do not break skills down into small enough components to be useful for lesson planning. For that reason, they often prefer to develop their own checklists. This can be done by proceeding as follows:

1. Choose a developmental area in which the child needs special instruction. Pick a specific skill from this area to assess.
2. Observe several older or normal children to determine what the specific components of the skill are. Use a commercial checklist to get you started, then fill in the gaps through your observations.
3. List the developmental steps in sequence.
4. Transfer your skill sequence to a checklist format with columns for recording date of first assessment, date of mastery, and comments.
5. Develop a criterion for each step to determine whether or not the child has mastered the skill at that step.

Table 7.4 presents an example of this process.

Skills checklists are among the most widely used assessment instruments in educational programs for both disabled and nondisabled children, because they are easy to administer, provide information that is useful for program planning, and are relatively reliable and free of bias. However, checklists are only one part of a good assessment program. Without information from both ends of the continuum as well as from the middle, we do not have a very complete picture of the child.

Rating scales are used to make judgments about a child's behavior or environment. They are not as useful as checklists, for they are not well-suited for assessing academic performance. In addition, because they require a judgment to be made and rarely provide criteria on which to base it, such scales tend to contain a great deal of bias. Nevertheless, a rating scale may be a useful time saver. Take, for example, the Pupil Behavior Rating Scale developed by Myklebust for as-

TABLE 7.4   Steps in Developing Skills Checklist

Guideline

1. Choose a developmental area in which the child needs special instruction. Pick a skill from this area to assess.

Self-help skills: feeding self

2. Observe several older children to find out what the specific components of the skill are. Use a commercial checklist to get you started. Lists the developmental steps in sequence.

Steps to self-feeding as presented in LAP	Observed
1.	a.
	b.
2.	a.
	b.
3.	a.
	b.
4.	a.
	b.

3. Transfer your skill sequence to a checklist format with room for recording date first assessed, date of mastery, and comments.

Skill	Date Assessed	Date Mastered	Comments
1.			
a.			
b.			
2.			
a.			
b.			

sessing the emotional behavior of young children. This instrument allows the observer to rate a child in terms of her attention span, activity level, and distractability in order to identify possible learning disabilities. The rating scale can be based on knowledge previously gained about the child or can be done through current observation. Either way, little time needs to be spent in direct observation compared to narrative or sampling techniques.

A portion of the Pupil Behavior Rating Scale is reproduced in Table 7.5 to illustrate the general format such scales take. Usually the observer is asked to rate the subject on a particular behavior on a numerical scale (e.g., one to five). Sometimes the scale is descriptive as in Table 7.5, ranging from *Never* through *Sometimes* to *Always*. The information gained may be useful in identifying areas for further testing, but it is usually too general to be very helpful in program planning. For this reason, rating scales are more useful during the screening process than they are for assessment.

TABLE 7.5   Pupil Behavior Rating Scale of H. Myklebust

Name _____ No. _____   School _____ Grade _____

Sex _____ Date _____   Teacher _____

PUPIL BEHAVIOR RATING SCALE*

1	2	3	4	5

I. Auditory comprehension and listening

Ability to follow directions

1	2	3	4	5
Always confused; cannot or is unable to follow directions	Usually follows simple oral directions but often needs individual help	Follows directions that are familiar and/or not complex	Remembers and follows extended directions	Unusually skillful in remembering and following directions

Comprehension of class discussion

1	2	3	4	5
Always inattentive and/or unable to follow and understand discussions	Listens but rarely comprehends well; mind often wanders from discussion	Listens and follows discussions according to age and grade	Understands well and benefits from discussions	Becomes involved and shows unusual understanding of material discussed

Ability to retain orally given information

1	2	3	4	5
Almost total lack of recall: poor memory	Retains simple ideas and procedures if repeated often	Average retention of materials; adequate memory for age and grade	Remembers procedures and information from various sources; good immediate and delayed recall	Superior memory for both details and content

Comprehension of word meanings

1	2	3	4	5
Extremely immature level of understanding	Fails to grasp simple word meanings; misunderstands words at grade level	Good grasp of grade level vocabulary for age and grade	Understands all grade level vocabulary as well as higher level word meanings	Superior understanding of vocabulary; understands many abstract words

TABLE 7.5   continued

II. Spoken language
Ability to speak in complete sentences using accurate sentence structure

Always uses incomplete sentences with grammatical errors	Frequently uses incomplete sentences and/or numerous grammatical errors	Uses correct grammar; few errors of omission or incorrect use of prepositions, verb tense, pronouns	Above-average oral language; rarely makes grammatical errors	Always speaks in grammatically correct sentences

*Adapted from a project developed under Research Grant, USPHS Contract 108-65-42, Bureau of Neurological and Sensory Diseases.

Information from Task Analysis

In developing our own checklist, we needed to break each skill into small components to provide information about the child's ability specific enough for teaching. This process of observing a behavior and breaking it into small steps is called task analysis and is discussed more fully in Chapters 8 and 9. It is especially important for teaching basic skills to severely handicapped, young children, who learn best by taking one small step at a time.

To understand task analysis it is helpful to analyze a task yourself. Take a task that you do every day, like putting on your shirt. List the steps in order as you do them. Do not omit any of your actions. Now, use the list to observe a child learning to dress himself. At what steps does he encounter difficulty? Putting his arm through the armhole? Matching correct button to buttonhole? Putting button through buttonhole? Wherever the breakdown occurs, it is obvious what steps need working on during skill-learning sessions.

Standardized Tests

In spite of their drawbacks, standardized tests provide certain information that is necessary for a complete assessment program. It is important when planning educational programs not only to identify those skills the child cannot perform but also to compare his performance with that of others his age in order to determine whether he is progressing normally. It might also be important to obtain an estimate of his potential ability in math, reading, or other achievement area. A standardized test performs these two functions quite well for children from the majority culture. A number of standardized testing instruments are described in the appendix.

Most standardized tests take special training to administer. They are norm-referenced, of course, which means that the child's performance is compared to those of children of comparable age levels. They are standardized in their rules for administration so that every presentation is as similar as possible to all previous and future administrations. This results in high reliability for such tests.

The most widely used of the standardized tests for infants and toddlers are the Brazelton Neonatal Assessment Scales, the Bayley Scales of Infant Development, and the McCarthy Scales of Children's Abilities. The Brazelton Scale requires extensive training before administration, as to a lesser extent do the Bayley and McCarthy Scales. All three instruments are usually administered by psychologists; the Brazelton Scales are often administered by pediatricians as well.

THE INTERDISCIPLINARY TEAM AND ECOLOGICAL ASSESSMENT

One of the most important mandates of P.L. 94–142 is that an IEP be developed for each child and that it be the result of interdisciplinary participation. As stated at the beginning of the chapter, our ability to evaluate children's educational needs at present appears to surpass our ability to provide programs to meet those needs. Interdisciplinary teams can produce a thorough needs assessment that can be translated into program objectives and program implementation.

Although teams vary in both composition and role depending upon in what part of the country and what type of institution they work, nevertheless some generalizations can be made. The interdisciplinary team is more fully discussed in Chapter 8.

CONCLUSION

This chapter has dealt with the processes of screening and assessment of young children and how those processes lead to the identification of children with developmental problems or with increased risk of developing problems. We have provided descriptions of various screening and assessment tools in the appendix. Other descriptions are available in a variety of sources (see Johnson, 1979). We have, however, concentrated on issues involved in the assessment of young children and have stressed more informal assessment techniques. In the chapters that follow, the reader will gain additional insights into assessment and, more importantly, will begin to see more clearly the relationship between assessment, program planning, and program implementation. We hope that this chapter has helped to put what follows into its proper perspective.

PROGRAM
PLANNING AND
IMPLEMENTATION

three

Individual Program Planning

1. What is the major premise of the ecological congruence model?
2. Why is the ecological congruence model compatible with a developmental approach?
3. What is the importance of task analysis in program planning?
4. What are the three components of a well constructed instructional objective?
5. Why is a team approach important when implementing the ecological congruence model?

three
8

Since the passage of Public Law 94–142, The Education for All Handicapped Children's Act, in 1975, there has been a legal mandate to develop individualized educational plans (IEPs) for all children classified by the public schools as requiring special services. The law requires that if services are provided by a public school system to any children who are between the ages of three and five, then the same services must be provided to all children ages three to five regardless of handicapping condition. According to a recent survey of the National Association of State Directors of Special Education, 17 states have mandated services for handicapped children down to the age of three years and 7 states have mandated services down to birth. Four other states provide services down to four years of age. Clearly, then, legislative mandates are applicable to a large number of children who fall within the birth to five years age range.

As a result of these mandates educational technology has been applied to the development of these individualized educational services. In this chapter, various aspects of educational technology are discussed as they facilitate the individual development of young handicapped children. Specifically, task analysis, developing instructional objectives, and data recording systems are discussed.

THE ECOLOGICAL CONGRUENCE MODEL

Before we can consider the technology of education, we must establish a context for that technology. Several years ago Thurman (1977) suggested the ecological congruence model for providing special educational services. His model is concerned with both the development of the child and the fit between the characteristics of the child and her environment. Thurman (1977) suggests that educational interventions must be concerned not only with changing the child to fit the environment but also with changing the environment to fit the child. When the child and the environment are in harmony, a state of ecological congruence exists.

According to Thurman, the ecological congruence model has three critical dimensions: deviancy, competency, and tolerance for difference. These dimensions are illustrated in Figure 8.1 and are explained below.

Deviancy, according to the ecological congruence model, is a function of the

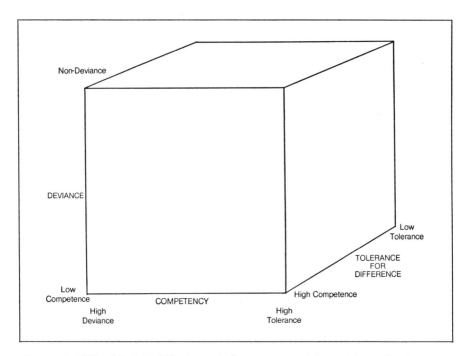

FIGURE 8.1 The Model of Ecological Congruence. Adapted from S. K. Thurman. The congruence of behavioral ecologies: A model for special education programming. *Journal of Special Education* 11, 329–333. Reprinted with permission.

label placed on an individual and/or his behavior. Essentially the model accepts Simmons' (1969) suggestion that no human behavior is inherently deviant as a valid basis for the conceptualization of deviancy. "The judgment made about a particular behavior or set of characteristics can be made relative only to the social context in which it has occurred. Thus, those conditions accounting for the label placed upon a behavior and, subsequently the individual himself, lie within the environmental context in which the behavior occurs" (Thurman, 1977, p. 330).

Competency can be defined, in the simplest terms, as functional behavior. "Just as every social setting defines parameters for deviance, so does it define a certain set of functional behaviors, or behaviors that lead to the completion of a task or job, within that setting. Competency/ incompetency, unlike deviance, is an attribute of the individual, since given a specific task a person either has or does not have the necessary behavior repertoire to perform the task" (Thurman, 1977, p. 330). Incompetence cannot be inferred solely from nonperformance, since performance of a task is a function of internal and external motivational factors as well as one's competence. Simply, lack of performance does not necessarily mean lack of competence.

Tolerance for difference is the dimension of the ecological congruence model which determines the goodness of fit between the individual and the environmental/social context. Within every social system there is a range of tolerance for difference. Each system defines its own range of what is or is not acceptable. An individual who is viewed as different enough, either because of her assigned degree of deviancy or her lack of competency in performing tasks within the system, is not tolerated by the system. Lack of tolerance by the system establishes an incongruent ecology.

Although not discussed in the original description of the ecological congruence model, incongruence in an ecology may result from intolerance of the individual for the system. If, in fact, the individual perceives systemic attributes he cannot tolerate, then a lack of ecological congruence results. For ecological congruence to be maximized, mutual tolerance of individuals for systems and systems for individuals must be brought about. Most often, human service interventions change individuals to make them more tolerable to social systems and thus create more congruent ecologies. On the other hand, interventions are rarely designed to make systems more tolerant of individual differences, be they in level of competence or degree of perceived deviance. Somewhat more frequent, although by no means commonplace, are interventions designed to increase individuals' tolerance of social systems.

Individual approaches to educational programming, the focus of this chapter, have dealt almost exclusively with the application of educational technology to changing individuals. Individualized educational approaches designed to increase ecological congruence must have three objectives: (1) to change individuals' patterns of behavior, (2) to change the tolerance for systemic difference of these individuals, and (3) to change the tolerance of the system for individual differences in competence and perceived deviancy. This approach does not alter the usefulness of the technology to be discussed, but rather modifies the way it is applied.

> When an individual's ecology is congruent, the stage has been set for maximization of his function and adjustment. Competent function brings along with it human dignity acceptance within the setting, and provides the basis for developing higher levels of competency. Congruence along the deviancy/nondeviancy dimension results in greater acceptance of the individual within the setting. [This coupled with the individual's tolerance for the setting leads to a feeling of security and nurturance.]
>   Congruence results in (a) the individual's expression of his maximum competence . . . (b) the acceptance of him with his individual differences [and (c) his feelings of security and comfort]. Congruence does not necessarily mean "normal," rather it can be seen as maximal adaptation [between the individual and the environment]. To borrow a term from biology, a homeostatic relationship exists between the individual and the environmental setting. As with all homeostatic situations, congruent behavioral ecologies will be in a state of dynamic equilibrium. . . . Such dynamic states are the basis of further adaptation and development of [both] the individual *and* his environment [and their continued interaction with each other]. [Thurman, 1977, pp. 332–333]

The ends inherent in the ecological congruence model are particularly relevant to preschool disabled and to at risk children whose perceptions of the environment and whose environment's perception of them may significantly alter their developmental course (Sameroff, 1979; Sameroff & Chandler, 1975; cf. Kearsley, 1979; Thurman & Lewis, 1979) and the ultimate nature of the ecological system of which they are part. In individual program planning for the young disabled child, the assumption is that program plans will improve ecological congruence rather than change individual patterns of behavior in order to increase individual levels of competence.

The previous sections of this book have been concerned primarily with development and assessment of disabled children between birth and five years of age. While the ecological congruence model suggests interventions which are designed to improve ecologies, it simultaneously recognizes the importance of individual development within the ecology. In fact, as will be seen in the ensuing discussion on program planning, assessment of an individual child within an ecological system is dependent upon adequate knowledge of a child's developmental progress and the various factors that account for it. Competence, in the ecological congruence model, represents the developmental status of the individual. A child's ability to perform a certain task or behavior (i.e., express competency) is clearly a function of her developmental status. It is the interrelationship of the individual's developmental status, degree of competency, and the setting's reaction to them which are of importance within the context of the ecological congruence model. Essentially the program planning strategy to be discussed is both developmental and ecological in nature and recognizes the unique contribution of each approach to the other.

USING THE ECOLOGICAL CONGRUENCE
MODEL IN EDUCATIONAL PLANNING

Thurman (1977) has suggested a nine-step process to assess degree of ecological congruence. The following steps are a modification of the original process.

1. Identify the major environmental settings that are important in the child's life.
2. Develop an inventory of critical tasks in those settings (i.e., those tasks which make the setting function).
3. Assess the child's competence to perform those tasks.
4. Assess motivational variables (i.e., contingency structures) and other factors that affect the child's ability to perform tasks.
5. Assess the child's tolerance of the environment.
6. Determine which of the child's behaviors and/or characteristics are outside of the level of tolerance of the system. (Note: These behaviors or characteristics may be those labeled as deviant or they may be the result of insufficient development of the child to perform necessary tasks.)
7. Identify objectives for each component of the ecology (i.e., child system) which, when accomplished, will lead to increased ecological congruence.
8. Identify strategies for accomplishment of the objectives.
9. Establish a means by which interventions are to be monitored and their effectiveness assessed.

Smith, Neisworth, and Greer (1978) have suggested that there is a range of educational environments, each of which has a role in the total education of the child. In discussing these environments, they suggest that "psychological and educational research [have] strongly documented the powerful influence of the environment on learning. Yet very little attention [has been] given to assessing the characteristics of the environment" (p. iv). They conclude that "astute diagnosticians are presently well beyond the point of focusing their assessment efforts exclusively on the child" (p. iii). The implementation of the ecological congruence model takes into account the points made by Smith and his colleagues and provides a useful context within which to examine existing aspects of educational technology. The remainder of this section elucidates the educational planning process as it is influenced by the ecological congruence model. In this discussion various aspects of educational technology will be brought to bear.

Identification of Major Environmental Settings

Each of us operates in a number of environmental settings each day. Only some of these settings provide major influences in one's life, for example, the daily family meal or weekly church service. Others are generally much less influential (e.g., the busy street corner or the shopping mall). The relative importance of any setting depends on the individual and his overall ecology. The shopping mall, for example, may hold great importance for a blind three-year-old who is just developing independent mobility skills.

To determine the most important environmental settings for any child, it is first necessary to identify the settings the child frequents. Although one should not assume *a priori* that an infrequently entered setting is not significant, as a rule those settings which young children occupy most frequently are the ones of greatest significance.

Roger Barker (1968) has provided a means for identifying individual units of the environment, which he terms *behavior settings*. Behavior settings can be used to define a person's behavioral ecology and the way her behavior is influenced by setting characteristics. For our present purpose, it is most useful to apply Barker's strategy to identify environmental settings within which child/setting congruence can then be determined. As a matter of fact, Barker himself expresses little concern about the goodness-of-fit between the individual and her behavior settings.

Behavior settings according to Barker (1968) have a *standing pattern of behavior* and a specific *milieu*. The standing pattern of behavior and milieu remain constant, regardless of the individuals occupying the setting. For example, in the behavior setting *family dinner* the standing pattern of behavior includes eating, sitting, passing food, and some degree of conversation. The milieu includes the physical features of the setting (i.e., the table, chairs, plates, utensils, etc.) The behavior setting is defined when the standing pattern of behavior and milieu come together in a functional manner at a given point in time. The behavior setting *family dinner* could not exist without all necessary utensils or enough chairs for all members of the family to be seated. Nor could it exist if people were sitting at the table but not engaging in eating, a critical aspect of the standing pattern of behavior. Thus, while the milieu is always present in space and time, it becomes part of a behavior setting only when it is surrounded by the proper standing pattern of behavior.

The identification of behavior settings begins with interviews with parents or primary caretakers of young, disabled children. Parents are asked to describe a typical day in their family and to tell where they go and what they do. Settings entered by older siblings, especially those who are closest in age to the child in question, may be of particular importance. These settings may provide useful insights into what the target child will be expected to do in the future. Interviews with parents can also include questions about the frequency of certain activities. Parents and other caretakers can also be asked to keep simple logs or diaries for a week or two to gain additional insights into the behavior settings the target child enters. A visit to the home can be useful in determining the milieu of those behavior settings occurring there. If the child has already entered a day program of some kind, visits can be made to the program and staff there can be asked about daily activities. Parents, teachers, and other caretakers can be asked to rate the importance of each setting identified for the child. For example, one family may see "Sunday Morning Church Service" as a very important behavior setting and one with which they seek congruence for their child. Another family, however, may be more concerned with ecological congruence during mealtimes or when visiting relatives.

Most families inhabit reasonably standard behavior settings. As a result, some may question spending time on interviews, diaries, and home visits. Each family is unique, however, and each may exhibit a different profile in its frequency of entrance of different behavioral settings. In addition, the relative importance of different behavior settings is made clear using interviews, diaries, and home visits. Keep in mind that individual program planning is the impetus for ecological congruence for ecologies that include preschool, disabled children.

Inventory Critical Tasks

Each behavioral setting is defined in part by a series of behavioral tasks. Once the most important settings have been identified, further analysis of these settings may be necessary. Since the ecological congruence model is concerned with the child's competence in those settings which make up his ecology, it is important to identify the competencies required for independent function of the individual within the setting. Using the earlier example, family dinner, one obviously necessary task for *independent* function is self-feeding. Self-feeding, however, may not be necessary for ecological congruence. The milieu and the behavior of other members of the setting often provide the individual modifications necessary to bring about congruence for the nine-month-old child who has not yet acquired independent feeding skills. Such modifications, quite obviously, include high chairs, bibs, down-size utensils, and the offer of individual bites of food by other members of the family. This example shows how naturally occurring systems modifications can bring about ecological congruence. The family system may or may not be as ready to make the necessary environmental modifications for a three-year-old, disabled child who possesses the same level of competence in self-feeding as a nine-month-old.

Critical competencies exist in most settings. If the same nine-month-old had developmental problems that did not permit her to sit independently in a high chair, she might have a more difficult time achieving congruence with her environment. Again, interviews with parents and caretakers as well as systematic observations of behavior settings can be useful for identification of task competencies for various levels of function. Further individualization is possible by assessing the individual level of competence the target child has in displaying these competencies. In a sense, the tasks included in the task inventory of the major behavior settings form the basic curriculum targets for the child's further development. This statement should not be taken to mean that certain systems modifications may not be necessary so that the child can express his maximum level of competence. In forgetting to examine and implement the necessary systems modifications, one would be abandoning the ecological congruence model.

Assessing the Child's Competencies

As has been discussed in the previous chapter there are a number of tools both standardized and informal which can be used in assessing the competency of various young, disabled children. These tools may be useful in getting a general picture of the child's level of competence and development. They may also provide information about the child's ability to perform tasks within given behavior settings. None of these assessment devices, however, is tied directly to competencies required in specific behavior settings. Task analysis is a way to assess children's competence to perform specific tasks in a given behavior setting.

Task analysis can be defined as breaking down a complex task into its component parts or behavioral steps. It is a way to develop instructional sequences and has been used extensively in the educational and vocational programming for both severely and profoundly retarded individuals (cf. Gold, 1976; Smith & Snell, 1978; Van Etten, Arkell, & Van Etten, 1980) and preschool, handicapped children. Within the context of the ecological congruence model, task analysis can be applied to specific tasks which are critical to function within a particular setting. These task analyses may then be used to assess the competency of an individual child.

Suppose a critical skill in a particular preschool classroom is a child's ability to enter the room, take off his coat, and hang it on a hook. A task analysis of this skill (competency) might be:

Step 1: Child removes coat.

Step 2: Child locates hook.

Step 3: Child hangs coat on hook.

These three steps are necessary to accomplish the critical competency and are indeed a task analysis of sorts. To be useful for assessment and instructional purposes, a greater degree of precision is necessary, however. These rather large steps must be broken into smaller, more discrete steps. A more appropriate task analysis of the skill "removing and hanging up a coat" might be:

Step 1: Child grabs one edge of coat at the chest.

Step 2: Child extends arm holding coat and lifts coat off of one shoulder.

Step 3: Child grabs other edge of coat at the chest with other hand.

Step 4: Child extends other arm lifting coat off at other shoulder.

Step 5: While still holding coat with one hand child pulls one arm out of the sleeve.

Step 6: With arm free of sleeve child reaches across body and grabs top of collar.

Step 7: While continuing to hold collar child pulls other arm from sleeve.

Step 8: Child continues to hold coat by collar and locates hook.

Step 9: Child places inside of collar over the hook.

Step 10: Child releases coat from hand.

This task analysis breaks down the task into much smaller and more discrete steps than did the previous one. As a result, it can be used to much more precisely assess a child's competence in taking off a coat. Keep in mind, however, that even this task analysis could be broken down into finer steps. For example, it can be further broken down as follows:

Step 1: Child bends arm at elbow at 90°.

Step 2: Child rotates arm so it is against the body.

Step 3: Child extends fingers.

Step 4: Child places fingers on the edge of the coat.

Step 5: Child flexes fingers around edge of coat.

This task analysis breaks the skill of grabbing the edge of the coat into its specific components. The degree of detail (i.e., the number of steps) in a task analysis depends upon the general nature of the task as well as the functioning level of the child. In the examples above, the second task analysis represents the level of detail necessary for most children. The steps in the first task analysis are clearly too large, while those in the third analysis are more detailed than is needed for most children. The third analysis probably would be of use for a child with particular difficulties in motor function or hand-eye coordination.

Task analyses for critical tasks in a setting can be used to determine a child's degree of competence. Suppose a new child entered a program and the teacher wanted to find out whether or not the child could remove a coat. He merely has to employ the task analysis developed above. The teacher may find that the child can do each step of the task, that the child can do some but not all of the steps, or that the child cannot do the task at all. To increase the level of ecological congruence, this teacher would probably want to develop an instructional program to increase the child's ability to remove a coat. If the other children in the class already had this competency, they might not be tolerant of the child who was just learning the skill. In that case, the teacher might have to develop a means by which the other children could become more tolerant of differences. The teacher might have to be tolerant of the extra time necessary to instruct the child and get the coat off and hung up, too.

Assessing Motivational Variables

An assessment may reveal that a child has the competency to perform a particular task, although observation of the child may reveal that she rarely performs the task spontaneously and independently. In this case, the child's performance deficits can be accounted for by motivational variables. The child simply lacks the motivation to perform competently. Motivation may be defined as a person's tendency to perform tasks and may be *intrinsic*, that is, come from inside the individual, or it may be *extrinsic*. Examples of intrinsic motivation are doing a task because it is expected or because it leads to a feeling of doing right. Examples of extrinsic motivation are doing a task because it leads to a compliment from another person or because it leads to a reward like food, money, or special considerations. Although almost no one is totally intrinsically or extrinsically motivated, children, especially those who are delayed cognitively, tend to be extrinsically motivated. Thus, our emphasis in this section is on identifying variables related to extrinsic motivation.

Extrinsic motivation is inherent in the environment. Put another way, children tend to behave (i.e., perform tasks) because their behavior results in certain consequences in the external environment. As is discussed in Chapter 9, these consequences may be arranged so that children are more likely behave in one way than another. Such arrangement of learning environments increases motivation, and concommitant increases in task performance (i.e., expression of competency) and learning (i.e., acquisition of new competency) come about.

As was stated above, lack of ecological congruence may be a result of lack of performance due either to lack of motivation or lack of having learned to do a task. In developing individual plans for the establishment of ecological congruence, it is important to assess how a child is best motivated. That is, what environment increases the child's tendency to perform critical tasks? To determine the answer to this question, it is necessary to observe both child and the environment.

Such observations should be structured to determine what consequences children receive for their behavior. Behavior that is followed by positive environmental consequences is probably desirable behavior. That which is followed by negative environmental consequences is probably undesirable behavior. By the same means, the consequences desired by particular children can be identified. When a child is observed in a free environment without any planned intervention on his behavior, it can be assumed that the child is behaving in the manner in which he is motivated to behave. Thus, if a child comes into the room and spontaneously hangs up her coat, it can be assumed that the child is motivated to perform in this manner. At the same time, if the child's behavior is followed consistently by verbal praise from the teacher, it is likely that the teacher's verbal approval is contributing to the child's motivation. Another child whose performance of coat hanging is not consistently followed by teacher praise and who continues to perform this task can be assumed to be motivated by other factors, which are probably more intrinsic in nature.

Consequences of a child's behavior that increase her tendency to behave in a certain manner are referred to as positively reinforcing consequences or *positive reinforcers*. Some reinforcers motivate each child more than others. As suggested above, the activities in which a child freely engages are activities reinforcing to that child. To increase the performance of certain tasks by the child (assuming, of course, such intervention is necessary for ecological congruence), it is important to establish a reinforcement hierarchy for the child. A *reinforcement hierarchy* is a list of consequences available in the environment which the child values. The more a particular consequence is valued by a child the higher that consequence appears in the hierarchy.

A reinforcement hierarchy can also be determined by asking the child's parents what the child likes best. Of course, the child, too, can be asked to tell what he likes, providing he has the necessary language skills to communicate likes and dislikes. Another means of finding effective reinforcers for a child is to test the effect of various consequences on the child's behavior. This can be done relatively simply by having a child perform a simple task (for example, finger tapping, hand clapping, jumping up and down, or the like), and counting the number of times the child performs the task in a minute. Several of these one-minute sessions can be followed by a particular consequence. Then several more by another consequence and so on until five or six different consequences have been employed. Those sessions in which the greatest number of behaviors (e.g., taps, jumping, etc.) occurred are assumed to be the sessions that were followed by the more reinforcing consequences. These consequences probably appear near the top of the child's reinforcement hierarchy.

An understanding of motivational factors is necessary for establishment of ecological congruence. The techniques discussed in this section are used to acquire information about the motivational structure of the child's environment and what specific factors are important for motivating a particular child. More will be said in Chapter 9 about the way the learning environment can be organized to make maximum use of motivational variables. Suffice it to say at this point that it is necessary to assess the child's competence in performing critical tasks, as well as the way her performance is affected by motivational variables. From the perspective of ecological congruence, the motivational aspects of the environment should maximize the child's expression of competence and support the learning of new critical competencies.

Assessing the Child's Tolerance of the Environment

Systematic observation is a major source of data about a young child's tolerance of his environment. The child should be observed in a number of different settings and during various activities within each setting. It is important to determine to what degree the child spontaneously interacts with people and objects in the environment. For example, is the child observed to make frequent or infrequent contacts with other children in the setting? How frequently the child makes contacts with adults in the environment also provides important information about the child's level of tolerance. Data may indicate that the child is more likely to approach and interact with some people in the environment than with others, thus indicating a higher degree of tolerance of some people by the child.

Another key to the child's tolerance of a particular environmental setting is the ease with which the child enters the setting. For example, a child who comes to the classroom and exhibits reluctance and makes protests suggests a rather low level of tolerance for the classroom setting. Such behavior is a primary source of incongruence between the child and the environment and requires an intervention designed to increase ecological congruence. Another child may enter the classroom freely but throw a tantrum at lunch time. While this child tolerates the classroom environment generally, his behavior suggests a low level of tolerance for lunch. Again some intervention to increase ecological congruence is probably necessary.

A child who is displaying a low level of tolerance for the system will, in most cases, become more tolerant over time. This is particularly true if the system is tolerant and responsive to the child's needs and if a trusting and nurturant environment is provided. Of course, educational interventions may be specifically designed to increase a child's tolerance for the environment. The common procedure of ignoring a child's temper tantrums is a case in point. While ignoring a child helps insure that she is not receiving any positive reinforcement for undesirable behavior (at least by the people in the classroom), ignoring also may be interpreted by the child as a sign of tolerance. Ignoring the child during a temper tantrum requires that the people in the environment tolerate the child's yelling and screaming until the child stops. Confrontation with the child increases the intensity of the tantrum not only because the child is receiving attention for his behavior but also because the people in the system are not being tolerant of the child's behavior. This confrontation often results in mutual intolerance, which creates an even greater level of incongruence in the ecology.

Assessing Tolerance in the Environment

The degree of tolerance in any environmental setting is defined by the people in that setting, both individually and collectively. For example, in a family setting, one parent may tolerate a five-year-old cerebral palsied child's inability to independently go to the bathroom while the other parent does not tolerate it at all and refuses to interact with the child during toileting times or in situations outside of the home where the child may have to be assisted with toileting needs. In another family, both parents may tolerate the child's inability to toilet independently. In still a third, neither parent may tolerate it. In the case of intolerance by both parents, it is likely that the child will be placed outside of the family.

In program planning for ecological congruence, it is important to assess the degree of tolerance in the social system for the preschool, handicapped child. This assessment can be done through observing how various individuals in the social system interact with the child. Do people approach the child, and if so in what circumstances? What behavior on the part of the child is followed by negative or aversive consequences? Negative consequences of a behavior suggest that the behavior is not desired or tolerated in a particular setting. Negative feedback suggests that the child is expected to behave differently if she is to be tolerated in the setting. This is not to suggest that negative consequences are necessarily effective in changing the child's behavior. Nor is it to suggest that the individual who provides the negative consequence to the child cannot become more tolerant of the child's current level of functioning.

People's expectations also measure their limits of tolerance. Through interviewing them, it is often possible to determine what people's expectations are for a particular child. This is especially true for individuals like parents, siblings, teachers, and other caretakers who have regular and intense opportunities to be with the child. The primary concern is the current expectations for a single child. In addition, some understanding of general expectations and limits of tolerance may also be determined through observation and interview techniques. These more general expectations and toleration limits may be important in maintaining ecological congruence over time. They are also important in developing long-term objectives for interventions.

Identifying Program Objectives

Interventions must be planned when there is incongruence between the individual preschool, handicapped child and his environment. This lack of congruence can come from either the system's intolerance of the child because of his perceived deviancy or incompetence *or* from the child's intolerance of the system. Of course, lack of tolerance can stem from both the system and the child simultaneously. Before program objectives can be identified, the sources of incongruence and the specific settings or situations where incongruence exists must be discovered. These data and the characteristics of the child are the basis of objectives.

Well articulated objectives underpin any successful intervention program. Objectives delineate what behaviors, values, attitudes, and physical modification must be brought about to establish ecological congruence. In addition, a well formulated objective can be used to gauge the effectiveness of a particular intervention.

Program objectives should be established by a team of professionals and parents. This team should identify which areas of incongruence are most important, so that increased congruence can be developed in these areas first. These priorities will be the result of the team's interaction and of negotiations concerning the assessment data gathered as well as of the perceptions of each member of the team. The role of the team in program planning is discussed more fully later in this chapter.

The important thing to remember in constructing objectives is that program planning must address both changes in the individual child and changes in the child's environment and social system. More traditional approaches to program planning have placed almost total emphasis on changes in the individual child. Some approaches have addressed certain interventions to parents (see Chapter 10), but these interventions most often have been designed to make parents more effective *change* agents for their children. Parent-oriented programs have not usually been concerned with increasing parental tolerance except as it is affected by the child's increased behavioral functioning.

The passage of Public Law 94–142, The Education for All Handicapped Children Act, provided an unparalleled impetus to individualized program planning. The mandate of P.L. 94–142, however, clearly has been one to develop individualized objectives to *change* the behavior of an *individual handicapped child*. Although P.L. 94–142 has been important, it has ignored substantially the need for both the child and his environment to change. If ecologically sound interventions are to be carried out, objectives that address both changes in the child's environment and changes in the child must be developed.

In the early 1960s, Mager (1962) introduced a way to prepare clearly stated, operationally defined instructional objectives. Mager's system has weathered the test of time and is still being advocated by people concerned with special education instruction (cf. Berdine & Cegelka, 1980; Safford, 1978; VanEtten, Arkell, & VanEtten, 1980). This system is, in fact, inherent in the requirements found in P.L. 94–142 for establishing individualized objectives. Mager suggests that a well constructed instructional objective has three essential characteristics. First, it stipulates the *specific behavior* expected. Second, it delineates the *conditions* under which the child is to emit the specified behavior. Third, it provides a *criterion* by which the accomplishment of learning the specified behavior can be assessed.

Consider the following examples of objectives.

Susie will identify her coat while it is hanging with 4 other coats.

Susie will take her coat off its hook.

Susie will identify her coat 5 out of 5 times for 3 consecutive days.

Each of these objectives meets a different one of Mager's criteria. The first example does not specify the behavior clearly enough, since identify could mean pick up, verbally label "that's mine," point to, or take the coat from its hook. This objective also does not include a criterion for acceptable learning performance. It does, however, express the conditions under which Susie must "identify" her coat viz., while it is hanging with four other coats. The second example provides an observable behavior by stipulating that Susie will take her coat off its hook. This example, however, fails to identify a criterion or the conditions under which the behavior will be performed. The third example provides a criterion but does not meet the other two conditions. The following objective meets all of Mager's criteria.

Susie will take her coat off the hook while it is hanging with 4 others, 5 out of 5 times for 3 consecutive days.

This objective is well constructed because it is based on an observable behavior, provides the conditions under which the behavior must be performed, and gives a criterion by which learning can be assessed.

Task analyses, used to establish a child's level of competence, can also be a basis for developing instructional objectives for a child. In our earlier example of task analysis the ability of the child to take off a coat was viewed as a critical competency for a particular preschool classroom. Suppose that through the assessment process we discover that Susie cannot take off her coat and that this is a skill that the team agrees she should learn. The accomplishment of that skill represents a terminal objective for Susie which could be stated as follows:

Given Susie with her coat on, and the verbal command "take off your coat" (conditions), she will remove her coat and hang it on a hook (behavior) within 2 minutes 5 out of 5 times for 3 consecutive days (criterion).

A terminal objective represents the learning of a complete task rather than any specific step in a task. Each step in a task can be expressed as an enroute objective; that is, one which takes the child closer to some terminal point. Thus, the first enroute objective for Susie in learning to take off her coat and hang it up might be:

Given Susie with her coat on and the verbal command "take off your coat," Susie will grab one edge of the coat at the chest within 10 seconds 5 out of 5 times for 3 consecutive days.

The next enroute objective might then be:

Given Susie with her coat on holding one edge of the coat at the chest and given the verbal command "take off your coat," Susie will extend her arm lifting the coat off of one shoulder within 10 seconds 5 out of 5 times for 3 consecutive days.

The rest of the enroute objectives would be developed from the next eight steps of the task analysis using a similar strategy.

The ecological congruence model mandates that objectives also be developed to change the setting to bring about congruence. The structure of these objectives can be essentially the same as that used for the development of objectives for individual children. Of course, the content of setting objectives is different from that of children's objectives. Suppose we return to our earlier example of the parent who was intolerant of a child's inability to independently toilet. Recall also that this child had cerebral palsy and lacked the physiological control to be completely independent in her toileting skills. She was toilet trained to the maximum extent possible and, so, increasing her competence for independent toileting was not possible. To increase the ecological congruence in the family setting, the parent lacking tolerance must become more tolerant of the child's level of competence. An objective for the parent might read:

Mr. Ray will take Ann to the bathroom given her request to go 3 times
during the day for 8 consecutive days.

Another objective might read:

Given Ann's lack of independent toileting behavior Mr. Ray will make
positive statements about Ann's ability at least 4 times a day for 4 consecutive days.

In this objective the positive statements might have to be further defined with
specific examples. These positive statements would be assumed to stem from
increased acceptance of Ann's ability and more good feelings toward her on the
part of her father. Notice, too, that an objective does not necessarily express the
means for intervention but merely the proposed outcome of intervention.

So far we have considered examples of objectives either to change the child or
to change aspects of the child's environment to establish congruence in the ecology. On many occasions, both child and environment will have to change for
congruence to increase. In that case, complimentary objectives are necessary—
some that address child change and others that address system change. Suppose
a four-year-old, developmentally delayed child has acquired only rudimentary
eating skills. That is, he can eat certain foods with his fingers but not with his
utensils. His older brothers would like to have friends come to dinner but are
embarrassed by their younger sibling's lack of competence in eating. Quite obviously an objective could be developed to increase the child's eating competence.
Such an objective might state:

Given meal time and a plate of cut up food in front of him, Bobby will use
a spoon to complete his meal for 6 consecutive meals.

At the same time, objectives might be developed which would help Bobby's
brothers deal more effectively with their embarrassment about his behavior. For
example an objective for them might be:

Given Bobby's poor eating behavior, his brothers will be able to express
their feelings verbally about it at least once a week for four consecutive
weeks.

In addition, the boys might be taught strategies to explain Bobby's behavior to
their friends should the need arise. An objective for this ability might be:

Given their friends at dinner and Bobby eating with his fingers, Bobby's
brothers will be able to answer questions about his behavior if asked.

The reader should be aware by now of the importance which the ecological congruence model places not only on changing the child but also on changing the
child's environment.

Identifying Strategies
for Accomplishing Objectives

Although the next chapter deals with program implementation, at least a word should be said here about the way potential change strategies can be identified. In general, an understanding of the individual's or system's particular characteristics and of the conditions accounting for the incongruence in the ecology are necessary to identify change strategies. The reader is reminded of the earlier discussion of conditions accounting for cognition in Chapter 3. The format of Figure 3.1 can be adapted easily for use in determining conditions that may account for the current characteristics of a particular child as well as the characteristics of the systems with which the child interacts. The same model is also applicable to identifying the conditions accounting for incongruence in the ecology.

Identifying Means for Monitoring Progress

In the planning process, some thought should also be given to how progress toward congruence may be monitored. The planning process should establish the frequency of and guidelines for monitoring activities. As was suggested earlier, properly constructed objectives in and of themselves are a means of program monitoring. Whether a particular objective has been met can be judged by whether the behavior specified in the objective is occurring at the level specified in the criterion.

One additional aspect of program monitoring that can take place as part of the planning process is the establishment of time lines for the accomplishment of objectives. For example, it may be decided that a particular terminal objective should be met in six months while another may require only three months. Time targets can be useful, but they must be flexible, since a number of different factors affect how quickly objectives are met.

THE TEAM APPROACH
TO PROGRAM PLANNING

The ecology of the preschool, disabled child is complex. Both the child and her environment are multifaceted. To effectively program for ecological congruence, as many aspects as possible for the child/environment system must be identified. Thus a holistic approach to program planning must be followed. Since no single individual possesses the professional expertise to analyze sufficiently the entire child/environment system, a team approach to program planning and implementation is necessary. Using a team approach increases the chances of considering all aspects of the child/environment system. Each professional can bring his expertise and perspective to the program planning process. Minimally, a program planning team for young, handicapped children should include representatives from the following professions: Education/Special Education, Health,

Social Work, Psychology, and Speech and Language Therapy. In addition, the program planning team should include the parent or guardian or other advocates for the child and her family. Each professional must be concerned with assessing the status of the child, the child's environment, and the interaction between the two. Each professional has unique skills to bring to the evaluation and planning process. At the same time, each professional must be open to suggestions and negotiations that bring about the best individualized plan for ecology being served.

Each professional on the team has a unique role in carrying out each step of the process. At the same time, different professionals have a more critical role in some steps than in others. The degree of involvement of each professional also depends on the features of the particular ecological system being assessed.

Education/Special Education

The members of the team evaluating preschool, handicapped children should become aware of both the education needs of the child and the opportunities which the child's environment provides. They must assess the child's competence within his environment and, at the same time, must analyze the various settings in which the child operates so that his competency can better be expressed. For example, an educational assessment may reveal that a child with spastic quadriplegia is not only able to complete but enjoys the challenge of wooden puzzles. However, if the classroom environment has only tables with slick tops that allow the puzzle boards to slide around when knocked by the child's random athetoid movements, an opportunity for the child to express her competence may be lost. An educational evaluator should recommend the necessary environmental modifications (e.g., placing the puzzle board in a frame that is attached firmly to the table).

The team's educator may also be important in assessing and identifying specific educational strategies for both behavior change in the child and other individuals in the child's environment. In essence, the educational personnel on the team must plan for the educational factors and needs to increase the ecological congruence for the child and other people in his environment.

Health

The health component of the interdisciplinary team may be either a physician or a nurse. The health professional assesses the health status of the child and of his family. He identifies the specific health needs in the child's ecology and suggests ways to meet these needs.

For example, the health professional may find that an orthopedically handicapped three-year-old has poor hygiene and is generally unkempt in appearance. Further investigation may indicate that the child's mother has not been taught proper lifting techniques and so finds it difficult to bathe the child as often as necessary. It may be important to teach the mother lifting techniques for several reasons, all of which would effect congruence in the child's environment. First, for health reasons the child's hygiene may need to be improved. Second, the mother may reduce her own fatigue by proper lifting techniques and thus have more energy to devote to the child and other members of the family. Finally, the unpleasantness of the child's poor state of hygiene may in fact not be well tolerated by teachers at school and could result in a lowering of ecological congruence in the classroom.

Health professionals also assess the status of preventive measures in the child's ecology. Sickness quite often leads to lack of congruency in the ecology, making prevention of health problems a major factor in the continued maintenance of ecological congruence.

Social Work

Professionals trained in social work probably understand family systems better than any other single profession. Their expertise should be used by the team to define the degree of ecological congruence within the family setting. Social work professionals can provide insight into family attitudes, expectations, and practices—which are of critical importance in defining the degree of ecological congruence within the family structure. Just as important is the social worker's ability to identify the conditions that account for the lack of congruence.

Another important role for the social work professional is to identify other sources of support and service for the *ecology being served*. For example, a social worker may observe that the lack of tolerance a mother has for her handicapped, preschool child is in part due to her generally poor coping skills. The social work professional may then suggest and arrange for babysitting services for the child so that the mother can have a respite. This break may increase the mother's overall tolerance of the child without significantly changing the child's characteristics. This example is a perfect instance of how ecological congruence might be increased without any direct intervention on the child or her behavior. Such interventions quite often will fall within the purview of the social work professional.

Psychology

Psychologists assess the child's functioning levels and psychological status. In addition, psychologists can identify the psychological needs of family members and the need for psychological supports to teachers and other service delivery professionals. Psychologists often can gain insight into the feelings of parents by interviewing them individually. These data can be used in conjunction with those gained by the social worker to assess and plan for changes needed in individual patterns of child/environment interaction.

Another important skill of psychologists is the ability to suggest how to approach a child or her family to achieve the desired outcome. Many school psychologists, in particular, have skills useful in consultation with individual teachers and with other agencies which might be involved in program planning and implementation.

Recall the earlier example of Ann and her father. It might well have been a psychologist who would have discovered Mr. Ray's inability to deal with Ann's lack of independent toileting and the lack of congruence it created. The team psychologist would have been instrumental in developing the objectives for Mr. Ray and might also have had primary responsibility for developing and implementing the interventions necessary to meet those objectives.

Speech and Language

A speech and language clinician has a primary role in determining the language competence of individual children. At the same time she assesses communication styles and communication interactions between the child and others in her environment. This is a critical function within the ecological congruence model, since lack of congruence can easily result from misunderstanding of communication styles or communicated messages. The regular kindergarten teacher who encounters a developmentally delayed child in her classroom for the first time finds that she must provide that child with additional or qualitatively different types of communicated cues. At the same time, she may have to be given information on the child's articulation errors in order to understand what the child is communicating. A speech and language clinician is a valuable resource to identify and remediate such sources of ecological incongruence.

Parents

Parents can and should be an integral part of the team that plans and implements services for them and their children. Parents are the greatest single source, outside of the child, of information about the child's characteristics and level of functioning. Parents, obviously, are important agents in the ecological system and can be a major source of both congruence and incongruence. Unfortunately, it is often difficult to include parents as totally functioning members of a team, because the parents may feel inferior to the professionals. To use parental expertise to its fullest, professionals must be mindful of the significant contribution parents can make to team planning and must communicate with and treat parents in a way that makes them feel that they are members of the team. Accomplishing this is sometimes difficult, not only because of parents' perceived inferiority, but also because it is not usually possible to confer with parents as often as it is with the professionals on the team.

Team Function and Case Management

For a team to function properly, it must have a leader. The leader can be permanent, or the responsibility can shift and be related to case management. Each program plan and its implementation must have a case manager. This responsibility is assigned to the professional with the most significant role in provision of services or who has the best rapport with the family involved. Regardless of which leadership strategy is employed, it must facilitate team decision making.

Johnston and Magrab (1976) have summed the essence of effective team function in the following statement:

> The problems of developmentally disabled children transcend the domain of any single profession. It is a challenge for all of us to develop creative and innovative modes for the many professionals involved to interact in an interdisciplinary way. ... At a minimum each of us can become aware of the kinds of contributions each discipline has to offer and, at the optimum, become open to the interdependent relationships that can develop. [p. 12]

Johnston and Magrab's statement has added meaning when the basic concern is programming for increased ecological congruence.

A FORMAT FOR PLANNING

A planning format should be used to effectively plan for increasing ecological congruence. Table 8.1 provides a planning format that allows team participants to summarize the program plan. This format is a guide, and you are urged to modify it to meet your needs. The main features of the planning format are explained here and illustrate how various intervention strategies can be employed based upon this planning format.

IDENTIFYING INFORMATION   At the top of the planning format is identifying information. This includes the family's name, child's name and date of birth, the specific ecological unit and/or activity for which the plan is being developed, the case manager, and the person primarily responsible for intervention in this particular ecological unit.

SOURCE OF INCONGRUENCE   In this column, the source of incongruence should be specifically identified. For example, in the case of Ann and her father, discussed earlier, the source of incongruence could be described as child has reached her highest level of toileting ability; father is not accepting of her less-than-independent toileting ability.

POSSIBLE NECESSARY CONDITIONS   This column would be listing of possible conditions to account for the lack of congruence. With Ann and her father these could include: father's frustration with Ann's condition; Ann's incompetence in independent toileting behavior; father's expectations of five-year-old children; father's incompetence in helping Ann.

OBJECTIVES FOR THE CHILD   Under this heading, specific objectives for the child are listed. Specific objectives include the components suggested by Mager

TABLE 8.1 Program Planning Sheet Based on the Ecological Congruence Model

Child's Name _____

Family's Name _____

Date of Birth _____

Ecological Unit/ Activity _____

Case Manager _____

Primary Interviewer _____

SOURCE OF INCONGRUENCE	NECESSARY CONDITIONS	OBJECTIVES FOR CHILD CHANGE	STRATEGIES FOR CHILD CHANGE	OBJECTIVES FOR SYSTEMS CHANGE	STRATEGIES FOR SYSTEMS CHANGE

(1962) and discussed earlier in this chapter. In our example, no specific objectives would be indicated for Ann.

STRATEGIES FOR CHILD CHANGE   In this column, suggested strategies for meeting the objectives developed for the child are listed. The list might include specific instructional techniques, like those discussed in the next chapter, as well as specific materials or curricular approaches. Since in the present plan no changes in Ann are expected, no strategies would be listed.

OBJECTIVES FOR THE SYSTEM   This category is analogous to the one listing objectives for the child except systems objectives are listed. Thus, the objectives delineated for Mr. Ray on page 180 would be listed in this column.

STRATEGIES FOR SYSTEM CHANGE   This category includes similar items to the ones listed for strategies for child change. That is, specific techniques and procedures that could bring about the desired changes in the environment are listed in this column. For Mr. Ray, these strategies might include individual counseling sessions to discuss his feelings and his daily recording of his statements regarding Ann and her toileting behavior. It might also include Mrs. Ray preparing special dinners for him on any day that he assisted Ann with her toileting needs three times or more.

EVALUATION   This category is for use in describing the evaluation strategy to be employed. The strategy should include assessment of both child change and system's change where appropriate and should indicate whether an increase in ecological congruence took place. Some statement about the length of time necessary for the achievement of the specified objectives also should be made. A description of evaluation for the present example might be that Mr. Ray was expected to meet his objectives within two months. Assessment might also include statements from the case manager or primary interventionist as well as data collected by Mr. Ray regarding his own assistance of Ann with her toileting. Quite possibly, the strategy would also include Mrs. Ray collecting data on her husband's assistance of Ann and his positive and negative statements regarding her. The strategy would also include a baseline before intervention began so that the effectiveness of the intervention could be measured. Finally, it might be desirable to assess the quality of Ann's interaction with her father as his level of tolerance of her increased.

SUMMARY AND CONCLUSIONS

This chapter has dealt with some of the issues and techniques involved in individualized program planning. The need for an approach that plans for both intervention designed for child change but also for systems change is put forth. Simply, intervention plans designed to increase ecological congruence as discussed by Thurman (1977) are suggested. This approach in many ways depends upon existing techniques and strategies but relies on the notion of the child's interaction with the environment. In essence, program planning should be designed with the entire environment of the child in mind and the purpose of the plan, therefore, should be how to best maximize the fit (i.e., congruence) between the child and her environment.

The next chapter discusses the way individual program plans can be implemented and monitored through specific instructional strategies. That chapter will also include a discussion of physical management of children with handicaps. Keep in mind that program planning is the framework for program implementation and that the two processes are interrelated. Assessment provides both a means of measuring changes brought about through intervention and the means by which existing program plans are modified. This assessment is the glue that brings planning and implementation together. The processes are inseparable if quality services are to be provided in ecologies that include preschool, handicapped children.

Implementing Individual Program Plans

1. How do major features of the learning environment affect the young child with special needs?
2. What are the potential negative side effects of punishment?
3. What is the role of antecedents in the implementation of individual program plans?
4. How are the strategies discussed in this chapter compatible with both the developmental approach and the ecological congruence model discussed in earlier chapters?

The previous chapter was devoted to a discussion of the program planning process and the way that process can be carried out in accordance with the ecological congruence model. This chapter addresses program implementation and deals with strategies for both child change and system change as well as factors relating to the physical management of preschool age, disabled children. The final section of this chapter addresses ways changes in both individual children and environmental systems can be assessed.

Any changes in a child result from his interaction with the environment. The way the child interacts with the environment is a function, in part, of the characteristics of the individual child. Effective change strategies for the child depend on an understanding of the typical patterns of development of young children. More important, however, is an understanding of the particular patterns of developmental characteristics of the child under consideration. The earlier chapters of this book provide this basic information.

THE LEARNING ENVIRONMENT

If one accepts that developmental changes in children result from their interaction with the environment, then it becomes important to examine features of the learning environment which may influence children's development. By *learning environment* we mean any setting where purposeful planned instructional intervention takes place. Such settings include classrooms, group homes, residential institutions, and natural homes. Virtually any setting can be a learning environment if purposeful instruction takes place there. This is not to suggest that learning and development do not take place without purposeful instruction. Certainly, they do. But it is most important to establish learning environments for disabled children to assure that these environments have the characteristics and resources necessary to maximize the child's development. The following aspects are important to consider in establishing an effective learning environment: (1) physical structure, (2) affective structure, (3) materials, and (4) human resources. Each of these factors is considered below.

Physical Structure

The physical structure of an effective learning environment provides open access to the child. Tables and chairs are of the proper size and arranged so that children can move about freely. Children with physical disabilities may require special equipment, such as walkers, wheelchairs, and standing tables, to take educational advantage of the environment. Other structural modifications for physically disabled children include wide doorways and entrance ramps.

In addition, children may require special equipment to assure that they are properly handled and positioned (Utley, Holvoet, & Barnes, 1977). Utley, Holvoet, and Barnes (1977) and Campbell, Green, and Carlson (1977) provide some excellent suggestions on how to position children correctly as well as how to provide them with the necessary prosthetic and adaptive equipment. Campbell, Green, and Carlson (1977, p. 307) provide the following suggestions for selecting and positioning equipment.

1. Make sure that the child's position is maximal for performing feeding or dressing skills. Sitting balance should be well developed (either independently or through equipment) to the point that the child is able to free both of his arms to use for the activity rather than for balance.
2. Make sure the child's position is such that [muscle] tone is normalized. If the child is very stiff or too hypotonic [flaccid], he will be unable to use his arms for function.
3. Know exactly what function you want the child to perform and exactly what motor action and skill are required. Select equipment to perform or to assist in performing those motor skills the child is unable to do on his own.

4. Equipment will not teach a child how to chew or hold a spoon, or take off his shirt. Equipment will only make it more possible for him to perform the motor skills. He still will have to be taught how to do the activity.

Classroom equipment must be appropriate to the task and, along with physical prostheses and braces, must be maintained in proper working order. Venn, Morganstren, and Dykes (1979, p. 54) have suggested that "the primary role of the teacher [or other learning environment manager] regarding ambulation devices is daily observation of the student's use and care of his or her equipment." They go on to provide checklists to assess leg braces, leg prostheses, and wheelchairs. These checklists are a useful aid to the learning environment manager and should be consulted by her in situations that require the use of these devices. In addition, physical and occupational therapists are valuable consultants in the proper use and maintenance of prosthetic and positioning devices and the learning environment manager is urged not to overlook their expertise. Finally, since special equipment often takes up large amounts of space, it may be necessary to serve fewer children in a given area or to make other arrangements to assure learning environments of the proper physical dimensions.

SPACE   The physical structure of the learning environment must be such that children have adequate space to move from place to place. In addition, crowding must be avoided. Animal studies like that of Calhoun (1962) suggest that crowding has adverse effects on behavior. Results with human populations are less definitive and, as Moos (1976) suggests in summarizing the literature:

> the age and individual characteristics of experimental subjects may affect the results of crowding studies. No research has compared the effects of density on individuals of various ages, yet children and adults may react to density differently. Similarly although the personal factors that mediate an individual's reaction to density have not been explored in depth, individuals undoubtedly differ in their reactions to density situations. . . . There is evidence that each individual has a "body-buffer-zone" or "personal space" surrounding him or her, and if this zone is invaded, feelings of stress appear. [pp. 160–161]

Smith, Neisworth, and Greer (1978) have also suggested that successful mainstreaming of handicapped and nonhandicapped children may require sufficient space so that "individuals and groups [can] keep their distance from each other while they are in the process of getting accustomed to each other" (p. 137).

LIGHT   Another factor affecting the structure of the physical environment is illumination. Smith, Neisworth, and Greer (1978) suggest that light levels should vary and should be appropriate for the activity being undertaken, "for example with brighter lighting at reading areas and softer lighting in areas used primarily for discussion" (p. 133). They believe that varying levels of light reduce the "institutional" look of a classroom.

TEMPERATURE   Hickish (1955) studied factory workers to determine their comfort zone for indoor temperature. His standard suggests a comfort zone of 69–74° during summer months. Since there is no evidence to the contrary, this is probably a reasonable comfort zone for most young children. High temperature, on the other hand, seems to be related to task performance and irritability. Pepler (1971) discovered that student performance in nonclimate controlled rooms was more variable than student performance in climate controlled rooms when temperatures were high both inside and outside. In another experiment Baron and Lawton (1972) showed an increased tendency of subjects to imitate modeled aggressive responses. The room they used in their experiment was extremely hot, however, being 100° F. With the trend toward energy conservation evident today, it is unlikely that higher temperatures present a problem in most learning environments. Unfortunately, the effects of relatively lower indoor temperatures are less well studied and the reader is urged to follow the advice of Smith, Neisworth, and Greer (1978) who suggest "that to the extent that rooms [in the learning environment] are individually controlled, the teacher [parent, or caretaker] may want to experiment with somewhat lower temperatures; this should be done gradually, however, so that the children have the opportunity to modify their clothing habits" (p. 133). It is also advisable to make sure that handicapped children's internal temperature maintenance mechanisms are intact, since changes in external temperature may pose significant problems in their ability to maintain body temperature.

NOISE   A well functioning learning environment may contain a certain amount of noise. This noise, however, should be related to learning activities and should not be extraneous noise from the environment. Extraneous noise can distract children. Since many young children, especially those with disabilities, are easily distracted, the degree of extraneous noise in the learning environment ought to be kept at a minimum. Research by Glass and Singer (1972) suggests that noise can have effects on human performance even after the noise has stopped. Moos (1976) has concluded that "the full extent of the psychic cost of the adaptation to noise is unknown" but cautions nonetheless about "the risk of underestimating the harmful consequences of noise" (p. 190).

Affective Structure

Just as important as the physical structure of a learning environment is the affective structure. The proper affective structure sets the stage for the trust and nurturance necessary for learning and development to occur at the most rapid pace. The person who controls the learning environment generally determines the nature of the affective structure. In the case of the classroom, the teacher is the main determiner of affective structure. In the home, the same role falls to parents, although it more often is ascribed to mothers. And, in a residential facility, it may fall to a charge aide or be a function of whoever is in control at a given point in time.

Smith, Neisworth, and Greer (1978) identified five continua that characterize the affective structure of a learning environment. While their major concern was in describing critical dimensions of teachers' behavioral styles, their conceptualization is equally applicable to any learning environment. The five dimensions that Smith and his colleagues identify are: (1) the positive-negative dimension, (2) the planned-haphazard dimension, (3) the flexible-rigid dimension, (4) the consistent-inconsistent dimension, and (5) the understanding-intolerant dimension. Each of these dimensions is discussed more fully in the following paragraphs.

POSITIVE-NEGATIVE DIMENSION   Some years ago a bumper sticker that read "Courtesy is Contagious" appeared in some areas of the country. The same might be said about being positive and, unfortunately, about being negative. Learning environment managers' attitudes are soon detected and imitated by the children. Positive affective structures lead to trust and comfort on the part of the child.

Lotman (1980) described what she labeled contingency climates. A contingency climate merely is the ratio of the number of positively reinforcing consequences a person receives to negative or punishing consequences. Thus, if a child received a positive consequence five times for every one time that he received a negative one, on the average, then this child's contingency climate would be a five to one positive climate. If the reverse were true, that is the child received five negative consequences for every one positive, then the contingency climate would be a five to one negative climate. Lotman's research demonstrated that severely retarded children exhibited better performance in a four to one positive climate than they did in a one to one climate and that their performance was even better in an eight to one positive climate. Positive attitudes in expectations have also been shown to favorably affect student outcome (cf., Rosenthal & Jacobson, 1968, 1975). Using Bandura's (1971) arguments on modeling effects as their foundation, Smith, Neisworth, and Greer (1978) conclude that "it is critical . . . that teachers be positive and enthusiastic whenever possible and that a continuing pattern of negative attitudes and behavior will inevitably affect the children in many unfortunate ways such as student passivity, withdrawal, and fear" (p. 85).

PLANNED-HAPHAZARD DIMENSION   A planned environment insures consistency and provides the child with a feeling of familiarity. When the environment is planned, children can more clearly see the purpose of activities and are more able to predict expected outcomes. Lewis and Goldberg (1969a, b) discussed the importance for children of learning generalized expectancies in infancy and preschool years. They suggest how consistent responding from the environment leads to children's recognition of their own effect on the environment. More recently, Thurman (1978) discussed the role of environmental contingencies and the development of expectancy in handicapped infants. Simply stated, planned environments provide more consistent contingency structures than do haphazard environments. Hence, in planned environments children develop a knowledge of their own effectiveness most readily. This knowledge is important for both the cognitive growth of the child and his recognition and awareness of self. Finally as Smith, Neisworth, and Greer (1978) suggest a planned learning environment promotes the participation of every child by giving her an opportunity to engage in appropriate learning activities.

FLEXIBILITY-RIGIDITY DIMENSION   Flexibility and rigidity also play an important role in establishing the affective structure of the classroom. Flexibility increases the fairness in the environment and creates a setting where new ideas, curricula, and techniques are tried in an open and objective manner. In short, a flexible climate is more responsive to the individual needs of the students. The variability in the needs and abilities of young, handicapped children makes flexibility a prerequisite for establishing effective learning environments for these children.

CONSISTENCY-INCONSISTENCY DIMENSION   Closely related to the conditions necessary for a planned environment is consistency. Like a planned environment, a consistent environment helps children feel comfortable and allows them to know what to expect. This in turn leads to feelings of trust and security and reduces the anxiety associated with learning situations. In a consistent environment, rules and standards are clearly stated and children receive consistent consequences for their behavior based upon those standards. It is important, however, to remain flexible, and flexibility should be used in setting up rules for the classroom. In addition, learning environment managers must be flexible enough to modify rules and standards when necessary. Consistency need not connote rigidity. The manager merely acts in accordance with established rules, retaining the ability to renegotiate them.

UNDERSTANDING-INTOLERANCE DIMENSION   Mutual tolerance and acceptance is a key factor in establishing a homeostatic balance and ecological congruence between a child and his environment. Learning environment managers must understand and accept their students if they are to provide meaningful programs matched to the characteristics of the individual child. Knowledge of the student's needs will not be gained by the person who is intolerant and who casts upon the child a series of expectations.

Materials and Equipment

Another important feature of the learning environment is the material and equipment that it contains. While they will not lead to an effective intervention program in and of themselves, materials and equipment are important in establishing meaningful learning environments. There are several considerations in choosing materials and equipment within the learning environment.

First, the materials chosen must meet the needs of the children being served. They must be appropriate to the developmental level of the child. That is, they must stimulate the child's involvement but not be so difficult that they lead to rapid frustration. As was suggested in the discussion of cognitive development in Chapter 3, cognition is advanced when the environment is just different enough to stimulate a child's natural curiosity to interact. Materials should be chosen with this principle in mind.

Children with sensory handicaps require materials with appropriate stimulus features. Young, visually impaired children relate best to auditory and tactile stimulation. Materials for young, visually impaired children should also be brightly colored and, when possible, have large, distinct features. This allows the child to make maximum use of his residual vision. Auditorially impaired children must rely more heavily on visual modes in order to learn. Materials for these children should also make use of any residual hearing.

As was discussed earlier, equipment can be important in providing access to the learning environment. Specialized wheelchairs and other physical prostheses should be used to provide the necessary learning experiences for physically handicapped children. Of course, many sensorily impaired children can benefit from hearing aids and eyeglasses. Learning environment managers should consult the proper professionals on their interdisciplinary team to make sure that they understand the use and maintenance of specialized equipment. Improper use of this equipment often can interfere with the child's learning.

In choosing materials, the learning environment manager should also consider factors like the cost and durability of the item. While there are many excellent materials on the market, materials can often be made at home which are of equal quality. Homemade materials usually cost less than purchased ones and have the added advantage of being designed for the particular child. With inflation, it is increasingly important to get the greatest benefit from one's materials budget. Most areas of the country have instructional materials centers funded by governmental sources that lend out materials for classroom use. Teachers and other learning environment managers are urged to borrow materials before spending money only to find that a material is not useful for the particular purpose or the type of child the teacher had in mind. You are urged to consult the work of Stowitschek, Gable, and Henrickson (1980) for suggestions on effective use of the materials budget as well as on the selection, management, and adaptation of instructional materials for exceptional children.

Human Resources

While the manager is a primary human resource in any learning environment, other human resources can also be used in the learning environment. These resources include parents, volunteers, aides, and the children themselves.

PARENTS　Using parents and other family members as change agents in learning environments is a well-established practice. Many programs for preschool age, handicapped children rely almost totally on parents as primary change agents for the children. Some of these programs are described in Chapter 11. These programs have demonstrated fairly conclusively that parents can create meaningful learning environments for the children reasonably independently. Even when parents are not the primary change agents in a program, their skills and talents can be put to use in the classroom. Parents can help prepare and develop materials as well as help implement instructional procedures. Just as important, however, is the information a parent can provide about a child. Whether parents are the primary change agents, in programs like that described by Shearer and Shearer (1976) (see Chapter 10), or whether they serve as informants and aides, as in the program described by Bricker and Bricker (1976) (see Chapter 11), parents are powerful and important human resources who should be part of the learning environments serving their children. Chapter 9 provides a number of strategies to make parents more effective resources in their children's learning environments.

VOLUNTEERS AND PARAPROFESSIONALS　Volunteers and paraprofessionals such as teacher's aides, client care workers, and assistant teachers, can also be useful human resources. Like parents, they can help develop and prepare materials as well as implement instructional programs. The PEERS Project (Losinno, n.d., see Chapter 11), serving disabled children from birth to three years of age, has been successful, in part, because of its effective use of volunteers. Use of volunteers has the additional advantage of extremely low cost. If properly recruited, trained, and recognized, volunteers of all ages can be an important human resource in programs serving preschool, handicapped children and their families. It should be stressed that volunteers and paraprofessionals must be given the support and, most of all, the recognition they need and deserve if they are to be active participants with ongoing involvement in programs for young, disabled children.

CHILDREN　One often overlooked human resource in learning environments is children. Program peers as well as older children who provide volunteer services can be important human resources for preschool, handicapped children. In the family setting, siblings can provide useful and constructive input into their handicapped brother's or sister's development. Hartup (1978) has discussed the importance of peers in the socialization process of young, disabled children. He suggests that peers influence each other through mechanisms like reinforcement, modeling, and tutoring. A number of authors have provided evidence that preschool peers can be effective models (e.g., Apolloni, Cooke, & Cooke, 1977; Guralnick, 1976; Peck, Cooke, & Apolloni, 1981; Strain, Kerr, & Ragland, 1981) and facilitators of social interaction (Devoney, Guralnick, & Rubin, 1974; Guralnick, 1981; Snyder, Apolloni, & Cooke, 1977; Strain & Timm, 1974) for their handicapped peers. The research of these authors clearly illustrates the important role that nonhandicapped children can play in the development of their handicapped peers. Simply, it is difficult to ignore the exciting human resources children can provide in any learning environment.

STRATEGIES FOR CHILD CHANGE

Having discussed a number of dimensions of learning environments, we can now shift our focus to specific strategies used to bring about changes in children's behavior. While the learning environment sets the stage for behavior change and provides the context for it, it is the development of specific strategies for modifying behavior that leads to effective behavior change. This is not to say that development will not occur without specific intervention. Certainly it will. But the types of behavior change required to bring about ecological congruence require specific, well-thought-out behavior change strategies.

Before beginning our discussion of specific behavior change techniques one more word needs to be said about variables that account for behavior. Just as a child's level of cognitive development or the lack of ecological congruence can be accounted for by some set of necessary and sufficient conditions, so, too, can a child's behavior. Thus, the learning environment manager should identify as many as possible of the conditions which might account for a child's behavior or developmental state. By so doing the manager may often save endless hours, conserve resources, and eliminate stress for herself and the child. Careful examination of conditions may reveal a simple, direct means of establishing congruence. The following story illustrates this point clearly.

A young boy residing in a state residential facility for retarded children was continually observed gouging his finger into his nose—a behavior that created enough incongruence in the ecology that his program management team decided to change his behavior. After consulting, they decided to verbally reprimand the boy whenever he began gouging in his nose. They found this procedure effective as long as it was used consistently. They found, however, that the boy would begin nose gouging as soon as they stopped consistently reprimanding him. They decided to use a "stronger" procedure. This time they coupled their verbal reprimands with 30 seconds of restraint to the boy's arm. Again, the procedure was effective. Gradually, however, even though the procedure was still in use, the boy's nose gouging behavior returned. Several other interventions were planned and implemented with similar results. Just as the program team ran out of ideas and was ready to concede failure, the boy was scheduled for his annual physical examination. While looking up the boy's nose, the physician discovered the spring from a ball point pen mechanism lodged in the boy's nostril. The next day, the boy was brought to the infirmary and the spring was removed. After that he was rarely seen gouging his fingers into his nose. The obvious point is that the program management team, in their desire to increase congruence, overlooked an important condition accounting for the boy's behavior. Had they examined more conditions, they could have saved themselves a lot of effort and have saved the boy a lot of discomfort and interference in his life. Before using any of the behavior change strategies discussed below, it is important to rule out other conditions that might account for or contribute to lack of ecological congruence and lack of expected behavior patterns or development levels in a child.

The Role of Environment

All behavior is partially a function of environmental events. Some of these events precede behavior and are referred to as *antecedents*. Others follow behavior and are referred to as *consequences*. These antecedents and consequences can be modified and controlled to change the behavior of an individual. This section deals with the systematic changes which can be introduced in antecedents and consequences to bring about desired behavioral change in young, handicapped children. The discussion begins with consequences.

Environmental Consequences

In the discussion of Piaget's theory in Chapter 3, it was pointed out that by the end of the Sensory Motor Period of development children have learned that their behavior affects the environment. The child's understanding of means-ends relationship comes from his action on the environment and the recognition that his behavior has an effect. Simply, the child's behavior provides the means to certain ends in the environment. Even children in the very earliest stages of the Sensory Motor Period modify their behavior in response to environmental consequences. For example, Sameroff (1968) demonstrated that five-day-old infants change their sucking responses depending upon which component of sucking was followed by the delivery of a nutrient solution. Thus, it can be seen that, virtually from the beginning of life, the consequences of our behavior affect the way we will behave in the future. For the most part, people emit behavior (i.e., exercise means) that lead to desired consequences (i.e., ends). Thus, the ebb and flow of behavior is a function of the interplay between the acquired means (behavior patterns) of the child and the ends (available consequences) in the environment.

The relationship between behavior and its consequence is referred to as a *contingency* or as being characterized by a *contingent relationship*. A contingency can be thought of as an if-then situation. That is, *if* a child behaves in a particular manner, *then* her behavior leads to a particular end. Through identifying and understanding the contingent relationships between a child's behavior and the consequences of her behavior, effective behavior change strategies can be developed.

Contingent consequences have three possible functions on a child's behavior. First, they may increase the behavior that they follow. Second, they may decrease the behavior that they follow. And third, they may have no effect on the behavior that they follow. A consequence that increases behavior is referred to as a *reinforcing consequence*. A consequence which decreases behavior is referred to as a *punishing consequence*. A consequence that does not affect behavior is

referred to as a *neutral consequence*. Reinforcing, punishing, and neutral consequences are defined in terms of their actual function on behavior, not on their
perceived or ascribed function. Thus, the parent who yells at her child systematically for kicking the dog and claims to be punishing him as a result, is, in fact,
not punishing the child at all unless the frequency with which the child kicks the
dog declines across time. This mother could even be reinforcing the child by
yelling at him if the yelling is linked to the child's continued kicking of the dog.
Simply, the nature of a contingent consequence is unknown unless the effects of
that consequence on behavior can be empirically demonstrated. Later in this
chapter we discuss data collection techniques that can be used to assess the function of various contingent consequences on behavior.

REINFORCING CONSEQUENCES   There are two basic types of reinforcing consequences, *primary reinforcing consequences* and *secondary* or *conditioned reinforcing consequences*. Primary reinforcing consequences are effective because
they provide a basic resource to the child's biological system. Primary reinforcing consequences include food, water, sleep, and sensory stimulation. In other
words, primary reinforcing consequences increase behavior in a child without
the child's need to learn that such consequences are reinforcing. Secondary or
conditioned reinforcing consequences, on the other hand, depend on learning.
Neutral consequences may be presented simultaneously with primary reinforcing consequences. As a result, these neutral consequences begin to take on the
reinforcing function of the primary reinforcing consequences. Many of the social
consequences that are reinforcing to us are conditioned this way. For example, in
training severely and profoundly retarded children or young, retarded children,
primary reinforcing consequences are used. Thus, if the child makes a correct
response to a discrimination problem, he is given a small edible treat or a sip of
juice or soft drink. At the same time, the child is verbally praised with a statement like "That's good work," or "I like the way you showed me the circle."
Over time, through being consistently paired with the food or liquid, these verbal
statements made by the trainer come to have reinforcing properties in and of
themselves. When that happens, verbal praise has become a secondary or conditioned reinforcing consequence. A child's mother often becomes a source of reinforcement in a similar way. During infancy and early childhood, a child's mother
is often the major source of primary reinforcing consequences. Because of this,
the child's mother herself can become reinforcing to the child. Her mere presence or her attention to the child can act as a reinforcing consequence, and a
powerful one at that. For this reason, a mother's attention may reinforce a
child's undesired behavior, even though she has put forth a consequence she
thinks of as punishing. This phenomenon explains the earlier suggestion that a
mother's yelling at her son for kicking the dog may actually maintain or increase
the child's kicking behavior, even though yelling is viewed as a negative consequence. In essence, the maternal attention the child receives as a result of the
yelling has a stronger effect on the behavior than does the yelling itself. This
phenomenon is more likely to occur when the mother provides attention to the

child primarily when the child is behaving in an undesired manner. Parents, teachers, and other learning environment managers must always keep in mind the powerful effects their attention can have on the behavior of children.

Reinforcing consequences can be used to develop and maintain desired behavior in preschool, disabled children. To do this, the learning environment manager must follow three steps. First, she must identify in specific terms the behavior to be changed. Second, she must identify the consequences that are reinforcing to the child. Third, she must set up a consistent contingent relationship between the desired behavior and a consequence desired by the child. Steps one and two were discussed in the previous chapter. Recall that any well-stated instructional objective includes a precisely defined, observable behavior and that strategies for identifying reinforcing consequences include observing the child and providing various consequences for the performance of simple tasks (e.g., hand clapping) to see which consequences result in the greatest increase in behavior.

Suppose an evaluation revealed a lack of congruence in the ecology because a three-year-old child failed to make social contact with other children in her class and the other children do not make contact with her. Two objectives to establish congruence might state:

Given a free play situation Sally, Belle, and Tanya will offer to share toys with Alice at least two times apiece for five consecutive days.

Given a free play situation, Alice will take a toy from Sally, Belle, or Tanya at least a total of four times for five consecutive days.

Alice is the child who is not making social contact. From these two objectives, the following observable behaviors can be defined:

Sally, Belle, or Tanya offers a toy to Alice. Offering a toy is defined as approaching Alice closely enough that she could take the toy and extending the arm toward Alice while holding the toy in the hand of the extending arm.

Alice takes the toy from Sally, Belle, or Tanya. Taking the toy is defined as Alice extending her hand, placing it on the toy, and removing the toy from the hand of the other child.

Next, the learning environment manager chooses a consequence to make contingent upon the identified behaviors. For Alice, an appropriate consequence might be a small bit of juice paired with verbal praise and several strokes on her arm or back. For Sally, Belle, and Tanya an appropriate consequence might be verbal praise alone. The contingencies, then, are verbally to praise Sally, Belle, or Tanya whenever they offer a toy to Alice and to give Alice a small tidbit of cereal along with physical and verbal praise if she takes the toy when offered. If over time Sally, Belle, and Tanya offer toys to Alice more frequently, then verbal praise is a reinforcing consequence. Likewise, if Alice takes the toy from the other girls more frequently the consequences arranged for her behavior are also reinforcing.

Reinforcement sometimes can occur when a particular behavior results in the contingent removal of or escape from a previously presented stimulus. Suppose a firm pressure is applied to a child's upper arm or shoulder when he wanders around the room. When he returns to his seat, the child is released. Thus, his behavior contingently results in the trainer letting go of the child. If this contingent consequence is effective, the child will return to his seat more quickly in the future. Ultimately, he may learn to avoid the firm grip altogether by not even leaving his seat unless told to do so. While techniques like this can be successful in increasing desired behavior (cf. Lovaas, Schaeffer, & Simmons, 1965), it is usually more desirable to present the child with positive consequence for her behavior. Thus, in the present example, the child would be given verbal praise for being in his seat or the teacher would stand by him and stroke his arm as long as he remains appropriately seated.

PUNISHING CONSEQUENCES As was noted above, contingent consequences can also lead to decreases in behavior. These consequences are said to be punishing consequences. Punishing consequences should be employed only when effective behavior change cannot be brought about using positively reinforcing consequence or when a decrease or cessation of a particular behavior is necessary for the safety or welfare of the child or others in the setting. Use of punishing consequences in situations other than these is, in our opinion, to be avoided. Inappropriate use of punishing consequences is at best an exercise of poor judgment and at worst a breach of basic human morality. Keep in mind, also, the punishment is almost always used to modify behavior viewed as deviant or intolerable. Before implementing a punishment procedure, program teams should assess the appropriateness of placing the burden of change solely on the child. Kazdin (1975) has summed up the use of punishment aptly. He states:

> that the best use of punishment in applied settings is an ancillary technique to accompany positive reinforcement. At best, punishment will only suppress undesirable responses but not train desirable behaviors. Reinforcement is essential to develop appropriate behaviors which replace the suppressed behaviors. [p. 167]

Kazdin (1975) has pointed out that punishment can lead to a number of undesirable side effects including: emotional reactions, escape and avoidance, aggression, modeled punishment, and perpetuation of punishment. Each of these deserves some additional elucidation.

Punishing consequences often lead to emotional reactions on the part of both the child being punished and the person doing the punishing. These emotional reactions interfere with the ongoing activities of the setting and lessen the opportunity for the child to learn an appropriate pattern of behavior. Kazdin (1975) suggests that the person offering the punishment may, over time, come to "elicit similar emotional reactions even in the absence of punishment" (p. 161). These reactions may adversely affect the relationship between the child and the learning environment manager and may eventually interfere with the child's opportunity to learn.

After repeated punishment, children learn to avoid or escape from punishing situations. This action may lessen their opportunities to learn more adaptive patterns of behavior because they avoid situations where punishment often occurs. At the same time, they may learn to avoid the person who issues the punishment. Such avoidance behavior can set the stage for significant levels of incongruency in the ecological system. It may, in fact, suppress the child's behavior to the point that he becomes "nonbehaving" in a sense. That is, the child withdraws from interaction with the environment to avoid the possibility of punishment.

Punishment can lead to aggressive interaction between punished parties. Early work of Azrin and Holz (1966) demonstrated that laboratory animals who were frequently punished using electrical shock were very prone to attack each other during nonpunishment periods. Kazdin (1975, p. 161) concludes that although "these phenomena have not been demonstrated with the wide range of punishing events used in applied settings . . . using punishment of any kind there is the possibility that the punished individual will aggress toward the punishing agent" and, thus, temporarily remove the punishing events.

Another potential drawback in the use of punishment is the model presented to the child by the punishing agent. That children imitate adult models has been well documented in the literature (cf., Bandura, 1971). Thus, children are prone to imitate patterns of behavior associated with punishment. They may come to use punishment as their mode of interacting with other children. The tendency to imitate the punishing model increases the likelihood of aggressive behavior, since many punishing events could be classified as aggressive.

A final undesirable side effect of punishment suggested by Kazdin (1975) is its tendency to perpetuate itself. He suggests that successful punishment almost immediately brings about reduction of undesired behavior. Consequently the punishing agent (e.g., the learning environment manager) is reinforced by the cessation of the child's undesired behavior. This reinforcement increases the likelihood that the person will use punishment in the future to manage or modify a child's behavior. Simply, the effectiveness of punishment in reducing undesirable behavior leads to the perpetuation of its use.

Punishing consequences can take many forms, some of which are milder and less dependent upon physical means. When punishment is necessary to bring about behavior change in young children, it is preferable to impose the mildest form of punishment which is effective, since these somewhat reduce the undesired side effects. Thus, if a two-year-old will stop beating on the goldfish tank with a wooden mallet (an obviously dangerous behavior) upon sharply being told "NO!", then it is not necessary to slap his hand, send him to the corner for five minutes, or deprive him of lunch. In point of fact, physical punishment is almost never needed with young, handicapped children. Learning environment managers other than parents should never use physical punishment and should get clearance from parents and program administrators before using any form of punishment other than the mildest kind. Parents should be instructed in ways to manage behavior without physical punishment. They, too, should depend on the mildest form of punishment which is effective and should be thoroughly familiarized with the negative side effects of punishment and the particular dangers of physical punishment.

Alternatives to physical punishment include techniques like verbal reprimands, time out, and response cost. All of these techniques can be used successfully with preschool age, handicapped children. Explanations and examples of their use with handicapped preschoolers follow.

Verbal reprimands consist of giving a child verbal feedback about his behavior. These can take the form of a sharply spoken word like "NO!" or "STOP IT!" or they can be affect-laden statements like "I don't like it when you hit children." The latter approach has the advantage of letting the child know specifically what he is doing that is undesirable. It is based on the assumption that expressed displeasure on the part of an adult is sufficiently aversive to decrease the child's behavior. This may or may not be the case. Sharply spoken words typically are more aversive for the child and are more likely to lead to decrease in behavior. A third approach to verbal reprimands is to combine a sharp word with an explanation of what the undesired behavior is, for example "STOP HITTING!" All three of these events can be effective verbal reprimands. The advantages of each should be weighed by the individual learning environment manager before she chooses the best one for the situation.

A technique referred to as *time out* can effectively punish a child without using physical punishment. Actually, time out is a shorthand notation for the more inclusive phrase time out from positive reinforcement. If a child emits an undesired behavior, he is not given *any* positive reinforcement for some period of time. There is no reason for the time out period ever to exceed more than five minutes, especially if the child is isolated in a stimulus-free room or cubicle. This type of physical isolation represents the extremest form of time out and should be used with the same precautions used for physical punishment procedures. It is rarely necessary to use a time out room with preschool age, handicapped children because their behavior can be managed with less drastic types of time out procedures. With young children, time out can be accomplished by adults in the learning environment halting their interaction with the child for a 30 to 60 second period of time. This technique is effective because adults are the primary source of positive reinforcement in the learning environment and control children's access to it. In addition, while it may not seem like a long period of time for an adult, 60 seconds can represent an "eternity" for a young child. Another effective means for implementing time out with young children is the traditional practice of standing or sitting in the corner. In implementing this procedure, the learning environment manager should arrange an area of the room where the child can sit or stand with his face to the wall and where the child is reasonably isolated from the ongoing activities. The child should be required to spend no more than two or three minutes in the "corner." Many managers find it effective to set a small kitchen timer for two or three minutes when the child goes to the corner. This tells both the child and the manager when the time is up and prevents forgetting that a child is in time out, which can result in his missing valuable learning activities. While most children will go to the time out corner upon command from the manager, some will not. These children should be guided firmly to the corner without fuss or fanfare. The manager may also find it necessary to monitor these children to prevent them from leaving the corner prematurely. Regardless of the type of time out used, the child should understand the contingency and be told specifically why he is being sent to time out. This enables the child to begin to distinguish appropriate behavior from inappropriate behavior and to begin to internalize the control of his own behavior.

Control of undesirable behavior can also be accomplished by a procedure known as response cost. *Response costs* are fines. That is, a particular behavior results in the loss of some portion of a desired resource or activity. In the preschool classroom, response cost could consist of withholding lunch time dessert, a portion of free play, or the opportunity to engage in a favorite activity or to play with a desired toy. In essence, the child pays the cost of emitting an undesired behavior by giving up something she desires. As with time out, it is important that the child understands the contingency and the exact reason for the response cost. While response cost can be effective, it also has certain drawbacks. First, it can set the stage for additional misbehavior by making the child angry. Since the child has already lost a desired activity or item, she may feel that nothing else can be lost by additional misbehavior. This is often a correct analysis by the child, so managers are urged to take away only a portion of a desired consequence. For example 5 minutes of a 15 minute free play period rather than the entire period can be removed. It is also more effective to make it the last 5 minutes rather than the first so the child pays her "fine" when it is felt most fully. In addition, children can be given the opportunity to earn the time or activity back through emitting desired behavior. Again, it is important for the child to know specifically what must be done to regain the lost resources. One cannot merely say to the child "if you're good you can gain your free play time back." Another drawback to response cost is the time which typically passes between the undesired behavior and the payment of the cost. Generally, contingent consequences are more effective if they are immediate. To get around this problem, response cost procedures are sometimes used in conjunction with token systems in which children receive tokens for desired behavior and give up tokens for undesired behavior. Tokens are then used to gain access to desired events, items, or activities. Unfortunately, token systems can be quite cumbersome and many young children have difficulty understanding the value of tokens and how they can be used. In spite of these limitations, response cost can be effective means for decreasing undesired behavior in preschool, handicapped children.

EXTINCTION   Extinction, like punishment, provides a means for decreasing undesired behavior. However, it does not bring with it the undesired side effects associated with punishment. *Extinction* occurs when a previously reinforced response is no longer reinforced. Allen and her colleagues (1964) offer an interesting example of extinction with a preschool child. In their study a four-year-old girl was socially withdrawn from other peers. Observation in the classroom revealed that her teacher attended to her whenever she was isolated from her peers. By ignoring the child when she was isolated and giving her attention when she played with other children, the teacher was able to significantly increase the child's social interaction. While extinction can be effective by itself, its effectiveness is usually increased when another more desirable response is reinforced simultaneously. Allen and colleagues were able to reinforce an alternative behavior that was also incompatible with the undesired behavior. This procedure is sometimes referred to as *differential reinforcement of incompatible behavior* or DRI. DRI is frequently used in conjunction with extinction or with various forms of punishment. Since extinction tends to decrease the rate of behavior more slowly than does punishment, it is good practice to combine extinction with a DRI procedure more rapidly to build behaviors which are desirable. Before using extinction, the learning environment manager should be sure that the reinforcer consequence that is maintaining the undesired behavior can be identified. In addition, the manager should be aware that when extinction is begun, an increase in undesired behavior may be noticed. For example, when extinction is used to decrease temper tantrums in young children, the length and intensity of the tantrums may increase for the first few days. The reason for this is the child's attempt to acquire the reinforcing consequence that usually follows the tantrum. The lack of expected reinforcers may also lead to frustration and anger, which can be minimized by increasing the amount of reinforcement for desired behavior.

Another technique which can decrease undesired behavior is called *differential reinforcement of other behavior* or DRO. DRO can be used alone or in conjunction with various forms of punishment. In a DRO procedure, a child is reinforced for any behavior other than the undesired behavior. The procedure usually is set up so that a child is reinforced after some period of time provided that the undesired behavior has not occurred. Suppose that a preschool, developmentally delayed child had periodic episodes of self-stimulating behaviors during the day. The learning environment manager could set up a DRO procedure by providing the child reinforcement for time periods during which self-stimulation did not occur. The more often the reinforcement occurred the more effective the procedure would be. Thus, the manager might elect to start by reinforcing the child for very brief periods of time, like 45 to 90 seconds and then to lengthen the time between reinforcement gradually. A small kitchen timer can be set for various lengths of time and reinforcement can be provided when the timer rings if the undesired behavior has not occurred. When it does occur, an undesired behavior can either be ignored (i.e., extinguished) or can be followed by a punishing consequence. In either case, the timer is reset so that the child is given a new opportunity for reinforcement.

Antecedent Events

Antecedent events can be just as important in bringing about effective behavior change in young children as can consequences. Antecedent events are particularly useful when a child is learning a behavior for the first time. They set the stage for behavior and provide models and cues for the child to follow. The effective use of antecedent events is necessary if young, handicapped children are to learn adaptive patterns of behavior.

TASK ANALYSIS AND INSTRUCTIONAL OBJECTIVES   The use of task analysis and instructional objectives was discussed in the previous chapter as it relates to the program planning process. These two techniques also play an important role in the actual instructional process. Recall that task analysis is the process by which relatively complex patterns of behavior are broken down into small, discrete steps. Each of these steps is the basis for enroute and terminal instructional objectives. In combination, these activities are the blueprint for instruction. More importantly, they are a way to identify the necessary antecedent events for effective instruction. Each behavioral step in a task is an antecedent to the step that follows it. For example, in the process of brushing one's teeth opening up the toothpaste is an antecedent event to placing the toothpaste on the toothbrush. Through task analysis, such events are identified and properly sequenced.

The givens or the conditions stated in a well constructed instructional objective simply identify antecedents. For example, consider the following objective.

> Given 2 red squares and a blue square and a verbal command "point to
> the one that is different," the child will point to the blue square 4 out of
> 5 times for 3 consecutive days.

The condition stated in this objective provides for several antecedent events before the child can emit the desired behavior. The trainer must provide three squares (two red and a blue) and a verbal command (point to the one that is different). Without these antecedent events, and, of course, without the child's attention to them, accomplishment of the objective stated above is impossible.

SETTING EVENTS   Setting events are those antecedents of behavior that cue the child that a response is expected or necessary. In the example, the setup of the materials and the placement of the child at a table opposite the trainer are considered general setting events. Each of these events suggests to the child "Now is the time to respond." The actual verbal command by the teacher (i.e., "Point to the one that is different") is the specific setting event that immediately precede the child's response. Over time, these setting events lead to the development of a *learning* or *response set* on the part of the child. That is, repeated exposure to these antecedents lead to a readiness on the part of the child to respond to cues provided. This is particularly true if the child is positively reinforced for responding.

DISCRIMINATIVE STIMULI   Discriminative stimuli or S^Ds are defined by the functional relationship between an antecedent event and the child's behavior. A *discriminative stimulus* (S^D) is an antecedent event in whose presence responding leads to positive reinforcement. In the example, the desired S^D is the blue square. Only as the child makes correct responses to the trainer's verbal command, does the blue square become an S^D, however. The child's correct response is followed by a reinforcing consequence and the blue square acquires the properties of an S^D. On the other hand, a punishing consequence would follow the child's incorrect responding (i.e., if she pointed to a red square). This punishing consequence would be of a mild nature and would be designed to correct the child's incorrect response. Thus, the trainer might say "No that's not right" and point to the blue square and say "This one is different." We hope that from this action the child would learn that the red squares were incorrect antecedents given the trainer's verbal command. Over time, in the same way the blue square becomes an S^D, the red squares become S^As, or antecedents in whose presence responding does not result in positive reinforcement.

Consistent use of setting events and S^Ds is critically important in establishing an effective learning environment because it helps the children learn when to respond. In addition, it lets the children know which responses are expected in which learning situations. A number of instructional techniques designed to develop new behavior patterns rely heavily on the effective use of antecedent events. We are not suggesting a more important role for antecedent events than for consequences, but we are asserting that antecedents must be considered in the instructional process. The next several paragraphs discuss various instruction procedures that depend on antecedent events. These procedures include: modeling, cueing, chaining, shaping, and fading.

MODELING   In modeling, a desired behavior is demonstrated by the trainer with the child watching. The intent is that the child will imitate the trainer and subsequently be reinforced. Some children, especially those with cognitive deficits, must actually be taught to imitate modeled responses (cf., Bricker & Dennison, 1978). Modeling is particularly useful in teaching social, self-help, and motor skills. Bricker and Dennison (1978) suggested it be used in teaching prerequisites to verbal language and Apolloni, Cooke, and Cooke (1977) have discussed techniques that can be used to establish a nonhandicapped peer as a model for a disabled peer in a preschool setting. The use of peer models is implicit in the integration of nonhandicapped and handicapped, preschool children (Bricker, 1978) although it is not necessarily a naturally occurring phenomenon (Snyder, Apolloni, & Cooke, 1977). It is important that models, both adult and child, be provided to preschool, handicapped children and that the necessary techniques to bring about imitation of these models be implemented. Shaping procedures to be discussed later in this chapter can be used to build imitative responses in preschool, handicapped children (cf., Baer, Peterson, & Sherman, 1967).

CUEING   Cueing, like modeling, uses antecedent events to bring about desired behavior change. Cueing consists of increasing the salience of an antecedent event. In the example where the child was to point to the different color, a cue can be provided by the trainer's pointing to the blue square while giving the verbal command. Other types of cues include physical prompts, instructions, and increasing the stimulus dimensions of an antecedent. In the case of a physical prompt, the trainer might actually hold the child's hands while performing a particular task or might give the child physical guidance by merely touching or pointing to the child's hands. Instructions like "Do this" or "Follow me" or "Pick the one that I point to" are also cues. Sometimes the physical properties of the antecedent event can be changed to provide a cue. In the example of the red and blue squares, the blue square could not only be blue but could also be bigger or lighter or darker in hue than the red squares. Thus, the blue square's salience could be increased. That is, its contrast or difference with the red squares could be made more obvious. Gordon and Haywood (1969) have shown that such stimulus enrichment (i.e., increasing in salience) can increase the performance of mentally retarded children.

CHAINING   Chaining grows out of task analysis and depends upon each step in the task analysis being established as an S^D for the preceding step. Chaining may start with the first step of a behavioral sequence and proceed to the last (i.e., forward chaining) or it may begin with the last step of the sequence and proceed to the first (i.e., backward chaining). In backward chaining the trainer completes the sequence except for the final step. Backward chaining is often the preferred procedure because it allows the child to complete the entire sequence by performing the last step, which is followed by a positive reinforcer. When the child learns the last response, he is expected to perform the last two responses, then the last three, and so on until the entire chain has been learned. Some behavior sequences (e.g., toileting) cannot be meaningfully taught using a backward chaining procedure. In these instances, the trainer employs forward chaining or graduated guidance. *Graduated guidance* consists of the trainer putting various degrees of pressure on the child's hands as he performs a behavior sequence from beginning to end. Popovich (1981) provides the following description of graduated guidance. She also provides an excellent discussion of the way chaining procedures are implemented. According to Popovich:

> During full graduated guidance, the instructor keeps her hands in full contact with the student's hands throughout the trial and praises the student continuously as long as the student is moving his hands in the desired direction. During partial graduated guidance, the instructor only guides the student's hands as necessary, while in shadowing the instructor does not physically touch the student's hands but keeps her hands within an inch of the student's hands as the student completes the trial. [p. 128]

Graduated guidance can be used effectively when the child has not learned all the specific behaviors necessary to complete the task being taught. Thus as Popovich (1981, p. 133) suggests, graduated guidance "is especially useful for students who do not understand simple verbal and gestural prompts and for students who need a great deal of physical prompting."

SHAPING   Shaping is used to develop new behaviors in children. It depends upon positive reinforcement rewarding closer and closer approximations of a desired behavior. Kazdin (1975, p. 40) contrasts chaining with shaping by suggesting that the former "is used to develop a sequence of behaviors based on responses that are already present in the individual's repertoire while shaping is used to develop new behaviors." Chaining and shaping often are used in concert since a child may have some but not all of the necessary behaviors for a particular behavior sequence. Shaping often uses models, cues, and prompts. These antecedents are used to encourage the performance of a particular behavior. If the child performs the behavior in even the grossest manner, reinforcement is given. However, future reinforcement is given only as the child's responses more and more closely approximate the response which is finally desired. Suppose, for example, a child is being taught to ask for things rather than to point. Since asking is a new behavior, shaping is an appropriate behavior change technique. The first time that a child is told "Ask for it, say I want" the child may do nothing more than make an inarticulate sound. Since such a sound is the first approximation of the desired response, reinforcement follows. Further reinforcement is contingent upon the child's more and more approximating the words "I want." In this particular example, the reinforcing consequence could be the child being given what was asked for. In other situations, shaping reinforcers may be either more primary or consist of social praise.

FADING   Up to this point, our discussion of environmental antecedents has focused on the importance of introducing antecedents that bring about desired responses in children. However, many of the antecedents used in the development of desired behavior outcomes are not readily available in many environmental settings. Thus, it is important that children's responses become more and more a function of internalized contingencies and the general recognition of the stimulus properties of various settings. Fading is often used to begin to meet this goal. Fading is a procedure by which the arranged antecedents for a child's behavior are gradually reduced or faded away. In our earlier example, the blue square might be illuminated in some manner at the same time the child was asked to "Point to the one that is different." As suggested earlier, this light is a cue, increasing the salience of the S^D being trained. As the child began to make more and more correct responses the degree of illumination could be gradually reduced. Thus, the cue would gradually be faded, in this case quite literally. Fading can also be used to reduce the amount of physical guidance necessary for a child to perform a task. The earlier discussion of graduated guidance illustrates this idea quite well. The degree of actual guidance given to a child in completing the behavioral sequence being trained depends on the degree of independence the child expressed in carrying out the sequences herself. In other cases, when more than one antecedent is arranged, one may be faded out while the other is left intact. Imitation training, referred to earlier, is a good example of this situation. When a child is being taught to imitate, it is important that she perform the same behavior as the model. In this training paradigm, the model usually performs a gross motor movement (e.g., placing the hands over the head) and simultaneously says to the child "Do this." The child may or may not imitate the model. If he does not, prompting is necessary. The trainer may have to take the child's hands and move them over his head. Gradually, however, these physical prompts are faded out and the child responds only to the model and the verbal command. Children who are taught to respond in this way to several different gross motor behaviors often learn to imitate spontaneously the model's behavior. Essentially, the child learns to emit the behavior that follows the command "do this." This procedure has been successful with severely and profoundly retarded young children and can be used to train both gross motor responses and manual and verbal communicative responses.

Behavioral Formula

Several authors (e.g., Bijou, Peterson, & Ault, 1968; Bijou et al., 1969; Lindsley, 1964) have suggested formulas for demonstrating the relationship between environmental antecedents and consequences and behaviors specifically targeted for behavioral change. Lindsley (1964), for example, puts forth the Is-Equation, which has been used recently to plan specific behavior change (cf., Kunzelmann, 1970). Program planning is a prerequisite to successful program implementation. The planning strategy inherent in the following behavioral formula is specific to the development of interventions designed to change a particular behavior in a given child. In addition, this formula gives an example of the relationship between antecedents, specific behavioral responses, and consequences. Table 9.1 is a planning format, which is discussed below. This format originates in suggestions made by Lindsley (1964) and Bijou and colleagues (1968, 1969). The reader should find this strategy useful in planning specific interventions.

This planning format is completed by asking a series of questions. These questions appear in the appropriate columns in Table 9.1. Tables 9.2 and 9.3 are examples of the way the planning format is used. These samples are based on earlier examples used in this chapter. Table 9.2 is based on the example of the red and blue squares. Table 9.3 is based on the example of a child receiving verbal reprimands for hitting other children. You are urged to develop your own plans with other techniques discussed in this chapter. These specific intervention plans are a useful supplement to the more general planning strategy discussed in the previous chapter.

Developmental Interaction

Behavioral technology, as described in the previous section, with its emphasis on the *process* by which a child may be taught a skill or concept, does not address

TABLE 9.1 Planning Format for Behavior Change

Name of Child _____

Name of Manager _____

Specific Objective:

PURPOSE	SETTING	ANTECEDENTS	DESIRED BEHAVIOR	CONSEQUENCE OF DESIRED BEHAVIOR	UNDESIRED BEHAVIOR	CONSEQUENCE OF UNDESIRED BEHAVIOR
What is being done and why	Where and when is the intervention taking place	What events are to occur which may increase the likelihood of the desired behavior	What specific behavior is it desired that the child do *more* often	What specific consequence will happen when the desired behavior occurs	What specific behavior is it desired that the child do *less* often	What specific consequence will happen when the undesired behavior occurs

TABLE 9.2 Use of the Planning Format to Teach the Concept Different From

Name of Child _____Billy R._____ Name of Manager _____Sandy L._____

Specific Objective: Given 2 red squares and a blue square Billy will point to the blue square 8 out of 10 times for 4 consecutive days when asked to point to the one that is different

PURPOSE	SETTING	ANTECEDENTS	DESIRED BEHAVIOR	CONSEQUENCE OF DESIRED BEHAVIOR	UNDESIRED BEHAVIOR	CONSEQUENCE OF UNDESIRED BEHAVIOR
To teach Billy the concept of different	The preschool class during individual instruction period	2 red squares and a blue square and the verbal request point to the one that is different	Billy points to the blue square	Verbal praise and a small bit of orange juice	Billy points to a red square	Verbal feedback "No Billy" and point to blue square and say "this one is different"

TABLE 9.3 Use of the Planning Format to Decrease Hitting Behavior

Name of Child _____ Patrice L. _____   Name of Manager _____ Allen W. _____

Specific Objective: Given Patrice in a classroom situation she will not hit other children all day for 5 consecutive days

PURPOSE	SETTING	ANTECEDENTS	DESIRED BEHAVIOR	CONSEQUENCE OF DESIRED BEHAVIOR	UNDESIRED BEHAVIOR	CONSEQUENCE OF UNDESIRED BEHAVIOR
To get Patrice to stop hitting other children	Preschool classroom during the entire day	None	Any appropriate behavior other than hitting	Periodic verbal praise and attention for appropriate behavior	Hitting other children	Verbal feedback "No hitting, Patrice"

the question of *content*, that is, the decision of what to teach or whether certain skills or concepts are appropriate for a given child at a given time. To make decisions concerning what to teach at any given time, the planner must examine normal developmental consequences and make a determination of what skills are appropriate for each child. This information can be provided through a sound assessment program as described in Chapter 7.

It is important to arrange the environment to motivate a child to learn the skill or concept. An important aspect of motivation is *readiness*. We do not apply this concept to handicapped children in the same way that Gesell and his associates (*see* Ilg and Ames, 1965) applied it to normally developing children. However, the idea that a child must be ready for a new learning in order for it to be meaningful is sound. For example, studies of children's spontaneous language acquisition have shown that children spontaneously imitate only those forms of adult grammar that they are about to incorporate into their own repertoires, ignoring other more complex forms (Bloom, 1973). It is doubly important, therefore, to be sure that whatever skill we are attempting to teach is developmentally appropriate. This will insure that the child herself will aid rather than resist the process.

Another aspect of motivation comes from Piaget's theory of the construction of knowledge. You will recall from Chapter 3 that Piaget (1952) considered cognitive development to be the result of a recurring state of *disequilibrium*. It is this state of disequilibrium, brought about when new information is at odds with previously held ideas, that is responsible for the child adapting her thinking to take into account the new information and thus attaining a higher level of knowledge. The state of disequilibrium is necessary, therefore, for new learnings to occur. Without this important process, the learning is likely to be restricted to a superficial rote level. It is important in program implementation to so engineer the environment that disequilibrium occurs.

In order to accomplish this, a developmental-interaction model (Biber, Shapiro, & Wickens, 1971; Bricker, Dennison, & Bricker, 1976) is suggested. This model combines the two basic ideas introduced above:

1. the need to base intervention on a sound developmental sequence
2. the need to organize the learning environment so that optimal interaction may occur. Optimal interaction occurs when the child is ready for the learning and when the interaction promotes a state of disequilibrium in the child which fosters the adaptive process

Shapiro and Biber (1972), of the Bank Street College of Education, have defined developmental interaction as follows:

Developmental refers to the emphasis on identifiable patterns of growth and modes of perceiving and responding which are characterized by increasing differentiation and progressive integration as a function of chronological age. Interaction refers, first, to the emphasis on the child's interaction with the environment

—adults, other children, and the material world—and second, to the interaction between cognitive and affective spheres of development. The developmental interaction formulation stresses the nature of the environment as much as it does the patterns of the responding child. [pp. 59–60]

This model emphasizes experiences that allow the child to try out new concepts, progress at his own pace, and engage in the kind of interaction that makes possible the assimilation of experience, the achievement of new integrations, and the resolution of conflict in both the cognitive and emotional realms (Shapiro & Biber, 1972).

In the Bank Street view, specific educational objectives for an individual child evolve from continuous analysis of the child's progress. Teachers must have a repertoire of teaching strategies from which to choose as individual situations dictate (Evans, 1975). The teacher is thus the most important variable in the child's learning environment. Other considerations for assuring appropriate environmental interactions include a flexible arrangement of classroom equipment, a large variety of materials, an atmosphere of trust, learning activities focused around concrete personal experiences, and an interweaving of work and play in the classroom (Evans, 1975).

Bricker's (1978) concept of the developmental interaction process is compatible with the traditional Bank Street model. In contrast to that of Bank Street, Bricker's model was conceived for use with disabled children. It stresses arranging the environment (curriculum) to ask more of the child each day in order to see change and growth. Behavior progresses from the simple to the complex in a specific developmental sequence. It is important, therefore, to base targets on normal development. By placing the child in a state of disequilibrium and then arranging the environment to promote meaningful interactions, the teacher assures maximum growth.

In summary, the planning and implementation of individual educational program for young, handicapped children must include considerations for both process and content. It must take account of both the child and the learning environment and provide for meaningful experiences at the proper developmental level. To accomplish this, we have suggested a combination of behavioral technology and developmental interaction strategies designed to maximize the effects of intervention.

STRATEGIES FOR SYSTEMS CHANGE

Having examined some of the major factors and techniques involved in changing and developing the behavior of the preschool, handicapped child, we can turn our attention to some means of bringing about systems change.

The ecological congruence model discussed in the previous chapter is as concerned with changing systems as it is with changing the behavior of individuals. Although a technology for changing systems has not been developed to the same

216 PROGRAM PLANNING AND IMPLEMENTATION

point as has individual behavior change technology, there are still some strategies that can be employed in an attempt to change systems. In fact, these strategies often use contingent consequences in the same way as does changing the behavior of a child. Systems, after all, are controlled by people, and people respond to changes in the contingency structure of their environments. Some readers may be familiar with a book by Saul Alansky (1971), called *Rules for Radicals*, which was popular in the early 1970s among persons interested in affecting social and political change. In the book, Alansky suggested that systems could be changed by identifying sacred or important elements in the system and then in some way interfering with the availability of these elements. For example, he maintained that O'Hare Airport is significant enough to the city of Chicago that one could bring about change in that city by effectively interfering with O'Hare's function. Alansky's suggestion was to muster a cadre of people and to occupy every stall of every bathroom at O'Hare until the city responded to whatever demands were being made. While Alansky's strategy is indeed a bit avant garde and to our knowledge has never been successfully used, it does illustrate a principle by which system change can be brought about. Essentially Alansky's strategy was one of negative reinforcement. Simply, when the city of Chicago behaved in the manner in which Alansky would desire, he would remove the aversive event (i.e., unoccupy the stalls at the airport). The point is that systems respond to contingent consequences just as do individuals and these consequences can be used to bring about desired systems change. Remember that contingencies can be used in a more positive manner to help bring systems changes needed to establish ecological congruence.

Systems change can often be brought about by effective negotiation leading to a compromise. Viewed from one perspective, a compromise is an agreed upon set of contingencies which will be offered by each party. Presumably, the rewards gained through negotiation are stronger in maintaining desired outcomes than is the punishment rendered through giving up some desired consequences.

Suppose you were case manager for Ann, the young, physically handicapped girl mentioned in the previous chapter. You may recall that Ann's father was intolerant of her inability to independently toilet herself and that his intolerance coupled with Ann's lack of function created an instance of incongruence in the family ecology. To increase Mr. Ray's tolerance of Ann, certain contingencies were implemented in the environment. For example, Ann's mother was to prepare special dinners for her husband on days when he assisted Ann with her toileting needs more than three times. Such contingencies might require negotiation to arrange. Mrs. Ray would need to be shown the benefits that she would receive from making special dinners. In this situation, Mrs. Ray's cooperation would no doubt depend on how much importance she placed on having her husband assist with Ann's toileting needs.

Negotiation, while an important skill in bringing about systems change, is not always easily learned; nor is it always easy to accomplish. Successful negotiation depends on:

1. understanding the nature of the system involved
2. understanding the individuals in the system
3. having a clear picture of the desired outcome of the negotiation
4. having a clear picture of what consequences you are willing to offer for desired ends
5. having a clear picture of what consequences you are *not* willing to offer for desired ends
6. being patient and tolerant of other people's view
7. being committed enough to take the time and make the effort to complete the negotiation

Even if these guidelines are followed, negotiation may not always be successful. Any negotiator must be willing to accept failure and to take reward in the fact that he did whatever could be done. In developing congruent ecologies, it is necessary to have a commitment to negotiation and to be an advocate for both systems and individual change.

Although it can be useful in bringing about necessary changes in the physical and contingency structures of a social system, negotiation is often less successful in creating necessary attitude change. Attitude change depends on modifying internal feelings and contingencies that mediate a person's behavior. Sometimes a change in attitude can result from a negotiation—if the negotiated outcome demonstrates a point. For example, if a Down's syndrome child's entrance into a regular kindergarten class could be successfully negotiated and implemented, the attitudes of the kindergarten teacher and other school personnel toward the acceptance of other developmentally disabled children in the future might become more favorable. Attitude change may also result from an examination of a person's internal state, an exercise that requires discussion and analysis over time. This is not to suggest that attitudes cannot also be changed by changing behavior, since the way we behave is a factor in determining the way we feel and the attitudes we express. The point is that attitude change usually requires relatively long-term interventions, which are carried out through systematic counseling and behavior change strategies. Chapter 10 discusses the use of these strategies as they apply to parents and other family members and so these strategies will not be talked about here.

SUMMARY AND CONCLUSIONS

The purpose of this chapter is to familiarize you with techniques and strategies for implementing individualized program plans. In addition, you learned about critical elements in the learning environments of young, disabled children and how antecedents and consequences can be arranged in the environment to bring about effective behavior change stressing a positive approach. Although changing the behavior of children was stressed, do not forget the importance of systems intervention and recognize that ecological congruence grows from both individual and systems intervention. Having examined some of the basic techniques for program planning and implementation, we will look at curriculum and methods for developing cognitive, motor, language, social, and self-care skills in young, disabled children in section IV. You should reflect on the developmental information found in the first several chapters of this book and how that information underlies many of the curricular activities that are discussed in the following chapters.

Involving Families in Programs

1. What are some of the ways parents of disabled, young children express their guilt and anger?
2. What are the unique effects on mothers, fathers, and siblings of young, disabled children?
3. What are the important features of successful parent training activities?
4. In what types of activities can parents engage in programs for their children?

Professional involvement with parents takes many forms. Especially when a child is newly identified as handicapped, but extending throughout a parent's life with his or her child, an empathetic and supportive professional can help parents adjust to the emotional demands of parenting a special child. The term *parent training* suggests a common role for professionals. Training parents to be effective educational change agents for their children is the goal of many parent programs. Professionals can be providers of information (referral agents), advocates, and collaborators working with parents on school organization, administrative issues, or special activities. Sometimes, direct involvement with parents is minimal, and professionals help parents most by providing children with a sound educational program and respecting parents' need to devote time to themselves, their spouses, and to their other children.

In this chapter we examine approaches to interacting with parents. These have typically been considered under the headings "parent counseling," "parent training," and "parent involvement." Often, one or another of these approaches

This chapter was written by Allen Sandler.

characterizes the parent program in a particular school. However, professionals need to possess the skills and understanding that will enable them to assume a variety of roles as they interact with parents. The information provided in the following pages will help you to work more effectively with parents who have differing backgrounds, emotional needs, abilities, and levels of interest in taking an active role in their child's educational program.

EMOTIONAL REACTIONS TO A HANDICAPPED FAMILY MEMBER

Early conceptualizations of parental reactions to a handicapped child tended to portray parents uniformly as neurotic—pathologically overcome by feelings of grief and guilt (Wolfensberger, 1967). These emotions are now more commonly viewed as among a range of emotional responses often experienced by essentially healthy individuals as they adjust to what Featherstone (1980) has termed "a difference in the family." We will look at these reactions in some detail. However, recognize that these responses are not experienced by all parents. Very few comparisons between parents of handicapped and nonhandicapped children have been made. One of the few control group studies reported (Boles, 1959), failed to support the commonly held views that mothers of handicapped children as a group were more anxious, more socially withdrawn, more rejecting, more unrealistic in their attitudes, or more guilt-ridden than mothers of nonhandicapped children. The bulk of work in this area has been theoretical, based upon anecdotal reports and case studies. Yet, familiarity with the available information in this area contributes substantially to one's ability to assist family members as they undergo what is often a continuing process of adjustment.

Grief

The period immediately after identification of a child as disabled is usually the most difficult for parents. When an infant is identified as handicapped at birth, parents are dealt a blow at a time that, even under the best of circumstances, is one of great physical and psychological stress. The birth of any child requires dramatic adjustments in the role and life styles of family members. The added stress of a handicapped newborn may cause shock, bewilderment, confusion, anxiety, and despair. Wolfensberger and Menolascino (1970) have suggested that the critical issue is not so much the reality of the situation (i.e., the fact that the child has a disability), but the sudden shattering of expectancies involved in learning of the disability. They termed this phenomenon "novelty shock."

Parents generally anticipate the birth of a child anxiously, with idealized expectations regarding the child-to-be. They often expect not merely a typical infant, but a perfect one. Grief is thought to result from the loss of this fantasized perfect child. Buscaglia (1975) describes the situation in this way:

To go through a time of self-pity and mourning is to be expected. All parents have a dream of a perfect child, a new life which will to some extent reflect their own but go beyond them. They have dreams of their child being the football hero or the belle of the ball. . . . These may be unconscious feelings, but they are known to be very human dynamics in the psychology of birth. They believe that these dreams have been permanently shattered. They pity the child. They pity themselves. They have a right to go through a time of mourning as they would mourn the death of a loved one—for to some extent, the reality of a disabled child is the death of a loved dream of the perfect child they hoped for. [p. 101]

There are, however, important differences between mourning the birth of a handicapped child and mourning a death (Featherstone, 1980, p. 233). The implications of a child's disability are not nearly so clear-cut as death's. Confusion and lack of certainty about the future may create ambiguity. Parents do not know what the future holds, because professionals are often unable to make definitive judgments regarding a child's future development at so early an age. Contradictory feelings may also be present; there may be sadness, but also love for the new infant. And, there are new caretaking demands:

Instead of an aching hole—the empty bed, the now-useless baby clothes—parents face the insistent demands of a child who needs even more care than an ordinary infant would. They must shoulder the heavy responsibility of leading the child into life, and love him as though he embodied all their dreams. While death provides a moment's respite from ordinary demands, disability generates new tasks and necessities. [Featherstone, 1980, p. 234].

The manner in which parents are informed by the physician of their child's condition may aggravate the difficult adjustment process. Parents look to the physician during this period for support and counsel. However, both the extent of the information conveyed by the physician and the way in which it is presented are often unsatisfactory. In two recent studies (Abramson et al., 1977; Pueschel and Murphy, 1976) only approximately 50 percent of the parents reported satisfaction with the advice they received. Twenty-five percent of the parents surveyed by Pueschel and Murphy indicated that their physician was abrupt and unsympathetic. Two parents were informed of their child's condition by mail. Providing the parents with the opportunity to express their sorrow and receive support for the legitimacy of their grief may be especially important at this critical time. The physician's lack of support and sensitivity may cause anger and resentment.

The identification of a child some time after birth is also likely to cause reactions of sorrow and grief. At this time, however, parents may also experience a sense of relief. A significant period of time often elapses between the time a problem is first suspected by the parent and the time the presence of a disability is confirmed. During this period of uncertainty, parents may remain unconvinced by the reassurances of friends and family and feel powerless in the face of their fears. Sorrow may accompany the confirmation of the child's disability, but, in the words of one parent, "I also was free now to proceed to do something, to gain some control over the situation, instead of feeling like a helpless victim" (Kovacs, 1972, pp. 29–30).

Anger

Parents may be angry with God, fate, society, and professionals. They also may feel anger toward the handicapped child. The birth of a handicapped child may cause parents to question and sometimes rebel against basic assumptions about life's meaning. A satisfactory answer to the question "Why me?" may evade parents previously secure in viewing the world as an orderly place in which good deeds are rewarded and only wrongdoing punished. Parents may rebel in anger at the unfair burden meted out to them by God or fate. Featherstone (1980, p. 49) describes one parent's reaction to another parent's observation "that God never gives you more troubles than you can bear." The parent raised a clenched fist and responded, "I don't even believe in God, but sometimes I look up and tell Him that I hate Him." Parents may feel "ripped off" by life—angry at life for violating the rules (Featherstone, 1980, p. 33).

Society's neglect of the problems of the handicapped may cause anger in parents. Inadequate funding and reductions in funding by government may make needed services unavailable. Services for preschool, handicapped children are especially vulnerable because they are not mandated in most states. The frustration caused by funding cuts is expressed in the following excerpt from a letter from the president of a parent group to a public official:

> With great dismay we learned of your directive to reduce our Early Intervention Program's budget by 10%. As parents of handicapped children, we feel such a reduction is deplorable. It is a set-back for our children because it means a reduction in personnel so vital to our Center's programming. Considering the total amount of our allocation, a 10% cut is devastating. Those who are in the program will receive less service, and many who are awaiting entrance will receive no services.
>
> William Baker, President
> Ken-Crest Growth and Development
> Center Parents' Association

The anger over threatened program cuts, however, may lead to action that positively affects parents' sense of competence and self-worth. In Featherstone's words, "Anger keeps us fighting. . . . We take a stand and raise ourselves to defend our own, like a mother bear with cubs" (1980, p. 49).

Medical and educational professionals are frequent targets of parents' anger. As we have already discussed, the manner in which a child's initial diagnosis is presented to parents may provoke anger. Parents may also experience considerable frustration as they seek accurate diagnosis of a child with a less readily identifiable problem. Too often a child's problem is minimized with statements such as "He's just a little bit slow," or "He'll outgrow it," and valuable time is lost. Parents may become angry when they are not given adequate direction—when the diagnosis is a dead-end without information about services available for the child and family.

Parents of autistic and severely emotionally disturbed children have been dealt the hardest blow by professionals, because they have often been blamed for their child's disability. This is how one father of an autistic child has responded to the National Society for Autistic Children's definition of autism:

Do you hear that out there Bruno Bettleheim? Are we getting through to you? We said: *No known factors in the psychological environment of a child have been shown to cause autism.* . . .

That means we didn't do it, Bruno. . . . It means that careful, objective, scientific people have carried out study after study . . . and have written paper after paper in journal after journal which show that we, the parents of autistic children, are just ordinary people. Not any crazier than others. Not "refrigerator parents" any more than others. . . . Not neurotic or psychopathic or sociopathic or any of those other words that have been made up.

It means, Dr. Bettleheim, that you, and all those others like you who have been laying this incredible guilt trip on us for over twenty years, you are wrong and ought to be ashamed of yourselves.

"Feral mothers" indeed! You are a feral mother, Bruno. Take that and live with it for awhile. It doesn't feel very good, does it?

And "parentectomy"? It is my considered professional opinion, after having carefully examined all of the facts, that nothing short of a Bruno-ectomy will improve conditions in this case. And a Freud-ectomy. And a psychiatrist-ectomy. And a jargon-ectomy. And a professional baloney-ectomy. [Warren, 1978, p. 195]

Finally, parents may feel anger toward their handicapped child. Feelings of resentment may build as extraordinary demands are made on parents' time, patience, physical endurance, and financial resources. Personal plans for the future may be thwarted, as parents look ahead to their child's continued dependence. Parents may be frustrated by their child's failure to progress at the pace they had anticipated; they may be angered by their child's apparent inability to learn. Behavior problems may cause anger, especially when they occur in public.

It may be difficult for parents to acknowledge anger toward their special child. In one of the few control group studies involving parents of handicapped children, Cummings, Bayley, and Rie (1966) found that mothers of mentally retarded children experienced greater difficulty handling anger at their children than mothers of nonretarded children. Reason would hold the child innocent, unable to intentionally control his or her behavior. As Featherstone puts it:

Because these children do not willfully choose to disobey or destroy, anger at them may appear as senseless as anger at fate itself. When disability magnifies a child's vulnerability, parents feel they owe him total devotion, unqualified and unremitting love. It takes courage to face rage and resentment . . . and the guilt these feelings bring. [p. 46]

Guilt

Redner (1980) recently found that college students' expectations about mothers of handicapped children are consistent with Featherstone's statement above. Students expected a mother to be affected negatively by having a handicapped child, yet expected her to be more devoted to her child. The conflict between personal/social expectations and the reality of a child who inevitably brings parents frustration may cause guilt. Unable to accept feelings of rejection or hostility, parents may blame themselves for experiencing emotions unbefitting a good and loving parent, especially a parent of a child so in need of love and exceptional care. Parents are not prepared to expect the ambivalence of feeling that frequently characterizes the emotional interplay between a parent and handicapped child. The emotional maturity required to feel confident of one's love in the face of anger or resentment may be difficult to achieve.

Guilt may lead to overprotection of the handicapped child, as parents attempt to compensate for anger or rejection. Self-sacrifice and martyrdom may help parents feel atonement for the perceived sin of failing to love their child wholeheartedly. However, overprotection may occur in response to reality factors such as immaturity of the child and uncertainty regarding his capabilities (Cummings, Bayley, & Rie, 1966). Overprotective behavior may also give a parent enhanced feelings of satisfaction and self-worth, gained through meeting the dependency needs of the child (Ryckman & Henderson, 1965).

Guilt may also be related to a parent's feeling that something he or she did, or failed to do, caused a child's disability. This may be particularly true of parents of autistic or severely emotionally disturbed children, for, as we have seen, professionals have often attributed the problems of these children to parental inadequacy. Parents of children identified at birth may feel guilt associated with some aspect of their pregnancy or the delivery: why didn't they refuse pain medication, or insist on a Caesarian—did they get enough rest, choose the right doctor, eat the right foods? Parents may feel guilt associated with their child's handicap simply because the child is theirs. Just as parents take pride in a healthy baby, they may feel guilt and shame because they have given birth to a child who is disabled, and thereby failed in the biological aspect of their role as parent.

Psychological Stress

Loss of self-esteem, loneliness, and what has been termed *chronic sorrow* (Olshansky, 1962) are among other possible reactions to a handicapped child. Cummings, Bayley, and Rie (1966) found that mothers of mentally retarded children expressed higher levels of depressive affect and lower levels of self-esteem relative to their role as parent than did mothers of nonretarded children. Sorrow, if not outright depression, and feelings of inadequacy often continue beyond the adjustment period immediately following a child's initial diagnosis. The presence of a handicapped child may provide parents with a continuing reminder that they have, in a sense, failed in their role as progenitor. Parents' self-esteem may also be affected negatively if they see a child's limited progress as evidence of their own lack of competence as parents. The opportunities for failure are as great for parents as they attempt to teach a child appropriate social behavior, language, or toileting skills, as they are for the child. The child's failure may reinforce an existing sense of failure in the parents. This may be especially true for fathers, who appear to view their role as guide and teacher as a fundamental aspect of their role as father (Boles, 1959).

Although it is over 20 years since Olshansky (1962) urged professionals to abandon "the simplistic and static concept of parental acceptance," theories that portray parents as progressing through various stages culminating in a final stage of acceptance continue to be popular. Olshansky instead offered the view that parents experience chronic sorrow associated with their child's lifelong state of dependency. The following passage written by Stanford Searle, the father of a mentally retarded child, supports Olshansky's position:

> Parents of retarded people, the theorists tell us, learn to live with their children's handicaps. They go through stages of reaction, moving through shock, guilt and rejection to the promised land of acceptance and adjustment.
>
> My own experience as the father of a retarded child did not fit this pattern. Instead, it convinced me that most people seriously misunderstand a parent's response to this situation. . . .
>
> Professionals could help parents more—and they would be more realistic—if they discarded their ideas about stages and progress. They could then begin to understand something about the deep, lasting changes that life with a retarded son or daughter brings to parents. And they could begin to see that the negative feelings . . . never disappear but stay on as a part of the parents' emotional life. [1978, p. 27]

In addition to the occasion of a child's initial diagnosis, later situations may evoke sorrow in parents of the disabled. Parents may accept their handicapped child. This state of acceptance, however, may be very different than the "final harmony" suggested by stage theories. It is an acceptance which includes periods of pain and sadness—"periodic sorrow" within an overall context of acceptance (Featherstone, 1980, p. 232; Wikler, Masow, and Hatfield, 1981). Some situations that might rekindle sorrow in parents of young, handicapped children include: (1) the child reaching the age when nonhandicapped peers begin to walk or talk, (2) a younger sibling overtaking the handicapped child's abilities, (3) the child beginning to attend a school program, and thus being publicly labeled as "different," and (4) parental management of a crisis (behavior problem, seizure disorder, other health problem) unique to the handicapped child (Wikler et al., 1981). Any situation that forces parents to confront their child's deviation from normal performance may cause sorrow.

There are a number of possible explanations for the social isolation and loneliness sometimes experienced by parents. Some isolation results from embarrassment. Parents may hesitate to take their child into public because of the child's appearance or behavior. The stigma associated with their child's disability may make parents themselves feel stigmatized and set apart from others. Parents may feel lonely because they are different, with problems and responsibilities unique to their role. Lack of understanding of these problems by others may intensify their feelings of aloneness. Katherine Morton described her rage in response to a stranger's suggestion that she let her four-year-old daughter walk independently:

> I explained that she couldn't walk, that she was severely retarded. The stranger's face softened; her attitude was warm and understanding. "Oh," she said, "they are such wonderful children, and all they need is loving." Perhaps I had a premonition even then of how many years of assistance and training it would take before she would be able to walk, not to mention toilet herself, feed herself, and dress herself which she still cannot do at age fifteen. One comes out of such interviews feeling very much alone, burdened by the obligation to explain, educate, and reassure others because they know so little about our children and so very little about how to help. [1978, pp. 145–146]

Parents may experience social isolation due to physical requirements of parenting a handicapped child. The time and energy needed to see friends, attend meetings, or enjoy an evening out with one's spouse may simply not be available to parents burdened with the extraordinary caretaking demands often required by a handicapped child. Holt (1975) found that in 30 percent of the 272 families he surveyed the parents never went out together, with the mother's only relief from care coming when the father took over. Many parents are either unwilling to leave their child with a sitter or unable to find a suitable sitter for their child. Gallagher, Cross, and Scharfman (1981) found changes in vacations, social activities, and recreation to be among the major sources of stress reported by parents of handicapped preschoolers.

Reality Sources of Stress

Care-giving demands were the best predictor of stress in a recent survey of mothers of handicapped infants (Beckman-Bell, 1981). When added to the ordinary responsibilities of maintaining a household and attending to the needs of nonhandicapped siblings, the additional demands of caring for a handicapped child can be overwhelming. Reality demands may be so excessive that parents experience "burn-out" (Boggs, 1978; Schell, 1981). Physical exhaustion may result from long hours of care without respite. Feeding, bathing, attending to special medical needs, carrying out home therapy programs, and providing other forms of therapeutic intervention—all may contribute to a state of chronic fatigue. Unfortunately, this aspect of parental stress has often been overlooked by professionals, who have focused instead on parental psychopathology:

> What goes on in training programs in the name of education is sometimes shocking. . . . I cringe at the thought of some of the course syllabi I have reviewed. In many of these courses, very little attention is directed toward helping parents solve

the day-to-day problems which almost invariably are encountered, yet weeks are devoted to the "psychological insight approach to parental guilt." Many such courses are a fraud and tend to insure further conflict and unsatisfactory relationships between parents and professionals. [Turnbull, 1978, p. 138]

Parents sometimes experience stress related to the need to provide stimulation and training to their child at home. This may be particularly true when a child is involved in a home-based program or in a program with a strong parent training emphasis. The pressure to provide training at home may prevent a mother from meeting her own needs for relaxation or time with friends and make it difficult for her to attend to other responsibilities around the home:

I think you are always going to feel more pressure if your little one is handicapped, there's no way around it. When you get a little one who doesn't do anything until you're the catalyst . . . it almost becomes an obsession . . . because you feel like he'd be sitting there, and you know that either you're going to sew . . . or you could get him to learn his "K" sounds. [Winton & Turnbull, 1981, pp. 14–15]

Other reality sources of stress include financial responsibilities, management of behavior problems, and efforts to obtain appropriate educational services. Severely handicapped children and children with physical disabilities are most likely to require medical care beyond that ordinarily covered by medical insurance. Regular visits to the pediatrician, neurologist, or orthopedist are often necessary and expensive. Specialized equipments such as an adaptive chair, prone board, or side-lyer are also costly. When financial resources are limited, the pressure to pay for needed services can be a significant source of stress (Beckman-Bell, 1981; Turnbull, 1978, p. 466).

The presence of severe behavioral problems may be a source of considerable stress for parents. Specialized procedures are often necessary to successfully remediate problems such as self-injurious behavior, stereotyped behavior, aggressive behavior, or tantrums. Parents may experience stress related to both the behavior problem itself and to the utilization of the intervention approach recommended to remediate the problem (Beckman-Bell, 1981; Bray, Coleman, & Bracken, 1981).

Events related to educational services were the most common source of stress among parents of a heterogeneous group of handicapped children participating in a recent survey reported by Bray, Coleman, and Bracken (1981). The impact of the child's initial diagnosis and the emotional impact of the child's disability on a specific family member were ranked as the next most common sources of stress. Parental concerns about educational services involved the suitability of placement; availability, relevance, or duration of services; and the child's adjustment to the educational program. In a related survey (Winton & Turnbull, 1981) parents of handicapped, preschool children indicated concern about the competence and sensitivity of their child's teacher. They were concerned not only because of the effect of the teacher's ability on their child's expected progress, but because the competence of their child's teacher affected their own ability to relax and obtain a break from the responsibilities involved in their child's care. Sixty-five percent of the mothers expressed the need for a break from the pressure of full-time educational responsibility for their child.

Marital Conflict

Marital stability may be seriously threatened by the presence of a handicapped child in a family. Especially when a relationship is already problematic, the added stress related to rearing a child with a disability may lead to severe marital discord. Love (1973) reported three times as many divorces among parents of mentally retarded children as among parents of nonretarded children. Fatigue may cause irritability and lack of tolerance for frustration, which may in turn lead to arguments and outbursts of temper. Anger associated with the handicapped child's behavior may be misdirected at a spouse. Featherstone offers the following insight from her own experience as a parent:

> As Jay and I struggle to understand the anger we felt toward one another in the second year of Jody's life, it seems to us that our inability to focus our frustration on Jody himself might have contributed. When our dreams lay in fragments at our feet, when a crying baby interrupted every activity, fury and frustration were inevitable. But how could we blame Jody, who suffered through no fault of his own, more than anyone else? Longing for solutions that no one could provide, we turned on one another. [1980, p. 98]

Another source of conflict may be disagreement about issues related to the handicap. Parents may disagree about the nature and extent of their child's disability and about implications for the future. This may be especially true in the case of children who are initially difficult to diagnose. Disagreements may concern the extent to which the needs of a handicapped child should be permitted to interfere with normal family routines and the needs of other family members. Another possible source of conflict, especially important due to its potential impact on the handicapped child, is parental disagreement about management of behavior problems. Parents may disagree about the extent to which the child should be held accountable for her own behavior and about the type of disciplinary approach, if any, to be used. Differences of opinion about other aspects of the child's training, especially as they affect the time and energy of other family members, may provide further ground for conflict.

Boles (1959) found significantly higher levels of marital conflict reported by mothers of cerebral palsied children than by mothers of nonhandicapped children, and offered two possible explanations. First, differences in traditional maternal and paternal roles may enable the mother to achieve greater fulfillment through mothering, sheltering, and sacrificing for the handicapped child. The father, however, may find the helpless dependency of a child with a severe handicap frustrating and more of a liability. The difficulty each parent has in understanding the satisfactions or frustration of the other may contribute to marital conflict. Boles also hypothesized that maternal involvement with the child may be so great that the husband and other children become neglected. This may result in feelings of resentment in the husband and lead to tension and unresolved conflict in the marriage. Other authorities have suggested similar explanations for marital discord among families with a handicapped child (Buscaglia, 1975, p. 122; Berger & Fowlkes, 1980; Featherstone, 1980, p. 109).

Borrowing the terminology and perspective of family therapy (Minuchin, 1974), the problem may be understood as stemming from a breakdown in the boundary that normally exists between the subsystem of husband and wife and the subsystem that includes their children. Maintaining the integrity of this boundary appears necessary for family stability. Problems may occur when the family system is unbalanced by an alliance between one parent and a child which isolates the other parent. Parent training programs that include only the mother may contribute to boundary problems in a family by promoting increased levels of interaction between the mother and her child at the expense of transactions between husband and wife (Sandler, Coren, & Thurman, 1983).

Fathers

Professionals have only recently turned their attention to fathers, the "forgotten parents" (Crowley, Keane, & Needham, 1982). "Parent" support groups and "parent" training programs have rarely been set up to accommodate both mothers *and* fathers. Although mothers and their children are far more accessible targets of intervention, and mothers generally do assume the major share of caretaking responsibility for a handicapped child, neglect of the needs of fathers can have an undesirable impact upon overall family adjustment and marital stability.

Cummings (1976) investigated the effect of a handicapped child on the father. As might be expected, he found that fathers of mentally retarded children experienced significantly greater levels of psychological stress than fathers of nonretarded children. Fathers of retarded children scored higher on measures of depressive affect and preoccupation with their child and scored lower on a measure of self-esteem related to paternal competence. The fathers of mentally retarded children also demonstrated a relative lack of gratification from relationships with their wives, with other children in the family, and with their handicapped child. Cummings suggests that the traditional paternal role of family provider limits a father's opportunities to act directly to help his handicapped child, thereby providing evidence of his love and concern, and counterbalancing the feelings of grief, frustration, and anger he may experience. Enacting other traditional paternal roles such as physical playmate and socializing agent/model, may also be difficult for fathers, especially when their handicapped child is a male (Gallagher, Cross, & Scharfman, 1981; Tallman, 1965).

Achieving greater satisfaction with their role in the family may be a most critical need of fathers. Their difficulty defining an appropriate role is underscored by findings reported by Gallagher, Cross, and Scharfman (1981). Fathers judged both "average" and "successful" in their overall adjustment to a handicapped child indicated that they felt they should be more actively involved in all six child care roles explored (teaching, nursing, child discipline, transporter, clothing selector, and recreation leader). Their wives agreed, and felt furthermore that the fathers should be more actively involved in 12 of 14 additional general family roles. Fathers appear to experience difficulty, however, discerning quite how to be involved with their handicapped child. The following responses by fathers of deaf children express a common need to know more about how they might assist in promoting the growth of their children: "Knowing what to do is half the struggle." "I need to know there is something I can do and to know what to do." "Tell us what to do and we'll do it." (Liversidge & Grana, 1973, p. 175).

The traditional image of the strong, silent male may further interfere with adjustment to a handicapped child. Mothers often complain that fathers do not talk about their feelings. Featherstone provides this example:

> Elizabeth Black's experience is not atypical. She described taking Kimberly in for an evaluation because she worried about the little girl's slow development. Gary went with her. The news was shattering. But Gary went off to work, straight from the appointment, leaving her to cope alone with the crying baby and her feelings. "No support," she remarked concisely. He returned home at 10 p.m., after work and overtime.
> "How are you?" Elizabeth asked.
> "Oh, I'm fine."
> "No, I mean how are you really?"
> "Oh. Well, I guess I'm not feeling so great, after what they said this morning."
> She waited, but that was all. [1980, p. 124]

The inability or lack of willingness to openly express feelings may make it difficult for fathers to reduce the burden of stress they bear. Participation in a group with other fathers, however, may help some fathers "open up" (Liversidge & Grana, 1973). Unfortunately, support groups for fathers are not generally available, and when they are organized, participation is often limited. Interested fathers may simply lack the energy after a typical day's work to attend an evening function. Successful groups for fathers have been described in the literature, however, and these descriptions are a valuable resource for professionals attempting to start a fathers' group (see Crowley, Keane, & Needham, 1982; Delaney, Meyer, & Ward, 1977; Erickson, 1974; Liversidge & Grana, 1973).

Fathers who do not feel comfortable participating in a sharing group may derive peer support through various activities centered around their children's school program. Group projects involving physical work, such as constructing a picnic table for the school yard or putting up a new piece of playground equipment, may allow fathers to experience comradeship and also may enhance fathers' self-esteem. Other avenues for involvement, which are consistent with traditional male roles, include participation in organizational functions such as serving as an officer of the Parent Group, actively engaging in fund raising, and joining in lobbying efforts directed at public officials.

Siblings

The effects of a handicapped child on the family are not limited to the parents. Such emotions as sorrow, anger, and guilt may be experienced by both parents and siblings. Intertwined with these reactions, however, are others more uniquely experienced by siblings. These include identification with the handicapped brother or sister, embarrassment, and resentment.

Based upon her experience conducting a support group for siblings, Kaplan (1969, p. 205) suggests that avoiding identification with a handicapped brother or sister is the most central concern of siblings. Just as the community views the family as a social unit, so children identify themselves as family members—sharing, internalizing, characteristics of their family. When a family's identity is heavily influenced by the presence of a handicapped child, siblings' identity cannot escape a similar influence. Children may also identify with their handicapped sibling because they physically resemble the sibling (Featherstone, 1980, p. 148). The process of identification may lead nonhandicapped brothers and sisters to question their own normalcy. They may fear that like their sibling they are in some way deficient.

Children often feel embarrassed and ashamed of their handicapped sibling. Efforts to conform to society's norms may be blocked by the stigma of a handicapped brother or sister. Embarrassment caused by the stares of strangers may be so painful that a brother or sister tries to avoid accompanying a handicapped sibling in public. Siblings who display obvious physical stigma or exhibit inappropriate social behavior such as self-stimulation are especially likely to cause embarrassment. The sister of the severely handicapped adult related her feelings at age 11 in this way:

> I can remember being actually embarrassed by the ill-concealed stares our family received. . . . I was certain that everyone was looking at my brother with his obvious handicap and their wondering what was wrong with the rest of us. As a result of the feelings aroused in me by these occurrences, I began to refuse to go out to dinner or shopping with my family and took precautions to avoid being seen on the street or in the yard with Robin.
>
> These avoidance procedures on my part were not taken without an accompanying sense of guilt. I knew that it was wrong for me to be ashamed of my brother. [Helsel et al., 1978, p. 110]

Significant amounts of time or money directed toward a disabled brother or sister may cause resentment among siblings. Children may feel deprived of the attention or resources they want and feel they need (Grossman, 1972, p. 176). They may resent the embarrassment they face and the extra responsibilities they must shoulder. Holt (1975) found approximately 10 percent of the siblings in 201 families he surveyed to be extremely resentful of the attention given to a retarded brother or sister.

In the past, parents were often counseled that keeping a mentally retarded child at home would harm the siblings. Although, as we have seen, responses to a disabled sibling may be negative in certain respects, positive reactions are also commonly reported (Cleveland & Miller, 1977; Farber, 1963; Featherstone, 1980; Schreiber & Feely, 1975). These reactions include increased maturity, compassion, tolerance for individual differences, patience, and sense of responsibility; a greater appreciation for family bonds and for good health; and increased sensitivity to prejudice and other social welfare issues. Grossman (1972) found positive reactions such as these to be about as commonly reported by college age siblings as various negative reactions.

At particular risk for the development of adjustment problems, however, may be the oldest female sibling (Cleveland & Miller, 1977; Fowle, 1968; Gath, 1973, 1974). This risk may be related to the increased likelihood that she assumes parent-surrogate responsibilities in relation to her handicapped brother or sister. Family supports such as respite care may help lessen this risk, allowing time for more normal peer relationships, dating, and the like. Many siblings benefit from participation in a group experience that provides information and a supportive atmosphere for the sharing of feelings. Sibling groups have been described by Kaplan (1969), Cansler, Martin, and Valand (1975), and Schreiber and Feely (1975).

MANAGEMENT

Although some parents may require the assistance of a professionally trained counselor or therapist, most families adapt with at least a fair degree of success to the stresses involved in coping with a handicapped child. It is the responsibility of early intervention program staff to help meet the still considerable needs of these parents who manage to cope without more specialized therapeutic intervention. Areas of assistance include providing information, emotional support, and help in response to reality sources of stress.

Both information and emotional support are needed following a child's initial diagnosis. Parents need the opportunity to express their grief and need to receive reassurance that their reaction is an acceptable one under the circumstances. Wolfensberger and Menolascino (1970) suggest the following approach to counseling parents experiencing what they have termed "novelty shock:"

> What parents in novelty shock need first and foremost is gentle, undramatic interpretation of the facts, provided in an atmosphere of maximal emotional support. . . . Interpretation should stress those elements which are realistically positive, such as the positive aspects of likely child development and the availability . . . of services and resources. To cope with their grief, parents should be helped to get to know fellow parents who have made model adjustments. [p. 480]

Reading material may be useful in conveying general information about the nature of a child's handicap, and review of evaluation data may help parents gain a more accurate view of their child's specific problem. It is often helpful to let parents talk about their experience when informed of their child's disability and to clarify any misconceptions related to the information they received at that time. The reasons for a child's handicap should be made clear whenever possible, because feelings of guilt may be reduced when a specific cause of a child's condition can be provided (Zuk, 1962).

Although parents are generally informed of their child's handicap in a single meeting, follow-up evaluations often provide additional information regarding the severity of a child's disability and his or her future potential. Contact with parents following these reevaluations should provide clarification, if necessary, and continuing support. Other times when parents are likely to need more intensified emotional support include the onset of medical problems such as a seizure disorder, hospitalization of a child, and when preparations are underway for entry into a program for school-age children.

To be an effective source of support for parents, a professional must be a good listener.

> Listening is the most helpful of all supportive roles. Before providing necessary information, the professional will need to provide a listening post for the parent; he should be a sensitive human being who is able to listen to the parents calmly, sympathetically, and nonjudgmentally. [Schlesinger & Meadow, 1976, p. 38]

Parents need an opportunity to ventilate—to clarify their feelings through talking and receive support for socially unacceptable feelings such as anger and resentment. They must be helped to understand that their reactions are a legitimate response to the situation they confront, and that other parents experience similar reactions.

The professional should listen carefully to parents, conveying a sense of respect for the uniqueness of each parent's experience. She should listen with curiosity, extending the parent's line of thought through questioning (Featherstone, 1980, p. 210). Nonverbal behavior such as leaning forward, maintaining eye contact, slight head nods, smiles, and the like can communicate acceptance and help the parent feel that it is all right to talk (Kroth, 1975, p. 28).

Interaction with other parents may be another valuable source of emotional support for parents, especially interaction with other parents who have coped successfully with children who have similar handicaps. Providing opportunities for interaction among parents is an important responsibility of an early intervention program. Pairing new parents with a more experienced "buddy" is often helpful. Parent group meetings, or coffee hours for mothers, while having as a focus the sharing of information, should also allow adequate time for informal socializing among parents. (An extended break for refreshments may help facilitate interaction). Parents may also derive support through the process of resocialization they undergo as they participate in a parent group and come to identify with the concerns of other special parents, adopting a shared perspective on their new role (Berger & Foster, 1976).

Husbands and wives should be encouraged to support *each other*. This includes not only actively listening to each other, but supporting each other's parenting decisions, especially in the area of behavior management. The use of newly learned behavior management skills by a mother will only have a positive effect on her child if the new approach is not sabotaged by the father, who may react to a perceived threat to his role in the family hierarchy by holding more firmly to existing ways of dealing with the child (Foster, Berger, & McLean, 1981). Professional intervention aimed at the mother and her handicapped child must be carried out with considerable sensitivity to the potential impact on other family members. Efforts should be made to include the father and, when this is not possible, the mother should be made aware of the importance of her husband's support and encouraged to actively enlist his cooperation before initiating any change in customary family approaches to discipline.

It is important for professionals to recognize the significant role played by grandparents in many families. Parents may experience considerable difficulty telling their parents about a child's disability. A supportive response by grandparents, however, may aid parents in coping with both their emotional needs and reality sources of stress. Grandparents may demonstrate their concern through helping out financially or by caring for the child at times so parents can obtain a break from child care responsibilities. Fathers of handicapped children may especially benefit from their parents' support. A recent study (Waisbren, 1980) indicated that fathers who felt their parents were highly supportive engaged in more activities with their handicapped child and had more positive feelings about their child.

Although the informational needs of parents are discussed in greater detail later in this chapter, there is one matter which warrants consideration here. Parents should be made aware of the effects their handicapped child may have on themselves as well as on their other children and/or family life in general. This information may give parents insight into both present and future conflicts, thereby achieving a better perspective on their situation as special parents. Group discussion of reading material such as that included in Featherstone's excellent book would be a good way to present this information and simultaneously provide an opportunity for peer interaction and support. Care should be taken to avoid portraying too bleak a picture, however. Positive aspects of parenting a special child should also be presented (see section later in this chapter), and the fact that most families adapt satisfactorily to a handicapped child should be stressed.

Parents can be helped to cope with reality stresses in a number of ways. First, the professional must help the parent understand that crises or conflicts related to excessive reality demands, and resulting symptoms of stress, are essentially normal reactions to the very real burdens often associated with parenting a handicapped child (Wolfensberger & Menolascino, 1970, p. 482). Next, concrete steps must be taken to help relieve these situational burdens. Parents should be encouraged to make use of respite-care services if available and helped to find competent babysitters. When sitters who feel comfortable with handicapped children are not available, as is often the case, professionals could encourage high school or community service groups to help out and could even provide training sessions. Professionals could also help organize a cooperative made up of parents in a program who are willing to take turns caring for each other's children (Turnbull, 1978, p. 474). Respite can take many forms, as described in this plea for help from the mother of a profoundly retarded daughter:

> If only practical offers of help were a traditional response to handicapped children—offers to baby-sit while we grocery shop, offers to take our children for a walk, offers to take them swimming, offers to give any reprieve, however short, which could give the parents, especially the mother, a chance to relax or tend to other things. Sympathy and pats on the back are nice, but . . . it's practical help, time and manpower we need . . . and those gifts must come from people who are less burdened than we. [Morton, 1978, p. 147]

It is important that all family members assist in the care of a handicapped child in order to avoid overwhelming the mother with sole responsibility for time-consuming and physically taxing child care duties. The participation of the father, and siblings where appropriate, fosters a sense of family unity and provides an opportunity for the demonstration of active concern for the well-being of the handicapped child. Mothers should be encouraged to request the help of other family members, as this alone may be sufficient to elicit their assistance (Buscaglia, 1975, p. 123).

A child's enrollment in a center-based educational program can also provide parents with needed relief from child care responsibilities, as well as from the pressure of full-time educational responsibility. Although they are administratively less expensive and may promote in parents a greater sense of their own importance as facilitators of their child's educational growth, home-based programs lack the respite function provided by center-based programs. This respite dimension of a center-based program is especially significant in the case of severely involved infants and young children, who represent a particularly heavy caretaking burden. A full day, center-based program, with a parent-training component, may best meet the needs of these children and their families.

Training in behavior management skills can help parents deal more effectively with behavior problems, another common source of stress. However, as discussed earlier, efforts should be made to involve fathers in such training programs to avoid possible conflict related to a change in existing disciplinary approaches. Professionals can help parents with other situational stresses by assuming the roles of advocate and referral/follow-up agent (Wolfensberger & Menolascino, 1970, p. 482). Assisting as an advocate can be extremely helpful as parents face their child's transition to a program for school-age children. The stress involved in leaving the familiar preschool and obtaining an appropriate program and related services in a school-age setting can be eased considerably through the assistance of a knowledgeable professional who is familiar with the child's needs and experienced in dealing with school administrative personnel.

Relief from other situational burdens can be achieved through helping parents make use of resources available in the community and through government agencies. Financial assistance may be available from the federal government through SSI (Supplemental Security Income), and other types of assistance are sometimes available through state or local government programs. Help is often needed to demonstrate eligibility for these programs. Information related to income tax deductions can often be valuable. Expensive equipment can sometimes be obtained through organizations such as Easter Seals or local community service groups. Free or low-cost medical services such as hearing, vision, and dental screening programs can often be recommended, as can enrollment in appropriate clinics. Parents often have difficulty finding pediatricians or other medical specialists with whom they feel comfortable; recommendations can be made regarding physicians with whom other parents have had positive experiences.

Positive Aspects of Exceptional Parenthood

As we noted at the beginning of this chapter, not all parents are similarly affected by a handicapped child. Variation in the amount of support needed by parents can be considerable. Here are quotes from two mothers moving from programs offering parent support groups to programs without active support groups:

> I cried for 2 months last spring. I knew what was going to happen. I didn't know it would be drastic. I was hoping that there would be some type of parental support but it just didn't happen.

> It is definitely refreshing. You really feel bad for the professionals that want to help you but don't know how. You know the psychologists and the social workers have this concept that every parent with a handicapped child wants to talk about it all the time—that's garbage! [Winton & Turnbull, 1981, p. 17]

The presence of a disabled child does not necessarily lead to debilitating levels of stress on parents. Gallagher, Cross, and Scharfman (1981) found measurable levels of stress reported by only 52 percent of fathers and 42 percent of mothers among a sample of 50 pairs of parents of moderately to severely handicapped children enrolled in specialized preschool programs. Positive reactions to a handicapped child are also reported. Helsel (Helsel et al., 1978, p. 113), both a parent and special education professional, advises that parents be told not only that it is all right to feel "resentful, embarrassed, uncomfortable, inadequate" in relation to their handicapped child, but that they also be told about "the joy, the love, the challenge, and the opportunities for growth and fulfillment that such a situation can offer."

Kramm (1963) found that 76 percent of the parents of Down's syndrome children he surveyed felt having a retarded child had been good for them, and a majority of parents felt that, except for the initial period, the experience had strengthened, rather than weakened, their marriage. Gath (1977) reported similarly that almost half the parents of Down's children she studied felt that their marriage had been strengthened by their experience raising a Down's child. When asked to indicate events they deemed critical in their family history, 15 percent of 169 parents of exceptional children responded positively (Bray, Coleman, and Bracken, 1981). Parents reported pride in the achievements of their children and affirmed the unifying influence of the child in their families.

The following passage from Pearl S. Buck's account of her experience as parent of a severely handicapped child probably sums up best the balance of happiness and pain involved in being an exceptional parent:

> Endurance of inescapable sorrow is something which has to be learned alone. And only to endure is not enough. Endurance can be a harsh and bitter root in one's life, bearing poisonous and gloomy fruit, destroying other lives. Endurance is only the beginning. There must be acceptance and the knowledge that sorrow fully accepted brings its own gifts. For there is an alchemy in sorrow. It can be transmuted into wisdom, which, if it does not bring joy, can yet bring happiness. [1950, p. 35]

PARENT TRAINING

As we have seen, parents vary considerably in their response to a handicapped child. Differences in the past experiences of parents, status of a marital relationship, the severity of a child's handicap, and other factors may influence not only the emotional adjustment of parents, but the degree to which they are able and willing to become actively involved in their child's educational program. As we turn next to parent training methods, we will pay special attention to the degree various approaches allow for differing levels of parent participation. We urge the reader to keep in mind as we examine this area that rigid adherence to any one professional role in working with parents is likely to lead to less than optimal results. Parents will often "open up" and express their feelings in the context of a parent training session. The professional must be willing to listen carefully as parents share their feelings, shifting easily from a parent training role to a supportive role more commonly associated with a counseling orientation. The approach used must depend upon the needs of a given parent at a particular point in time. Sensitivity and an open mind are required to discern adequately what these needs may be.

Training programs for parents are generally provided within either a center-based or a home-based context. In either case, the following components are among those likely to be included (Welsh & Odum, 1981):

1. a review of normal child development and developmentally sequenced instruction
2. explanation of handicapping conditions and an overview of their treatment
3. instruction in child management techniques
4. instruction in teaching techniques, often including data collection
5. observation of modeled teaching sequences involving child
6. opportunity to practice teaching and receive feedback from professional staff

It is important that parents understand the basis for selecting skills to be taught to their child. Meaningful parent involvement in formulating goals and objectives requires familiarity with the concept of developmentally sequenced instruction. This may be facilitated by providing parents with a copy of a developmental checklist, and using it with them as a resource in choosing skills for their child. Parents often lack a clear understanding of the nature of their child's handicap and its implications for the future. A review of the causes and characteristics of the major handicapping conditions and their treatment may help parents to develop more realistic expectations and to better understand their role in promoting their child's growth.

Training in Child Management

The bulk of parent training research has involved training parents to remediate behavior problems in their children (Johnson & Katz, 1973; O'Dell, 1974). Parents often take their children's good behavior for granted and respond with negative attention to undesirable behavior. Thus, the child receives attention, albeit negative attention, following behavior that is disturbing to parents. This strengthens the disturbing behavior. Intervention involves teaching the parent to praise or otherwise reinforce appropriate behavior and to replace negative attention (scolding, repeated commands, reprimands, threats, and the like) with either systematic ignoring or an effective punishment procedure, such as time-out. The effort required to teach appropriate use of time-out in the home should not be underestimated; repeated home visits are often required.

Among the most common behavior problems at home are noncompliance (refusal to follow commands) and tantrums. Procedures for reducing noncompliant behavior include a) reinforcing compliance, b) teaching the parent to provide clear commands and to limit the number of the repetitions of an initial command, and either c) putting the child through the desired behavior without attention, or d) providing a warning, e.g., "If you don't _____, you'll go in time-out," and, if the child does not comply after the warning, using time-out. Children tantrum either to avoid something aversive (going to bed, taking a bath, and the like), or to obtain something they desire (a cookie, a chance to go outside, and the like). When a mother "gives in" to her child's demand, her behavior is negatively reinforced by termination of the child's tantrum, and she will therefore be more likely to give in again in the future. The child's tantrum behavior is also reinforced when the mother gives in, because the child either gets something pleasant or avoids something which is unpleasant. Intervention involves teaching parents to avoid giving in to demands made during a tantrum episode and to otherwise ignore tantrum behavior.

Despite research support for the effectiveness of techniques such as these in treating behavior problems at home, prominent researchers in this area have questioned the generality of parent training results (Bernal, Klinnert, & Schultz, 1980; Wahler, 1980). Not all parents are likely to profit equally from training; Bernal, Klinnert, and Schultz suggest that a large proportion of parents with children who have conduct problems may fail to become effective change agents for their children.

Training Parents to Teach Their Children

A combination of small group and individual sessions is effective for providing instruction in teaching techniques involved. General information may be conveyed through group sessions, which use professional time economically and enable parents to benefit from the encouragement and support of their peers. Individual sessions give parents an opportunity to observe as their child receives training and to themselves work individually with their child and receive feedback from the parent trainer or other staff person. A variety of instructional methods may be used. Reading material, such as the *Steps to Independence Series* (Baker et al., 1976) is helpful for presenting basic information (other parent training manuals are reviewed by Bernal & North, 1978). Videotaped sequences demonstrating various instructional techniques can be used (see Koegel, Glahn, & Niemiren, 1978) as can live modeling and role playing. Videotaping parents as they teach their child and reviewing the taped sequence afterwards is a most effective way to provide feedback to parents.

Data Keeping

Parent training programs often include instruction in data-keeping procedures (Bricker & Bricker, 1976; Fredericks, Baldwin, & Grove, 1974; Hayden & Haring, 1976; Shearer & Shearer, 1976). Although some parents' experience with data keeping is quite positive (see Figure 10.1), others find data keeping burdensome, and question its necessity for adequate instruction at home. Parents may feel under too much pressure to record data, and may even fabricate data in response to program pressure (Sandler & Coren, 1981). We agree with Lansing and Schopler (1978, p. 449) that data keeping by parents may be unnecessary "for the development of a consistent and rational approach with the child." It is recommended that instruction in data keeping be provided to only those parents who express an interest in this procedure, rather than be included within a standard parent training "package." Here, as in other areas of work with parents, the diversity of parent interests must be respected.

Home-Based and Center-Based Approaches

The overall structure of a parent training program depends upon whether the program has been established to supplement a center-based program or to stand alone in a home-based program. Home-based programs, discussed in greater detail in Chapter 11, are generally centered around regularly scheduled meetings between the parent and home-teacher, either exclusively in the home, or alternating between home and center. Regular sessions with clinical staff, such as the language therapist and occupational or physical therapist, may also be

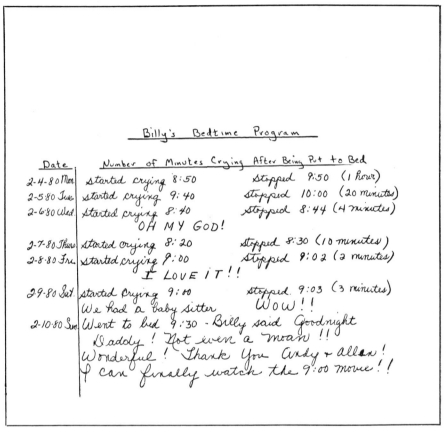

FIGURE 10.1   Example of Data Keeping by parents.

scheduled. These sessions generally include a demonstration of teaching skills in the child's individual program followed by observation of the mother as she works with her child. It is expected that the parent will work with her child on a regular basis at home between contacts with school staff.

Parent training programs provided in conjunction with a center-based program should involve close coordination between home and school. Sandler and Coren (1981) have described a parent training program intended to encourage instruction at home on the same skills worked on at school. Parents participated in a team meeting approximately every six weeks to review and update the short-term objectives included in their child's individual educational program. Following this team meeting, parents observed through a one-way mirror as their child's teacher provided instruction on the new or revised objectives. The parent also had an opportunity to receive feedback from the parent trainer as she herself taught these skills to her child. Educational materials were sent back and forth daily between home and school, as was a home-center data sheet (Fredericks,

Baldwin, & Grove, 1974), which included space for both parent and teacher to record data on each skill being worked on. Parent and teacher also met briefly each week to review child progress (see Figure 10.2). Although this program required a considerable degree of participation, mothers reported high levels of satisfaction with each of its components.

Lovaas and his associates at U.C.L.A. (Lovaas, 1978) have developed a training program for parents of autistic children which requires a large degree of parent involvement. One parent is expected to devote most of the day for a period of at least one year to working with the child. The couple must postpone having additional children and if both parents work one parent must quit his or her job. Program commitments are further spelled out in a legal contract signed by parents. Parents are permitted to miss no more than two clinic visits per month and they must learn to record reliable data within the first month of the program, learn to shape a behavior independently during the second month, and so on. Early in the program new behaviors are trained in the clinic. Parents visit the clinic two to three times per week and then attempt to transfer skills to the home with the assistance of a therapist who works with them at least ten hours per week. After a few months in the program, clinic visits may decrease to only once a week, and the major responsibility for teaching new skills is assumed by the parent; home visits totaling 10 to 20 hours per week continue, with student interns assisting the parent with home programming.

Home Programming and the Family

The family sacrifice involved in implementing a home program as demanding as this has caused Lovaas's program to be seriously questioned (Hemsley et al., 1978; Schopler, 1978). Indeed, a major drawback of most home programs is the time commitment required of parents. As we have seen, for some parents the pressure to provide structured programming at home can be stressful. A mother may not have the time or energy to carry out routine housekeeping chores, adequately meet her own personal needs and the needs of her husband and her other children, and also perform both caretaking and teaching roles with her handicapped child. This is especially true in families in which both parents work. In a follow-up study of a home program involving teaching manuals for parents of mentally retarded children (Baker, 1977) it was found that most home teaching following completion of the program 14 months earlier was incidental (incorporated into daily routines), despite the fact that the program had encouraged more formal training sessions lasting 10 to 20 minutes each, involving repeated trials. The major obstacle to programming by parents was limited time—reported by approximately 75 percent of the mothers. Approximately 25 percent of the mothers cited as obstacles items related to rejection of the role of home teacher; one in five indicated that they found teaching uninteresting or of dubious value (most children in this program were enrolled in full-time school placements).

CHILD'S NAME _____ TEACHER _____

DATE	OBJECTIVE:		OBJECTIVE:		OBJECTIVE:		OBJECTIVE:		OBJECTIVE:		OBJECTIVE:	
	TEACHER	PARENT	TEACHER	PARENT	TEACHER	PARENT	TEACHER	PARENT	TEACHER	PARENT	TEACHER	PARENT

FIGURE 10.2 Example of a Home-centered Program Data Sheet

Alternate Models

We will look next at three program models which are unique because their development was guided by the desire to intervene in such a way that normal family routines and family relationships are supported or enhanced, while at the same time parent-initiated activities are undertaken to maximize child progress. Incorporation of various elements from these programs into a more traditional parent training model may do much to broaden the range of parents a program is able to serve.

The parent/family participation program of the Madison, Wisconsin Metropolitan School District's Early Childhood Program (Branston, Vincent, & Salisbury, 1978) was designed to enable parents to teach their children during daily routines at home, such as mealtime, bathtime, and the like. Advantages cited for this approach are: (1) more parents are able and willing to participate because no extra time commitment is required and (2) acquisition, maintenance, and generalization of skills is facilitated by providing instruction in the natural environment, rather than in a structured teaching situation. The initial step in program implementation involves assessment of the family's daily routine, which is carried out through constructing a grid showing days of the week broken into half-hour intervals, with the activity listed for each interval. Potentially valuable times for home programming include bath time, after dinner, dessert time, traveling in the car, bedtime, and during daily chores such as cooking, dusting, and doing dishes or the laundry (dinner may not be an optimal time because many families use dinner as a time for exchanging information, or "eat on the run"). It is suggested that the initial skill chosen for instruction be a skill the child already demonstrates at school but has not yet generalized to the home environment. Gradually skills that have not yet been accomplished at school or that are unique to the home situation may be selected.

The incidental teaching approach used in the Madison program may be illustrated by examining activities which might be worked on during clean-up time after dinner. Depending upon a child's developmental level, the parent might work on sorting spoons from dirty dishes, sorting big spoons from little spoons, or teaching the child that dirty cups go in the sink and dirty napkins go in the garbage. The program has developed a manual containing ideas for incorporating training into daily activities (Hugdahl et al., 1978), although parents and program staff are encouraged to be creative in developing new home programming ideas.

Parent involvement is often difficult to achieve in low-income families, probably at least in part due to the substantial time and energy requirements involved in simply meeting basic family survival needs in this population. Levenstein's (1970, 1972, 1975) Verbal Interaction Project successfully involved mothers of environmentally at risk two and three year olds in a home program which had as a primary aim achieving input to the child through the mother with the least possible disruption to the child and family. The program involved twice-weekly, half-hour home visits carried out over a two-year period by staff members called

Toy Demonstrators. Each week a different toy or book was brought to the home as a gift for the child, from a set of 24 books and 22 toys sequenced according to increasing complexity. The Toy Demonstrator modeled appropriate verbal interaction utilizing the toy or book, based upon suggestions provided in a handbook illustrating techniques for promoting conceptual development for each stimulus material. The approach was distinctly non-didactic and low-key; after demonstrating during a session, the Toy Demonstrator withdrew into the background, and the mother was free to adopt the modeled behavior or not as she wished. It was suggested to the mothers, but not stressed, that they play and read with their children each day. The program produced sizeable and lasting gains in cognitive growth (see Tjossem, 1976, p. 19). The very non-intrusive nature of this program suggests that a similar approach may promote increased involvement of certain parents.

At the Family Intervention Project affiliated with Georgia State University (Berger & Fowlkes, 1980), intervention is based upon an assessment of both family and child needs. Tasks that promote the handicapped child's development are assigned to family members based upon their abilities, interests, and available time. When appropriate, tasks are assigned in order to help bring about a restructuring of the family system, with the goal of enabling its members to function more effectively as a family unit. For example, the father of a young boy with a motor deficit who has been distant from his son might be assigned motor activities to carry out designed to reduce the child's motor delay and also optimally lead to more pleasurable interactions between father and son. A sibling resentful of the attention given a handicapped infant might be trained to teach fine and gross motor games or self-help skills to the infant. This activity would enhance the sibling's feelings of pride, competence, and importance in the family, while simultaneously facilitating the handicapped infant's development. Other needs dealt with by the Family Intervention Project staff include: (1) supporting family members in being appropriately separate, (2) facilitating "collaboration" with "generational subsystems" (i.e., between husband and wife, or handicapped and nonhandicapped siblings), and (3) helping parents successfully meet the demands of the various family roles they must play (e.g., mother *and* wife).

The Family Intervention Project is especially interesting because it represents a departure from exclusive focus on the mother-child dyad characteristic of most parent training programs. Few additional reports of training programs for other family members have appeared in the literature. Miller and Cantwell (1976) have described procedures used to train siblings to ignore inappropriate behavior exhibited by their emotionally disturbed brother or sister. The siblings had been effectively undoing their parents' efforts to provide behavioral programming by attending to behavior their parents were attempting to ignore. Miller and Cantwell suggest that training sessions for siblings be short and combine didactic teaching with role playing and behavior rehearsal. Adubato, Adams, and Budd (1981) attempted to overcome some of the practical problems inherent in working with fathers. A mother was trained in procedures for improving her severely developmentally delayed son's independent dressing skills, and was then asked to teach these same procedures to her husband. The mother was successful in communicating the procedures to her husband, as indicated by improvement in father-child interaction during structured teaching sessions. This approach appears promising, since without active encouragement of the sort provided by Adubato and colleagues, mothers and fathers may not spontaneously share the knowledge gained by the mother through participation in parent training activities (Sandler, Coren, & Thurman, 1983). Effective intervention at home requires a coordinated effort by all family members. The continued development of approaches involving family members other than the mother is clearly needed.

Other Avenues for Involvement

Fredericks, Baldwin, and Grove (1974) have suggested that in an average center program only about 50 percent of the parents can be expected to actively participate in programming at home; a level greater than 60 percent indicates an extraordinary program. A flexible program offers ways for those parents to become involved who are not interested in participating in a structured parent training program. Both the parents and program may benefit from this involvement.

An excellent example of the variety of areas in which parents may participate is provided in the following list of activities engaged in by parent task forces at the Madison, Wisconsin Early Childhood Program (Branston, Vincent, & Salisbury, 1978):

1. development of a project evaluation questionnaire
2. development of a community resources handbook
3. student files and record keeping
4. current legislation
5. program materials
6. touring visitors
7. an informational parent handbook
8. publicity

Other activities in which parents might engage include fundraising, publication of a school newsletter, equipment maintenance (a good way to involve fathers!) and planning of class trips and events at holiday times (e.g., a visit to Santa Claus, Halloween party, Easter egg hunt, and the like).

Many programs use parents as volunteers in the classroom. This provides extra labor and may allow more individualized programming to occur. Assisting in the classroom also provides an opportunity for parents to learn skills which will help them to work more effectively with their child at home. An effective volunteer program, however, cannot be approached casually. Some guidelines for a successful program include (Fredericks, Baldwin, & Grove, 1974): (a) providing a brief initial training experience, including a description of the program, volunteer responsibilities, and review of some basic teaching principles, followed by practicum experience in which the parent can observe and teach under supervision of a teacher; (b) providing teaching tasks appropriate to a parent's teaching ability through initially having the parent teach in a single area only (e.g., self-help, fine motor, etc.); (c) providing regular feedback regarding performance through observation by supervisory staff; and (d) flexible scheduling so that inevitable missed days will not be overly disruptive to classroom programming.

Regularly scheduled meetings for sharing information, which also allow opportunities for social interaction, are of interest to many parents. A coffee-hour format may be used, with an initial lecture on a relevant topic, followed by refreshments and informal discussion. Topics might include legislative issues, legal issues such as wills and guardianship, resources for financial assistance, interpreting professional reports and understanding professional roles (e.g., neurologist, psychologist, physical and occupational therapist, etc.), and health issues such as child dental care or methods of treating common childhood illnesses. Similar topics might be addressed by speakers at evening parent group meetings, which also provide an opportunity for conducting parent group organizational business.

Involvement in Program Policy Issues

An active parent group can be a valuable training ground for future parent participation in policy decisions affecting their children and can contribute toward the maintenance and continued development of current programs. As consumers and taxpayers, parents have a right to be involved in program policy issues. A program's philosophy will determine whether this involvement is in an advisory capacity only, or whether parents actually participate equally with professionals in the decision making process. Parent input concerning possible program changes contributes to the likelihood that a program will meet actual parent/family needs. With the best of intentions, professionals sometimes make program decisions that are overly influenced by administrative concerns or considerations related to a handicapped child's needs viewed in isolation from the needs of the parents and other family members.

At the Ken-Crest Growth & Development Center (Sandler & Coren, 1981), Parent Group representatives regularly participate in hiring new staff and in reviewing proposed yearly budget submissions to the funding source, including determination of how limited resources will be spent. Vigorous fund-raising efforts have enabled this Parent Group to support center staff positions, including at various times a Parent Trainer, Speech/Language Therapist, and Assistant Teacher. An example of a policy issue in which parent input was especially important is a proposed change from full-day to half-day center programming for severely handicapped three to five year olds. Center professionals felt that the more time a child spent with his or her parents, the greater the rate of child progress would be (a comprehensive parent training program was available in this setting). Parents, however, felt that their children benefited more from the expertise of the center's professionally trained teaching staff, and also felt they needed the respite from child-care responsibilities which a full-day program provided. By obtaining the perspective of parents, program staff gained important insight into the impact of this proposed change on the families they served.

Involvement in Social Policy Issues

Parent groups often are the base from which parents become involved in social policy issues. Right-to-education litigation and passage of P.L. 94–142 have been the result of joint parent-professional efforts. But getting a law "on the books" is not enough—parents must often continue their involvement to make sure laws and court decisions are properly implemented. In the recent Armstrong v. Kline (1979) case, three parents brought a class action suit on behalf of their own severely handicapped children and all other Pennsylvania residents who faced a similar program against the Pennsylvania Department of Education. At issue was the Department of Education's policy of refusal to provide programs to any handicapped child in excess of 180 days—the length of the program provided to nonhandicapped children. It was decided in U.S. District Court, and the decision upheld in the U.S. Third Circuit Court of Appeals (Battle v. Commonwealth, 1980), that blanket use of the "180 day rule" denied the right of certain children to receive an appropriate educational program as guaranteed under P.L. 94–142.

Lobbying efforts by parents are often helpful in preventing planned cuts in funding, or in seeking increases in funding levels required to provide adequate programming. Few states currently mandate educational services for handicapped children from birth through age five; this is an area of particular priority for continued parent/professional lobbying efforts. Although their children may be very young, parents of handicapped, preschool children should be encouraged to support advocacy efforts on behalf of expanded services for school-aged and adult handicapped persons. They should be encouraged to view their parental role as encompassing advocacy on behalf of their child throughout the child's life span (Cartwright, 1981).

Involvement in the
Educational Planning Process

Team meetings to update a child's program provide professional staff at the preschool level with an opportunity to instill in parents a sense of their importance as collaborators in the development of an appropriate program for their child. Because programs for school-aged children rarely encourage the degree of parent involvement typically present in programs for preschool, handicapped children, experiences at the preschool level are especially important if parents are to assume an active role in the educational team planning process throughout their child's school career. Some suggested strategies for eliciting active parent participation include (Turnbull, Strickland, & Goldstein, 1978): (a) model question-asking and the statement of diverse opinions at the team meeting; (b) directing questions to parents; (c) verbally reinforcing parent responses; and (d) eliciting from parents any special concerns related to their child's program. Turnbull, Strickland, and Goldstein also suggest that *parents* be encouraged to (a) engage in active decision-making strategies such as initiating questions and asking for clarification of unclear issues; (b) be persistent in getting answers to questions; and (c) state any special concerns, and be sure these concerns are considered carefully by the other team members. Assigning one team member the role of parent advocate, with responsibility for directing questions to parents, verbally reinforcing their contribution, and so on may be an effective strategy for facilitating active parent participation (Goldstein & Turnbull, 1982). The conflict of interest inherent in school personnel assuming an advocacy role, however, limits the feasibility of this model in the event of a difference of opinion regarding needed services.

If parents themselves are to advocate for their children, they must be knowledgeable concerning their child's educational needs, understand state and federal laws related to the provision of special education and related services, and also be *assertive*! The last of these three ingredients for effective advocacy may be the most difficult to develop in parents. Sandler and McNulty (1979) described an advocacy training program for parents of handicapped preschool children about to enter school-aged programs. The program included the viewing of a set of videotaped sequences involving modeled interactions between assertive parents and school district personnel. An excellent resource for those interested in training parents to be more assertive is the handbook *How To Get Services by Being Assertive* (Jardis et al., 1980). Following are some typical nonassertive statements and their assertive counterpart taken from this guide:

NON-ASSERTIVE STATEMENT	*ASSERTIVE STATEMENT*
"My child needs services, but I don't want to push too much. They'll think I'm a trouble maker."	"If they think I'm pushing because I keep asking about services—then I'll have the kind of reputation that brings action."
"I don't think this program is right for my child—but it's better than nothing."	"I don't think this program is right for my child. And I will not accept a program that is not appropriate."
"If I stick my neck out and rock the boat . . . they'll take it out on my child."	"I'm willing to stick my neck out to get the services my child needs. And I won't allow anyone to punish me or my child for doing what's right."

"Our School District has such financial problems, I can't possibly ask for the services my child needs. They'll say 'no' for sure."

"Our School District has severe financial problems but I intend to ask for the services my child needs which he has the right to by law. He'll never get services if I don't. And the schools will never get the money they need if I don't insist."

In periods of dwindling public resources, it is especially important that parents be assertive in seeking services for their children. It is only through the combined advocacy efforts of parents and professionals that present programs will be maintained and expanded services put into place.

SUMMARY AND CONCLUSIONS

This chapter has reviewed the emotional feelings of family members when a young, disabled child is present in the home. Family members often cope with guilt, anger, and psychological stress. At the same time, families must be concerned with acquiring the services their young, disabled child requires.

Several means by which parents can become involved with programs for their children are discussed. In addition, the chapter describes some parent training programs.

Since the family is one of the main ecological systems to include special needs young children, it is important to analyze how congruence can be effectively established. Many of the programs and techniques discussed in this chapter should be useful to that end.

MAJOR PROGRAM APPROACHES

four

Preschool Models for Young Special Needs Children

1. What are the major differences in Anastasiow's classification scheme as compared with Beller's classification scheme?
2. What are the features common to early intervention programs for disabled children?
3. Do those programs that depend on parents seem to be mindful of the issues discussed in Chapter 10?
4. What features would you want to be sure to include in an early intervention program which you were planning?

As far back as ancient times human society has had a commitment to educate and protect its children. This is the way the mores and values of a culture are passed from generation to generation. It is through education that socialization and acculturation of individuals takes place; that is, individuals come to understand the rules and limits of the culture in which they live. While very early socialization usually takes place in families, there have always been young children whose families were unable to care for them. In such cases alternatives to natural families, such as orphanages and foster homes, have been provided. While the quality of these placements have varied greatly they have continued to exist because "the [perceived] role of adult society, be that parent or homes for children, has been considered to be one of protection . . . carrying out elementary socialization tasks related to biological needs of the infant" (Beller, 1979, p. 852) and young child.

In the last 75 to 100 years society has seen significant shifts in the roles of women. More women are expressing their independence, working out of the home, or pursuing more education. As a result, their traditional role in the basic socialization process has shifted. Because of the changes in the nuclear family brought about by the economic and moral necessities of women leaving the home, alternative socialization structures have a major influence on infants and young children. These structures have recently taken form as day centers, kindergartens, and preschool education programs. All have grown out of society's historical commitment to provide socialization experiences to young children.

Early childhood programs had their beginnings in the theories of Montessori and Freud and later drew empirical support from authors like Spitz (1945) and Goldfarb (1943). It was in the 1960s, however, that early childhood education really blossomed. The forceful theoretical writings of Hunt (1961, 1964) and Bloom (1964) provided impetus for changes. The new social consciousness and the resulting governmental funding of preschool programs provided a major thrust for the development and maintenance of preschool programs. The establishment of Head Start in 1965 epitomizes the trend which began in the 1960s.

Preschool programs initially were developed to reach populations deemed "culturally deprived" or, more precisely, those subject to poverty or having lower socio-economic status. The rationale for prototypic programs like Head Start and Demonstration and Research Center for Early Education (DARCEE) (Klaus & Gray, 1968) was that the deleterious effects of poverty in the preschool years could be prevented and/or remediated by effective, intensive, preschool programming. This belief was important in shifting the emphasis of preschool and infant programs from one of custodially oriented caretaking to one of programming for developmental change.

Preschool education can minimize the effects of risk and lead to fewer manifestations of handicap in later years. This rationale was strong enough to lead to the establishment of the Early Childhood Assistance Program of the Bureau of Education for the Handicapped (BEH) in 1968. This program provided funds for the development of model preschool programs for handicapped children. From this mandate the Handicapped Children's Early Education Programs (HCEEP) was born and special education for the preschool age child began to flourish. HCEEP led to the development of a number of prototypic models for providing educational services to handicapped children birth to six years of age. In addition, the Program provided a means for disseminating critical aspects of these prototypic models to other sites. Throughout the early and mid-1970s HCEEP was a major source of support for innovated program development for preschool, handicapped children, and in 1979, 86 percent of the 24 originally funded programs were still operational (DeWeerd, 1980). Several Titles (e.g., I and II) of the Elementary and Secondary Education Act (ESEA) also had provision for funding preschool programs for handicapped children. These funds, however, were distributed and monitored through State Education Agencies and generally did not have as significant an impact as HCEEP. This is not to say that some innovative and worthwhile programs were not developed via ESEA provisions. Rather because of the linking of these funds to State Education Agencies, visibility and dissemination of programs was quite often not as great as of those funded through HCEEP. Some early childhood programs for handicapped children were also funded in the 1970s through the Social Security Act and its Amendments. Initially this funding was provided via Title IV-A and then later through Title XX. Many local programs were supported through these Titles, which were distributed and monitored through State Welfare programs. These funds were often critical in establishing and maintaining local social welfare programs and so led to the provision of educational programs for handicapped preschool children within the broader context of social services provision to low income populations. Title IV-A and Title XX funds were also often important in providing ongoing program support after programs had completed their funding cycles through HCEEP—whose funds were strictly for model development, *not* long term program maintenance. HCEEP now operates as part of the Office of Special Education and Rehabilitation Services in the Department of Education.

Starting in the late 1970s a new form of funding for preschool programs for handicapped children appeared. This funding stream was made possible through Public Law 94–142, the Education for All Handicapped Children Act passed in 1975. This legislation and the appropriation that followed it made funding available to local districts to provide programs for preschool, handicapped children. P.L. 94–142 create a means by which local school districts can receive an incentive of $300 per child per year for every preschool, handicapped child served. They receive this $300 in addition to the funding they would receive for any handicapped child. In December 1983 with the passage of P.L. 98-199 (The Education of the Handicapped Act Amendments of 1983) preschool incentive funds can now be used to support programs for handicapped children down to birth. In addition, these amendments make grants available to states to develop and implement comprehensive plans to provide early childhood education to all handicapped children from birth to five years of age. More and more local school districts are developing services for preschool, handicapped children as a result of these incentive grants. In addition, several states have statutes requiring that educational services be provided to handicapped infants from birth. Generally, however, the preschool, handicapped population is underserved and poorly defined (Lessen & Rose, 1980). New federal priorities in this area should begin to eliminate this problem.

As a result of the impetus provided by these various funding sources, many programs for preschool, handicapped children have been developed throughout the country. The remainder of this chapter is devoted to a discussion of the major models for preschool education of handicapped children which have emerged as a result of these program development efforts of the last decade and a half. In addition, some major programs for preschool, handicapped children will be described.

MODELS OF PRESCHOOL EDUCATION

Beller (1979) recently described several models of preschool education. While these models are discussed in terms of early intervention programs designed primarily to serve children from lower socio-economic groups, they are generally applicable to handicapped or other high-risk young children.

Beller (1979) provides a categorization based upon the service delivery strategy employed by various programs. Service delivery models are home-based or center-based and parent-oriented or child-oriented. *Home-based* programs provide services in the homes of individual clients, whereas *center-based* programs provide services primarily in some central location like a church or school. *Parent-oriented* programs give parents skills to more effectively facilitate the development of their children. That is, these programs see parents as the major agents for intervention. Professional staff provide training and support to parents. *Child-oriented* programs, on the other hand, emphasize direct intervention with the child. In general, home-based programs tend to be parent-oriented, although this does not necessarily have to be the case. At least one child-oriented, home-based program has been described by Schaefer and Aaronson (1972). They relate how tutors were sent into the home to facilitate the cognitive development of infants from lower income families.

Beller (1979) suggested that home-based infant programs are equally effective to center-based programs. The choice of service delivery model, then, may not be based as much on empirical verification as it is on practical constraints like geography, costs, and philosophical orientation toward parental involvement in infant and preschool programs. For example, the Portage Project (Shearer & Shearer, 1976) used a home-based approach because geography prevented transporting children to a central location. Home-based models often have additional flexibility and have the advantage of providing children with intervention in their natural environments. On the other hand, home-based programs often put additional stress on parents, especially mothers, because they do not provide a means for them to have a respite from their children. In addition, parent-oriented programs, especially home-based ones, put a good deal of added responsibility for successful intervention onto parents. While proper support can reduce the degree of parent failure, when parents do fail to effectively intervene they may feel guilty and inadequate. A number of programs have begun to incorporate both home-based and center-based activities, minimizing the weaknesses of both approaches while maximizing their strengths.

Like Beller (1979), Anastasiow (1978) has taken a broad categorical approach to the classification of preschool models. Anastasiow's conceptualization differs from Beller's in two significant aspects. First, it is clearly directed to programs which may include handicapped, preschool children and, second, and perhaps more importantly, it provides a basis for categorization based upon the theoretical and conceptual basis of programming rather than the service delivery structure. Anastasiow describes four basic preschool models, namely the behavioral, normal developmental, cognitive developmental, and cognitive learning models. A brief description of each model follows.

BEHAVIORAL MODEL   The behavioral model is based in large part on the work of Skinner and his followers (e.g., Bijou & Baer, 1961; Bijou, 1966). Thus, it suggests an intervention strategy based on the manipulation of environmental contingencies. Desired behavior is reinforced and undesired behavior is extinguished (ignored) or in some cases punished. This model views the child as a passive learner whose dignity is dependent upon overt manipulation of the environment by the teacher or interventionist. As Anastasiow (1978) points out, the model has its greatest usefulness with children exhibiting severe behavior problems or very significant delays in development.

NORMAL DEVELOPMENTAL MODEL   This model finds its basis on a belief in the natural unfolding of development. The model is guided by maturational sequences like those delineated by Gesell (1940). This model provided the impetus for maturational preschools—which provided the environments for children to be nurtured sufficiently that their development would unfold as a matter of course. In the normal developmental model, the child is seen as naturally active and engaging the environment. The teacher's role is to provide a nurturant environment full of learning opportunities. The teacher provides guidance and the child learns and develops as a result of her maturational readiness to do so. There is heavy emphasis on group instruction and socialization.

Since this model is based upon a belief in the natural ontogenesis of development, it is, in a sense, antithetical to the early education of high risk or handicapped, preschool children. These children, by definition, are displaying developmental patterns noticeably different from the norm. Consequently a normal developmental model is not likely to be effective with them, unless the teacher is willing to individualize his instructional approach. In fact, Anastasiow (1978, p. 102) "believe[s] that the failure of the normal developmental model to provide for individual differences is what led parents of impaired children to set up their own schools and experiment with ways to facilitate impaired children's learning."

COGNITIVE DEVELOPMENTAL MODEL   The cognitive developmental model gets its support from Piaget and in some respects parallels the normal developmental model. As was discussed in Chapter 3, Piaget's theory suggests a relatively fixed unfolding of cognitive structures as the child gets older. These structures unfold because of the child's active seeking of information from the environment. As with the normal developmental model, the teacher becomes a facilitator whose role it is to arrange the environment to assure that the child has the experiences necessary for cognitive growth to take place. Where the normal developmental model is more concerned with socialization and conformity, the cognitive developmental model emphasizes cognitive growth. Knowledge of the social world is believed to come about through the development and application of existing cognitive structures. This model is applicable to children with delays in development to the extent that the teacher provides experiences novel enough to the child to stimulate curiosity and application of existing cognitive structures to the environment. It is only through further assimilative and accommodative processes that development occurs.

COGNITIVE LEARNING MODEL   Anastasiow (1978) credits the Brickers (1974, 1976) with the development of what he has termed the cognitive learning model. Anastasiow chooses this name "because the Brickers integrate the utilization of operant procedures for lesson strategies and remediation while drawing upon cognitive, psycholinguistic, and perceptual theories to diagnose the child's level of development and to plan intervention programs" (p. 105). With significantly delayed children, it may first be necessary to teach exploratory strategies to facilitate further development. At the same time, the child can be taught specific cognitive skills using contingency management. These skills are the basis for the development of more complex cognitive abilities. Thus, in a sense the child begins as a passive learner as in the behavioral model but is transformed into an active mode both by structuring the necessary contingencies into the environment and by providing small instructional steps leading to more complex cognitive abilities. A strict Piagetian viewpoint (e.g., Duckworth, 1979) would question whether such a strategy could be employed. Rather, Duckworth might suggest that such instruction will not benefit the child if she is not ready (cognitively) for it or that such instruction will come too late as the child had already begun to exhibit cognitive skills in the developmental sequence without any formal instruction. Programs like those of the Brickers (1974, 1976) and others (e.g., Robinson & Robinson, 1978) are accumulating data that attest to the success of this approach.

A Synthesis

Since the categorizations presented by Beller (1979) and Anastasiow (1978) address different dimensions of preschool models, they can be combined into a single classification. Such a classification system is useful for comparing preschool programs for handicapped children. The two systems when combined provide a framework for categorizing both the service delivery strategy (i.e., Beller's system) and the conceptual base (i.e., Anastasiow's system). Of course, like any classification scheme, there is not total mutual exclusiveness between categories within a given dimension. For example, a program could employ both home-based programming and center-based programming on a cognitive developmental and normal developmental conceptual base. Figure 11.1 presents a matrix which intersects Beller's categories with Anastasiow's. This matrix provides the basis for analyzing programs as to both their service delivery model as well as their conceptual base. It not only provides a framework from which to view the program description which follows, but it also should be useful to anyone who must spend time assessing various preschool programs for handicapped children.

SOME ILLUSTRATIVE PROGRAMS

This section is devoted to descriptions of various infant and preschool programs for handicapped children. These programs are chosen for illustrative purposes and are meant to provide the reader with an overview not an exhaustive look.

Service Delivery Mode (Beller)

	Home-based Child Oriented	Home-based Parent Oriented	Center-based Child Oriented	Center-based Parent Oriented
Behavioral				
Normal Developmental				
Cognitive Developmental				
Cognitive Learning				

Conceptual Base (Anastasiow)

FIGURE 11.1   A Matrix for Analyzing Preschool Programs for Handicapped Children

The programs described include home-based and center-based programs which are either child-oriented or parent-oriented. They cut across various conceptual models and they serve a variety of handicapped children. Each program will be described in terms of its conceptual/theoretical orientation; population; program goals; general program activities; assessment strategies; and relative strengths and weaknesses. Basically, programs will be categorized as center-based or home-based, however, the reader should easily see where the programs fit according to the preschool analysis matrix presented in Figure 11.1.

Center-Based Programs

THE INFANT, TODDLER, AND PRE-SCHOOL RESEARCH AND INTERVENTION PROGRAMS   The Infant, Toddler and Pre-school Research and Intervention Program (Bricker & Bricker, 1971, 1972, 1973, 1976) began as a model program based at George Peabody College in Nashville, Tennessee in 1970. As was suggested earlier, the program employed a cognitive learning model by incorporating developmental theories with operant technology. The program was designed originally to serve toddler age children (18 to 36 months) and was later expanded to serve children from birth to five years. The program spread "its service base across the pre-school development range, across the economic continuum from poverty to affluence, and across a broad range of ethnic backgrounds" (Bricker & Bricker, 1976, p. 546). The program included children whose developmental progress was within normal limits as well as those who had identifiable delays in development (e.g., Down's syndrome, autistic-like behavior, or brain damage). Approximately 25 percent of the children served were "normal," 25 percent were "normal" but "at risk" and the remaining 50 percent were noticeably delayed in development.

Bricker and Bricker (1976) identified the following goals for the infant component of their programs: "1) the creation of individual programs to develop the child's competencies in the areas of gross motor skills, fine motor skills, sensorimotor, self-help, and social skills; 2) the operationalization and empirical validation of such Piagetian concepts as causality, means-end, object permanence, imitation and functional usage; 3) the development of a library of video tapes of infant behavior to be used for research, teaching, and parent training; and 4) the provision for each child to develop certain prerequisite forms of behavior necessary for adaptive functioning in the toddler unit" (p. 560). Activities for each infant were very flexible and individualized to meet her needs.

Goals for the toddler unit included: "1) daily group or individual language training, 2) individually programmed gross and fine motor activities, 3) the opportunity to engage in self-directed activities, 4) a consistent environment established and maintained through the application of contingency management techniques, 5) opportunities to develop appropriate cognitive skills such as labeling, problem solving, and concept formation, and 6) adaptive skills necessary for entrance into the pre-school unit" (Bricker & Bricker, 1976, p. 561). The day's activities typically consisted of opening group time, individual and small group programming and skill building, free play, gym, snack, and closing activities.

The goals for the preschool unit in large measure represented an upward extension of the goals of the infant and toddler units. Like the earlier goals, they reflect a cognitive learning model. These goals included: "1) to develop preoperational cognitive skills, 2) to develop further and refine more difficult self-help skills, 3) to develop increasingly independent behavior without teacher supervision or continuous reinforcement, 4) to correctly formulate three-word phrases, and 5) to develop certain prerequisite or useful early elementary education skills" (Bricker & Bricker, 1976, p. 562). Daily activities were similar to those of the toddler unit with more stress being placed on language and concept training as well as more independence on the part of the children.

Although this program was essentially child-oriented, a heavy emphasis was placed on parental involvement. Parents were asked to participate in their

child's classroom at least once a week. At the same time, project staff were expected to provide parent training and generally support parents through counseling and advocacy in acquiring additional services outside the project (e.g.,
medical services, welfare services, and the like).

Assessment strategies employed a number of informal classroom measurement systems like precision teaching (Kunzelmann, 1970). Through such systems, instruction and assessment become an ongoing and interrelated process.
In addition, more standardized means of assessment such as the Bayley Scales of
Infant Development (Bayley, 1969) or the Cattell Infant Intelligence Scale (Cattell, 1960) were used.

The strengths of the Brickers' (1976) project include its application of services
to both handicapped and nonhandicapped children, a practice whose rationale
has been well documented (Guralnick, 1978) from social-ethical, legal-legisla-
tive and psychological-educational points of view (Bricker, 1978). The ability to
provide individualized programming with the cognitive learning model adds to
its efficiency in serving both handicapped and nonhandicapped children by
making it "most adaptable to environmental changes required to successfully
integrate" (Anastasiow, 1978, p. 108) these children.

Another strength of the program is the level of support provided for parents.
Parents not only receive training designed to enhance their understanding of
their child and his development, but they also learn skills which help them further facilitate their child's education and training in the home. In addition, families received emotional support through counseling, referral, and advocacy
services.

One obvious weakness is the program's rather loosely defined evaluation
strategy. No evaluation design is reported by the Brickers which would substantiate the benefits of the program for both handicapped and nonhandicapped
children. In essence, the standardized measure employed documented that the
normal children's development "was progressing as expected or better with no
regression effects noted (Bricker & Bricker, 1971, 1972)" (Bricker, 1978, p. 20)
although no data indicate that the development of the nonhandicapped children's education was in any way facilitated.

Another weakness of this model is its highly idealized nature. Since this program was affiliated with a university complex, high levels of expertise and student participation created a situation that cannot be replicated in the "real
world" service delivery system. While this high level of resources was probably
quite beneficial for the children being served, it also reduced the replicability of
the program in non-university settings.

One further note of caution concerning the Brickers' program seems in order.
Although it is theoretically adaptable to diverse populations of young children as
suggested above, some data suggest that the delayed children and the non-
delayed children in this program were, perhaps, not as well integrated as an initial perusal of the program would lead one to believe (cf., Ray, 1974a; and Porter
et al., 1978).

THE DOWN'S SYNDROME PROGRAM   The Down's Syndrome Program at the University of Washington's Experimental Education Unit has been described by Hayden and Dmitriev (1975) and Hayden and Haring (1976). Hayden and Dmitriev (1975) state that the program is concerned with bringing the Down's syndrome child's development as close to normal as possible. Thus, "the children's progress [is measured] in relation to established developmental norms for *normal* children the same age, on precisely the same activities and learned tasks" (p. 194). This program then approximates what Anastasiow (1978) has termed a normal developmental model, although like the Brickers (1976), Hayden and Dmitriev (1975) do report some dependence on task analysis and reinforcement contingencies to facilitate learning.

The program was designed to serve Down's syndrome children exclusively and included children from birth to six years of age. Children were subdivided into four age groupings resulting in an Infant Class (children 5 weeks to 18 months); an Early Pre-school Class (18 months to 3 years); an Advanced Pre-school (3 to 5 years); and a Kindergarten (4-1/2 to 6 years). The Infant Class met once a week and provided "30 minutes of individualized training in early motor sensory development" (Hayden & Dmitriev, 1975, p. 199) with the parent(s) and infant together. The other classes met four days a week, two hours a day.

All four classrooms in the program had the following common goals relating to children:

1. to increase the rate of sensory, vocal, and motor development of Down's syndrome children to more nearly approximate the sequential development of normal children
2. to increase the subsequent rate of pre-academic, academic, and social performance of these children with the goal of including them in regular and special education programs in the schools
3. to involve parents in full participation and full cooperation with the intervention team in the training of their children
4. to promote full cooperation of educators and child peers in accepting these children in school and community programs
5. to record continuous measurement data on the children's progress and to base all decisions and teaching activities on such data (Hayden & Dmitriev, 1975, p. 195)

Activities for the infant program were highly individualized and involved parents. Training goals were developed individually for infants based on the Denver Developmental Screening Test (Frankenburg & Dodds, 1969) and on the norms provided by Gesell and Amatruda (1969) (Hayden & Haring, 1976). Specific training activities were then developed based on the goals for each infant.

In the early preschool class, activities are designed to enhance fine and gross motor skills, self-help skills, individual concept learning, and social interaction. Children are given exercises to aid development of standing and walking. In addition, manipulative and creative materials like crayons, dolls, and puzzles are made available. Concept development is facilitated through one-to-one instruction and all children are trained in toileting and hand washing when ready. Daily activities also include: an opening routine, snack time (used for developing eating and communication skills), story time, and music and departure routine. Activities in the advanced preschool class are similar to those in the early preschool class but are designed to deal with more complex developmental skills.

In the kindergarten class activities continue to stress self-help and motor development, however, there is an added emphasis on cognitive development. Children are exposed to calendars, seasons, and holidays. They are also given instruction in academics including sight words, basic number concepts, letter recognition, simple printing (e.g., their names), and phonics. Finally, it should be mentioned that parents are involved in all phases of the program from the time their child is enrolled until he is placed elsewhere.

Besides individualized continuous data systems, the program has used standardized tests of development. These have included the Denver Developmental Screening Test and Gesell norms for infants, and the Peabody Picture Vocabulary Test (PPVT) (Dunn, 1959) for preschool and kindergarten children. The PPVT was administered once a year and used because it "enables children with low verbal skills to demonstrate their receptive and associative capabilities without penalizing them for their verbal deficits" (Hayden & Haring, 1976, p. 595).

The greatest strength of this program is the commitment of the staff to approximate normal development in Down's syndrome children. Many children in this program have made significant developmental progress which probably would not have occurred without the existing program orientation toward normal development. The success of the Down's Syndrome Program has done a great deal toward modifying the expectations of both parents and professionals as to the developmental potentials of Down's syndrome children. This success has been so far-reaching that the program has been replicated in Australia (De-Weerd, 1980).

The program also has a strength in its overriding concern with parental involvement. Parents are critical members of the program's team. They are viewed as "powerful educators [who require] training, encouragement, and acknowledgement of [their] contribution to their child's development" (Hayden & Haring, 1976, p. 589).

THE MILWAUKEE PROJECT   One of the best known preschool projects for high-risk children is described by Heber and Garber (1975). Beller (1979) characterized this program as being equally oriented to the child and the parent. The program is based on the prediction that certain children will exhibit characteristics associated with cultural-familial mental retardation if significant changes are not made in their life situations in their first six years. *Cultural-familial retardation* is associated most often with children from lower socio-economic families who show no biological or organic basis for displaying mental retardation. In addition, one or more of their family members is classified as mentally retarded.

People who are cultural-familially retarded typically fall within the mild to moderate range of retardation exhibiting IQ scores between 50 and 75 (see Table 3.4).

Because of the belief that cultural-familial retardation results largely from environmental factors, Heber and Garber (1975) set up selection criteria which were based on family characteristics for the infants to be included in their program. Infants were selected from low SES, black families in which the mother's measured IQ scores on the Wechsler Adult Intelligence Scale (Wechsler, 1955) was 75 or less. Thus, these mothers themselves could be classified as exhibiting cultural-familial retardation. Families selected were assigned to either an experimental or a control group.

The program which was implemented was a "family intervention program which was designed to modify adverse factors in the environments of the experimental infants. The objective was to provide the kind of learning opportunities that facilitate the acquisition of cognitive skills" (Heber & Garber, 1975, p. 406). To meet this goal, two parallel intervention programs were developed. One, directed to mothers, had as its purpose to provide them with better vocational, homemaking, and child rearing skills. The other, directed to infants, was designed to facilitate the development of cognitive, language, and social abilities. The program was designed to start in infancy and continue to the time that the children entered first grade. While general goals were the same for each child, programs were individualized "to maximize the effects of the educational experiences for each child" (Heber & Garber, 1975, p. 408). During infancy, babies were assigned to one primary caretaker during program hours. This practice assured a secure environment for each infant and provided for one-to-one programming.

During the preschool years the program stressed a combination of small group learning and individual child directed activities. Most activities were geared toward cognitive and language development. Language was taught through the use of the Peabody Language Development Kit and "each child participated in informal reading, science, music, and art activities" (Heber & Garber, 1975, p. 413). Each child was assessed every two weeks using the goals in the curriculum sequence.

Both experimental and control children were assessed periodically in physical development, language development, and measured intelligence. In addition, the mother-child interaction of each family was assessed through observation. Physical development was assessed by periodic medical examinations. These assessments showed no overall differences in the experimental and control groups relative to height, weight, or abnormal birth conditions.

The Gesell Developmental Schedule revealed the first significant differences in language development at 18 months. These differences in favor of the experimental groups were manifested from that point on. Analysis of language samples also revealed differences between experimental and control children in amount of conversation and lexical growth. Articulation was better in the experimental group as was grammatical comprehension. All children were given the Illinois Test of Psycholinguistic Abilities (ITPA) (Kirk, McCarthy, & Kirk, 1968) at 54 months of age. The control group was one-and-a-half years behind the experimental group in psycholinguistic development.

Periodic measurement of intelligence using standardized tests like the Cattell (Cattell, 1960), Stanford-Binet (Terman & Merrill, 1973), and the Wechsler Preschool and Primary Scale of Intelligence (Wechsler, 1967) yielded differences in IQ in the magnitude of 20 to 30 points between 24 and 66 months of age. "Thus, the performance [of these children] on standardized tests of measured intelligence indicates a remarkable intellectual development on the part of Experimental subjects who have been exposed to the infant stimulation program" (Heber & Garber, 1975, p. 429). This statement assumes, of course, that IQ tests are valid measures of intellectual development and not just measures of learning outcomes.

The Milwaukee Project has a strong conceptual base, recognizing the need for family-based intervention. The project drew its strength from improving the performance and competence of both children and their parents. Although the theory of such an approach can hardly be disputed, at least one critic, Page (1975), has questioned the validity of Heber's results. Page suggests that there were significant sampling errors resulting in non-equivalence of the experimental and control groups. He further contends that measurements may have biased through children's specific skills measured by the IQ tests employed. He further points out the lack of clarity in describing the intervention program and the curriculum employed. Heber, however, has since indicated where this information is available (see Heber & Garber, 1975, footnote p. 409). To our knowledge, the Milwaukee Project has not been widely replicated. Perhaps through such replications the ultimate effectiveness of this conceptually sound model can be elucidated.

THE YPSILANTI HIGH SCOPE PROGRAM   The Ypsilanti High Scope Program had its origins in the early 1960s and was initiated by Weikart and his associates as the Ypsilanti Perry Pre-school Project and was designed "as a long-term effort to assist educationally disadvantaged Negro children in developing the concepts and abilities necessary for academic success in the public schools" (Weikart et al., 1971, p. 1). The program used a cognitive developmental model based on Piaget's theory. Several excellent accounts of Piagetian based curricula have been formulated (e.g. Weikart et al., 1971; Weikart, 1974; Kamii, 1972) and the interested reader is referred to these sources for more detailed information. More recently, Ispa and Matz (1978) described how handicapped children have been integrated into a preschool program employing the High Scope curriculum.

Classrooms were set up with 2 teachers and 15 children, 10 of whom were nonhandicapped and 5 of whom were handicapped. The handicapped had a variety of difficulties including heart defects, hemiplegia, spine curvature, language delay, Down's syndrome, and partial hearing loss.

Daily activities allowed children to plan and execute their own activities. During planning time each child planned activities to do during work time. In the work time that followed, children carried out their plan "with the support and assistance of adults and peers [they] actively pursue[d] the ideas, activities, and projects they [had] planned for at planning time" (Ispa & Matz, 1978, p. 169). Work time was followed by snack and small group activity. Children were also given an outdoor activity designed to include large motor activities when possible. The last activity of the day was circle time, which typically included songs and musical games. Because the Cognitively Oriented Curriculum is universalistic, Ispa and Matz (1978, p. 171) believe it can be adapted with equal success to both handicapped and nonhandicapped children. They state that "because each child works at activities that are developmentally appropriate, he or she has the opportunity to grow and experience success without infringing on the needs of other children for a faster (or slower) pace or for an activity that is more personally interesting" (p. 171).

To assess the effects of integrating handicapped and nonhandicapped preschool children Ispa and Matz (1978) developed an observation scheme for assessing naturally occurring interactions. Each child was observed for a total of 48 minutes divided into four 12 minute observations. Observations were carried out during work time only "and only when at least two handicapped children were present" (Ispa & Matz, 1978, p. 175). Analysis of the data collected by these procedures indicated that the handicapped children less frequently: (1) conversed with peers, (2) verbally expressed pride to peers, and (3) gave and showed materials to peers. In addition Ispa and Matz (1978) report that the observed and expected number of times children interacted with disabled and nondisabled children were similar. Thus, they conclude that the children are socially integrated. These results, while somewhat different than those of Ray (1974a), Porter and colleagues (1978), Guralnick (1976), and Devoney, Guralnick, and Rubin (1974), may be accounted for by differences in the populations studied and by the ratio of handicapped to nonhandicapped children. Finally, it is also possible that the dependent variables accounted for these differences. As Guralnick (1980) suggested, all of these factors may be important in determining the degree of social integration between handicapped and nonhandicapped preschool children in the same classroom.

Ispa and Matz report the use of the McCarthy Scales of Children's Abilities (McCarthy, 1970) as means of assessing developmental progress in the children. Children were pretested and posttested with this scale. The handicapped and nonhandicapped children made equivalent gains on all areas of the McCarthy except for the motor areas. Ispa and Matz (1978) account for this result by the physical disabilities of some children which may have made it "unreasonable to expect progress analogous to that of non-handicapped children [in the motor area]" (p. 187).

Ispa and Matz (1978) presented an effective model of educating relatively mildly handicapped preschool children. That social integration seems to have occurred is of particular interest and supports the effectiveness of child-directed programs for both handicapped and nonhandicapped preschool children.

If parents were involved either in classroom programming or in counseling or training sessions, Ispa and Matz fail to mention it in their report. Weikart and colleagues point to the importance of home visits in the implementation of the High Scope Model. It is reasonable to conclude that Ispa and Matz chose to stress the effects of classroom activities on social integration rather than to deal with parent components. The role of parents in the program (assuming there was one) may have in part contributed to the program's apparent success. Ispa and Matz therefore would have been well advised to make some mention of parental involvement.

THE MAMA LERE HOME   The Mama Lere Home has been described by Horton (1976) as having been planned "to give parents of hearing impaired infants immediate and continuing help in developing their child's ability to develop spoken language in that period before formal educational experiences begin" (p. 374). The program was designed to serve children from birth to three years with a parent oriented training experience. Specifically the program's objectives were "1) to provide a parent-oriented program appropriate to the needs of the very young child in which skills basic to the attainment of language may be practiced on an extensive basis in the child's home and 2) through intensive audiological management to take early advantage of his hearing potential by use of wearable amplification so that all possible assistance is given through the auditory channel" (Horton, 1976, p. 374).

This program clearly views the parents as the primary agent of change. This orientation is quite evident from the major goals of the program. These include "1) to teach parents to optimize the auditory environment for their child, 2) to teach parents how to talk to their child, 3) to familiarize parents with the principle stages and sequence of normal language development and to apply this frame of reference in stimulating their child, 4) to teach parents the strategies of behavior management, and 5) to supply affective support to aid the family in coping with their feelings about their child and the stresses that a handicapped child places on the integrity of the family" (Horton, 1976, p. 375).

This program was based in a "teaching house," where teacher, parent(s), and infant interacted during the day in a home-like environment. Parents then stayed with the child during evening hours in the house. The length of stay varied from several days to a week or more. The teacher-parent interaction is informal in nature and "the teacher spends a great deal of time during each session working in the kitchen as the mother would at home or sitting on the floor with the child, while the parents are led to join in these activities" (Horton, 1976, p. 374). All of these activities are designed to increase parents' skills and awareness of their hearing impaired infant. The teacher acts as a role model for the parents, especially the mother, by engaging in routine activities of daily living with the child as the mother would, *but* she stresses the use of language and "demonstrates that every such activity offers a vehicle for communication" (Horton, 1976, p. 375). Because a basically oral-aural approach to educating hearing impaired children is used in the Mama Lere Program, much heavier emphasis is placed on sound stimulation than on visual stimulation.

Unfortunately, Horton (1976) fails to mention any ongoing assessment of children in the program (save audiological examination). Nor does she give any indication that parents' acquisition of the skills being taught is measured in any way. This lack of information, which we hope does not represent a lack of practice, makes it difficult to assess the effectiveness of the Mama Lere Program. Horton (1976) does report some preliminary results of a study by Liff (1973) which indicate increased language competence in children who were in the Mama Lere Program as compared with ones who were not. Unfortunately, these comparison groups had only six children each, greatly limiting the meaningfulness of Liff's results. In essence then, while Horton (1976) suggests "there is a 'new breed' of deaf child emerging from these efforts" (p. 376) she presents little in the way of empirical data to substantiate this claim.

This program is center-based and parent-oriented. While the approach as described has a strong conceptual base, one must ask the question whether a home-based approach based on the same conceptual assumptions would not be just as effective. While it is true that children coming to the Mama Lere Home could get supportive audiological and speech services, it is also likely that the unfamiliar environment of the Mama Lere Home interfered with the typical patterns of interaction and exchange between parents and children. Although the effectiveness of the Mama Lere Model remains somewhat clouded by lack of assessment and program evaluation data, it nonetheless has some unique features which make it worthy of discussion in the present context.

REGIONAL INTERVENTION PROGRAM (RIP)   RIP falls in the category of a center-based, parent-oriented program and first gained distinction as one of the earliest programs funded by HCEEP in 1969 at George Peabody College. RIP is now run through the Tennessee Department of Mental Health, Division of Children and Youth Services. Anastasiow (1978) has classified RIP as a behaviorally oriented project. RIP was originally designed to serve autistic, behavioral disordered, and oppositional, preschool-age children. More recently, however, it has expanded to include the full range of "developmentally disabled and behaviorally disordered preschool children from birth to 5 years of age" (Wiegerink, Parrish, & Buhl, 1979, p. 153). RIP essentially has adopted a zero reject model and includes any children whose parents feel they can benefit from the program. In addition, RIP services are flexible enough that any family can be responded to within a 48 hour period.

Although RIP was originally conceived in a traditional manner with professional staff providing services to families, its founder, John Ora, soon saw the necessity to have families provide services to each other. As a result, RIP evolved into and has continued to be a program in which direct service to clients is almost exclusively provided by parents. Professionals act as resources to the parents and provide supervision and management.

As families enter the program, parents are taught techniques of contingency management intake, assessment, home visits, classroom teaching, and individual tutoring (Wiegerink, Parrish, & Buhl, 1979). With the growth of their individual competence, parents take over more and more responsibility for providing services to new families as they enter the program. Of course, through learning these skills parents become better able to manage their own children and provide an environment both at home and at school which facilitates their children's development. Wiegerink, Parrish, and Buhl (1979) have summed up parents' involvement in RIP stating that:

> Once their child is making steady progress and parents have demonstrated competency in some of the basic skills, they begin to offer volunteer services [for a period of 6 months], which can be the beginning of a new career for some. If the parent has demonstrated mastery in individual tutoring or generalization training, he can begin as an assistant in these modules. If parents showed interest in one of the pre-school classrooms, they could begin an assistantship there. In some cases, the parents teach others to collect basic behavioral data, but if they show programming and decision making competencies they can take on more and more responsibilities in one of the service modules. [p. 157]

These services modules include: intake, individual tutoring, generalization training, intake classroom, language classroom, community classroom, and liaison. Parents provide services in all of these modules.

RIP's primary objective "is to prepare the family and the child's maintenance and developmental progress outside of institutional care" (Wiegerink, Parrish, & Buhl, 1979, p. 153). The activities of each of the several modules mentioned above are designed to bring about the realization of this objective. Individual goals and objectives are set for each family. The intensive nature of the programming can be seen from the fact that children remain in the program for an average of 8.1 months, entering at an average of 41 months. Individual data collection systems are devised for each child in order to monitor his progress. Like other aspects of the program, parents have the responsibility for collecting and interpreting the data collected on each child.

Overall program evaluation and policy making are the purview of the RIP Evaluation Committee. Both professional and parent personnel meet monthly with the Committee to review individual family progress. Program evaluation is facilitated by the establishment of management objectives based on a format established by Reddin (1971). Staff performance can then be assessed against these established objectives.

The strict adherence to a behavioral approach can be seen as both a strength and weakness of the RIP model. While there is little doubt that this approach is effective with developmentally delayed and behaviorally disordered preschool children, it can also be narrow in focus and concerned primarily with control of undesirable behaviors. Another advantage to the behavioral approach is the relative ease with which it can be taught to and implemented by parents. The resource utilization of RIP is among the best of any program operating for preschool, handicapped children. Parents are the program and because they volunteer their time in exchange for services the cost effectiveness of RIP remains quite high. In addition, by using professional staff in consultation and support roles fewer professionals are needed and cost per student is again minimized.

The RIP experience has clearly demonstrated how parents can be involved effectively in the planning, development, implementation, and evaluation of preschool programs for handicapped children. While it is probably desirable to include parents in all of these activities, we must remain mindful of placing too much burden on parents whose children are developmentally handicapped. Such handicaps, after all, strain the coping mechanisms of parents and extra responsibilities for programming without the necessary supports may, in some cases, be more than a parent is able to tolerate.

Home-Based Programs

THE PORTAGE PROJECT   Shearer and Shearer (1976) described the Portage Project, which began in 1969 as a model program under HCEEP. More recently, the project has operated as a P.L. 91–230, Title IV-C project in cooperation with a regional education agency in rural Wisconsin. Because of the relative geographic isolation of the population being served, the Portage Project is home-based. In addition, the project employs a behavioral model, specifically one based on precision teaching (Kunzelmann, 1970) and uses parents as teachers of their own children. This latter practice is characteristic of most home-based programs for preschool, handicapped children. The project serves any child to six years old who lives within the project's catchment area.

Besides the pragmatic necessity for a home-based project in a rural area like that served by the Portage Project, the project staff has come to believe "that there are inherent *educational* advantages utilizing the home-based precision teaching model" (Shearer & Shearer, 1976, p. 336). Shearer and Shearer (1976) list these educational advantages as: (1) that learning occurs in the natural environment; (2) that there is constant access to the full range of child's behavior as it naturally occurs; (3) that because learning is occurring in the natural environment there is more likelihood of maintenance and generalization; (4) that in the home environment all members of the family can participate in the teaching process and support the child's learning; (5) that training parents will presumably provide them with skills to deal more effectively with new behaviors as they arise in the child's repertoire; and (6) that individualization is enhanced because the teacher is able to work on a one-to-one basis with the parent who in turn works on a one-to-one basis with the child. All in all the home-based approach is thought to better the ability of the project children to gain competencies in language, cognitive, self-help, motor, and socialization skills.

Activities vary from child to child in the program and are prescribed on an individualized basis. Each home teacher spends about an hour and a half a week with each child assigned to her. Instruction during the remainder of the week is the responsibility of the parent. Prescriptions are modified according to each child's individual progress from week to week. Three new behavior targets are identified each week and it becomes the parent's responsibility to provide instruction on these behaviors between the weekly visits of the home teacher. The home teacher collects data both before and after instruction to monitor the progress of each child. The home teacher, in addition, helps parents sharpen their teaching skills. Model techniques are presented by the home teacher and parents are given an opportunity to try them out and receive feedback each week. All project staff act as home teachers even though they come from varied professional disciplines (e.g., special education, speech, psychology). In addition, some home teachers are paraprofessionals.

Ongoing assessment of children is accomplished through the individualized data charts referred to above. In addition the Alpren-Boll Developmental Profile (Alpren & Boll, 1972) is administered to all children for screening and curriculum planning. The Portage Guide to Early Education (Bluma et al., 1976) was developed by project staff to aid in curriculum planning and to assess ongoing progress of the children. This assessment procedure is based on a series of developmental checklists which cover the age range from birth to six years. The Portage Guide has been widely accepted and suggested for older children who are severely or profoundly delayed (cf. Van Etten, Arkell, & Van Etten, 1980) and for handicapped, young children.

The Stanford-Binet and Cattell Infant Test have both been used to assess the progress made by children in the Portage Project Program. These measures were employed on a pre-post test basis and showed that "the average child in the Project gained 15 months in an 8 month period" (Shearer & Shearer, 1976, p. 348). Project children also showed significantly greater gains on these measures and on the Alpren-Boll Developmental Profile and the Gesell when compared with a group of control children who were drawn randomly from preschool classes serving culturally and economically disadvantaged children. Shearer and Shearer (1976) suggested that the use of these standardized, norm referenced measures would be phased out of the Program since "the staff believes that the only purpose for testing should be to program curriculum more effectively for children" (p. 338). They stress instead "informal assessment, which includes observing and recording how a child accomplishes a task, or why he fails to accomplish it, as well as behavioral checklists" (p. 338).

The success of the Portage Model can be seen in its wide dissemination and replication. DeWeerd (1980) reports that a program modelled after the Portage Project has been implemented in Japan. Another strength of the Portage Project can be seen in the development and dissemination of the Portage Guide to Early Education (Bluma et al., 1976), the assessment aspect of which was discussed above. The Guide also includes a set of curriculum cards that correspond to the assessment checklist and incorporate almost 600 objectives in the area of infant stimulation, self-help, language socialization, and cognitive skills. While the manual gives overall instructions on the use of the Guide, each card provides a specific "how to do it" statement related to each curriculum goal.

According to the Shearers (1976), the project also has the advantage of being low in cost. They reported in 1976 that the cost per child was $622 annually with about half that cost being borne by the local district. They suggested that the cost per child would continue to be reduced as more children were served. This conclusion seems logical in that the primary source of training is the children's parents.

The Portage Project puts significant responsibility on the shoulders of the parents by casting them in the role of teacher. High expectations are held for parents in carrying this and the amount of support provided by project staff is relatively low. The support that is provided tends to be centered around the development of teaching and data collection skills by parents. Parent support in the emotional and affective domain is seen as coming from other service agencies suggested by project staff. In spite of the advantages of this home-based approach, it is difficult to determine whether the lack of socialization with other children hinders the development of children served by the Project. While the Shearers present data suggesting advances in socialization, this may actually refer to adaptive interaction with other children. The home-based approach of the Portage Project seems to overlook the significant contribution of peers to the development of handicapped children.

PROJECT EDGE   The project for Expanding Developmental Growth through Education (EDGE) has been described by Rynders and Horrobin (1975) as a program designed to facilitate the development of Down's syndrome children through home instruction in infancy. After a period of home instruction, children enter the EDGE preschool at 30 months of age. Like several of the projects already described, Project EDGE received its initial funding through HCEEP and was based at the University of Minnesota's Research, Development and Demonstration Center in Education of Handicapped Children.

Several important principles undergird Project EDGE and provide the basis for the program's activities. According to Rynders and Horrobin (1975) these principles are:

1. Each activity shall engage the child and his mother in affectionate, focused, sensorimotor interaction (p. 178).
2. Each activity shall engage mother and child in sensorimotor activity and is to require, at the same time, that the mother talk with her child about the activities (p. 180).
3. Mothers will be taught to use a hierarchy of teaching strategies (p. 181).
4. A child should be exposed systematically to the fact that three-dimensional objects, photographs of the objects, and their printed labels have related meaning (p. 181).
5. When a mother is asked to work with her Down's syndrome child for an hour each day, she may be able to involve normal preschool children in the lesson so as to minimize the risk of sibling jealousy (p. 182).
6. One of the crucial considerations in a maternal tutoring program is to ensure that sufficient structure guides the mother's activities so that the execution of curricular principles can be guaranteed but, at the same time, does not stifle her unique maternal style (p. 182).

7. The reinforcement value of relative novelty will be capitalized on by pairing every lesson in all possible lesson combinations (p. 183).

These principles recognize the important role of the mother in the education and development of Down's syndrome infants. In addition, they are indicative of a cognitive learning model and stress the development of language and cognitive skills in particular.

Mothers of children enrolled in the infant program are expected to engage in specified training activities for one hour daily. Individual daily lessons are based on the EDGE curriculum and each mother is provided with 20 sets of simple materials which could be used in carrying out the daily lessons. "The lessons provide enough structure to help the mother to be goal-directed by allowing considerable freedom for her to use materials to suit her style preferences" (Rynders & Horrobin, 1975, p. 178). The mother continues conducting daily lessons with the child until he reaches 30 months of age at which time the child enters the EDGE preschool which continues to place emphasis on the development of communication skills. Even after the child enters the preschool program, the mother is expected to continue to provide him daily stimulation by working with the child for 30 minutes daily. Thus the EDGE approach in reality combines a home-based approach for infants with a center-based approach for preschool age children (i.e., those 2-1/2 to 5 years).

While mothers are seen as the hub of the program, Project EDGE staff recognized the necessity to augment maternal tutoring with other services. This recognition led to the implementation of certain ancillary services which lessened the burden of mothers in providing education and training to their children while also seeing their importance. In addition to the preschool program mentioned above for the older children in the project, several other services were provided to support the efforts of the mothers with infants. These included an itinerant teacher, provision of respite care, and a mobile education unit. The itinerant teacher conducted lessons in the home and provided "counseling and instructional support for parents" (Rynders & Horrobin, 1975, p. 184). Through their activity, the itinerant teachers provided mothers a certain amount of free time and at the same time sharpened mothers' skills through modeling and feedback.

Respite care services provided parents an opportunity to get away from their child for short periods of time. Respite care must be provided in safe home-like settings if it is to be maximally effective (cf. Ray, 1974b).

A mobile unit was used as a classroom on wheels and was taken around to various locations. The unit was a base for instruction in a classroom-like environment. Mothers were initially included in the instructional activities but were gradually faded out. Instruction was carried out by two undergraduate students who "were selected because of their ability to relate to young children effectively, for their careful driving habits, excellent language skills, and willingness to help create and then carefully implement lesson plans" (Rynders & Horrobin, 1975, p. 187). Three hours of instruction were provided weekly to 8 children through the mobile unit. Rynders and Horrobin (1975) conclude that a mobile unit is an effective and reasonably inexpensive means for providing educational services to Down's syndrome infants. They suggest that mobile units may be particularly useful in rural areas, although theirs was used in a primarily metropolitan setting. Finally, they make the point that the "mobile program was used to *augment* a mother's teaching, not to supplant it" (p. 189).

Project EDGE used a strong evaluation design by assigning 20 children to the intervention group and 20 children to a control (non-intervention) group. It is unclear from the description provided by Rynders and Horrobin (1975) what level of intervention, if any, the control children received. While such control groups provide an opportunity to collect more meaningful data, we would personally question the advisability of not providing services to a group of Down's syndrome infants merely for the benefit of research design. According to preliminary data, experimental children were showing positive performance differences in concept formation, expressive language, on-task behavior, and IQ score as compared with their non-enrolled (control) counterparts" (Rynders & Horrobin, 1975, p. 184). Rynders and Horrobin (1975) do not report the means by which these data were collected nor do they mention the specific assessment instruments employed. In a more recent presentation of their data Rynders, Spiker, and Horrobin (1978) state:

> we would point out that the 17 children in our early education treatment programs have shown, on the average, gains in I.Q. score (on the Stanford-Binet). Nevertheless, in the group of 18 Down's syndrome children not receiving our experimental treatment, fully 45 percent scored at or above the educable level. (Most of these children received differing forms of early intervention) [p. 446].

Clearly, a strength of the EDGE program is the recognition by its staff that although mothers can provide an important link in education of Down's syndrome infants, they must have additional services to augment their efforts at home. An examination of Project EDGE will demonstrate that service delivery to families with Down's syndrome infants and young children is a challenging and complex task and that multiphasic modes must be employed to carry out this task well.

Perhaps a weakness of the project is its university base, for although the university provides a multitude of resources, its context is not easily replicable in the world beyond its campus. In general, Project EDGE represents an innovative and well-thought-out approach to preschool education of handicapped children, has positive implications for providing educational services to other groups of developmentally disabled infants and young children.

PARENTS AS EFFECTIVE EARLY EDUCATION RESOURCES (PEERS)   Like several projects already described, the PEERS project (Losinno, n.d.) received funding through HCEEP after its inception as a volunteer program. More recently, it has been funded through P.L. 89–313 and the County Office of Mental Health and Mental Retardation in Philadelphia, Pennsylvania. PEERS is currently run by a community service agency in northeast Philadelphia and maintains a basic philosophy "that any child who is developmentally delayed must be involved in a consistent training program as soon as a delay in any developmental area is identified" (Losinno, n.d., p. 4). The basis of the PEERS program lies in the following beliefs:

1. Parents, given proper information and training, can best serve as the child's teacher during the early years.
2. Parents and volunteers are effective primary intervention agents. Early intervention can alleviate developmental delay. (Losinno, n.d., p. 5)

Thus, the PEERS program employs a home-based, parent-oriented model of service delivery and adheres to what Anastasiow (1978) would classify as a cognitive developmental model.

The PEERS project has operated on a zero reject model of acceptance and has been able to serve between 20 and 40 families a year. These families all have children who are between the ages of three weeks and three years and who are manifesting developmental delays in one or more areas. Many of these children also attend other training programs. The basic goals of the program are (1) to provide stimulation and create an optimum learning environment for the child in-home and (2) to provide intensive training for the child's parents and family. Project staff believe that attainment of these goals will minimize the degree of handicap exhibited by a child when she reaches preschool or kindergarten age.

The program activities are arranged in three components—parent training, home visits, and individualized child evaluations and prescriptive programming. Parent training is accomplished through seminars and lectures when parents come together as a group on Saturday mornings. These Saturday sessions are arranged to coincide with the individualized prescriptive/evaluative program sessions held for the children. About 80 percent of the families enrolled in the program attend these Saturday sessions on the typical Saturday and about 60 percent of the time both parents attend (Losinno, n.d.). These sessions are both a means for formal instruction and a social and emotional support group for the parents. The course of instruction for parents is designed to last two years and covers "basic concepts in child development; a review of methods and means of assessment; a discussion of community resources; and guidelines in dealing with sibling problems, parent/child problems, child problems, future planning, toy selection, child management, and other related topics" (Losinno, n.d., pp. 8–9).

Home visits are conducted by a project teacher once a month. The home visit centers around parent concerns and the teacher provides parents with input concerning prescriptions and procedures for implementing them. New lesson plans are explained to parents and are left for their use in training sessions. Parents are urged to set aside thirty minutes for training every day and are encouraged to keep a log of their child's activities and progress. These anecdotal records are seen as important sources of data for assessing both parent and child progress.

As alluded to above, children also come in on Saturdays for evaluation and individualized prescriptive programming. These sessions last for three hours and are conducted by community volunteers and project staff. Children are worked with individually and in small groups. These Saturday sessions provide the children with an opportunity to become socialized to other children and give project staff an opportunity to formally assess children's progress. In addition, parents are excused from their training session periodically and given an opportunity to work with their child with all project staff available for feedback and to provide information. This opportunity occurs approximately once every six weeks. Saturday morning sessions are also used by staff to assess and update individual prescriptions for children about once every three months.

Formal evaluation of each child is done every six months. Children are evaluated with standardized tests like the Bayley Scales of Infant Development (Bayley, 1969), the Vineland Scale of Social Maturity (Doll, 1964), and Bzoch-League Receptive-Expressive Emergent Language Scales (Bzoch & League, 1971). In addition, children's progress on self-help skills, fine motor skills, gross motor skills, cognitive concepts, social skills, and expressive and receptive language skills is assessed using an internal evaluation device known as the PEERS instrument which Losinno (n.d.) reports correlates in the range of .83 to .96 with the standardized measures used.

Sower (1978) compiled an extensive report on the effectiveness of the PEERS project. The method of compensated and non-compensated post ages developed by Irwin and Wong (1974) was used as the major means of evaluating gains in children's development. A multivariate analysis of pre and post scores of the Bayley, Vineland, Bzoch-League, and the seven domains on the PEERS instrument revealed an overall significant effect for both compensated and non-compensated scores. This analysis included 17 subjects. Sower (1978) concludes that:

> these multivariate analyses suggest that the total impact of the PEERS program on the 17 subjects as evaluated by the seven sub-tests is indeed considerable. Note that even the analysis that employs the compensated post ages [scores] is significant. This analysis is more rigorous from their conventional post analysis because it subtracts from the actual increase the mathematical projection of the increase that could have been predicted by maturational factors alone [p. 21].

Even using compensated scores, it is difficult to interpret the "real" effects of the PEERS project since many of the children were also served by other programs.

One strength of the PEERS project is the support that parents of the project provide for each other. The regularly scheduled, Saturday morning meetings greatly facilitate the development of this support. These types of group meetings are unique and do not usually occur in parent-oriented programs, which are typically oriented to the individual family. In essence, the PEERS project provides a means by which parents become resources to their own children and to each other. In general, the PEERS project staff realizes that parents need not only training but psychological and emotional support in dealing with their handicapped children.

A relative weakness of the project is the infrequency with which parents were visited by home teachers. While this deficiency was offset to some degree by the weekly Saturday meetings, which provided access to staff, it must be remembered that these meetings were typically of a general nature and were designed to give group input to the parents. Another point of weakness is the relatively long time span (three months) between changes in prescription. A child who spends a full two years in the program has only 8 different prescriptions during his tenure in the program.

Finally, the PEERS Project reports annual direct service costs of $2,000 per child which "is indeed economical when . . . contrasted with the traditional five-day-a-week center-based costs which are significantly higher" (Losinno, n.d., p. 14).

THE UCLA INFANT STUDIES PROGRAM   According to a description of the UCLA Infant Studies Program provided by Bromwich and Parmelee (1979), "the educational intervention program . . . was oriented primarily to support and enhance the quality of interaction between parent and infant in light of considerable research evidence regarding the powerful influence of parent-infant interaction on the development of the infant" (p. 389). The program serves high-risk, preterm infants between the ages of ten months and two years. To be eligible for the program, infants had to be less than 37 weeks in gestational age and weigh less than 2500 grams at birth. In addition, they had to be evaluated as being at risk using the cumulative risk measures described by Parmelee, Sigman, Kopp, and Haber (1975, 1976) and Sigman and Parmelee (1979). The families of these infants ran across the spectrum of ethnic and socio-economic groups. The program employed a home-based, parent-centered approach which followed cognitive developmental models.

The overall goal of the program was to enhance the parents' enjoyment of and sensitivity and responsiveness to their infants and thus to increase their motivation and ability to provide opportunities and experiences that would further the infant's development (Bromwich & Parmelee, 1979, p. 390). The staff was concerned with infant development in the social-affective, cognitive-motivational, and language areas. To reach its goal with parents and infants, the staff developed an individualized plan to carry out with each family. In general, goals centered around making parents responsive to cues given by the infant; giving parents ways of motivating infant responses, giving parents observational skills enabling them to assess the infant's competence and then select appropriate materials and play activities; increasing parents' awareness of prelinguistic skills and the necessity for reciprocal communication; and providing parents with skills to motivate infant language.

The activities of the intervention program were centered around home visits. During the several home visits, staff were primarily concerned with establishing rapport with the family and completing a baseline assessment on the infant.

After the first three sessions, an intervention plan for the family was developed. Every four months staff prepared case summaries which "included: (a) an assessment of the infant, parenting behavior, parent-infant interaction, and home environment of the infant; (b) a discussion of changes in any of the areas that were assessed; and (c) an evaluation of the concept and process of intervention with subsequent revisions of the intervention plan as indicated by the evaluation" (Bromwich & Parmelee, 1979, p. 392).

Bromwich and Parmelee (1979) point out that the staff followed a number of "guidelines" which they suggest "were central to our approach" (p. 394). These guidelines were:

1. parent remains in control
2. dealing with parent's priorities and concerns
3. avoiding the "authority-laymen" gap
4. respecting parent's goals for infant
5. respecting individual styles of parent-infant interaction
6. parent participation in planning
7. building on strengths of parents
8. reinforcement is not enough
9. parent as observer of infant's play
10. giving parents an "out"
11. experimenting can be fun for parent (pp. 394–396).

Two instruments were developed by project staff to assess the effectiveness of the intervention program in modifying parent-infant interaction. The first of these was the Parent Behavior Progression (PBP) designed to assess parenting behavior at six levels. These levels ranged from assessing a parent's basic enjoyment of her infant to assessing the parent's ability to independently generate developmentally appropriate and interesting experiences for the infant. In addition to the PBP, the Play Interaction Measure (PIM) was developed by project staff. Unlike the PBP, the PIM was designed for use in the laboratory rather than the home. The PIM is divided into three sections which measure (1) play-related behaviors; (2) social-affective behaviors, and (3) language behaviors. In addition, children were assessed using the Gesell and the Bayley.

The program employed a control group which did not participate in the intervention program. As with the EDGE project (Rynder & Horrobin, 1975) discussed above, the issue must be raised as to the suitability of having children not receive interventions for the primary purpose of program evaluation designs. It is interesting to note that Bromwich and Parmelee found no significant differences between the one-year or two-year Gesell or Bayley scores for the intervention and the non-intervention groups. They conclude that "it is clear that the intervention did not alter this trend" (p. 400).

Staff assessed the intervention program as being successful for families in the intervention group. Fourteen were rated as mixed successes and 5 were considered unsuccessful. From these cases, the 11 most successful were compared with the 10 least successful on percentage gain on the PBP and the PIM. The total gain on all levels of the PBP was 46 percent for the successful group as compared with an average gain of only 10 percent for the unsuccessful group. On the PIM, the average gain for the successful group was 34 percent as compared with 23 percent for the unsuccessful group. These results may be confounded by the fact that the staff may have known PBP and PIM scores and that that knowledge affected which families were viewed as successful and which families were not.

While the philosophical tenets of this program appear sound, the data that Bromwich and Parmelee (1979) present raise some questions as to the actual effectiveness of the intervention program. Since these authors do not specify precisely what procedures are employed in their intervention program, it is difficult to assess why the evaluation data do not show a higher degree of successes. The authors suggests that the effects of the program may be in the long term rather than in the short term. In addition, they relate that the "nontreatment" group actually received certain medical and social services through the time of the program. These services may have been as effective in facilitating development as those offered through the intervention program. In summary, the strength of this program lies in its theoretical and philosophical underpinnings, which were drawn from a substantial literature on the relationship between mothers and their infants and how these relationships can foster optimal infant development.

ANALYSIS AND CONCLUSIONS

This chapter has dealt with the major models of preschool education of handicapped children. The illustrative programs described should allow the reader to see how different approaches can be employed to provide educational services to preschool, handicapped children. No program described is without its individual strengths and weaknesses. And, quite frankly, it is often the individual commitment and integrity of a program's staff that accounts for its success as much as the theoretical or service delivery approach employed.

In spite of the inherent differences in the programs, certain basic tenets of early intervention for preschool, handicapped children can be extracted from these program descriptions. These basic tenets are:

1. Parents are seen as having a significant role in the education and development of their handicapped child.
2. With few exceptions, programs for preschool, handicapped children are concerned with a broad spectrum of developmental targets not just a specific area of development.
3. Early intervention is viewed as means for enhancing development and/or lessening the degree of manifested delay.

On the other hand, programs vary greatly in the way they identify curriculum targets, the means they use for assessing children and measuring program outcomes, their underlying theoretical base, and the degree to which they provide a full range of services. What emerges is a pattern that suggests a commitment to some basic tenets in all programs but a variety of means and methods by which those tenets are translated into action.

In analyzing the state of the art of early intervention for the handicapped child, Gallagher (1980) has suggested that as we move into the next decade certain policies will emerge that will change the face of preschool education of handicapped children. These policies clearly emerge from our present views and practices. Gallagher (1980) suggests that future policies affecting early intervention programs should include:

1. Assign specific responsibility to key state agencies for program development for young, handicapped children.
2. Explore the viability of environmental modifications as an addition to strategies for helping young, handicapped children and their families.
3. Entertain proposals on how to aid "at risk" children who can be identified only on an actuarial basis at young ages.
4. Extend demonstration and outreach models illustrating agency cooperation and interdisciplinary cooperation.
5. Consider extention of P.L. 94–142 to cover handicapped children 3 to 5 and encourage work from birth to 3 (p. 43)

In summary, while we have come a long way in the provision of services to handicapped, young children since the inception of Head Start in 1965 and HCEEP in 1969, there are still frontiers to cross. We hope the programs illustrated in this chapter provide a picture of where the frontier begins and suggest where it has still to go.

Mainstreaming and Young Children

1. What has been the role of litigation in bringing about mainstreaming among the preschool population?
2. Why is imitation thought to be important in mainstreamed preschool settings?
3. What major arguments have been put forth against mainstreaming and how do these arguments apply to preschool populations?

The term *mainstreaming* seems to be on everybody's lips these days. Administrators, parents, teachers, and sometimes even children can be found discussing the relative merits of this concept, usually with great fervor. There is a good deal of emotional investment in the term by both parents and professionals, and this is sometimes accompanied by misinterpretations of the laws which fostered mainstreaming as well as by rather cloudy understandings of the concept itself. It is the purpose of this chapter, therefore, to clarify the concept of mainstreaming as it applies to preschool, handicapped children. We will begin with a look at the legal precedents which established the concept, then briefly examine the historical context, some pros and cons, and finally review various ways in which the concept has been implemented.

LITIGATION AND LEGISLATION

Bricker (1978) stated that the prevailing social philosophy in the United States has been gradually changing to include more and more children in public education programs. Whereas formerly only a select group was eligible, today all children from ages 3 to 21 must be provided services. This change had particularly strong impact in two areas: the education of preschool children with handicaps and the education of severely handicapped children in kindergarten through twelfth grade. As the public schools have adjusted to accommodate these two groups into special, usually self-contained, programs, the same social philosophy has prompted a movement of mildly handicapped youngsters from segregated into integrated or mainstreamed programs.

The social philosophy to which Bricker (1978) refers is reflected in a series of court and legislative decisions during the past ten to fifteen years that reach back to the Fourteenth Amendment. The equal protection clause of that amendment has been used repeatedly in the litigation and legislation discussed below to justify the extension of educational services to handicapped children. That clause simply states that any opportunity provided by a state must be made available to all citizens on an equal basis. Court decisions relating to mainstreaming may be divided into two groups, those mandating right to treatment for institutionalized children (deinstitutionalization) and those mandating right to education in the least restrictive environment (mainstreaming) for non-institutionalized children. Combined, these decisions constitute a strong movement toward normalization (Wolfensberger, 1975) of life for all handicapped citizens. They are briefly reviewed here.

Right to Appropriate Education

Cases dealing with the right to an appropriate education involved two factors. First, the contention was made that many handicapped children were being denied a free public education because they were being denied access to the public schools. These were primarily children who were labeled moderately to severely mentally retarded and who were either living in institutions or remained at home with no schooling. Second, there were large numbers of children placed inappropriately in special classes for the mentally retarded. These children, while served by the public school system, were not being provided an *appropriate* education. Many of these children were from minority backgrounds. For example, the Children's Defense Fund in 1974 published statistics (Children Out of School in America) from a study of 505 southern school districts. Over 80 percent of the children in classes for the mentally retarded in those districts were black.

The major litigation dealing with these two issues took place between 1968 and 1973:

> 1968 *Arreola et al. vs. Board of Education.* This case involved seven Mexican-American children in Santa Ana, California, who had been placed in special classes for the mentally retarded. Their placement had been based on IQ scores obtained from tests administered in English. The children were retested in Spanish and scored within the normal range on an individually administered intelligence test.

1970 *Diana vs. Board of Education.* In a case similar to Arreola vs. Board of Education, nine Mexican-American children who had been tested by means of a group IQ test and found mentally retarded were retested individually in English and/or Spanish. Seven of the children scored well above 70, the eighth scored 70 and the ninth 67, for an average gain of 15 points each. The court ruled that a group IQ test score could not be used for the purpose of labeling a child mentally retarded.

1970 *Stewart vs. Philip* was a classification suit which involved seven children from low SES, black families in Boston who had been classified mentally retarded. Retesting found them to be functioning within the average intellectual range. The court's decision was based on the following points: 1) The children had been placed outside the regular classroom because they were considered behavior problems; 2) They had been classified on the basis of a single test; 3) Standarized tests discriminate against children who are not of white, middle-class backgrounds; 4) Standardized tests fail to discriminate among various learning disorders, only one of which is mental retardation.

1971 *Hobson vs. Hansen* was a suit filed by a group of black parents in Washington, D.C., against the tracking system in which children were tested at an early age and sorted into ability groups. The court found that the low track consisted predominantly of low SES, black children and that the low track program was of poor quality. The court further found that the aptitude test used for sorting was biased in favor of white, middle-class children, and its use for tracking purposes violated the Fourteenth Amendment.

1972 *Mills vs. Board of Education* was a class action suit brought against the Washington, D.C. Board of Education on behalf of nine handicapped children who had not been allowed to enroll in the public schools. The court ruled that the children must be provided educational services by the public school system, that lack of funds could not be used as an excuse for not educating handicapped children, and that due process procedures must be instituted to protect children from arbitrary administrative decisions.

1972 *Larry P. vs. Riles*, a landmark case in San Francisco, involved six black, elementary school children who had been tested and improperly placed in classes for the mentally retarded. Stating that the children were "victims of a testing procedure which fails to recognize unfamiliarity with white middle class culture," the judge ruled that a second criterion in addition to the IQ test was necessary in order to classify a child mentally retarded. He instructed the educational system to find an IQ test that was not culturally biased against minority children. Seven years later when such a test had still not been developed, he ruled (in 1979) that IQ tests could not be used at all in the classification of minority children.

1972 *Pennsylvania Association for Retarded Children vs. Commonwealth of Pennsylvania*, another landmark case in the right to education litigation, challenged the constitutionality of the state law which excluded mentally retarded children from public schools. Basing its decision on both Fifth and Fourteenth Amendments, the court mandated free, public programs for all retarded children in Pennsylvania between the ages of 6 and 21. These programs were stipulated to be appropriate to the needs of the child and to be carried out in the least restrictive environment. Due process protections were included.

1973 *Lebanks vs. Spears*, a case brought in Louisiana on behalf of children in special education classes, resulted in an opinion that the regular classroom with support services is preferable to special class placement. The decision called for a written individual educational plan for each handicapped child.

Right to Treatment

Whereas the five years from 1968 to 1973 were years of significant progress in the delineation of educational rights of some handicapped children, it wasn't until 1972 that an important case was brought on behalf of those severely handicapped children who were not only left out of the mainstream but were spending their lives in institutions without adequate treatment. In *Wyatt vs. Stickney* (1972) the court stated that citizens in a state institution have the right to appropriate treatment, education, and habilitation, and that these services must be in the form of an individual program fitted to their needs. This landmark case was affirmed by the United States Supreme Court, making it a decision of national impact. Two similar cases, *Welsch vs. Likens* in Minnesota (1974) and *New York Association for Retarded Citizens vs. Carey* (1975) affirmed the right to treatment based on the Eighth Amendment protection against cruel and unusual punishment.

The result of the decade or so of court decisions broadening access to free, ᴨppropriate education was a series of state and federal laws culminating in Public Law 94–142, the Education for All Handicapped Children Act of 1975. This law established the following mandates:

1. All handicapped children between the ages of 3 and 21 must be provided free, appropriate educational programs. Only those states already serving normal 3 to 5 year olds in public schools need serve handicapped preschoolers.
2. These programs must be based on an individualized educational plan developed for each handicapped child and revised at least annually.
3. The individualized educational plan must be developed by means of assessment procedures that take account of the child's cultural background, primary language, and previous experience.
4. The educational program chosen must be the least restrictive alternative. This means that the child must be placed in as normal a setting as he or she can prosper in, with nonhandicapped children as much of the time as possible. This will vary according to the individual capabilities of each handicapped child.
5. Parents must be involved in the planning of their child's educational program. They are accorded carefully defined, due process procedures for appealing educational decisions that they find inappropriate and must be consulted whenever program changes are made.

The law certainly makes clear its intent in regard to the education of preschool handicapped children. It clearly intends that mildly handicapped preschoolers be mainstreamed, or placed in programs with their nonhandicapped peers for most or all of their program. The expectation for more severely impaired youngsters is that they be integrated for certain portions of their program with normally developing children. The question arises whether this is an appropriate, feasible way of educating both handicapped and nonhandicapped children. It is a question we will explore in the remainder of this chapter.

HISTORICAL PERSPECTIVE

The history of educational programs for young, handicapped children is a short one. Traditionally, handicapped children have been kept at home or placed in institutions soon after birth. They were not considered educable and so the expenditure of funds for this purpose was generally considered wasteful (Hutt & Gibby, 1976). It was seen to be in the best interests of handicapped and nonhandicapped alike to keep the handicapped at home, either to prevent them from harming the nonhandicapped or to protect them from a too-demanding environment.

Until the early twentieth century, the public schools had a limited role in the education of handicapped children. Their major function was seen as the socialization and education of normal children. Gradually that view changed, and mentally retarded children were accepted into the public school system in segregated classes. By 1910 there were classes for mentally retarded children in 99 cities in the United States (Hutt & Gibby, 1976). The twenties, thirties, and forties saw an expansion of such programs, but preschool children were generally excluded. During the 1950s and 1960s, there was a gradual movement to provide public educational programs for other handicapped, school age children—physically handicapped, visually and hearing impaired, and learning disabled children. However, although the public school system finally accepted responsibility for these children after the age of six, it has been only recently that a similar commitment to preschool youngsters has been made, and this is the result of strong encouragement from lawmakers in the form of P.L. 94–142. At present, most public educational programs for preschool, handicapped children are federally funded and are conducted in segregated settings.

Educational programs for preschool age children during the past 20 years have fallen into three general categories: 1) private nursery schools for children from middle and upper class families, 2) early intervention programs for children from lower class families who were considered to be "culturally deprived," and 3) programs sponsored by community and private agencies for the benefit of young, handicapped children. The latter category has included some hospital-based, short-term programs.

While it is beyond the scope of this chapter to discuss programs based on social and economic class, it is important to note that during the 1960s much national attention was focused on efforts to help lower class children "catch up" with the middle class majority. The provision of public programs for these children (Head Start, Follow Through) provided some legitimacy for the public education of handicapped preschoolers. Indeed, Head Start's requirement that 10 percent enrolled children be labeled handicapped not only sanctioned services to preschool, handicapped youngsters but sanctioned mainstreamed services at that.

In summary, mainstreaming programs have been more difficult to achieve for preschool age children than for school age children. Whereas the same attitudes that account for the mainstreaming movement in public schools are present, the machinery—classes of normally achieving children—are not so readily available at the preschool level. This has meant that mainstreamed programs for young children are much less common and will probably continue to be so until public schools become more involved in the education of all children below age five.

ARGUMENTS FOR MAINSTREAMING

Surely the goal of serving all children within the public sector is a noble one against which few argue. But should handicapped and nonhandicapped be educated together? Unless mainstreaming is beneficial to both groups of children, it cannot be wholeheartedly supported. While much has been written on this topic, a few references stand out. Dunn (1968) was among the first to question the education of mildly retarded children in segregated classes. In an article that has since become a classic in the field of special education, Dunn presented educational and social arguments suggesting that special classes generally provided inadequate programs for handicapped children. Expectancy studies during the late 1960s and early 1970s (Avery, 1971; Beez, 1968; Scott, 1969) indicated that teacher expectations are lower for labeled children than for those without handicap labels. Lowered expectations lessen the chance of handicapped children achieving average levels in their academic and social performance.

Evidence certainly suggests that handicapped children do not necessarily receive an appropriate education within the special class setting. Ethical considerations, too, have provided much of the rationale for mainstreaming children of all ages. The traditional segregation of handicapped children is as much a result of negative social attitudes toward mentally retarded, cerebral palsied, or neurologically impaired children as it is motivated by a desire to improve conditions for such children. Bartel and Guskin (1980) point out that society creates handicapped children by selecting certain attributes (e.g., normal intelligence) and calling them desirable while labeling others (e.g., mental retardation) undesirable. They further maintain that whether a child is labeled handicapped depends on her social class, parents, income, educational level, and race. Those children from socially less desirable backgrounds tend to be labeled handicapped more often (Mercer, 1973) and segregated from the mainstream as a result. Thus our society has tended to deal with difference or deviance by separating it out so that it can be ignored.

Placing a handicapped child in an environment with only other handicapped children for companionship may result in an inadequate environment for that child. Since an impoverished environment may have caused the handicap in the first place, a segregated environment can only maintain that impoverishment and continue the handicap (Bartel & Guskin, 1980). Such an environment does not provide normal role models for the handicapped child and so prevents the child's return to normal. Bartel and Guskin claim that, indeed,

> Segregation of handicapped children in special programs is one aspect of a larger social phenomenon: the formal management of deviance by our society. It includes prisons for the behaviorially different, mental institutions for the emotionally different, residential institutions and special classes for the intellectually different, hospitals for the physically different, and ghettos for the ethnically and racially different. [p. 64]

Mainstreaming is more compatible with the recent emphasis in this country on a multicultural approach to education which values differences between individuals. Multicultural education and mainstreaming share the same goal: To achieve acceptance by the public school system of children who may for reasons of cultural, intellectual, or behavioral difference deviate from the norm significantly enough to be noticed. However, public schools are only a reflection of the larger society they serve. We must ask whether expectations for social reform can be realistically posited in them. Surely the attitudes of all citizens, not only children, must be changed if people who are different are to be allowed to lead normal lives; this seems a fearsome and unrealistic responsibility to place on public schools.

In review of developmental or psychological arguments for mainstreaming, the work of Harlow and his colleagues with rhesus monkeys is a good starting place. For nearly twenty years, Harlow and associates studied the social relationships of monkeys in order to gain a better understanding of primates in general. Their conclusions regarding the role of peer relationships in social development have implications for mainstreaming. Suomi and Harlow (1975) believe, for example, that peer friendships traditionally have been underestimated in importance by researchers in social development. They present evidence that competent and adaptive social activity in the adult monkey is predicated on the development and maintenance of peer friendships immediately following infancy and throughout the developmental years. They found peers to be the most salient influence in a monkey's everyday life after infancy; this influence is primarily in the form of play, through which social roles are established and maintained. Suomi and Harlow maintain that peer interactions have an important developmental purpose not only for rhesus monkeys but for other primates, including humans, as well. They believe that as humans we share with other primates a genetically acquired potential for social activity which is shaped by peer interactions.

The role of play in children's cognitive and moral development (Piaget, 1932, 1954; Vandenberg, 1978) and social and affective development (Bruner, Jolly, & Sylva, 1976; Hartup, 1978; Lee, 1975; Weisler & McCall, 1976) as discussed in

Chapter 5 has been well documented. It is through play that children try out new roles, experiment with their environment, and test their limits in physical and mental activity.

Play also provides a safe forum in which a child may experiment with aggression and sexual arousal as a means of learning how to handle these feelings, without fear of adult antagonism. Hartup (1978) points out that play is a uniquely child-child activity and that peer interaction is therefore a better means of eliciting play behavior than adult-child interaction. In play activity with peers, children encounter an equalitarian environment with fewer constraints than in adult-child relationships, and this environment facilitates many kinds of learning: social, cognitive, moral, language, and motor. Indeed, inadequate peer relations are prognostic indicators of social and emotional trouble in young children, for loners more often end up as delinquents or develop adjustment difficulties in adulthood.

Evidence suggests that differentiated social relationships develop early in infancy. Lee (1973) found that infants of eight to ten months of age differed in the amount of approach behavior directed toward them by other babies in the day care group; the most approached infants seemed already to have developed a responsive, reciprocal style of interacting with peers. Other research (Hartup, Glazer, & Charlesworth, 1967) indicates that reciprocity is an important aspect of toddler friendship, and that imitation plays a role in establishing peer interactions during the first and second years of life (Mueller & Lucas, 1975). Thus, peer interaction or lack of it becomes an important issue early in a child's life.

Peer interactions in the form of play are important to preschool children. They might be even more important to handicapped children, who have experienced deprived environments as Bartel and Guskin (1980) have suggested. Before we address the question of whether mainstreaming preschoolers increases their peer interaction, let us examine for a moment some aspects of peer relationships.

According to Mueller and Lucas (1975), young children between the ages of 12 and 18 months go through three stages in their development of peer interactions. Stage one is an outgrowth of sensorimotor behavior. It consists of two children acting on an object in an identical fashion. Because one-year-olds are used to acting on objects, the object, which is naturally admired by both children, becomes the focus of contact. This stage is, therefore, dyadic and three-person interactions are not observed until age two. This stage is sometimes known as parallel play, terminology that actually ignores the peer interaction involved. The beginnings of imitative behavior are seen here, as the two children behave in similar fashion with the object.

By stage two, children are actively seeking and receiving what Mueller and Lucas term contingencies, that is, actions contiguous in time and space. These are compared to Piaget's idea of secondary circular reactions. That is, child A initiates an action such as laughing and child B's response to that action causes child A to repeat the action. A circular reaction that involves a good deal of imitation is set up. The children's behaviors gradually become reciprocal. For example, child A honks a horn, child B then honks the horn, then child A honks it again. As the imitation and the reciprocal activity increase, both children notice each other and actively seek more interaction.

By stage three the interchanges have become complementary in nature. The participants do different but intercoordinated things. The activity is reciprocal in the sense that child B now does the opposite of what child A does or responds with his own action. Therefore, by definition stage three is no longer imitative. The activities at stage three require a sensitivity between the children to each other's movements. For example, two children playing a game of catch, rolling a ball back and forth between them, requires one to throw and the other to catch and each must be sensitive to the movements of the other. Thus, Mueller and Lucas have identified a developmental sequence that begins with sensorimotor intelligence and develops through imitation to reciprocal interactions, all during the first 18 months of life.

Hartup has identified three ways in which peers influence each other. The first and earliest to develop is *peer modeling*. We have noted previously that imitation plays an important part in the socialization of young children. Peer modeling, Hartup reports, is influential in the development of problem-solving behavior, sex-role activity, and social interaction. It is evidently enhanced if the child sees the peer model receive a reward (Bandura & Menlove, 1968) and if the child and the model are of the same sex. Hartup notes that children enjoy being imitated and are more apt to be friendly toward the imitator, a factor to be considered in mainstreaming handicapped children.

A second kind of peer influence is that of *peer reinforcement*. Peer reinforcement is related to the efficacy of peer modeling. Hartup (1978) found that children who had experienced positive interactions with their peers were better able to imitate models than those who had not. He cites many examples from research showing how effective peer reinforcement can be for shaping behaviors. Finally, Hartup suggests *peer tutoring* as a means of providing opportunity for social interaction between preschool children. Both children benefit from the peer tutoring experience. The tutor gains in self-esteem due to the increased status the role provides and has an opportunity to experience a nurturing role, which helps to increase his sensitivity to others. The tutored child benefits from the individual attention that is provided and has an opportunity for increased cognitive growth.

Hartup (1978) maintains that these forms of peer interaction are all helpful in the socialization process. He cautions, however, that peer interactions must be carefully planned if they are to help handicapped children get along with non-handicapped. This brings us to our previous question, that is, does mainstreaming preschoolers increase their social interaction with their normal peers? Research evidence does not provide a clear answer to this question. Nevertheless, some interesting work has been done. Cavellaro and Porter (1980), for example, found that in a free-play situation preschool children selected playmates with similar cognitive levels. That is, normal children tended to select normal children for playmates and retarded children tended to select other retarded children. Guralnick has done a great deal of work in this area. He reports that simply introducing nonhandicapped children into a play setting does not automatically guarantee that handicapped and nonhandicapped children play together. In an early study (Devoney, Guralnick, & Rubin, 1974), it was found that handicapped children could be encouraged to play both with each other and with nonhandicapped children if the teacher structured the environment to promote interactions. When this was done it was observed that the handicapped children played in a more organized way and with more sophistication and more fantasy than had been noted before their contacts with nonhandicapped children. In a later study, Guralnick (1976) found that peer modeling and peer reinforcement by nonhandicapped children significantly increased the cooperative play of handicapped children.

Two factors have been identified by Guralnick (1980) and others (Peck, Apolloni, Cooke, & Raver, 1978) which have an important effect on how much handicapped and nonhandicapped, preschool children interact when they are in a mainstream situation. The first of these is training. It appears that developmentally disabled, preschool children imitate normal children if they are trained to do so and reinforced for it. Peck, Apolloni, Cooke, and Raver (1978) found, moreover, that this training generalized to other situations. In their experiment, they trained retarded children to imitate normal children and found that the behaviors learned from peer models were displayed in other situations. They noted that the generalization was more successful when the children were closest in developmental level. And this is the second factor to emerge from the research. Children seem to choose playmates who are at similar developmental levels. This suggests that older, handicapped children should be integrated with younger, normal children so that they might approximate the same developmental level and share similar interests and ability levels. As a matter of fact the interest in mixed-age peers is not restricted to handicapped and nonhandicapped children. Hartup (1978), for example, reports research on normal, preschool children in mixed-age classes that indicates that such situations produce more mature play and may contribute to a child's greater socialization.

Another area where influence of peers may be important for handicapped preschoolers is language acquisition. Here again, the evidence is not clearcut. Bates (1975) has noted that normal children who spend more time with peers than with adults are at a disadvantage in learning language. She cites research to show that twins who talk only to each other tend to be retarded in language development, that first-borns have better language than younger siblings because they talk more to adults than to peers, and that institutional children have poor language if adult speech is not available to them. But the same children show no effects from peer talk or the lack of it. Thus the level of language development has been found to be highest in children who associate primarily with adults.

It would seem from this information that peers are not a great influence on a handicapped child's language acquisition. Nevertheless, evidence suggests that other children are an important source of communication for a child, and that children are sensitive to the communicative needs of each other. In continuing her discussion of this topic, Bates (1975) cites an important monograph by Shatz and Gelman (1973) in which four-year-olds were found to speak differently to adults, to peers, and to two-year-olds. All the four-year-olds in that study adjusted their speech for the two-year-olds, making it shorter, simpler, and more directive. In a study of three-and-one-half to five-and-one-half-year-olds, Mueller (1972) found that more than half of the utterances by children were responded to appropriately by their peer listeners.

Since language acquisition appears to depend on availability of simple, clear, grammatically correct, and redundant language, known as "motherese" by language acquisition researchers, the fact that young children can apparently provide this sort of language to their peers is important. Guralnick (1978) reported that nonhandicapped children adjust their speech when addressing handicapped children to match their listener's cognitive and linguistic levels. He concludes that nonhandicapped peers can provide a linguistic environment for handicapped children that is sufficiently complex to stimulate language development and still remain at the appropriate developmental level for the listener. Evidence suggests, then, that the benefits of peer modeling extend to language development as well.

In summary, there appear to be many benefits available to the handicapped child in a mainstreamed, preschool classroom, as long as the environment is properly structured and the child is provided some training and reinforcement in order to take advantage of the nonhandicapped peer models available. None of the research reported above found any ill effects for the handicapped children in their studies. But the question remains whether the effects on the nonhandicapped children involved are as positive. Although little study has been done on this subject, what evidence there is suggests that the effects on nonhandicapped children are beneficial. Studies by Bricker and Bricker (1971), Guralnick (1978), and Peck and colleagues (1978) suggest that nonhandicapped children benefit from integrated programs to at least the same degree and sometimes to a higher degree than would be expected if they had attended non-integrated preschools. These studies did not find negative effects on the nonhandicapped children in these programs. Guralnick (1978) compares the positive effects on nonhandicapped children to similar effects found for tutors in peer tutoring situations, namely that the child who is tutoring receives different but just as significant benefits from the experience as does the tutored, handicapped child.

ARGUMENTS AGAINST MAINSTREAMING

The principal arguments against the mainstreaming of handicapped children come from data based on elementary school and high school aged children. We stated earlier that some of these data reveal the inadequacy of segregated programs for handicapped children of elementary school age. Such children, however, also encounter problems in the regular classroom, and these appear to be primarily related to teacher attitude. Palmer (1979, 1980), for example, studied instructional prescriptions teachers prepared for normally achieving, learning disabled, and mentally retarded children, and found that teachers prescribed more remedial lessons for labeled children than for normally achieving children even if all were performing at grade level. They evidently expected the labeled children to perform less ably. In another study, MacMillan, Meyers, and Yoshida (1978) found that regular classroom teachers perceived mainstreamed students formerly in classes for the mentally retarded to be significantly lower than regular classroom students in both academic achievement and social acceptance, even though there was little measured difference between the two groups of students. In a study of teacher attitudes toward mainstreaming, Moore and Fine (1978) reported that regular classroom teachers were less accepting of mainstreaming than other teachers, and that they were less positive about mentally retarded than learning disabled children being mainstreamed.

These studies suggest that teacher attitudes may adversely affect the classroom environment for the mainstreamed child. Although there is no direct evidence of this at the preschool level, it must be inferred that a negative attitude on the part of preschool teachers toward handicapped children in their mainstream classrooms would have similar adverse effects.

A fear of parents of handicapped children is that a mainstream classroom will not provide the individual attention that children have traditionally enjoyed in segregated settings (Sarason & Doris, 1979). It is true that teacher-child ratios for segregated classrooms are generally established by law and are usually quite favorable, whereas regular classroom settings tend to be less strictly regulated. Nevertheless, mainstreamed, preschool programs generally have a higher teacher-child ratio than normal programs because the need for more individual attention is recognized.

Finally, an argument raised against mainstreaming by parents of nonhandicapped children is that their children will suffer a reduction in attention and instructional time because the handicapped children use up more than their share. There does not appear to be any basis for this fear, as an examination of some successful mainstreaming programs at the preschool level demonstrates. Indeed, our personal experience indicates that the individualized programming that handicapped children need, and must be provided, often spills over into the instructional environment of the nonhandicapped child as well. Regular classroom teachers who previously thought in terms of group activities and group achievement have learned through their work with handicapped children to plan for individual needs much more successfully.

And now with the main arguments for and against mainstreaming in mind, let us examine some specific ways in which handicapped children have been integrated into mainstreamed programs.

INTEGRATED PRESCHOOL PROGRAMS

Sonoma, California

Three integrated intervention projects directed by the Sonoma County Office of Education, with assistance from a nearby junior college and state college, serve youngsters from six months to six years of age in infant, toddler, and preschool groups. The children range in developmental level from severely impaired to normal; they are grouped so that there are typically two to four nonhandicapped children integrated with six to eight handicapped youngsters.

The Sonoma programs are behavioral in approach. The most interesting and innovative aspect of the programs is the peer imitation training (PIT) that takes place with toddlers and preschoolers. Thomas Cooke and Tony Apolloni, designers of PIT, were cognizant of the ordinarily low levels of peer interaction and imitation between handicapped and nonhandicapped, preschool children (Allen, Benning, & Drummon, 1972; Devoney, Guralnick, & Rubin, 1974; Ray, 1974a) and so determined to increase those levels through training. Behavior modification techniques consisting of verbal and physical prompts followed by reinforcement are used to train the handicapped child to imitate desirable behaviors of the normal peer. In the classroom the children work in dyads or triads with one normally developing child acting as peer model for one or two handicapped children.

The classrooms in the Sonoma project are organized around the five traditional areas of development: 1) language, 2) motor, 3) perceptual-cognitive, 4) self-help, and 5) social-emotional. Curriculum is based on individual developmental data gathered for each child, handicapped or not, from which instructional objectives are determined. Instruction is then either individual adult/child, small group led by adult, or peer tutoring, which is adult-supervised. Handicapped children of varying skill levels are often used in peer tutoring sessions as behavioral models for their peers just as normal children are.

An advantage of the Sonoma classes is the availability of teachers and paraprofessionals in training at the associated college and junior college. Their presence in the classroom makes a one-to-one ratio possible much of the time.

In regard to the effect of PIT on the normal children participating in the program, Apolloni and Cook (1975) report that they do not imitate behaviors of handicapped children unless reinforced. Moreover, Apolloni and Cooke question whether such imitation should necessarily be considered detrimental.

The strength of the Sonoma projects lies in the individual planning of each child's program in the structuring of learning activities and materials to maximize opportunities for handicapped children to observe and imitate their nonhandicapped peers. The fact that parents are trained to work on skill development with their own child as well as others in the classroom adds to the success of the programs.

Head Start

As noted above, Head Start programs have been required by Congress to reserve 10 percent of their enrollment space for children identified as handicapped. Head Start classes tend to be small in keeping with their performance standards, which require procedures for individual planning and evaluation of each child's growth (Cardenas, n.d.). As a result of this emphasis on meeting the special

294   MAJOR PROGRAM APPROACHES

needs of each child, such classes have been conducive to mainstreaming. Because the children come from low-income families, the majority have special needs, and so there is a tradition in Head Start of identifying children's specific skill areas that need extra remedial effort. This tradition extends readily to handicapped children. As a result, mainstreaming has become a major activity for Head Start; more than any other preschool institution, Head Start has promoted the mainstreaming of handicapped children.

Because of the grass roots nature of the Head Start experience, it is difficult to generalize about programs. Local autonomy has been the rule, and so different regions may approach mainstreaming differently. Nevertheless, some general observations may be made.

In a recently published (DHEW No. OHDS 78-311110) series of manuals for Head Start teachers, the role of the classroom teacher was delineated as:

1. developing and putting into effect an educational program that meets the special needs of a handicapped child
2. helping parents implement the learning program at home as a carry-over from the classroom
3. taking advantage of special services available to aid in program diagnosis, program planning, and implementation (handicap coordinator, social services coordinator, educational consultant)

Head Start teachers have a wealth of resources to draw on to fulfill these responsibilities. Medical, dental, mental health, and nutritional consultants provide full-time or part-time services. Social workers are often available full-time. Public school evaluation teams may be responsible for Head Start children through the Child Find outreach mandated by P.L. 94-142. Resource Access Projects (RAP) were established throughout the country to provide local Head Start staff with training and technical assistance to meet the special needs of handicapped children. Training, technical assistance, or equipment may be made available through public health departments, community mental health centers, speech and hearing clinics, universities and colleges, and developmental disabilities programs or through private agencies.

SUMMARY

Specific descriptions of other integrated preschool programs have been discussed in Chapter 11. In addition, many handicapped children are being accepted into public school kindergartens, where supplementary services are generally available, and into community and private day care centers, where they generally are not. As we extend publicly funded educational programs to a greater number of young, handicapped children during the coming decades, it is important to consider the availability of support services to aid teachers in individualizing instruction. The Head Start experience provides an excellent model. By contrast, the lack of commitment to adequate day care funding by the federal government may result in continuing inadequate educational programs for many handicapped preschoolers. It is incumbent upon us in the field of preschool education to put our support behind those in the day care field who are working for better programming for both nonhandicapped and handicapped children.

APPENDIX

TABLE   Age Ranges for Selected Screening and Assessment Instruments

TESTS	AGES IN MONTHS					
	0–12	12–24	24–36	36–48	48–60	60–over
ABC Inventory		x	x	x	x	x
Animal Crackers					x	x
Assessment of Children's Language Comprehension			x	x	x	x
Austin Spanish Articulation Test			x	x	x	x
Basic Concept Inventory				x	x	x
Bayley Scales of Infant Development	x	x	x			
Behavioral Developmental Profile	x	x	x	x	x	x
California Preschool Social Competency Scale			x	x	x	x
Carrow Elicited Language Inventory			x	x	x	x
Cattell Infant Intelligence Scale	x	x	x			
Circus				x	x	x
Columbia Mental Maturity Scale				x	x	x
Communicative Evaluation Chart	x	x	x	x	x	
Cooperative Preschool Inventory			x	x	x	x
Denver Developmental Screening Test	x	x	x	x	x	x
Detroit Tests of Learning Aptitude				x	x	x
Developmental Task Analysis			x	x	x	x
Developmental Test of Visual-Motor Integration			x	x	x	x
Developmental Test of Visual Perception			x	x	x	x
French Pictorial Test of Intelligence				x	x	x
Gesell Action Agent Test				x	x	x
Gesell Developmental Schedules	x	x	x	x	x	x
Goldman-Fristoe Test of Articulation			x	x	x	x
Goldman-Fristoe Test of Auditory Discrimination					x	x

Table Con't. TESTS	AGES IN MONTHS					
	0–12	12–24	24–36	36–48	48–60	60–over
Goodenough-Harris Draw-A-Man				x	x	x
Houston Test for Language Development	x	x	x			
Illinois Test of Psycholinguistic Ability			x	x	x	x
Key Math Diagnostic Test				x	x	x
Leiter International Performance Scale			x	x	x	x
McCarthy Scales of Children's Abilities			x	x	x	x
Pre-School Screening System				x	x	x
Merrill-Palmer Language Scale		x	x	x	x	x
Minnesota Pre-School Scale		x	x	x	x	x
Movement Skills Survey				x	x	x
Oseretsky Tests of Motor Proficiency					x	x
Peabody Picture Vocabulary Test			x	x	x	x
Physician's Handbook Screening for MBD	x	x	x	x	x	x
Porteus Mazes				x	x	x
Preschool Attainment Record	x	x	x	x	x	x
Preschool Embedded Figure Test				x	x	x
Preschool Language Scale		x	x	x	x	x
Primary Self-Concept Inventory					x	x
Pupil Record of Educational Behavior				x	x	x
Rutgers Drawing Test					x	x
Santa Clara Inventory of Developmental Tasks	x	x	x	x	x	x
Screening Test for Auditory Comprehension of Language				x	x	x
Slosson Intelligence Test					x	x
Stanford-Binet Intelligence Test			x	x	x	x
STEPS					x	x

	AGES IN MONTHS					
TESTS	0–12	12–24	24–36	36–48	48–60	60–OVER
TARC Assessment System				x	x	x
Templin-Darley Tests of Articulation					x	x
Test for Auditory Comprehension of Language				x	x	x
Tests of Basic Experiences					x	x
Utah Test of Language Development		x	x	x	x	x
Verbal Language Development Scale	x	x	x	x	x	x
Vineland Social Maturity Scale	x	x	x	x	x	x
Wechsler Preschool & Primary Scale					x	x
Winterhaven Test					x	x
Y.E.M.R.				x	x	x
Yellow Brick Road				x	x	x

TABLE Areas of Use for Selected Screening and Assessment Instruments

	SCREENING	ASSESSMENT	SOCIAL-EMOTIONAL DEVELOPMENT	AFFECTIVE	COGNITIVE	AUDITORY	VISUAL MOTOR	GROSS MOTOR	SPEECH AND LANGUAGE	BILINGUAL	MATH
ABC Inventory	x				x						
Animal Crackers	x			x							
Assessment of Children's Language Comprehension		x							x		
Austin Spanish Articulation Test		x							x	x	
Basic Concept Theory	x				x						
Bayley Scales		x	x	x	x		x		x		
Behavioral Development Profile		x	x	x			x		x		
California Preschool Social Competency Scale		x		x							
Carrow Elicited Language Inventory		x							x	x	
Cattell Infant Intelligence Scale		x			x						
Circus	x	x	x	x	x	x	x	x			x
Columbia Mental Maturity Scale		x			x	x				x	
Communicative Evaluation Chart	x						x				
Cooperative Preschool Inventory	x				x		x				
Denver Developmental Screening	x			x	x		x		x		

Test	1	2	3	4	5	6	7	8
Detroit Tests of Learning Aptitude	X		X		X	X	X	X
Development Task Analysis			X	X	X	X	X	
Developmental Test of Visual-Motor Integration					X			
Developmental Test of Visual Perception					X			
French Pictorial Test of Intelligence			X				X	X
Gesell Action Agent Test			X		X		X	X
Gesell Developmental Schedules			X		X		X	X
Goldman-Fristoe Test of Articulation			X		X			
Goldman-Fristoe Test of Auditory Discrimination						X		
Goodenough-Harris Draw-A-Man			X				X	
Houston Test for Language Development			X					X
I.T.P.A.			X		X	X	X	X
Key Math Diagnostic Test	X		X				X	X
Leiter		X	X			X		X
McCarthy Scales	X		X	X	X		X	X
Preschool Screening System			X	X	X		X	X
Merrill-Palmer Language Scale			X			X		X
Minnesota Preschool Scale			X				X	
Movement Skills Survey			X	X				
Oseretsky Tests of Motor Proficiency			X	X				

TABLE Continued

	SCREENING	ASSESSMENT	SOCIAL-EMOTIONAL DEVELOPMENT	AFFECTIVE	COGNITIVE	AUDITORY	VISUAL MOTOR	GROSS MOTOR	SPEECH AND LANGUAGE	BILINGUAL	MATH
Peabody Picture Vocabulary		x			x				x		
Porteus Mazes		x					x				
Preschool Attainment Record		x		x	x			x			
Preschool Embedded Figures Test		x			x		x				
Preschool Language Scale		x							x		
Primary Self-Concept Inventory		x		x							
PREB		x			x	x	x	x	x		x
Rutgers Drawing Test	x						x			x	
Santa Clara Inventory		x			x	x	x	x			
Screening Test for Auditory Comprehension of Language	x					x			x	x	
Slosson Intelligence Test	x				x						
Stanford-Binet		x			x				x		
STEPS	x				x				x		
TARC Assessment System	x			x				x	x		
Templin-Darley Test of Articulation	x	x							x		

Test for Auditory Comprehension of Language		x				x			x	x	
T.O.B.E.	x		x		x		x		x	x	x
Utah Test of Language Development		x			x				x		
Verbal Language Development Scale		x							x		
Vineland		x	x	x							
WPPSI		x		x	x						
Winterhaven Test	x						x				
YEMR	x		x	x	x		x	x			
Yellow Brick Road		x		x	x	x	x	x	x		

EARLY CHILDHOOD ASSESSMENT LIST

ABC Inventory

Publisher: Norman A. Adair and George Glesch, Muskegon, Michigan

Age Range: K–1; 3 yrs. 6 mos.–6 yrs. 7 mos.

There are no data on reliability and validity for predicting success. There are no norms on first grade entrants. The inventory is not adequately developed and researched. "It was constructed to identify children who are immature for a standard school program, suggesting a readiness concept based on the passage of time rather than the acquisition of experience. It can be administered by teachers. Instructions for administering are clear and brief. Vital information such as sex, geographical location, socioeconomic status, and ethnic composition are not presented" (Buros, 1978).

Animal Crackers: A Test of Factors of Motivation to Achieve

Publisher: CTB/McGraw Hill, Del Monte Research Park, Monterey, California 93940

Age Range: Pre-K, K-1

30–45 minutes

Set

Information derived from Animal Crackers should assist a teacher in providing learning and social experiences likely to optimize the development of achievement-oriented behavior and positive attitudes toward learning. Animal Crackers provides a measure of those aspects of achievement-oriented behavior that are not attributable to intellectual abilities. The test's premise is that a young child's success in school is a result of both his intellectual capacity and his motivation for learning.

Assessment of Children's Language Comprehension (ACLC)

Publisher: Consulting Psychologist's Press, 577 College Ave., Palo Alto, California 94306

Age range: 2–6 yrs.

10–15 minutes

Specimen set; pictures; manual; 25 record sheets

There are no data on reliability or norms. The assessment is recommended for research use. ACLC was developed to define receptive language difficulties in young children, and to indicate guidelines for correction of language disorders. The test uses a core vocabulary of fifty common words combined into 2, 3, and 4-element phrases. No oral responses are required from the child who points to an appropriate picture in response to a word or phrase from the examiner. It is a diagnostic tool for normal and handicapped children.

Austin Spanish Articulation Test

Publisher: Learning Concepts, 2501 North Lamar, Austin, Texas 78705

Age range: 3–12 yrs.

25 minutes

Examiner's kit

The test was developed under the supervision of Dr. Elizabeth Carrow-Woolfolk. The test is designed to evaluate the principal phonemes and phoneme combinations of the Spanish language. It is used by speech clinicians and therapists to identify articulation problems of Spanish-speaking children. Measures are single consonants and vowel sounds, major dipthongs, and consonant clusters.

Basic Concept Inventory (Englemann)

Publisher: Follett Publishing Company, 1010 W. Washington Blvd., Chicago, Illinois 60607

Age range: Pre-K–1

15–25 minutes

Picture cards; manual; tests

There are no norms for reliability and validity. The population is supposedly "culturally disadvantaged," preschool, K, slow learners, E.D., M.R. The test is based on behavioral theory. There is information for classroom application, but it appears over-simplified. Much verbalization is required of the child. It tests the understanding of basic concepts needed to be successful in school. It is a criterion referenced checklist.

Bayley Scales of Infant Development

Publisher: Psychological Corporation, 304 East 45th St., New York, New York 10017

Age range: 2 mos.–30 mos.

45 minutes

Set

There is broad coverage of behavior repertoire. The scales are recommended for clinical and research purposes. There is no predictive validity. It is used in recognition and diagnosis of sensory and neurological defects. There is high reliability, excellent standardization—representative U.S. population, controlled for sex, race, and education of head of household.

Behavioral Developmental Profile
(Marshalltown)

Publisher: Marshalltown Project, J. Mongomery, 507 East Anson, Marshalltown, Iowa 50158

Age range: 0–6 yrs.

The authors state that the test is designed to measure the development of handicapped and "culturally deprived" children, ages 0–6 years, in order to facilitate individualized teaching of preschool children within the home setting. The items are based upon normal child development. The profile consists of specifically stated skills divided into three scales: Communication, Motor, and Social. The guides list behavioral objectives reduced into sequential steps and activities to accomplish each objective.

California Preschool Social Competency Scale

Publisher: Consulting Psychologists Press, 577 College Ave., Palo Alto, California 94306

Age range: 2 yrs. 6 mos.–5 yrs. 6 mos.

Specimen set; manual; scales package of 25

The scale is easy to use, thirty item teacher's rating scale to obtain objective numerical evaluations of the social competency of preschool children. The items insure high reliability by calling for specific behaviors. A special feature of the manual is to provide percentile norms for children from high and low occupational levels for four age groups (by sex) from 2-½ to 5-½ years. The scale is a tool for diagnosis, placement, or measurement of developmental progress of young children.

Carrow Elicited Language Inventory

Publisher: Learning Concepts, 2501 North Lamar, Austin, Texas 78705

Age range: 3–8 yrs.

30 minutes approximately

Examiner's kit

The inventory is a diagnostic procedure for obtaining performance data on the child's grammatical system. In addition, it allows the speech pathologist to determine specific linguistic structures contributing to inadequate language performance. It is designed for individual administration only. The test includes practice materials. The inventory is composed of 52 stimuli, ranging from 2–10 words in length and covering twelve grammatical categories.

Cattell Infant Intelligence Scale

Publisher: Psychological Corporation, 304 East 45th St., New York, New York 10017

Age range: 3 mos.–30 mos.

20–40 minutes

Set

The scale is a downward extension of the Stanford-Binet. It has been modified by observations of the Merrill-Palmer, Minnesota Preschool and Gesell scales. The Binet yields MA scores and IQs. It was published in 1940. The scale has five items and one or two alternate items for each age level. The score obtained is the child's mental age. A number of props are needed. The test is untimed and individually administered by a person with a sound background in child psychology, including mental testing of children and a nursery school training course. Item response rates for various ages of infants are reported. Spearman-Brown reliabilities and predictive validities with Stanford-Binet scores (36 mos.) are available.

Circus

Publisher: Educational Testing Service, Rosedale Road, Princeton, New Jersey 08540

Age range: Pre-K–K

The test was developed by ETS in response to a need for a comprehensive array of assessment devices for use in nursery schools and kindergartens. The test is designed in a practical form for use by classroom teachers. There are 17 Circus instruments: Direct Child Measures—receptive vocabulary, quantitative concepts, visual discrimination, perceptual motor-coordination, discrimination of real word sounds, auditory discrimination, aspects of functional language, comprehension of oral language, productive language, general information, visual and associative memory, problem solving, and divergent pictorial production; Indirect Child Measures—activities inventory, behavior inventory; Teacher Program Measure—educational environmental questionnaire. The Circus sample over-represents children in the northeast region, and children in cities with less than 50,000. It under-represents children in the southeast, children in cities over 50,000, and black children.

Columbia Mental Maturity Scale

Publisher: Psychological Corporation, 304 East 45th St., New York, New York 10017

Age range: 3 yrs. 6 mos–9 yrs. 11 mos.

15–20 minutes

95 cards and guide for administering

The scale requires no verbal response and a minimum of motor response. It is suitable for cerebral palsy patients and others with impaired verbal or physical functioning. Age deviation scores and a supplemental maturity index indicate the child's rank on a developmental age scale. A bilingual edition includes directions in Spanish.

Communicative Evaluation Chart from Infancy to Five Years

Publisher: Educators Publishing Service, 75 Moulton St., Cambridge, Massachusetts 02138

Age range: 0–5 yrs.

Four charts

There is no manual or data on reliability and validity. The norms are based on other tests. The chart is a screening device that gives an impression of the child's overall abilities. From 12 to 15 items are given for the ages: 3 mos.; 6 mos.; 9 mos.; 1 yr.; 1 yr. 6 mos.; 2 yrs.; 3 yrs.; 4 yrs.; and 5 yrs. This is essentially a checklist of items categorized by age.

Cooperative Preschool Inventory

Publisher: Educational Testing Service, Rosedale Road, Princeton, New Jersey 08540

Age range: 3–6 yrs.

20 tests; manual; technical report

There is no hard data for predicting validity. The inventory has strong verbal emphasis. There are inadequate norms. "The test was designed for individual use. While not a culture-fair instrument, the test was developed to give a measure of achievement in areas regarded as necessary for success in school. The inventory is comprised of items of the information type and to a lesser extent, items requiring ability to label quantities, identify serial position, perceive shapes, and execute visual-motor basic drawing skills. The test has a strong verbal emphasis, but is relatively light on tasks such as short term memory, motor development and visual perception" (Buros, 1978).

Denver Development Screening Test

Publisher: Laradon Hall, East 51st Avenue and Lincoln, Denver, Colorado

Age range: 2 wks.–6 yrs.

15–20 minutes

100 tests; kit of objects; manual (cash orders only)

The test was sampled in Denver and has limited norms. The test may not be appropriate to be used for minority children. It is not to be used to determine mental age. Reliability, validity, and norms are not adequate. Contrary to claims, the test should be given by one experienced with children. It evaluates four aspects of a child's personal-social development. The results in each sector are categorized as normal, abnormal, and questionable. The test allows the examiner to look at the range of behavior in each infant and to interpret information to parents (Buros, 1978).

Detroit Tests of Learning Aptitude

Publisher: Bobbs-Merrill Company, Box 558, 4300 W. 62 St., Indianapolis, Indiana 46202

Age range: 3–19 yrs.

Pictorial material; record books; handbook

Detroit Tests are a series of 19 subtests designed to measure abilities in reasoning and comprehension, practical judgment, verbal ability, time and space relationships, number ability, auditory attentive ability, visual attentive ability, and motor ability. The range of mental ages measured is 3–19 years. Six subtests are recommended for the preschool age level. The test can be suitable for use with mentally retarded children. The tests yield a general mental age as well as subtest mental ages. It was standardized in the Detroit public schools on a population typical of large metropolitan cities. The 1967 revision of the manual is based on 1955 forms. No data on reliability of part scores are available.

Developmental Task Analysis (Valett)

Publisher: Fearon Education, Pitman Learning Inc., 6 Davis Dr., Belmont, California 94002

Age range: 2–7 yrs.

Single copy.

This is a form listing a hundred behavioral tasks basic to success in learning (most children accomplish these by the time they reach the intermediate grades). A scale is included for rating a child's accomplishment level in each of the tasks and space for comments. The tasks cover seven basic areas: Motor Integration and Physical Development; Tactile Discrimination; Auditory Discrimination; Visual Motor Coordination; Visual Discrimination; Language Development and Verbal Fluency; and Conceptual Development. It is helpful in determining whether complete diagnostic evaluation is indicated, and in planning tentative educational programs for the child.

Developmental Test of Visual-Motor Integration (Beery)

Publisher: Follett Publishing Company, 1010 W. Washington Blvd., Chicago, Illinois 60607

Age range: 2–8 yrs., 2–15 yrs.

10 minutes

Tests; manual

Reliability and validity are not very useful. The test is good for detecting visual-motor integration. Test contains 24 geometric forms that a pupil is asked to copy, reflecting problems in visual perception, hand control, and coordination between the two. The aim is to facilitate classroom screening of the perceptual motor development of young children. There are a short form and a long form. Both can be easily administered by the classroom teacher. There are developmental norms with each geometric figure as well as for the entire test. "Scoring procedures are not so straightforward and contain a high degree of subjectivity" (Buros, 1978).

Developmental Test of Visual Perception
(Forstig, Lefever, Whittlesey)

Publisher: Consulting Psychologists Press, 577 College Ave., Palo Alto, California 94306

Age range: 2–8 yrs.

This is a test of visual motor skills to be administered to groups of children between the ages of 2 to 8 years. It may be given individually. The test should be given by an experienced tester, but can be given by classroom teachers if directions are followed carefully. The subtests include: eye-motor coordination, figure-ground discrimination, form constancy, position in space, and spatial relationships. This test can be scored with a high degree of objectivity, but careful attention to the scoring instruction is mandatory. The test may be given in one or up to four sittings, depending on the age and conditions.

French Pictorial Test of Intelligence

Publisher: Houghton Mifflin, 53 West 43rd St., New York, New York 10036

Age range: 3–8 yrs.

45 minutes

Complete set

This test contains: picture vocabulary, information and comprehension, form discrimination, similarities, size and number, and immediate recall. It follows Binet, and has similar kinds of responses. The subtests are arranged in order of difficulty. There is adequate validity. The test is good for motor, speech, and language problems. It samples behavior relevant to psycho-educational demands.

Gesell Action Agent Test

Publisher: Psychological Corporation, 304 East 45th St., New York, New York 10017

Age range: 3–6 yrs.

This is a vocabulary test which consists of forty items such as, "what runs?" "what flies?" etc. The child is to supply the agent of the action. The test is more informative with the upper half of preschool range. It provides information about language comprehension as well as social and emotional maturity.

Gesell Developmental Schedules

Publisher: Psychological Corporation, 304 East 45th St., New York, New York 10017

Age range: 4 wks.–6 yrs.

20–30 minutes

Set of test materials; manual

The schedules give developmental age to contrast with chronological age and are good for screening procedures for school entry and initial class assignments. They avoid emotional factors and give simplified behavior scales. The Gesell should be used by trained personnel.

Goldman-Fristoe Woodcock Test of Articulation

Publisher: American Guidance Service, Publisher's Building, Circle Pines, Minnesota 55014

Age range: 2 yrs. and over

less than 10 minutes

Kit; filmstrip

This is a systematic assessment of the articulatory skills of children from 2 years on. Three subtests are provided to obtain a complete picture of a child's articulatory skills. It is appropriate for distractable, mentally retarded, and very young children. "The test is not in keeping with new psycholinguistic knowledge. The test gives uniformity in observation of speech patterns. Reliability and validity are not consistent" (Buros, 1978).

Goldman-Fristoe Woodcock Test of Auditory Discrimination

Publisher: American Guidance Service, Publisher's Building, Circle Pines, Minnesota 55014

Age range: 4 yrs. and over

10–15 minutes

Kit

This test evaluates speech-sound discrimination under both quiet and distracting noise conditions. There are nine clinical samples which measure speech and language problems, learning problems, and hearing defects. There are clear and

APPENDIX   315

detailed procedures for administration and interpretation in the manual. Reliability is low, and validity is questionable, especially for mentally retarded children.

Goodenough-Harris Draw-A-Man

Publisher: Harcourt, Brace, Jovanovich, Test Department, 757 3rd Ave.,
New York, New York 10017

Age range: 3–5 yrs.

Specimen set; tests

The Goodenough-Harris is a nonverbal test of mental ability. The child is asked
to draw a man, a woman, and himself. Norms are available for 3–15 years, separately for boys and girls in the form of standard scores and percentile ranks.
Buros states the user of the test should use Harris' guide book for accurate interpretation. More information is needed on the reliability and validity of the test.
There are many good suggestions for art educators.

Houston Test for Language Development
(Part I and Part II)

Publisher: Houston Test Company, Houston, Texas

Age range: 0–3 yrs.

This test measures the growth of language in children in order to determine the
level of therapy needed and in addition to determine progress with therapy. This
test was constructed to measure the development of language in children up to
three years of age. It is not consistent with new language theories. Buros recommends the use of another instrument for younger children. Categorized remarks
are used in scoring.

Illinois Test of Psycholinguistic Ability (ITPA)

Publisher: James McCarthy and Samuel Kirk, University of Illinois
Press, Box 5081, 54 E. Gregory Dr., Station A, Champaign, Illinois

Age range: 2–10 yrs.

90 minutes maximum (test can be interrupted)

Complete set

The ITPA is a complicated diagnostic test for use by the trained examiner only.
There are ten tests and two supplementary tests. Wide discrepancies between
abilities and disabilities help to identify the child with learning disabilities and

help outline areas requiring remediation. The ITPA actually tests cognitive functioning more than language. It omits reading, spelling, and other school associated tests. Test reliability is good, but standardization is questionable (middle class, white, average IQ). No data for learning disabled children are available. They must be compared to the norms.

Key Math Diagnostic Test

Publisher: American Guidance Service, Publisher's Building, Circle Pines, Minnesota 55014

Age range: Pre-school–grade 6

30 minutes approximately

Complete set

The Key Math provides a comprehensive assessment, utilizing fourteen subtests organized in three major areas: Content, Operations, and Applications. Each subtest contains items arranged in order of increasing difficulty. In the operations area the four subtests on fundamental computations (add., subt., multip., div.) contain some pencil and paper items. Other subtests in Key Math require the child to respond orally to open-ended items that are presented by the examiner. Total test score reliabilities are reported for each grade from K through 7th. The obtained correlations are in the .94 to .97 range.

Leiter International Performance Scale
(Russell G. Leiter)

Publisher: Western Psychological Services, 12031 Wilshire Blvd., Los Angeles, California 90025

Age range: 2 yrs. and over

The Leiter is a widely used non-verbal intelligence test, designed for use with individuals from two years through adults. It is excellent for use with speech handicapped, auditory-handicapped, illiterates, foreign born, and for persons of all cultural backgrounds. It is administered without language. The Leiter correlates very highly with other individual intelligence tests. The IQ has to be figured manually. There are no extrapolated tables such as in the Binet.

McCarthy Scales of Children's Abilities

Publisher: Psychological Corporation, 308 East 45th St., New York, New York 10017

Age range: 2 yrs. 6 mos.–8 yrs. 6 mos.

45 minutes age 5 and under, 60 minutes others

Set

The McCarthy assesses the intellectual and motor development of children 2-½ to 8½. It yields scores for verbal ability, short term memory, numerical ability, perceptual performance, motor coordination, lateral dominance, and overall intellectual competence. Tasks are suitable for both sexes, as well as for children from various ethnic, regional, and socioeconomic groups. It was standardized on a stratified sample controlled for age, sex, color, region of the country, and father's occupation.

Preschool Screening System

Publisher: Preschool Screening System, P.O. Box 1635, Pawtucket, Rhode Island 02862

Age range: Preschool

15–20 minutes

Record forms; developmental questionnaires; manual

This is an individually administered screening test of learning efficiency combined with a parent questionnaire, which is used as a first step toward recognizing and responding to the special learning needs of the child entering school. The primary use of this screening system is for a quick survey of the learning skills of large numbers of entering school children, so that the school curriculum can better meet their needs. This system can be used as part of a more detailed evaluation. The screening of the child includes: Information Processing Skill in Language, visual-motor and gross motor areas, and two supplementary subtests, namely, Draw-A-Person and Verbal Reasoning. The parent fills in a Developmental Questionnaire covering: Behavioral Characteristics or the skills and behavior of the child at home, plus a short Medical History and a Developmental History. Norms for ages 4 yrs. 4 mos., 4 yrs. 7 mos., 4 yrs. 8 mos., 4 yrs. 11 mos., 5 yrs., and 5 yrs. 4 mos. are provided for the above six areas (three child scores, three parent question sections).

Merrill-Palmer Language Scale

Publisher: C.H. Stoelting and Company, Chicago, Illinois

Age range: 1 yr. 6 mos.–7 yrs.

This scale measures receptive and expressive language abilities and articulation. It provides age equivalent scores for auditory comprehension, verbal ability, and overall language ability.

Minnesota Pre-School Scale (MPS)

Publisher: American Guidance Service, Publisher's Building, Circle Pines, Minnesota 55014

Age range: 1 yr. 6 mos.–6 yrs.

30 minutes or less

Complete set; specimen set with manual

The MPS is a series of 26 short subtests which provide an estimate of verbal and non-verbal intelligence. The scale is administered individually because of the early age of the children tested. Raw scores may be converted into C scores, which are approximately equally spaced as to difficulty of attainment, or converted to percentile placement scores or IQ equivalents. The scale is standardized on 100 children at each of the half year points between 1 year 6 months and 6 years. The reliability coefficients of the MPS approximate .90 for all age levels within an age range of 6 months. The scale has a probable error of 2 months.

Movement Skills Survey

Publisher: Follett Publishing Company, 1010 W. Washington Blvd., Chicago, Illinois 60607

Age range: 3–7 yrs.

Over a period of several weeks observation

This survey assists classroom teachers, movement education supervisors, school psychologists, and other professional school personnel in evaluating selected aspects of a child's motor development. It is intended to be used with the Frostig-Maslow Move-Grow-Learn Program. It assesses children's abilities in coordination and rhythm, agility, flexibility, strength, speed, balance, and body awareness.

Oseretsky Test of Motor Proficiency

Publisher: American Guidance Service, Publisher's Building, Circle Pines, Minnesota 55014

Age range: 4–16 yrs.

20–30 minutes

Set

This is a year by year scale of fine and gross motor development of children. Six basic tasks are included for each age: General Dynamic Coordination; Motor Speed; Simultaneous Voluntary Movements; and Performance without Extraneous Movement. Pantomine demonstrations of the instructions reduce the intellectual component in performance on this test. There are no American norms, but it can be administered by a trained examiner.

Peabody Picture Vocabulary Test (PPVT)

Publisher: American Guidance Service, Publisher's Building, Circle Pines, Minnesota 55014

Age range: 2 yrs. 6 mos.–18 yrs.

15 minutes or less

Set with plastic plates

The PPVT is an easily administered, quick, individual intelligence test that is appropriate for speech impaired, cerebral palsied, withdrawn, distractable, mentally retarded, and remedial reading cases. It is non-verbal and requires no special training to administer other than close attention to the manual and scoring directions. This test is untimed and takes less than 15 minutes. This test has a high correlation with both the Binet and Wechsler.

Physician's Handbook Screening for M.B.D.

Publisher: CIBA Pharmaceutical Company, Division of CIBA-GEIGY Corporation, P.O. Box 608, Summit, New Jersey 07901

Age range: 6 mos.–6th grade

time varies

This handbook was developed primarily for physicians and is designed to increase awareness of minimal brain dysfunction and to present guidelines and diagnostic aids for office screening and case management. The guidelines are organized into sections dealing with medical, social, psychological, educational, and language evaluations. These guidelines are designed to offer physicians a framework for evaluation and treatment. It is written in a manner that enables teachers and other staff to use the handbook.

Porteus Mazes, Vineland Revision

Publisher: Psychological Corporation, 304 East 45th St., New York, New York 10017

Age range: 3–12 yrs., year 14 and adult

15–60 minutes

12 pads with pad of score sheets

The mazes are a non-language test of mental ability used with the verbally handicapped, in anthropological studies, and in research on the effects of drugs and psychosurgery. It is a series of twelve mazes. It is easily administered and scored. It is included as part of the Arthur Point Scale. This test is good for children and adults who might be considered untrainable. It was designed to provide a more accurate diagnosis of mental retardation. It does discriminate between severe and moderate TMR. "While there is much about the predicative validity of the test which is known, the full development of the test potential has suffered from a lack of clearly focused validation research" (Buros, 1978).

Pre-School Attainment Record
(Research Edition)

Publisher: American Guidance Service, Publisher's Building, Circle Pines, Minnesota 55014

Age range: 6 mos–7 yrs.

20–30 minutes

25 record blanks; manual; specimen set

The informant-interview method is used. Eight areas are tapped: Ambulation, manipulation, rapport, communication, responsibility, information, ideation, and creativity. It is intended for determining the level of children for whom verbal intelligence tests are not appropriate, i.e., learning disabled, cerebral palsied, emotionally disturbed, culturally deprived, deaf, blind, aphasic. "It is divided into eight areas with fourteen age items under each category. As a scale which does not require language, and includes motor and social as well as intellectual competencies, it should prove useful in evaluating the developmental strengths and weaknesses of young children with physical, emotional or culturally-based developmental disabilities" (Buros, 1978).

Pre-School Embedded Figures Test (PEFT)

Publisher: Consulting Psychologists Press, 577 College Avenue, Palo Alto, California 94306

Age range: 3 yrs.–5 yrs. 10 mos.

15 minutes approximately

Manual; plates; 25 sheets; 25 recording forms

This is a series of devices to study the disembedding process. The PEFT has been used with children as young as 2 years 6 months. Normative data are based on 248 children aged 3 years to 5 years 10 months. It consists of 27 black and white plates all with an embedded triangle. This test requires the use of a stop watch.

Pre-School Language Scale (Zimmerman)

Publisher: Charles E. Merrill Publishing Company, 1300 Alum Creek Dr., Columbus, Ohio 43216

Age range: 1–6 yrs.

This scale is designed to detect language strengths and deficiencies. It consists of two main parts: auditory comprehension and verbal ability. It also includes a supplementary articulation section. Developmental ages are given. An auditory comprehension quotient and a verbal ability quotient can be derived as well as a general language quotient. Buros states this is a "naive instrument." It seems to be more confusing than helpful. It is a compilation of items from many traditionally used tests and is not a thorough language inventory.

Primary Self-Concept Inventory

Publisher: Learning Concepts, 2501 North Lamar, Austin, Texas 78705

Age range: 4–12 yrs.

Test manual; male and female test booklets; specimen set; technical report

The Primary Self-Concept Inventory is composed of twenty pictorial stimuli designed to measure six factors in three domains of self-concept. The instrument can be used as a pre/post test for program evaluation, and as a screening instrument to identify children with potentially low self-concepts. Reliability and validity data have been collected on black, Mexican-American, American Indian, and Anglo-American children.

Pupil Record of Educational Behavior (PREB)

Publisher: Teaching Resources, 100 Boylston St., Boston, Massachusetts 02116

Age range: Preschool–upper primary

30 minutes–2 hours

Kit

This is a tool to aid the teacher in early identification of a child's strengths and weaknesses. It profiles a student's performance over a wide range of developmental skills including coordination in both gross and fine motor skills, visual motor integration, auditory and visual perception, and higher cognitive functions related to association, generalization, and problem solving, language development, and mathematical concepts. It is not a test with norms. The child is not compared to other children. It is not designed to be used as the basis for placement of children in special class. It is useful to indicate possible difficulties and lead to further indepth evaluations.

Rutgers Drawing Test

> Publisher: Anna Starr, PhD., 126 Montgomery St., Highland Park, New Jersey 08904
>
> Age range: 4–6 yrs., 6–9 yrs.
>
> No time limit
>
> Manual for each level; test

This is a non-verbal copying test of visual perceptual and motor ability. Its norms are not adequately represented. Reliability is acceptable. More work is needed on predictive validity. It may be helpful in making subjective observations of perceptual-motor dysfunction or emotional disturbance. It can be used as a supplement to the Bender and Frostig. It is good for establishing rapport. The Rutgers Drawing Test can be used with non-English speaking, preschool, and speech impaired children.

Santa Clara Inventory of Developmental Tasks

> Publisher: Richard L. Zweig Associates, 520 Richey Ave., West Collingswood, New Jersey 08107
>
> Age range: 0–7 yrs.

This is an observational guide of developmental tasks. The areas measured are: motor coordination, visual-motor performance, visual perception, visual memory, auditory perception, auditory memory, and conceptual development. There are accompanying remedial activities for each task. The inventory and the tasks can be used by the classroom teacher.

Screening Test for Auditory Comprehension of Language

> Publisher: Learning Concepts, 2501 North Lamar, Austin, Texas 78705
>
> Age range: 3–6 yrs.
>
> Specimen set

The test for Auditory Comprehension of Language can be used as a rapid method of identifying children for an indepth listing. Composed of 25 items, it is designed for easy small group administration by the classroom teacher. Responses to the oral stimuli are marked directly in individual test booklets. Spanish and English versions are available.

Slosson Intelligence Test (SIT)

Publisher: Slosson Educational Publications, 140 Pine St., East Aurora, New York 14052

Age range: 4 yrs. and over, can be used for younger children

10–20 minutes

The SIT can be used by teachers, principals, psychometrists, psychologists, guidance counselors, social workers, school nurses, and other responsible persons who need to evaluate a person's mental ability. Items are similar to the Stanford Binet. The validity of the IQs obtained on infants and children under four years of age is unsatisfactory. If IQs are very high or very low they may be useful for screening purposes. Items and tasks used in the infant and early childhood section of this test were taken directly, or adapted, from the Gesell Developmental Schedules since the Stanford Binet does not contain an infant section. It yields sufficient validity for IQs for children four years to adulthood. The SIT is good as a quick screening device. It should not be substituted for the WISC or Binet. There is heavy emphasis on the verbal component. "Validity studies leave much to be desired. Extreme caution should be taken in relying on SIT test scores in situations where important diagnostic decisions are required, such as special class placements" (Buros, 1978).

Stanford-Binet Intelligence Scale

Publisher: Houghton Mifflin, 53 West 43rd St., New York, New York 10017

Age range: 2–18 yrs.

Varies with age to maximum of 90 minutes to two hours

In its present version (1960) the Stanford-Binet is a result of successive refinements of the original Binet Scales. It is composed of tasks which require a variety of responses from children, including the identification of common objects, hand-eye coordination, work definition, practical judgements, arithmetic computations, sentence completion, and problem interpretations. The test taps verbal abilities primarily. "This is an old, old vehicle. It has led a distinguished life as a pioneer in the bootstrap operation, that is the assessment enterprise. Its time is just about over" (Buros, 1978).

System for Teacher Evaluation for Pre-reading Skills (STEPS)

Publisher: CTB/McGraw Hill, Del Monte Research Park, Monterey, California 93940

Now in the research state, STEPS has 37 objectives. It includes parent assistance cards. The parent cards are written on a fifth and sixth grade reading level.

TARC Assessment System (Topeka Association for Retarded Children)

Publisher: H and H Enterprises, P.O. Box 3342, Lawrence, Kansas 66044

Age range: 3–16 yrs.

Time varies

A new test just printed in 1975. The publishers are interested in having professionals review the assessment. The TARC system provides a short-form behavioral assessment of the capabilities of retarded, or otherwise severely handicapped, children, on a number of skills related to education (self-help, motor, communication, and social skills). The system provides a quick assessment that stresses observable behavioral characteristics. The standardization population was 238 severely handicapped children of both sexes, ranging in ages from 3 to 16 years. The inventory is most discriminative at lower ranges of retardation.

Templin-Darley Tests of Articulation

Publisher: Bureau of Educational Research and Service, State University of Iowa, Iowa City, Iowa

Age range: 3 yrs. and over

5–15 minutes screening; 20–40 diagnostic

This test is good for a large group screening inventory in order to obtain a phonemic inventory. Competency requirements of the test administrator are not specified in the manual. The norms are based on a general American Caucasian dialect. It does not give degrees or frequencies of misarticulation.

Test for Auditory Comprehension of Language

Publisher: Learning Concepts, 2501 North Lamar, Austin, Texas 78705

Age range: 3–6 yrs.

Examiner's kit, Spanish or English version

The test measures the child's understanding of English or Spanish language structure. The test is composed of 101 plates of pictorial referents. The child responds to each of the examiner's oral stimuli by pointing to one of three line drawings. Test results can be used to diagnose the language competence of bilingual and mentally retarded children as well as those with hearing, articulation, or language disorders. The test is designed for individual administration by speech or testing specialists.

Tests of Basic Experiences (TOBE)

Publisher: CTB/McGraw Hill, Del Monte Research Park, Monterey, California 93940

Age range: Pre-K, K, 1st grade

25 minutes approximately (five sections)

The TOBE measures educationally relevant concepts, experiences, and differences among children which are directly related to the child's environment. It identifies concepts that children have and have not mastered. The format is unique because there is only one test item per page. The TOBE was standardized with children from four community types (inner city, urban, suburban, and small city) throughout the U.S. Spanish directions for administering the TOBE have also been developed. The five tests are: mathematics, language, science, social studies, and general concepts. It can be administered by the classroom teacher.

Utah Test of Language Development

Publisher: Communication Research Associates, Box 11012, Salt Lake City, Utah 84111

Age range: 1 yr. 5 mos.–14 yrs. 5 mos.

30–48 minutes

Complete; record sheets; manual

This test was normed on 273 normal, white children in Utah. It measures expressive and receptive verbal language skills. Language "milestones" are sampled. It is not recommended for children with visual-perceptual problems or non-white, urban children. Buros states that more research is needed if it is to be used as a diagnostic instrument.

Verbal Language Development Scale (VLDS)

Publisher: American Guidance Service, Publisher's Building, Circle Pines, Minnesota 55104

Age range: 1 month–16 yrs.

30 minutes

Specimen set; manual; score sheets

The VLDS is an expansion of the verbal portion of the Vineland Social Maturity Scale. Information is obtained by an interview method. It yields a language age equivalent based on a child's level of communication. The scale was standardized on 237 children selected as representative in respect to urban-rural residence, socioeconomic level, and sex. It would be appropriate to use as an interview technique with parents to determine their perception of their children's language skills.

Vineland Social Maturity Scale

Publisher: American Guidance Service, Publisher's Building, Circle Pines, Minnesota 55104

Age range: birth–adulthood

20–30 minutes

Specimen set; manual; record blanks

The Vineland is an interview type test. It outlines performances in which the individuals show progressive capacity for looking after themselves and for participating in those activities which lead toward ultimate adult independence. The items are arranged, like a Binet-type scale, in order of increasing average difficulty in six categories: self-help, self-direction, occupation, communication, locomotion, and socialization. Unless the examiner knows the subject intimately, he is dependent upon information furnished by an informant, i.e., mother, father. It can be used as a record of developmental history; as a measure of growth or deterioration; a guide for child training; and vocational and educational guidance. (See Measurement of Social Competence below)

Measurement and Social Competence (Doll)

Publisher: American Guidance Service, Publisher's Building, Circle Pines, Minnesota 55104

Text

This text thoroughly describes the Vineland Social Maturity Scale. It covers in detail the philosophy of the scale, its development, construction, procedures, scoring, standardization, item and scale validation, reliability, applications, and lists research available. Twenty-four case studies are also provided. It is essential in order to obtain maximum precision and usefulness from the Vineland Social Maturity Scale. (See Vineland Social Maturity Scale.)

Wechsler Preschool and Primary Scale of Intelligence (WPPSI)

Publisher: Psychological Corporation, 304 East 45th St., New York, New York 10017

Age range: 4 yrs.–6 yrs. 6 mos. (overlaps WISC in the 5–6½ year range)

Set with carrying case

The WPPSI is standardized on a sample at each of the six age levels, controlled for sex, color, father's occupation, geographic region, and urban vs. rural residence. It yields separate Verbal and Performance IQs, and a Full Scale IQ. For this reason the intelligence scale might be preferable to the Stanford-Binet.

Winterhaven Perceptual Forms Test

Publisher Author: Dr. M. Wold, 353 H Street, Chula Vista, California 92010

Age range: 4–9 yrs.

The Winterhaven is a visual-motor screening test. It can be used separately or together with the Winterhaven program. Visual memory is also tested. Results will indicate possible sensory motor problems in terms of actual reproduction, spatial orientation, organization, and angulation. Norms are suggested for chronological ages.

The Yellow Brick Road

Publisher: Learning Concepts, 2501 North Lamar, Austin, Texas 78705

Age range: 3–6 yrs.

Examiner's kit

The Yellow Brick Road is a screening instrument used to identify functioning strengths and weaknesses in preschool children. The program evaluates motor, visual, auditory, and language functioning. The program is designed for group administration but allows for each child to be tested individually. After receiving admission tickets to the Land of Oz, the children follow The Yellow Brick Road to take game-like tests at four testing stations. Administration requires four to eight examiners. Aides, volunteers, and parents can assist the examiners by directing children from one test station to another, or by detaining them when a test area is momentarily occupied. The test is used in research at Morehead and Peabody Colleges.

Y.E.M.R. Performance Profile for the Young Moderately and Mildly Retarded

> Publisher: Reporting Service for Children, 563 Westview Avenue, Ridgefield, New Jersey 07657
>
> Age range: Pre-K–primary
>
> Time varies

This is an evaluative scale of an individual's performance based upon teacher observation. It is designed to identify performance levels of the pupil in a wide variety of the daily tasks in the curriculum. The child is evaluated on each item on the basis of level of performance alone, regardless of the age factor. The six major areas in the profile are: social behavior; self-help; intellectual development; academics; imagination and creative expression; and emotional behavior.

References

Abramson, P., M. Gravink, L. Abramson, and D. Sommers. 1977. Early diagnosis and intervention of retardation: A survey of parental reactions concerning the quality of services rendered. *Mental Retardation* 15: 28–31.

Abroms, K. I. and J. W. Bennett. 1980. Current genetic and demographic findings in Down's syndrome: How are they presented in college textbooks on exceptionality? *Mental Retardation* 18: 101–107.

Adelson, E. and S. Fraiberg. 1975. Gross motor development in infants blind from birth. In *Exceptional infant: Assessment and intervention*. Vol. 3, edited by B. Z. Friedlander, G. M. Sterrit, and G. E. Kirk. New York: Brunner/Mazel.

Adubato, S., M. Adams, and K. Budd. 1981. Teaching a spouse in child management techniques. *Journal of Applied Behavior Analysis* 14: 193–205.

Alansky, S. D. 1971. *Rules for radicals*. New York: Random House.

Allen, K. E., P. M. Benning, and W. T. Drummond. 1972. Integration of normal and handicapped children in a behavior modification preschool: A case study. In *Behavioral analysis and education*, edited by G. Semb. Lawrence: University of Kansas Press.

Allen, K. E et al. 1964. Effects of social reinforcement on isolate behavior of a nursery school child. *Child Development* 35: 511–518.

Alpren, G. and T. Boll. 1972. *The developmental profile*. Indianapolis: Psychological Development Publishers.

Anastasi, A. 1976. *Psychological testing*. 4th ed. New York: Macmillan.

———. 1958. Heredity, environment and the question of "how?" *Psychological Review* 65: 197–208.

Antastasiow, N. J. 1981. Socioemotional development: The state of the art. *New Directions for Exceptional Children* 5: 1–12

———. 1978. Strategies and models for early childhood intervention programs in integrated settings. In *Early intervention and the integration of handicapped and nonhandicapped children*, edited by M. J. Guralnick. Baltimore: University Park Press.

Anatov, A. N. 1947. Children born during the siege of Leningrad in 1942. *Journal of Pediatrics* 30: 250.

Apgar, V. 1965. Drugs in pregnancy. *American Journal of Nursing* 65 (3), 104–105.

———. 1953. A proposal for a new method of evaluation of the newborn infant. *Anesthesia and Analgesia* 32: 260–267.

Apgar, V. and L. S. James. 1962. Further observations on the newborn scoring system. *American Journal of the Diseases of Children* 104: 419–428.

Apgar, V. et al. 1958. Evaluation of newborn infants—second report. *Journal of the American Medical Association* 168: 1958–1988.

Apolloni, T., S. A. Cooke and T. P. Cooke. 1977. Establishing a normal peer as a behavioral model for delayed toddlers. *Perceptual and Motor Skills* 44: 231–241.

Apolloni, T. and T. P. Cooke. 1975. Peer behavior conceptualized as a variable influencing infant and toddler development. *American Journal of Orthopsychiatry* 45: 4–17.

Armstrong v. Kline. 476 F. Supp. 583 (E.D. Pennsylvania, 1979).

Atkinson, R. C. and R. M. Shiffrin. 1968. Human memory: A proposed system and its control processes. In *The psychology of learning and motivation: Advances in research and theory*. Vol. 2, edited by K. W. Spence and J. T. Spence. New York: Academic Press.

Avery, C. D. 1971. A psychologist looks at the issue of public versus residential school placement for the blind. In *Problems and issues in the education of exceptional children*, edited by R. L. Jones. Boston: Houghton Mifflin.

Ayres, J. 1972. *Sensory integration and learning disorders*. Los Angeles: Western Psychological Services.

Azrin, N. H. and W. C. Holz. 1966. Punishment. In *Operant behavior: Areas of research and application*, edited by W. K. Honig. New York: Appleton-Century-Crofts.

Baer, D. M., R. F. Peterson, and J. A. Sherman. 1967. The development of imitation by reinforcing behavioral similarity to a model. *Journal of Experimental Analysis of Behavior* 10: 405–409.

Baker, B. L. 1977. Support systems for the parent as therapist. In *Research to practice in mental retardation*. Vol. 1, edited by P. Mittler. Baltimore: University Park Press.

Baker, B. L., A. J. Brightman, L. J. Heifetz, and D. M. Murphy. 1976. *Steps to independence series*. Champaign, Ill.: Research Press.

Baldwin, A. 1968. *Theories of child development*. New York: Wiley.

Bandura, A. 1971. Psychotherapy based on modeling principles. In *Handbook of psychotherapy and behavior change: An empirical analysis*, edited by A. Bergin and S. L. Garfield. New York: Wiley.

Bandura, A. and F. L. Menlove. 1968. Factors determining vicarious extinction of avoidance behavior through symbolic modeling. *Journal of Personality and Social Psychology* 8: 99–108.

Barker, R. G. 1968. *Ecological psychology*. Stanford: Stanford University Press.

———. 1955. *One boy's day*. New York: Harper & Row.

Barnes, A. C. 1968. *Intra-uterine development*. Philadelphia: Lea & Febiger.

Baron, R. A. and S. F. Lawton. 1972. Environmental influences on aggression: The facilitation of modeling effects by high temperatures. *Psychonomic Science* 26: 80–82.

Bartel, N. R. and S. L. Guskin. 1980. A handicap as a social phenomenon. In *Psychology of exceptional children and youth*. 4th ed., edited by W. M. Cruickshank. Englewood Cliffs, N.J.: Prentice-Hall.

Bates, E. 1976a. *Language and context*. New York: Academic Press.

———. 1976b. Pragmatics and sociolinguistics in child language. In *Normal and deficient child language*, edited by D. Morehead and A. Morehead. Baltimore: University Park Press.

———. 1975. Peer relations and the acquisition of language. In *Friendship and peer relations*, edited by M. Lewis and L. Rosenblum. New York: Wiley.

Battle v. Commonwealth. 79–2158, 79–2188–90, 79–2568–70, (3rd Cir., July 18, 1980).

Bayley, N. 1970. Development of mental abilities. In *Carmichael's manual of child psychology*. Vol. 1, edited by P. H. Mussen. New York: Wiley.

———. 1969. *Bayley scales of infant development*. New York: Psychological Corporation.

———. 1935. The development motor abilities during the first three years. *Monographs of the Society for Research in Child Development* 1: 1935.

Beckman-Bell, P. 1981. Child related stress in families of handicapped children. *Topics in Early Childhood Special Education* 1: 45–53.

Beckwith, L. 1979. Prediction of emotional and social behavior. In *The handbook of infant development*, edited by J. D. Osofsky. New York: Wiley.

Beez, W. V. 1968. Influence of biased psychological reports on teacher behavior and pupil performance. *Proceedings of the Seventy-fifth American Psychological Association Annual Convention*. Washington, D.C.: American Psychological Association.

Bell, R. Q. 1968. A reinterpretation of the direction of effects in studies of socialization. *Psychological Review* 75: 81–95.

Beller, E. K. 1979. Early intervention programs. In *Handbook of infancy research*, edited by J. D. Osofsky. New York: Wiley.

Belmont, J. M. and E. C. Butterfield. 1971. Learning strategies as determinants of memory deficiencies. *Cognitive Psychology* 2: 411–420.

Benoit, E. P. 1959. Towards a new definition of mental retardation. *American Journal of Mental Deficiency* 63: 559–565.

Berdine, W. H. and P. T. Cegelka. 1980. *Teaching the trainable retarded*. Columbus, Ohio: Charles Merrill.

Berg, W. K. and K. M. Berg. 1979. Psychophysiological development in infancy: State, sensory function and attention. In *The handbook of infant development*, edited by J. D. Osofsky. New York: Wiley.

Berger, M. and M. Foster. 1976. Families with retarded children: A multivariate approach to issues and strategies. *Multivariate Experimental Clinical Research* 2: 1–21.

Berger, M. and M. A. Fowlkes. 1980. Family intervention project: A family network model for serving young handicapped children. *Young Children* 35: 22–32.

Bernal, E. M., Jr. 1977. Introduction: Perspectives on nondiscriminatory assessment. In *Psychological and educational assessment of minority children*, edited by T. Oakland. New York: Brunner/Mazel.

Bernal, M. E., M. D. Klinnert, and L. A. Schultz. 1980. Outcome evaluation of behavioral parent training and client centered parent counseling for children with conduct problems. *Journal of Applied Behavior Analysis* 13: 677–691.

Bernal, M. E. and J. A. North. 1978. A survey of parent training manuals. *Journal of Applied Behavior Analysis* 11: 533–544.

Biber, B. E., E. Shapiro, and D. Wickens. 1971. *Promoting cognitive growth: A developmental-interaction point of view*. Washington, D.C.: National Association for the Education of Young Children.

Bijou, S. W. 1966. A functional analysis of retarded development. In *International review of research in mental retardation*. Vol. 1, edited by N. R. Ellis. New York: Academic Press.

Bijou, S. W. and D. M. Baer. 1965. *Child development*. Vol. 2. *Universal stages of infancy*. New York: Appleton-Century-Crofts.

———. 1961. *Child development: A systematic and empirical theory*. Vol. 1. New York: Appleton-Century-Crofts.

Bijou, S. W., R. F. Peterson, and M. H. Ault. 1968. A method to integrate descriptive and experimental field studies at the level of data and empirical concepts. *Journal of Applied Behavior Analysis* 1: 175–191.

Bijou, S. W. et al. 1969. Methodology for experimental studies of young children in natural settings. *Psychological Record* 19: 177–210.

Bixler, R. H. 1980. Nature versus nurture: The timeless anachronism. *Merrill-Palmer Quarterly* 26: 153–159.

Bloom, B. S. 1964. *Stability and change in human characteristics*. New York: Wiley.

Bloom, L. 1973. *One word at a time: The use of single-word utterances before syntax*. The Hague: Mouton.

———. 1970a. *Language development: Form and function in emerging grammars*. Cambridge, Massachusetts: The Massachusetts Institute of Technology Press.

———. 1970b. Child language, adult model. Review of P. Menyuk, Sentences children use. *Contemporary Psychology* 15: 182–184.

Bloom, L. and P. Lahey. 1978. *Language development and language disorders*. New York: Wiley.

Bloom, L., P. Lightbrown, and L. Hood. 1975. Structure and variation in child language. *Monographs of the Society for Research in Child Development* 40 (Serial No. 160).

Bluma, S. M., M. S. Shearer, A. H. Frohman, and J. M. Hillard. 1976. *Portage guide to early education*. Portage, Wis.: Cooperative Educational Service Agency 12.

Bogdan, R. 1980. What does it mean when a person says, "I am not retarded"? *Education and Training of the Mentally Retarded* 15: 74–79.

Boggs, E. M. 1978. Who is putting whose head in the sand or in the clouds as the case may be? In *Parents speak out: Growing with a handicapped child*, edited by A. P. Turnbull and H. R. Turnbull, III. Columbus, Ohio: Charles E. Merrill.

Boles, G. 1959. Personality factors in mothers of cerebral palsied children. *Genetic Psychology Monographs* 59: 195–218.

Bourne, L. E., Jr., R. L. Dominowski, and E. F. Loftus. 1979. *Cognitive processes*. Englewood Cliffs, N.J.: Prentice-Hall.

Bovet, M. C., P. R. Dasen, and B. Inhelder. 1974. Etapes de l'intelligence sensorimotrice chez l'enfant Baoule. *Archives de Psychologie* 41: 363–371.

Bower, E., K. Bersamin, A. Fine, and J. Carlson. 1974. *Learning to play, playing to learn*. New York: Human Sciences Press.

Bowerman, M. 1973. *Early syntactic development: A cross-linguistic study with special reference to Finnish*. London: Cambridge University Press.

Bowlby, J. 1969. *Attachment*. New York: Basic Books.

Brackbill, Y. 1979. Obstetrical medication and infant behavior. In *Handbook of infant development*, edited by J. O. Osofsky. New York: Wiley.

Brandt, R. M. 1972. *Studying behavior in natural settings*. New York: Holt, Rinehart & Winston.

Branston, M. B., L. J. Vincent, and C. Salisbury. 1978. *User's guide for using families' daily activities as teaching times: A parent manual*. Madison, Wis.: Madison Metropolitan School District.

Bray, N. M., J. M. Coleman, and M. B. Bracken. 1981. Critical events in parenting handicapped children. *Journal of the Division for Early Childhood* 3: 26–33.

Brazelton, T. B. 1973. *Neonatal behavioral assessment scale*. Philadelphia: Lippincott.

————. 1969. *Infants and mothers: Difference in development*. New York: Delacorte Press.

Brazelton, T. B., B. Koslowski, and M. Main. 1974. The origins of reciprocity: The early mother-infant interaction. In *The effect of the infant on its caregiver*, edited by M. Lewis and L. A. Rosenblum. New York: Wiley.

Bricker, D. D. 1978. A rationale for the integration of handicapped and nonhandicapped preschool children. In *Early intervention and the integration of handicapped and non-handicapped children*, edited by M. J. Guralnick. Baltimore: University Park Press.

Bricker, D. D. and W.A. Bricker. 1973. Infant, toddler and preschool research and intervention project report: Year III. *IMRID Behavioral Science Monograph* (No. 23). Nashville, Tennessee: Institute on Mental Retardation and Intellectual Development, George Peabody College.

————. 1972. Toddler research and intervention project report: Year II. *IMRID Behavioral Science Monograph* (No. 21). Nashville, Tennessee: Institute on Mental Retardation and Intellectual Development, George Peabody College.

————. 1971. Toddler research and intervention project report: Year I. *IMRID Behavioral Science Monograph* (No. 20). Nashville, Tennessee: Institute on Mental Retardation and Intellectual Development, George Peabody College.

Bricker, D. D. and L. Dennison. 1978. Training prerequisites to verbal behavior. In *Systematic instruction of the moderately and severely handicapped*, edited by M. E. Snell. Columbus, Ohio: Charles E. Merrill.

Bricker, D. D., L. Dennison and W. A. Bricker. 1976. *A language intervention program for developmentally young children*. University of Miami, MCCD Monograph (Series No. 1).

Bricker, W. A. and D. D. Bricker. 1976. The infant, toddler, and preschool research and intervention project. In *Intervention strategies with high risk infants and young children*, edited by T. D. Tjossem. Baltimore: University Park Press.

————. 1974. An early language training strategy. In *Language perspectives: Acquisition, retardation, and intervention*, edited by R. L. Schiefelbusch and L. L. Lloyd. Baltimore: University Park Press.

Bromwich, R. M. and A. H. Parmelee. 1979. An intervention program for pre-term infants. In *Infants born at risk: Behavior and development*, edited by T. M. Field. New York: Spectrum Publications.

Brown, A. L., J. C. Campione, N. W. Bray, and B. L. Wilcox. 1973. Keeping track of changing variables: Effects of rehearsal training and rehearsal prevention in normal and retarded adolescents. *Journal of Experimental Psychology* 101: 123–131.

Brown, R. 1973. *A first language: The early stages*. Cambridge, Mass.: Harvard University Press.

Brown, R. and U. Bellugi. 1964. Three processes in the child's acquisition of syntax. *Harvard Educational Review* 34: 133–151.

Brown, R., C. Cazden, and U. Bellugi. 1969. The child's grammar from one to three. In *Minnesota Symposia on Child Psychology*. Vol. 2, edited by J. P. Hill. Minneapolis: University of Minnesota Press.

Brown, R. and C. Fraser. 1963. The acquisition of syntax. In *Verbal behavior and verbal learning: Problems and process*, edited by C. N. Cofer and B. Musgrave. New York: McGraw Hill.

Bruner, J. S. 1975. The ontogenesis of speech acts. *Journal of Child Language* 2: 1–19.

————. 1972. Nature and uses of immaturity. *American Psychologist* 27: 687–708.

Bruner, J. S., A. Jolly and K. Sylva (eds.) 1976. *Play: Its role in development and evolution*. New York: Basic Books.

Buck, P. S. 1950. The child who never grew. *Ladies' Home Journal* May: 35–169.

Buncic, J. R. 1980. Disorders of vision. In *Child development and developmental disabilities*, edited by S. Gabel and M. Erickson. Boston: Little, Brown.

Buros, O. K. (ed.) 1978. The eighth mental measurements yearbook. Highland Park, N. J.: Gryphon Press.

Buscaglia, L. 1975. *The disabled and their parents: A counseling challenge.* Thorofare, N.J.: Charles B. Slack.

Buss, A. H. and R. Plomin. 1975. *A temperamental theory of personality development.* New York: Wiley.

Butler, N. R. and E. D. Alberman (eds.) 1969. *Perinatal problems: The second report of the 1958 British Perinatal Mortality Study.* Edinburg: Livingston.

Butterfield, E. C., C. Wambold and J. M. Belmont. 1973. On the theory and practice of improving short-term memory. *American Journal of Mental Deficiency* 77: 654–669.

Byers, P. and H. Byers. 1972. Nonverbal communication in the classroom. In *Functions of language in the classroom,* edited by C. Cazden and J. Hymes. New York: Teachers' College.

Bzoch, K. and R. League. 1971. *Receptive-expressive emergent language scales.* Baltimore: University Park Press.

Calabro, J. J. 1970. Management of juvenile rheumatoid arthritis. *Journal of Pediatrics* 77: 355–365.

Calhoun, J. B. 1962. Population density of social pathology. *Scientific American* 206: 139–148.

Cansler, D. P., G. H. Martin and M. C. Valand. 1975. *Working with families.* Winston-Salem, N.C.: Kaplan Press.

Cameron, J. R. 1978. Parental treatment, children's temperament, and the risk of childhood behavioral problems. *American Journal of Orthopsychiatry* 48: 140–147.

———. 1977. Parental treatment, children's temperament, and the risk of childhood behavioral problems: Relationships between parental characteristics and changes in children's temperament over time. *American Journal of Orthopsychiatry* 47: 568–576.

Campbell, P. H., K. M. Green and L. M. Carlson. 1977. Approximating the norm through environmental and child-centered prosthetics and adaptive equipment. In *Educational programming for the severely and profoundly handicapped,* edited by E. Sontag. Washington, D.C.: Council for Exceptional Children, Division on Mental Retardation.

Capobianco, R. J. and D. A. Cole. 1960. Social behavior of mentally retarded children. *American Journal of Mental Deficiency* 64: 638–651.

Carey, W. B. 1970. A simplified method of measuring infant temperament. *Journal of Pediatrics* 77: 188–194.

Carter, C. H. (ed.) 1975a. *Medical aspects of mental retardation.* 2nd ed. Springfield, Ill.: Charles C Thomas.

———. 1975b. *Handbook of mental retardation syndromes.* 3rd ed. Springfield, Ill.: Charles C Thomas.

Carter, S. 1975. Assessing prognosis after a child's first febrile seizure. *National Spokesman* April: 5.

Cartwright, C. A. 1981. Effective programs for parents of young handicapped children. *Topics in Early Childhood Special Education* 1: 1–9.

Cassarett, L. J. and Doull, J. (eds.) 1975. *Toxicology, the basic science of poisons.* New York: Macmillan.

Cattell, P. 1960. *The measurement of intelligence of infants and young children.* New York: The Psychological Corporation.

Cavallaro, S. and R. Porter. 1980. Peer preferences of at-risk and normally developing children in a preschool mainstream classroom. *American Journal of Mental Deficiency,* 84 (4): 357–366.

Chomsky, N. 1965. *Aspects of the theory of syntax.* Cambridge, Mass.: The M.I.T. Press.

————. 1959. Review of *Verbal Behavior* by B. F. Skinner. *Language* 35: 26–58.

Christopherson, J. 1972. The special children in the regular preschool: Some administrative notes. *Childhood Education* 49: 138–140.

Cleveland, D. W. and N. Miller. 1977. Attitudes and life commitments of older siblings of mentally retarded adults: An exploratory study. *Mental Retardation* 15: 38–41.

Cohen, G. and M. Martin. 1975. Hemisphere differences in an auditory stroop test. *Perception and Psychophysics* 17: 79–83.

Cohen, L. B., J. S. DeLoache, and M. S. Strauss. 1979. Infant visual perception. In *The handbook of infant development*, edited by J. D. Osofsky. New York: Wiley.

Cole, M. and J. Bruner. 1971. Cultural differences and influences about psychological processes. *American Psychologist* 26: 867–876.

Cooper, L. Z. and S. Krugman. 1966. Diagnosis and management: Congenital rubella. *Pediatrics* 37: 335.

Corter, C. Infant attachments. 1974. In *New perspectives in child development*, edited by B. Foss. Baltimore: Penguin.

Craik, F. I. M. and R. S. Lockhart. 1972. Levels of processing: A framework for memory research. *Journal of Verbal Learning and Verbal Behavior* 11: 671–684.

Cratty, B. J. 1970. *Perceptual and motor development in infants and children*. New York: Macmillan.

Crowley, M., K. Keane, and C. Needham. 1982. Fathers: The forgotten parents. *American Annals of the Deaf* February: 38–40.

Culatta, R. and B. K. Culatta. 1981. Communication disorders. In *An introduction to special education*, edited by A. E. Blackhurst and W. H. Berdine. Boston: Little, Brown.

Cummings, S. T. 1976. The impact of the child's deficiency on the father: A study of fathers of mentally retarded and chronically ill children. *American Journal of Orthopsychiatry* 46: 246–255.

Cummings, S. T., H. Bayley, and H. Rie. 1966. Effects of the child's deficiency on the mother: A study of mothers of mentally retarded, chronically ill, and neurotic children. *American Journal of Orthopsychiatry*, 36: 595–608.

Dale, P. S. 1976. *Language development: Structure and function*. New York: Holt, Rinehart & Winston.

Dansky, J. L. 1980. Cognitive consequences of sociodramatic play and exploration training for economically disadvantaged preschoolers. *Journal of Child Psychology and Psychiatry and Allied Disciplines* 21: 47–58.

Darley, B., and M. May (eds.) 1979. *Infant assessment: Issues and applications*. Proceedings of conference sponsored by Western States Technical Assistance Resource, 1978–1979.

Davidson, C. 1980. Parents' and teachers' response to mainstreaming. *Education Unlimited* 2: 33–35.

Delaney, S. W., D. J. Meyer and M. J. Ward. 1977. *Fathers and infants class: A model for facilitating attachment between fathers and their infants*. Seattle: University of Washington, Experimental Education Unit, Child Development and Mental Retardation Center.

Dennis, W. 1960. Causes of retardation among institutional children: Iran. *Journal of Genetic Psychology* 96: 47–59.

Dennis, W. and P. Najarian. 1957. Infant development under environmental handicap. *Psychological Monographs* 71 (No. 7).

Deutsch, M. 1966. Facilitating development in the pre-school child: Social and psychological perspectives. In *Preschool education today*, edited by F. Hechings. New York: Doubleday.

Devoney, C., M. J. Guralnick, and H. Rubin. 1974. Integrating handicapped and nonhandicapped preschool children: Effects on social play. *Childhood Education* 50: 360–364.

DeWeerd, J. 1980. Handicapped children's early education program: A retrospective. In *Handicapped children's early education program: 1979 conference proceedings*, edited by S. Friedman. Washington, D.C.: Bureau for the Education of the Handicapped.

Dexter, L.A. 1964. On the politics and sociology of stupidity in our society. In *The other side: Perspectives on deviance*, edited by H. S. Becker. New York: Free Press.

Doll, E. A. 1964. *The Vineland scale of social maturity.* Minneapolis: American Guidance Service.

Dore, J. 1975. Holophrases, speech arts, and language universals. *Journal of Child Language* 2: 21–40.

Drage, J. S. et al. 1966. Five-minute Apgar scores and 4-year psychological performance. *Development, Medicine and Child Neurology* 8: 141.

Drillien, C. M. 1964. *The growth and development and the prematurely born infant.* Baltimore: Williams and Wilkins.

Duckworth, E. 1979. Either we're too early and they can't learn it or we're too late and they know it already: The dilemma of "applying Piaget." *Harvard Educational Review* 49: 297–312.

Dunn, L. M. 1968. Special education for the mildly retarded—Is much of it justifiable? *Exceptional Children* 35: 5–22.

———. 1959. *Peabody picture vocabulary test.* Minneapolis: American Guidance Service.

Edgar, E. and Davidson, C. 1979. Parent perceptions of mainstreaming. *Education Unlimited* 1: 32–33.

Edmonds, M. 1976. New directions in theories of language acquisition. *Harvard Educational Review* 46: 29–40.

Edwards, C. P. and M. Lewis. 1979. Young children's concepts of social relations: Social functions and social objects. In *The child and its family*, edited by M. Lewis and L. A. Rosenblum. New York: Plenum.

Ellis, N. R. 1970. Memory processes in retardates and normals. In *International review of research in mental retardation.* Vol. 4, edited by N. R. Ellis. New York: Academic Press.

Erickson, M. P. 1974. Talking with fathers of young children with Down's Syndrome. *Children Today* Nov.–Dec.: 22–25.

Erikson, E. H. 1963. *Childhood and society.* 2nd ed. New York: Norton.

Erlenmeyer-Kimling, L. 1968. Studies on the offspring of two schizophrenic parents. In *The transmission of schizophrenia*, edited by D. Rosenthal and S. Kety. New York: Pergamon Press.

Escalona, S. K. and H. H. Corman. 1969. *Albert Einstein scales of sensorimotor development.* New York: Department of Psychiatry, Albert Einstein College of Medicine.

Evans, E. D. 1975. *Contemporary influences in early childhood education.* 2nd ed. New York: Holt, Rinehart & Winston.

Fallen, N. H. and J. E. McGovern. 1978. *Young children with special needs.* Columbus, Ohio: Charles E. Merrill.

Farber, B. 1968. *Mental retardation: Its social context and social consequences.* Boston: Houghton-Mifflin.

———. 1963. Interaction with retarded siblings and life goals of children. *Marriage and Family Living* 25: 96–98.

Featherstone, H. 1980. *A difference in the family.* New York: Basic Books, Inc.

Feitelson, D. and G. S. Ross. 1973. The neglected factor—play. *Human Development* 16: 202–223.

Ferguson, C. 1977. Baby talk as a simplified register. In *Talking to children*, edited by C. Snow and C. Ferguson. Cambridge: Cambridge University Press.

Fillmore, C. 1968. The case for case. In *Universals in linguistic theory*, edited by E. Bach and R. T. Harms. New York: Holt.

Fiorentino, M. 1972. *Normal and abnormal development: The influence of primitive reflexes on motor development*. Springfield, Ill.: Charles C Thomas.

Fisher, M. A. and D. Zeaman. 1973. An attention-retention theory of retardate discrimination learning. In *The international review of research in mental retardation*. Vol. 6, edited by N. R. Ellis. New York: Academic Press.

Fitzhardinge, P. M. and M. Ramsey. 1973. The improving outlook for the small prematurely born infant. *Developmental Medicine and Child Neurology* 16: 709–728.

Flavell, J. 1977. *Cognitive development*. Englewood Cliffs, N. J.: Prentice-Hall.

Foster, M., M. Berger and M. McLean. 1981. Rethinking a good idea: A reassessment of parent involvement. *Topics in Early Childhood Special Education* 1: 55–65.

Fowle, C. M. 1968. The effect of the severely mentally retarded child on his family. *American Journal of Mental Deficiency* 73: 468–473.

Fox, N. 1978. *Infant "at risk": The consequences of low birth weight on the physical and mental health of the child*. Princeton, N.J.: Institute for the Study of Exceptional Children, Educational Testing Service.

Fraiberg, S. 1975. Intervention in infancy: A program for blind infants. In *Exceptional infant: Assessment and intervention*. Vol. 3 edited by B. Z. Friedlander, G. M. Sterritt, and G. E. Kirk. New York: Brunner/Mazel.

———. 1971. Intervention in infancy: A program for blind infants. *Journal of the American Academy of Child Psychiatry* 10: 381–405.

Fraiberg, S. and E. Adelson. 1973. Self representation in language and play: Observations of blind children. *Psychoanalytical Quarterly* 42: 539.

Fraiberg, S., M. Smith, and E. Adelson. 1969. An educational program for blind infants. *Journal of Special Education* 3 (2): 121–139.

Frankenburg, W. and B. Camp (eds.) 1975. *Pediatric screening tests*. Springfield, Ill.: Charles C Thomas.

Frankenburg, W. and J. Dodds. 1969. *Denver developmental screening test*. Denver: University of Denver.

Fredericks, H. D., V. L. Baldwin, and D. Grove. 1974. A home-center based parent training model. In *Training parents to teach: Four models*, edited by J. Griggs. Chapel Hill, N.C.: Technical Assistance Development System. (EC 071447)

Freedman, D. G. 1974. *Human infancy: An evolutionary perspective*. Hillsdale N.J.: Lawrence Erlbaum.

Freud, S. 1926. *Inhibitions, symptoms, and anxiety*. London: Hogarth Press.

———. 1915. *Instincts and their vicissitudes*. London: Hogarth Press.

Furey, E. M. 1982. The effects of alcohol on the fetus. *Exceptional Children* 49: 30–34.

Gallagher, J. J. 1980. The next decade for the young handicapped child. In *Handicapped children's early education program: 1979 conference proceedings*, edited by S. Friedman. Washington, D.C.: Bureau of Education for the Handicapped.

Gallagher, J. J., A. Cross, and W. Scharfman. 1981. Parental adaptation to a young handicapped child: The father's role. *Journal of the Division for Early Childhood* 3: 3–14.

Gallagher, J. M. and D. K. Reid. 1981. *The learning theory of Piaget and Inhelder*. Monterrey, California: Brooks/Cole.

Garnica, O. 1977. Some prosodic and paralinguistic features of speech to young children. In *Talking to children*, edited by C. Snow and C. Ferguson. Cambridge: Cambridge University Press.

Garwood, S. G. 1979. *Educating young handicapped children: A developmental approach*. Germantown, Maryland: Aspen Systems.

Gath, A. 1977. The impact of an abnormal child upon the parents. *British Journal of Psychiatry* 130: 405–410.

———. 1974. Sibling reactions to mental handicap: A comparison of the brothers and sisters of mongol children. *Journal of Child Psychology and Psychiatry* 15: 187–198.

———. 1973. The school-age siblings of mongol children. *British Journal of Psychiatry* 123: 161–167.

Gazzaniga, M. 1970. *The bisected brain.* New York: Appleton-Century-Crofts.

Gazzaniga, M. S. and C. Blakemore (eds.) 1975. *Handbook of psychobiology.* New York: Academic Press.

Gazzaniga, M. S. and J. E. LeDoux. 1978. *The integrated mind.* New York: Plenum.

Gearheart, B. R. 1972. *Education of the exceptional child: History, present practices, and trends.* Scranton, Pennsylvania: International Textbook Co.

Gesell, A. 1949. *Gesell developmental schedules.* New York: Psychological Corporation.

———. 1940. *The first five years of life.* New York: Harper & Row.

Gesell, A. and C. Amatruda. 1969. *Developmental diagnosis.* New York: Harper & Row.

Gianascol, A. J. 1973. Psychodynamic approaches to childhood schizophrenia: A review. In *Clinical studies in childhood psychosis: 25 years in collaborative treatment and research,* edited by S. A. Szurek and I. N. Berlin. New York: Brunner/Mazel.

Ginsburg, H. and S. Opper. 1979. *Piaget's theory of intellectual development.* 2nd ed. Englewood Cliffs, N. J.: Prentice-Hall.

Glass, D. C. and J. E. Singer. 1972. *Urban stress: Experiments on noise and social stressors.* New York: Academic Press.

Gleason, J. 1973. Code switching in children's language. In *Cognitive development and the acquisition of language,* edited by T. Moore. New York: Academic Press.

Gold, M. W. 1976. Task analysis of a complex assembly task by the retarded child. *Exceptional Children* 43: 78–84.

Golden, M. and B. Birns. 1976. Social class and infant intelligence. In *Origins of intelligence,* edited by M. Lewis. New York: Plenum.

Goldfarb, W. 1943. The effects of early institutional care on adolescent personality. *Journal of Experimental Education* 12: 106–129.

Goldschmid, M. L. and P. M. Beatler. 1968. *Manual: Concept assessment kit—conservation.* San Diego: Educational and Industrial Testing Service.

Goldstein, J. and A. P. Turnbull. 1982. Strategies to increase parent participation in IEP conferences. *Exceptional Children* 48: 360–361.

Goodwin, W. and L. Driscoll. 1980. *Measurement and evaluation in early childhood education.* San Francisco: Jossey-Bass.

Gordon, J. E. and H. C. Haywood. 1969. Input deficit in cultural-familial retardates: Effect of stimulus enrichment. *American Journal of Mental Deficiency* 73: 604–610.

Gorman, J. J., D. G. Cogan and S. S. Gellis. 1957. An apparatus for grading the visual acuity of infants on the basis of optokinetics. *Pediatrics* 19: 1088.

Gottlieb, G. 1965. Prenatal auditory sensitivity in chickens and ducks. *Science* 147: 1596–1598.

Graham, M. D. 1967. *Multiply-impaired blind children: A national problem.* New York: American Foundation for the Blind.

Green, H. B. 1974. Infants of alcoholic mothers. *American Journal of Obstetrics and Gynecology* 118: 713–716.

Gregg, N. M. 1941. Congenital cataract following German measles in the mother. *Transactions of the Opthalmological Society of Australia* 3: 35.

Grossman, F. K. 1972. *Brothers and sisters of retarded children: An exploratory study.* Syracuse, N.Y.: Syracuse University Press.

Grossman, J. J. (ed.) 1973. *Manual on terminology and classification in mental retardation.* Washington, D.C.: American Association on Mental Deficiency.

Gruenwald, P. 1965. Some aspects of fetal distress. In *Gestational age, size, and maturity,* edited by M. Dawkins and W. G. MacGregor. London: Spatics Society.

Guralnick, M. J. 1981. Peer influences on the development of communicative competence. In *The utilization of classroom peers as behavior change agents*, edited by P. S. Strain. New York: Plenum.
———. 1980. Social interactions among preschool children. *Exceptional Children* 46: 248–253.
———. (ed.) 1978a. *Early intervention and the integration of handicapped and non-handicapped children*. Baltimore: University Park Press.
———. 1978b. Integrated preschools as education and therapeutic environments: Concept, design and analysis. *Early intervention and the integration of handicapped and nonhandicapped children*, edited by M. J. Guralnick. Baltimore: University Park Press.
———. 1976. The value of integrating handicapped and nonhandicapped preschool children. *American Journal of Orthopsychiatry* 42: 236–245.
Guthrie, R. D. et al. 1977. The newborn. In *Introduction to clinical pediatrics*, edited by D. W. Smith. Philadelphia: W. B. Saunders.

Hallahan, D. P. and J. M. Kauffman. 1982. *Exceptional children: Introduction to special education*. 2nd ed. Englewood Cliffs, N.J.: Prentice-Hall.
Halliday, M. A. K. 1975. *Learning how to mean—Explorations in the development of language*. London: Edward Arnold.
Hansen, H. 1978. Decline of Down's syndrome after abortion reform in New York state. *American Journal of Mental Deficiency* 83: 183–185.
Hanson, M. J. 1978. *Teaching your Down's syndrome infant: A guide for parents*. Baltimore: University Park Press.
Harbin, G. 1977. Educational assessment. In *Identifying handicapped children: A guide to casefinding, screening, diagnosis, assessment and evaluation*, edited by L. Cross and K. Goin. New York: Walker & Co.
Hare, B. A. and J. M. Hare. 1979. Learning disabilities in young children. In *Educating young handicapped children: A developmental approach*, edited by S. G. Garwood. Germantown, Maryland: Aspen Systems.
Harley, R. D. (ed.) 1975. *Pediatric ophthalmology*. Philadelphia: Saunders.
Harnad, S. et al. (eds.) 1977. *Lateralization in the nervous system*. New York: Academic Press.
Hart, V. 1979. Crippling conditions. In *Children with exceptional needs*, edited by M. S. Lilly. New York: Holt, Rinehart & Winston.
Hartup, W. W. 1978. Peer interaction and the processes of socialization. In *Early intervention and the integration of handicapped and nonhandicapped children*, edited by M. J. Guralnick. Baltimore: University Park Press.
———. 1975. The origins of friendship. In *Friendship and peer relations*, edited by M. Lewis and L. Rosenblum. New York: Wiley.
Hartup, W. W., J. Glazer, and R. Charlesworth. 1967. Peer reinforcement and sociometric status. *Child Development* 38: 1017–1024.
Hayden, A. and G. R. Beck. 1982. The epidemiology of high-risk and handicapped infants. In *Finding and educating high-risk and handicapped infants*, edited by C. T. Ramey and P. L. Trohanis. Baltimore: University Park Press.
Hayden, A. H. and V. Dmitriev. 1975. The multidisciplinary preschool program for Down's syndrome children at the University of Washington Model Preschool Center. In *Exceptional infant: Assessment and intervention*. Vol. 3, edited by B. Z. Friedlander, G. M. Sterritt, and G. E. Kirk. New York: Brunner/Mazel.
———. 1974. New perspectives on children with Down's syndrome. Paper presented at Down's Syndrome Congress, Milwaukee, Wisconsin.
Hayden, A. H. and N. G. Haring. 1976. Early intervention for high risk infants and young children: Programs for Down's syndrome children. In *Intervention strategies*

for high risk infants and young children, edited by T. D. Tjossem. Baltimore: University Park Press.

Hebb, D. O. 1949. *The organization of behavior.* New York: Wiley.

Heber, R. F. 1961. A manual on terminology and classification in mental retardation. Rev. ed. *American Journal of Mental Deficiency Monograph* (Supp. 64).

————. 1959. A manual on terminology and classification in mental retardation. *American Journal of Mental Deficiency Monograph* (Supp. 64).

Heber, R. and H. Garber. 1975. The Milwaukee Project: A study of the use of family intervention to prevent cultural-familial mental retardation. In *Exceptional infant: Assessment and intervention*. Vol. 3, edited by B. Z. Friedlander, G. M. Sterritt, and G. E. Kirk. New York: Brunner/Mazel, Inc.

Heckinger, F. (ed.) 1966. *Preschool education today.* New York: Doubleday.

Held, R. and A. Hein. 1963. Movement-produced stimulation in the development of visually guided behavior. *Journal of Comparative and Physiological Psychology* 56: 872–876.

Hellman, L. M. and J. A. Pritchard. 1971. *Williams obstetrics.* 14th ed. New York: Appleton-Century-Crofts.

Helsel, E., B. Helsel, B. Helsel, and M. Helsel. 1978. The Helsels' story of Robin. In *Parents speak out: Growing with a handicapped child*, edited by A. P. Turnbull and H. R. Turnbull, III. Columbus, Ohio: Charles E. Merrill.

Hemsley, R. et al. 1978. Treating autistic children in a family context. In *Autism: A reappraisal of concepts and treatment*, edited by M. Rutter and E. Schapler. New York: Plenum Press.

Heward, W. L. and M. D. Orlansky. 1980. *Exceptional children.* New York: Merrill.

Hickish, D. 1955. Thermal sensations of workers in light industry in Southern England. *Journal of Hygiene* 53: 112–123.

Hill, R. M. et al. 1977. Utilization of over-the-counter drugs during pregnancy. *Clinical Obstetrics and Gynecology* 20: 381–394.

Hirshhorn, K. 1973. Chromosomal abnormalities I: Autosomal defects. In *Medical genetics*, edited by V. A. McKusick and R. Claiborne. New York: Hospital Practice Publishing.

Hobbs, N. (ed.) 1975. *Issues in the classification of children.* San Francisco: Jossey-Bass.

Holden, R. H. 1972. Predictions of mental retardation in infancy. *Mental Retardation* 10: 28–30.

Holt, K. S. 1975. Home care of severely retarded children. In *Community services for retarded children*, edited by J. J. Dempsey. Baltimore: University Park Press.

Honig, A. S. and J. R. Lally. 1970. *Piagetian infant scales.* Syracuse, N.Y.: Syracuse University Children's Center.

Horowitz, F. and M. Dunn. 1978. Infant intelligence testing. In *Communication and cognitive abilities—early behavioral assessment*, edited by F. Minifrie and L. Lloyd. Baltimore: University Park Press.

Horton, K. B. 1976. Early intervention for hearing-impaired infants and young children. In *Intervention strategies with high-risk infants and young children*, edited by T. D. Tjossem. Baltimore: University Park Press.

Hugdahl, L. et al. 1978. *Using familiar daily activities as teaching times: A parent manual.* Madison, Wisconsin: Madison Metropolitan School District.

Hulme, I. and E. A. Lunzer. 1966. Play, language and reasoning in subnormal children. *Journal of Child Psychology and Psychiatry* 7: 107.

Hunt, J. McV. 1972. Heredity, environment and class or ethnic differences. In *Assessment in pluralistic society*.

————. 1964. The psychological basis for using preschool as an antidote for cultural deprivation. *Merrill-Palmer Quarterly* 10: 209–248.

————. 1961. *Intelligence and experience.* New York: Ronald Press.

Hunt, J. V. 1976. Environmental risk in fetal and neonatal life. In *Origins of intelligence*, edited by M. Lewis. New York: Plenum.

Hutt, C. and C. Ounsted. 1970. Gaze aversion and its significance in childhood autism. In *Behaviour studies in psychiatry*, edited by S. J. Hutt and C. Hutt. New York: Pergamon Press.

Hutt, M. L. and R. G. Gibby. 1976. *The mentally retarded child: Development, education and treatment.* 3rd ed. Boston: Allyn and Bacon.

Huttenlocher, P. R. 1974. Dendritic development in neocortex of children with mental defect and infantile spasms. *Neurology* 24: 203–210.

Ingalls, R. P. 1978. *Mental retardation: The changing outlook.* New York: Wiley.

Ingram, D. 1976. Current issues in child phonology. In *Normal and deficient child language*, edited by D. Morehead and A. Morehead. Baltimore: University Park Press.

Inhelder, B. 1968. *The diagnosis of reasoning in the mentally retarded.* New York: Day.

Ilg, F. L. and L. B. Ames. 1965. *School readiness.* New York: Harper and Row.

Ireland, W. W. 1900. *The mental affections of children: Idiocy, imbecility, and insanity.* Philadelphia: Blakiston.

Irwin, D. M. and M. Bushnell. 1980. *Observational strategies for child study.* New York: Holt, Rinehart, and Winston.

Irwin, J. V. and S. P. Wong. 1975. Compensation for maturity in long range intervention studies. *Acta Symbolica* 5: 47–66.

Ispa, J. and R. D. Matz. 1978. Integrating handicapped preschool children within a cognitively oriented program. In *Early intervention and the integration of handicapped and nonhandicapped children*, edited by M. J. Guralnick. Baltimore: University Park Press.

Jakobson, R. 1968. *Child language, aphasia and phonological universals.* The Hague: Mouton.

Jardis, C. D. et al. 1980. *How to get services by being assertive.* Chicago, Ill.: Coordinating Council for Handicapped Children.

Jervis, G. A. 1952. Medical aspects of mental deficiency. *American Journal of Mental Deficiency* 57: 175–188.

John, E. R. 1976. A model of consciousness. In *Consciousness and self-regulation: Advances in research.* Vol. 1, edited by G. E. Schwartz and D. Shapiro. New York: Plenum.

Johnson, C. A. and R. C. Katz. 1973. Using parents as change agents for their children: A review. *Journal of Child Psychiatry and Psychology* 14: 181–200.

Johnson, H. W. 1979. *Preschool test descriptions.* Springfield, Ill.: Charles C Thomas.

Johnson, S. W. and R. L. Morasky. 1980. *Learning disabilities.* 2nd ed. Boston: Allyn and Bacon.

Johnston, J. R. and T. K. Schery. 1976. The use of grammatical morphemes by children with communication disorders. In *Normal and deficient child language*, edited by D. M. Morehead and A. E. Morehead. Baltimore: University Park Press.

Johnston, R. B. and P. R. Magrab. 1976. *Developmental disorders: Assessment, treatment, education.* Baltimore: University Park Press.

Jones, K. L. and D. W. Smith. 1974. Recognition of fetal alcohol syndrome in early infancy. *Lancet* 2: 999–1001.

Jones, K. L., D. W. Smith, C. N. Ulleland, and A. P. Streissguth. 1973. Pattern of malformation in offspring of chronic alcoholic mothers. *Lancet* 1: 1267–1271.

Kagan, J. 1968. On cultural deprivation. In *Environmental influences*, edited by D. Glass. New York: Rockefeller University Press.

Kagan, J., R. B. Kearsley, and P. R. Zelazo. 1978. *Infancy: Its place in human development*. Cambridge, Mass.: Harvard University Press.

Kahn, J. V. 1976. Utility of the Uzgiris-Hunt scale of sensori-motor development with severely and profoundly retarded children. *American Journal of Mental Deficiency* 80: 663–665.

Kamii, C. 1972. An application of Piaget's theory to the conceptualization of preschool curriculum. In *The preschool in action*, edited by R. K. Parker. Boston: Allyn and Bacon.

Kanner, L. 1943. Autistic disturbances of affective contact. *Nervous Child* 2: 217–250.

Kaplan, E. and G. Kaplan. 1971. The prelinguistic child. In *Human development and cognitive processes*, edited by J. Elist. New York: Holt, Rinehart and Winston.

Kaplan, F. 1969. Siblings of the retarded. In *Psychological problems in mental deficiency*, edited by S. B. Sarason and J. Doris. New York: Harper and Row.

Kaplan, R. L., T. S. Glahn, and G. S. Nieminen. 1978. Generalization of parent-training results. *Journal of Applied Behavior Analysis* 11: 95–109.

Karnes, M. and J. Teska. 1975. Children's response to intervention programs. In *Application of child development research to exceptional children*, edited by J. Gallagher. Reston, Virginia: Council for Exceptional Children.

Kauffman, J. M. 1980. Where special education for disturbed children is going. *Exceptional Children* 46 (7): 516–522.

Kauffman, J. M. and J. S. Payne. 1975. *Mental retardation: Introduction and personal perspectives*. Columbus, Ohio: Charles E. Merrill.

Kazdin, A. E. 1975. *Behavior modification in applied settings*. Homewood, Ill.: The Dorsey Press.

Kearsley, R. B. 1979. Iatrogenic retardation: A syndrome of learned imcompetence. In *Infants at risk: Assessment of cognitive functioning*, edited by R. B. Kearsley and I. E. Sigel. Hillsdale, N.J.: Lawrence Erlbaum.

Kearsley, R. B. and I. E. Sigel. (eds.) 1979. *Infants at risk: Assessment of cognitive functioning*. Hillsdale, N.J.: Lawrence Erlbaum.

Keogh, B. and L. D. Becker. 1973. Early detection of learning problems: Questions, cautions, and guidelines. *Exceptional Children* 40: 5–11.

Keogh, B. and C. Kopp. 1978. From assessment to intervention an elusive bridge. In *Communication and cognitive abilities—early behavioral assessment*, edited by F. Minifrie and L. Lloyd. Baltimore: University Park Press.

Ketchum, B. 1977. The day care alternative: Facilitating normalization of preschool multihandicapped children. *Journal of Clinical Child Psychology* 6(3): 45–47.

Kiff, A. D. and C. Lepard. 1966. Visual responses in premature infants. *Archives of Ophthalmology* 75: 631.

Kinsbourne, M. and F. Wood. 1975. Short-term memory processes and the amnesic syndrome. In *Short-term memory*, edited by D. Deutch and J. A. Deutch. New York: Academic Press.

Kirk, S. A. and J. J. Gallagher. 1983. *Educating exceptional children*. 4th ed. Boston: Houghton-Mifflin.

Kirk, S. A., J. J. McCarthy, and W. D. Kirk. 1968. *Examiner's manual: Illinois test of psycholinguistic abilities*. Rev. ed. Urbana, Ill.: University of Illinois Press.

Klaber, M. 1970. Institutional programming and research: A vital partnership in action. In *Residential facilities for the mentally retarded*, edited by A. A. Baumeister and E. C. Butterfield. Chicago: Aldine.

Klaus, R. A. and S. W. Gray. 1968. The early training project for disadvantaged children: A report after five years. *Monographs for the Society for Research in Child Development* 33 (serial No. 120).

Knapczyk, D. R. and J. O. Yoppi. 1975. Development of cooperative and competitive play responses in developmentally disabled children. *American Journal of Mental Deficiency* 80(3): 245–255.

Knoblock, H. and B. Passamanick (eds.) 1974. *Gesell and Amatruda's developmental diagnosis*. 3rd ed. New York: Harper and Row.

Kodera, T. L. and S. G. Garwood. 1979. The acquisition of cognitive competence. In *Educating young handicapped children: A developmental approach*, edited by S. G. Garwood. Germantown, Maryland: Aspen System.

Kovacs, D. 1972. Josh: The lonely search for help. *Exceptional Parent* April/May.

Kramm, E. 1963. *Families with mongoloid children*. Washington, D.C.: United States Government Printing Office.

Kroth, R. L. 1975. *Communicating with parents of exceptional children: Improving parent-teacher relationships*. Denver, Colorado: Love Publishing Co.

Kunzelmann, H. P. (ed.) 1970. *Precision teaching: An initial training sequence*. Seattle: Special Child Publications.

Lackner, S. R. 1968. A developmental study of language behavior in retarded children. *Neuropsychologia* 6: 301–320.

Lansing, M. D. and E. Schopler. 1978. Individualized education: A public school model. In *Autism: A reappraisal of concepts and treatment*, edited by M. Rutter and E. Schopler. New York: Plenum Press.

Laosa, L. 1977. Nonbiased assessment of children's abilities: Historical antecedents and current issues. In *Psychological and educational assessment of minority children*, edited by T. Oakland. New York: Brunner/Mazer.

Lee, L. C. 1975. Toward a cognitive theory of interpersonal development: Importance of peers. In *Friendship and peer relations*, edited by M. Lewis and L. Rosenblum. New York: Wiley.

———. 1973. Social encounters of infants: The beginning of popularity. Paper presented at the biennial meeting of the International Society for the Study of Behavioral Development, Ann Arbor, Michigan.

Leonard, L., J. Bolders, and J. Miller. 1976. An examination of the semantic relations reflected in the language usage of normal and language-disordered children. *Journal of Speech and Hearing Research* 19: 371–392.

Lerner, J., C. Mardell-Czudnowski, and D. Goldenberg. 1981. *Special education for the early childhood years*. Englewood Cliffs, N.J.: Prentice-Hall.

Lessen, E. I. and T. L. Rose. 1980. State definitions of preschool handicapped populations. *Exceptional Children* 46: 467–469.

Levenstein, P. 1975. Message from home: Findings from a program for non-retarded, low income preschoolers. In *The mentally retarded and society: A social science perspective*, edited by M. J. Begab and S. A. Richardson. Baltimore, Maryland: University Park Press.

———. 1972. But does it work in homes away from home? *Theory Into Practice* 11: 157–162.

———. 1970. Cognitive growth in preschoolers through verbal interaction with mothers. *American Journal of Orthopsychiatry* 40: 426–432.

Levitt, E. and S. Cohen. 1975. An analysis of selected parent intervention programs for handicapped and disadvantaged children. *Journal of Special Education* 9(4): 345–374.

Levy, J. 1974. Psychobiological implications of bilateral asymmetry. In *Hemisphere function in the human brain*, edited by S. J. Dimond and J. G. Beaumont. New York: Halsted Press.

Levy, J., C. Trevarthen, and R. W. Sperry. 1972. Perception of bilateral chimeric figures following hemispheric deconnexion. *Brain* 95: 61–78.

Lewis, M. 1976a. Infant intelligence tests: Their use and misuse. *Human Development* 16: 108.

———. (ed.) 1976b. *Origins of intelligence*. New York: Plenum.

Lewis, M. and J. Brooks. 1978. Self-knowledge and emotional development. In *The development of affect*, edited by M. Lewis and L. A. Rosenblum. New York: Plenum.

Lewis, M. and C. Feiring. 1969. The child's social network: Social object, social functions, and their relationship. In *The child and its family*, edited by M. Lewis and L. A. Rosenblum. New York: Plenum.

Lewis, M. and S. Goldberg. 1969a. The acquisition and violation of an expectancy: An experimental paradigm. *Journal of Experimental Child Psychology* 7, 70–80.

————. 1969b. Perceptual-cognitive development in infancy: A generalized expectancy model as a function of the mother-child interaction. *Merrill-Palmer Quarterly* 15: 81–100.

Lewis, M., J. Kagan, H. Campbell, and J. Kalafat. 1966. The cardiac response as a correlate of attention in infants. *Child Development* 37: 63–71.

Lewis, M. and L. A. Rosenblum (eds.) 1974. *The origins of fear*. New York: Wiley.

Lewis, M. and S. J. Spaulding. 1967. Differential cardiac response as a correlate of attention in the young child. *Psychophysiology* 3: 229–238.

Lezine, I., M. Stambak, and I. Casati. 1969. *Les etapes de l'intelligence sensorimotrice (Monographie No. 1)*. Paris: Les Editions du Centre de Psychologie Appliquee.

Li, A. K. F. 1981. Play and the mentally retarded child. *Mental Retardation* 19(3): 121–126.

Liff, S. 1973. Early intervention and language development in hearing impaired children. Unpublished Master's Thesis, Vanderbilt University, Nashville, Tennessee.

Lilienfeld, A. M. and B. Pasamanick. 1956. The association of maternal age and fetal factors with the development of mental deficiency II. *American Journal of Mental Deficiency* 60: 557–569.

Lillie, D. 1977. Screening. In *Identifying handicapped children: A guide to casefinding, screening, diagnosis, assessment and evaluation*, edited by L. Cross and K. Goin. New York: Walker and Co.

Lindsay, P. H. and D. A. Norman. 1977. *Human information processing*. 2nd ed. New York: Academic Press.

Lindsley, O. R. 1964. Direct measurement and prosthesis of retarded behavior. *Journal of Education* 147: 62–81.

Liversidge, E. B. and G. M. Grana. 1973. Hearing impaired child in the family: Parent's perspective. *The Volta Review* March.

Longhurst, T. and S. Grubb. 1974. A comparison of language samples collected in four situations. *Language, Speech and Hearing Service in the Schools* 5: 71–78.

Lorenz, K. 1972. Psychology and phylogeny. In *Studies in animal and human behavior*. Translated by R. Martin. Cambridge, Mass.: Harvard University Press.

————. 1957. Companionship in birdlife. In *Instinctive behavior*, edited by C. H. Schiller. New York: International Universities Press.

Losinno, T. (ed.) no date. *The P.E.E.R.S. program: An overview*. Philadelphia: Special People in the Northeast.

Lotman, H. A. 1980. Effects of three contingency reinforcement climates on increasing on-task behavior in a classroom for trainable retarded. Unpublished Doctoral Dissertation, Temple University, Philadelphia, Pennsylvania.

Lovaas, O. I. 1978. Parents as therapists. In *Autism: A reappraisal of concepts and treatments*, edited by M. Rutter and E. Schopler. New York: Plenum Press.

————. 1973. Behavioral treatment of autistic children. *University Programs Modular Studies*. Morristown, N.J.: General Learning Press.

Lovaas, O. I. and B. D. Bucher. 1974. *Perspectives in behavior modification with deviant children*. Englewood Cliffs, N.J.: Prentice-Hall.

Lovaas, O. I., B. Schaeffer, and J. Q. Simmons. 1965. Building social behavior in autistic children by use of electric shock. *Journal of Experimental Research in Personality* 1: 99–109.

Love, H. 1973. *The mentally retarded child and his family.* Springfield, Ill.: Charles C Thomas.

Lowenfeld, B. (ed.) 1973. *The visually handicapped child in school.* New York: Day.

Luria, A. R. 1973. *The working brain: An introduction to neuropsychology.* Translated by B. Haigh. New York: Basic Books.

———. 1963. Psychological studies of mental deficiency in the Soviet Union. In *Handbook of mental deficiency*, edited by N. R. Ellis. New York: McGraw-Hill.

MacMillan, D. L. 1977. *Mental retardation in school and society.* Boston: Little, Brown.

Mager, R. F. 1962. *Preparing instructional objectives.* Palo Alto, California: Fearon.

Mahler, M. S. 1952. On child psychosis and schizophrenia: Autistic and symbiotic infantile psychoses. *The psychoanalytic study of the child.* Vol. 7. New York: International Universities Press.

Maratosos, M. 1973. Nonegocentric communication abilities in preschool children. *Child Development* 44: 697–700.

McCall, R. 1971. New directions in psychological assessment of infants. *Proceedings of the Royal Society of Medicine* 64: 465–467.

McCall, R. B. 1979. Qualitative transitions in behavioral development in the first two years of life. In *Psychological development from infancy: Image to intention*, edited by M. H. Bornstein and W. Kessen. Hillsdale, N.J.: Lawrence Erlbaum Associates.

McCall, R. B., M. Appelbaum, and P. S. Hogarty. 1973. Developmental changes in mental performance. *Monographs of the Society for Research in Child Development* 38(150).

McCall, R. B., D. H. Eichorn, and P. S. Hogarty. 1977. Transitions in early mental development. *Monographs of the Society for Research in Child Development* 42(171).

McCall, R. B., P. S. Hogarty, and N. Hurlburt. 1972. Transitions in infant sensorimotor development and the prediction of childhood I.Q. *American Psychologist* 27: 728–748.

McCarthy, D. 1972. *McCarthy scales of children's abilities.* New York: The psychological Corporation.

———. 1970. *Manual for the McCarthy scales of children's abilities.* New York: Psychological Corporation.

McGraw, M. B. 1966. *The neuromuscular maturation of the human infant.* New York: Hafner.

McLean, J. E. and L. K. Snyder-McLean. 1978. *A transactional approach to early language training.* Columbus, Ohio: Charles Merrill.

Meier, J. 1976. Screening assessment—Intervention for young children at developmental risk. In *Intervention strategies for high risk infants and young children*, edited by T. Tjossem. Baltimore: University Park Press.

Mellin, G. W. and M. Katzenstein. 1962. The saga of Thalidomide. *New England Journal of Medicine* 267: 1184–1193, 1238–1264.

Menyuk, P. 1964. Comparison of grammar of children with functionally deviant and normal speech. *Journal of Speech and Hearing Research* 7: 109–121.

Menyuk, P. and P. Looney. 1972. A problem of language disorder: Length versus structure. *Journal of Speech and Hearing Research* 15: 264–279.

Mercer, J. R. 1973. *Labeling the mentally retarded: Clinical and social systems perspectives on mental retardation.* Berkeley: University of California Press.

Meyers, C. E., D. L. MacMillan, and R. K. Yoshida. 1978. Validity of psychologists' identification of EMR students in the perspective of the California decertification experience. *Journal of School Psychology* 16: 3–15.

Miller, J. and D. Yoder. 1974. An ontogenetic language teaching strategy for retarded children. In *Language perspectives: Acquisition, retardation and intervention*, edited by R. Schiefelbusch and L. Lloyd. Baltimore: University Park Press.

Miller, L. B. and J. L. Dyer. 1975. Four preschool programs: Their dimensions and effects. *Monographs of the Society for Research in Child Development* 40 (162): 5–6.

Miller, N. B. and D. P. Cantwell. 1976. Siblings as therapists: A behavioral approach. *American Journal of Psychiatry* 133: 447–450.

Miller, W. and S. Erwin. 1964. The development of grammar in child language. In *The acquisition of language*, edited by U. Bellugi and R. Brown. *Monographs of the Society for Research in Child Development* 29 (Serial No. 92).

Minuchin, S. 1974. *Families and family therapy.* Cambridge: Harvard University Press.

Moerk, E. L. 1975. Verbal interactions between children and their mothers during preschool years. *Developmental Psychology* 11: 788–794.

Mogford, K. 1977. The play of handicapped children. In *Biology of play*, edited by B. Tizard and D. Harvey. Philadelphia: Lippincott.

Montagu, A. 1971. *The elephant man: A study in human dignity.* New York: Ballantine Books.

Moore, J. and M. J. Fine. 1978. Regular and special class teachers' perception of normal and exceptional children and their attitudes toward mainstreaming. *Psychology in the Schools* 15: 253–259.

Moores, D. F. 1982. *Educating the deaf: Psychology, principles and practices.* 2nd ed. Boston: Houghton-Mifflin.

Moores, D., K. L. Weiss, and M. W. Goodwin. 1978. Early education programs for hearing-impaired children: Major findings. *American Annals of the Deaf* 123: 925–936.

———. 1976. *Early education programs for hearing impaired children.* Minneapolis: University of Minnesota Research and Development Center in Education of Handicapped Children, Research Report No. 104.

Moos, R. H. 1976. *The human context: Environmental determinants of behavior.* New York: Wiley.

Morehead, D. and D. Ingram. 1973. The development of base syntax in normal and linguistically deviant children. *Journal of Speech and Hearing Research* 16: 330–352.

Morton, K. 1978. Identifying the enemy—A parent's complaint. In *Parents speak out: Growing with a handicapped child*, edited by A. P. Turnbull and H. R. Turnbull, III. Columbus, Ohio: Charles E. Merrill.

Mueller, E. 1972. The maintenance of verbal exchange between young children. *Child Development* 43(3): 930–938.

Mueller, E. and T. Lucas. 1975. A developmental analysis of peer interactions among toddlers. In *Friendship and peer relations*, edited by M. Lewis and L. Rosenblum. New York: Wiley.

Muma, J. R. 1978. *Language handbook: Concepts, assessment, intervention.* Englewood Cliffs, N.J.: Prentice-Hall.

National Advisory Committee on the Handicapped. 1976. *The unfinished revolution: Education for the handicapped.* Washington, D.C.: United States Office of Education.

National Society for the Prevention of Blindness. 1966. *N.S.P.B. fact book: Estimated statistics on blindness and visual problems.* New York: The Society.

Neisser, U. 1976. *Cognition and reality: Principles and implications of cognitive psychology.* San Francisco: Freeman.

Neisworth, J. T. and R. M. Smith. 1978. *Retardation: Issues, assessment and intervention.* New York: McGraw-Hill.

Newcomer, B. L. and T. L. Morrison. 1974. Play therapy with institutionalized mentally retarded children. *American Journal of Mental Deficiency* 78: 727–733.

Nihara, K., R. Foster, M. Shellhaas, and H. Leland. 1974. *AAMD adaptive behavior scale*. Rev. ed. Washington, D.C.: American Association on Mental Deficiency.
————. 1969. *AAMD adaptive behavior scale*. Washington, D.C.: American Association on Mental Deficiency.

Oakland, T. 1977. *Psychological and educational assessment of minority children*. New York: Brunner/Mazel.
O'Brien, J. S. 1971. How we detect mental retardation before birth. *Medical Times* 99: 103–108.
O'Dell, S. 1974. Training parents in behavior modification: A review. *Psychological Bulletin* 81: 418–433.
Olshansky, S. 1962. Chronic sorrow: A response to having a mentally defective child. *Social Casework* April: 190–193.
Ornitz, E. M. and E. R. Ritvo. 1977. The syndrome of autism: A critical review. In *Annual progress in psychiatry and child development*, edited by S. Chess and A. Thomas. New York: Brunner/Mazel.

Page, E. B. 1975. Miracle in Milwaukee: Raising the I.Q. In *Exceptional infant: Assessment and intervention*. Vol. 3, edited by B. Z. Friedlander, G. M. Sterritt, and G. E. Kirk. New York: Brunner/Mazel.
Palmer, D. J. 1980. The effect of educable mental retardation descriptive information on regular classroom teachers' attributions and instructional prescriptions. *Mental Retardation* 18: 171–175.
————. 1979. Regular classroom teachers' attributions and instructional prescriptions for handicapped and nonhandicapped pupils. *Journal of Special Education* 13: 325–337.
Parker, R. K. and M. D. Day. 1972. Comparisons of preschool curricula. In *Preschool in action*, edited by R. K. Parker and M. D. Day. Boston: Allyn and Bacon.
Parmelee, A. H. and A. Haber. 1973. Who is the "Risk Infant"? *Clinical Obstetrics and Gynecology* 16: 376–387.
Parmelee, A. H., C. B. Kopp, and M. Sigman. 1976. Selection of developmental assessment techniques for infants at risk. *Merrill-Palmer Quarterly* 22: 177–199.
Parmelee, A. H., M. Sigman, C. B. Kopp, and A. Haber. 1976. Diagnosis of the infant at risk for mental, motor, or sensory handicap. In *Intervention strategies for high risk infants and young children*, edited by T. D. Tjossem. Baltimore: University Park Press.
————. 1975. The concept of a cumulative risk score for infants. In *Aberrant development in infancy: Human and animal studies*, edited by N. R. Ellis. Hillsdale, N.J.: Lawrence Erlbaum.
Parten, M. B. 1932. Social participation among preschool children. *Journal of Abnormal and Social Psychology* 27: 243–269.
Pavlov, I. P. 1927. *Conditioned reflexes*. London: Oxford University Press.
Peck, C. A., T. Apolloni, T. P. Cooke, and S. Raver. 1978. Teaching retarded preschoolers to imitate the free-play behavior of non-retarded classmates: Trained and generalized effects. *Journal of Special Education* 12: 195–207.
Peck, C. A., T.P. Cooke, and T. Apolloni. 1981. Utilization of peer imitation in therapeutic and instructional contexts. In *The utilization of classroom peers as behavior change agents*, edited by P. S. Strain. New York: Plenum.
Penrose, L. S. 1949. *The biology of mental defect*. New York: Grune and Stratton.
Pepler, R. 1971. Variations in students' test performances and in classroom temperatures in climate controlled and non-climate controlled schools. *ASHRAE Transactions* 77 (pt. 2): 35–42.
Phemister, M. R., A. M. Richardson, and E. V. Thomas. 1978. Observations of young

normal and handicapped children. *Child Care, Health and Development* 4(4): 247–259.

Phillips, J. 1973. Syntax and vocabulary of mother's speech to young children: Age and sex comparisons. *Child Development* 44: 182–185.

Piaget, J. 1975. *The development of thought: Equilibrium of cognitive structures.* New York: Viking Penguin, 1977 (original French edition, 1975).

———. 1954. *The construction of reality in the child.* New York: Basic Books.

———. 1952. *The origins of intelligence in children* (2nd ed.). New York: International Universities Press.

———. 1951. *Play, dreams, and imitation in childhood.* New York: Norton.

Piaget, J. and B. Inhelder. 1969. *The psychology of the child.* New York: Basic Books.

Pick, H. L., Jr. 1976. Development in complex perceptual activities. In *Psychopathology and child development: Research and treatment,* edited by E. Schopler and R. J. Reichler. New York: Plenum.

Popovich, D. 1981. *Effective educational and behavioral programming for severely and profoundly handicapped students: A manual for teachers and aides.* Baltimore: Paul H. Brookes.

Porte, R. H. et al. 1978. Social interactions in heterogeneous groups of retarded and normally developing children: An observational study. In *Application of observational/ethological methods to the study of mental retardation.* Vol. 1, edited by G. P. Sackett. Baltimore: University Park Press.

Provost, M. and T. Decarie. 1974. Modifications du rhthme cadique chez des enfants de 9–12 mois au cours de la recoutre avec la personne etrangere. *Canadian Journal of Behavioral Science* 6: 154–168.

Peuschel, S. M. and A. Murphy. 1976. Assessment of counseling practices at the birth of a child with Down's syndrome. *American Journal of Mental Deficiency* 81: 325–330.

Rawlings, G., E. O. R. Reynolds, A. Stewart, and L. B. Strange. 1971. Changing prognosis for infants of very low birth weight. *Lancet* 1: 516–519.

Ray, J. S. 1974a. Behavior of developmentally delayed and non-delayed toddler-age children: An ethological study. Unpublished Doctoral Dissertation, George Peabody College, Nashville, Tennessee.

———. 1974b. The family training center: An experiment in normalization. *Mental Retardation* 12(1): 12–13.

Reddin, W. J. 1971. *Effective management by objectives.* New York: McGraw-Hill.

Redner, R. 1980. Others' perceptions of mothers of handicapped children. *American Journal of Mental Deficiency* 85: 176–183.

Riesen, A. 1964. Effects of early deprivation on photic stimulation. In *The biosocial basis of mental retardation,* edited by S. F. Osler and R. E. Cooke. Baltimore: Johns Hopkins Press.

Rimland, B. 1964. *Infantile autism.* New York: Appleton-Century-Crofts.

Ringler, N. 1973. Mothers' language to their young children and to adults over time. Unpublished Doctoral Dissertation, Case Western Reserve University.

Robinson, C. C. and J. H. Robinson. 1978. Sensorimotor functions and cognitive development. In *Systematic instruction of the moderately and severely handicapped,* edited by M. E. Snell. Columbus, Ohio: Charles E. Merrill.

Robinson, N. M. and H. B. Robinson. 1976. *The mentally retarded child.* 2nd ed. New York: McGraw-Hill.

Rogers, S. J. 1982. Developmental characteristics of children's play. In *Psychological assessment of handicapped infants and young children,* edited by G. Ulrey and S. Rogers. New York: Thieme-Stratton.

———. 1977. Characteristics of the cognitive development of profoundly retarded children. *Child Development* 48: 837–843.

Rosen, C. E. 1974. The effects of socio-dramatic play on problem-solving behaviors among culturally disadvantaged preschool children. *Child Development* 45: 920–927.

Rosenthal, R. and L. Jacobsen. 1975. What teacher behavior mediates. *Psychology in the Schools* 12: 454–461.

———. 1968. *Pygmalion in the classroom: Teacher expectation and pupils' intellectual development.* New York: Holt, Rinehart, and Winston.

Rubin, K. H., T. L. Maioni, and M. Hornung. 1976. Free play behavior in middle- and lower-class preschoolers: Parten and Piaget revisited. *Child Development* 47: 414–419.

Ruder, K. and M. Smith. 1974. Issues in language training. In *Language perspectives— Acquisition, retardation and intervention*, edited by R. Schiefelbusch and L. L. Lloyd. Baltimore: University Park Press.

Rutter, M. 1975. *Helping troubled children.* New York: Plenum.

Ryckman, D. B. and R. A. Henderson. 1965. The meaning of a retarded child for his parents: A focus for counselors. *Mental Retardation* 3: 4–7.

Rynders, J. and J. M. Horrobin. 1975. Project EDGE: The University of Minnesota's communication stimulation program for Down's syndrome infants. In *Exceptional infant: Assessment and intervention.* Vol. 3, edited by B. Z. Friedlander, G. M. Sterritt, and G. E. Kirk. New York: Brunner/Mazel.

Rynders, J. E., D. Spiker, and J. M. Horrobin. 1978. Underestimating the educability of Down's syndrome children: Examination of methodological problems in recent literature. *American Journal of Mental Deficiency* 82: 440–448.

Sachs, J. 1977. Adaptive significance of linguistic input to prelinguistic infants. In *Talking to children*, edited by C. Snow and C. Ferguson. Cambridge: Cambridge University Press.

Safford, P. L. 1978. *Teaching young children with special needs.* St. Louis: Mosley.

Saltz, E., D. Dixon, and J. Johnson. 1977. Training disadvantaged preschoolers on various fantasy activities: Effects on cognitive functioning and impulse control. *Child Development* 48: 367–380.

Sameroff, A. J. 1979. Etiology of cognitive competence. In *Infants at risk: Assessment of cognitive functioning*, edited by R. B. Kearsley and I. E. Sigel. Hillsdale, N.J.: Lawrence Erlbaum.

———. 1968. The component of sucking in the human newborn. *Journal of Experimental Child Psychology* 6: 607–623.

Sameroff, A. J. and M. J. Chandler. 1975. Reproductive risk and the continuum of caretaking casualty. In *Review of child development research.* Vol. 4, edited by F. D. Horowitz, M. Hetherington, S. Scarr-Salapatek, and G. Siegel. Chicago: University of Chicago Press.

Sameroff, A. J. and M. Zax. 1978. In search of schizophrenia: Young offspring of schizophrenic women. In *Nature of schizophrenia: New findings and future strategies*, edited by L. C. Wynne, R. Cromwell, and S. Matthysse. New York: Wiley.

Samuda, R. J. 1975. *Psychological testing of American minorities.* New York: Harper and Row.

Samuels, S. 1981. *Disturbed exceptional children: An integrated approach.* New York: Human Sciences Press.

Sandler, A. and A. Coren. 1981. Integrated instruction at home and school: Parents' perspective. *Education and Training of the Mentally Retarded* 16: 183–188.

Sandler, A., A. Coren, and S. K. Thurman. 1983. A training program for parents of handicapped preschool children: Effects upon mother, father, and child. *Exceptional Children* 49: 355–358.

Sandler, A. and D. McNulty. 1979. Training parents to be effective members of the educational planning team: A videotape training approach. Presented at the Pennsylvania Federation Council for Exceptional Children Annual Conference, Pittsburgh, Pennsylvania.

Sanford, A. 1974. *Learning accomplishment profile.* Winston-Salem, North Carolina: Kaplan.

Sanford, A. and J. Zelman. 1981. *Learning accomplishment profile.* , M.Winston-Salem, N.C.: Kaplan.

Sarason, S. B. and J. Doris. 1979. *Educational handicap, public policy and social history.* New York: The Free Press.

Scarr-Salapatek, S. 1976. An evolutionary perspective on infant intelligence. In *Origins of intelligence*, edited by M. Lewis. New York: Plenum.

Schaefer, E. S. and M. Aaronson. 1972. Infant education research project: Implementation and implications of the home tutoring program. In *The preschool in action*, edited by R. K. Parker. Boston: Allyn and Bacon.

Schell, G. C. 1981. The young handicapped child: A family perspective. *Topics in Early Childhood Special Education* 1: 21–27.

Schlesinger, I. 1971. Production of utterances and language acquisition. In *The ontogenesis of grammar*, edited by D. Slobin. New York: Academic Press.

Schlesinger, H. J. and K. P. Meadow. 1976. Emotional support for parents. In *Teaching parents to teach: A guide for working with the special child*, edited by D. L. Lillie, D. L. Trohanis. and K. W. Goin. New York: Walker and Company.

Schopler, E. 1978. Changing parental involvement in behavioral treatment. In *Autism: A reappraisal of concepts and treatments*, edited by M. Rutter and E. Schopler. New York: Plenum Press.

Schreiber, M. and M. Feely. 1975. Siblings of the retarded: A guided group experience. In *Community services for retarded children*, edited by J. J. Dempsey. Baltimore: University Park Press.

Schwartz, E. 1974. Characteristics of speech and language development in the child with myelomingocele and hydrocephalus. *Journal of Speech and Hearing Disorders* 39: 465–468.

Schwartz, M. and R. H. Day. 1979. Visual shape perception in early infancy. *Monographs of the Society for Research in Child Development* 44 (No. 7).

Scott, K. 1978. The rationale and methodological considerations underlying early cognitive and behavioral assessment. In *Communication and cognitive abilities—Early behavioral assessment*, edited by F. Minifrie and L. Lloyd. Baltimore: University Park Press.

Scott, R. A. 1969. *The making of blind men.* New York: Russell Sage Foundation.

Searle, S. J. 1978. Stages of parental reaction. *Exceptional Parent* April: 27–29.

Sears, R. R., E. E. Maccoby, and H. Levin. 1957. *Patterns of child rearing.* New York: Harper and Row.

Self, P. A. and F. D. Horowitz. 1979. The behavioral assessment of the neonate: An overview. In *Handbook of infant development*, edited by J. D. Osofsky. New York: Wiley.

Shapiro, E. and B. Biber. 1972. The education of young children: A developmental-interaction approach. *Teachers College Record* 74: 55–79.

Share, J., R. Koch, A. Webb, and B. Graliker. 1964. The longitudinal development of infants and young children with Down's syndrome. *American Journal of Mental Deficiency* 68: 689–692.

Shatz, M. and R. Gelman. 1973. The development of communication skills: Modifications in the speech of young children as a function of listener. *Monographs of the Society for Research in Child Development* 38 (Serial No. 152).

Shearer, D. E. and M. S. Shearer. 1976. The Portage Project: A model for early childhood intervention. In *Intervention strategies for high risk infants and young children*, edited by T. D. Tjossem. Baltimore: University Park Press.

Shepard, C. H. 1976. Teaching language to mentally retarded deaf children: Review of literature and description of one classroom program. *American Annals of the Deaf* 121(4): 366–369.

Sheridan, M. D. 1975. The importance of spontaneous play in the fundamental learning of handicapped children. *Child Care, Health and Development* 1(3): 118–122.

————. 1968. *The developmental progress of infants and young children*. London: H. M. S. D.

Sigel, I. E. 1979. On becoming a thinker. A psychoeducational model. *Educational Psychologist* 14: 70–78.

————. 1972a. Assessment in pluralistic society. *Proceedings of the Invitational Conference on Testing Problems*. Princeton, N.J.: Educational Testing Service.

————. 1972b. Where is preschool education going? Or are we enroute without a road map? *Proceedings of the Invitational Conference on Testing Problems*. Princeton, N.J.: Educational Testing Service.

Sigman, M. and A. H. Parmelee. 1979. Longitudinal evaluation of the pre-term infant. In *Infants born at risk: Behavior and development*, edited by T. M. Field. New York: Spectrum Publications.

Simmons, J. L. 1969. *Deviants*. Berkeley, Calif.: Glendessary Press.

Sinclair, H. 1973. Language acquisition and cognitive development. In *Cognitive development and the acquisition of language*, edited by T. Moore. New York: Academic Press.

————. 1971. Sensorimotor action patterns as a condition for the acquisition of syntax. In *Language acquisition: Models and methods*, edited by R. Huxley and E. Ingram. New York: Academic Press.

————. The transition from sensory motor behavior to symbolic activity. *Interchange* 1: 119–126.

————. 1969. Developmental psycholinguistics. In *Studies in cognitive development*, edited by D. Elkind and J. Flavell. New York: Oxford University Press.

Skeels, H. M. and H. B. Dye. 1939. A study of the effects of differential stimulation on mentally retarded children. *Proceedings and Addresses of the American Association on Mental Deficiency* 44: 114–136.

Skeels, H. M., R. Updengraff, B. L. Wellman, and H. M. Williams. 1938. A study of environmental stimulation: An orphanage preschool project. *University of Iowa Study of Child Welfare* 15 (No. 4).

Skinner, B. F. 1957. *Verbal behavior*. New York: Appleton-Century-Crofts.

Smilansky, S. 1968. *The effects of sociodramatic play on disadvantaged preschool children*. New York: Wiley.

Smith, B. J. 1978. P. L. 94–142 and the child below age 5. *Division of Early Childhood Communicator* 4(2): 11–15.

Smith, D. D. and M. E. Snell. 1978. Classroom management and instructional planning. In *Systematic instruction of the moderately and severely handicapped*, edited by M. E. Snell. Columbus, Ohio: Charles E. Merrill.

Smith, D. W. 1976. *Recognizable patterns of human malformation: Genetic, embryologic and clinical aspects*. 2nd ed. Philadelphia: Saunders.

Smith, D. W. and A. A. Wilson. 1973. *The child with Down's syndrome (mongolism)*. Philadelphia: Saunders.

Smith, R. M., J. T. Neisworth, and J. G. Greer. 1978. *Evaluating educational environments*. Columbus, Ohio: Charles E. Merrill.

Snow, C. 1972. Mothers' speech to children learning language. *Child Development* 43: 549–565.

Snyder, L. 1975. Pragmatics in language deficient children: Prelinguistic and early verbal performatives and presuppositions. Unpublished Doctoral Dissertation, University of Colorado.

Snyder, L., T. Apolloni, and T. P. Cooke. 1977. Integrated settings at the early childhood level: The role of nonretarded peers. *Exceptional Children* 43: 262–266.

Solnit, A. J. and S. Provence. 1979. Vulnerability and risk in early childhood. In *Handbook of infant development*, edited by J. D. Osofsky. New York: Wiley.

Sower, R. (ed.) 1978. *Parents teaching children: The P.E.E.R.S. Model.* Philadelphia: Special People in the Northeast.

Sperry, R. W. 1974. Lateral specialization in surgically separate hemispheres. In *The neurosciences, third study program,* edited by F. O. Schmitt. Cambridge, Mass.: M.I.T. Press.

Spitz, R. A. 1946a. Hospitalism: An inquiry into the genesis of psychiatric conditions in early childhood: A follow-up report. *The Psychoanalytic Study of the Child* 2: 113–117.

———. 1946b. Anaclitic depression. *The Psychoanalytic Study of the Child* 2: 313–342.

———. 1945. Hospitalism: An inquiry into the genesis of psychiatric conditions in early childhood. *The Psycho-Analytic Study of the Child* 1: 53–74.

Springer, S. and G. Deutsch. 1981. *Left brain, right brain.* San Francisco: W.H. Freeman.

Sroufe, L. A. 1979. Socioemotional development. In *The handbook of infant development,* edited by J. D. Osofsky. New York: Wiley.

Stein, Z., M. Susser, G. Saenger, and F. Marolla. 1972. Nutrition and mental performance: Prenatal exposure to the Dutch famine of 1944–1945 seems not related to mental performance at age 19. *Science* 178: 708–713.

Stephens, T. M. and B. L. Braun. 1980. Measures of regular classroom teachers attitudes toward handicapped children. *Exceptional Children* 46: 292–294.

Stewart, A. L., D. M. Turcan, G. Rawlings, and E. O. R. Reynolds. 1977. Prognosis for infants weighing 1,000 gm or less at birth. *Archives of Diseases in Childhood* 52: 97–104.

Stewart, R. B., L. E. Cluff, and R. Philip. 1977. *Drug monitoring: A requirement for responsible drug use.* Baltimore: Williams and Wilkins.

Stowitschek, J. J., R. A., Gable, and J. M. Hendrickson. 1980. *Instructional materials for exceptional children: Selection, management, and adaptation.* Germantown, Maryland: Aspen Systems.

Strain, P. S. 1975. Increasing social play of severely retarded preschoolers with sociodramatic activities. *Mental Retardation* 13(6): 7–9.

Strain, P. S., M. M. Kerr, and E. V. Ragland. 1981. The use of peer social initiations in the treatment of social withdrawal. In *The utilization of classroom peers as behavior change agents,* edited by P. S. Strain. New York: Plenum.

Strain, P. S. and M. S. Timm. 1974. An experimental analysis of social interaction between a behaviorally disordered preschool child and her classroom peers. *Journal of Applied Behavior Analysis* 7: 583–590.

Strauss, A. and L. Lehtinen. 1947. *Psychopathology and education of the brain injured child.* New York: Grune and Stratton.

Strauss, A. and H. Warner. 1942. Disorders of conceptual thinking in the brain injured child. *Journal of Nervous and Mental Disease* 96: 153–172.

Stremel, K. and C. Waryas. 1974. A behavioral psycholinguistic approach to language training. In *Developing systematic procedures for training children's language,* edited by L. McReynolds. *American Speech and Hearing Association Monograph* No. 18.

Stuckless, E. and J. Birch. 1966. The influence of early manual communication on the linguistic development of deaf children. *American Annals of the Deaf* 111: 425–460, 499–504.

Suomi, S. J. and H. F. Harlow. 1975. The role and reason of peer relationships in rhesus monkeys. In *Friendships and peer relations,* edited by M. Lewis and L. A. Rosenblum. New York: Wiley.

Suran, B. G. and J. V. Rizzo. 1979. *Special children: An integrative approach.* Glenview, Ill.: Scott Foresman.

Sylva, K. 1977. Play and learning. In *Biology of play,* edited by B. Tizard and D. Harvey. Philadelphia: Lippincott.

Taffel, S. 1978. *Congenital anomalies and birth injuries among live births; United States,*

1973–74. Vital and Health Statistics: Series 21, No. 31, DHEW Publication No. (PHS) 79–1909.

Taft, L. T. and H. J. Cohen. 1967. Neonatal and infant reflexology. In *Exceptional infant*, Vol. 1, edited by J. Hellmuth. New York: Brunner/Mazel.

Tallman, I. 1965. Spousal role differentiation and the socialization of severely retarded children. *Journal of Marriage and the Family* February: 37–42.

Terman, L. M. and M. A. Merrill. 1973. *The Stanford-Binet Intelligence Scale.* 3rd rev. Boston: Houghton Mifflin.

Thomas, A., S. Chess, and H. Birch. 1968. *Temperament and behavior disorders in children.* New York: New York University.

Thomas, A. et al. 1963. *Behavioral individuality in early childhood.* New York: New York University.

Thurman, S. K. 1978. *A review of contingency in infants: Avenues for the handicapped infant.* Princeton, N.J.: Institute for the Study of Exceptional Children, Educational Testing Service.

———. 1977. The congruence of behavioral ecologies: A model for special education programming. *Journal of Special Education* 11: 329–333.

Thurman, S. K. and M. Lewis. 1979. Children's responses to differences: Some possible implications for mainstreaming. *Exceptional Children* 45: 468–470.

Thurman, S. K. and A. Widerstrom. 1979. A methodological synthesis for the study of social behavior. Unpublished manuscript, Temple University.

Thurstone, L. and T. Thurstone. 1954. *Science Research Associates primary mental abilities.* Rev. ed. Chicago: Science Research Associates.

Tizard, B. and D. Harvey. 1977. *Biology of play.* Philadelphia: Lippincott.

Tizard, J. 1964. *Community services for the mentally handicapped.* Oxford: Oxford University Press.

Tizard, J. and B. Tizard. 1971. The social development of two-year-old children in residential nurseries. In *The origins of human social relations*, edited by H. R. Schaffer. New York: Academic Press.

Tjossem, T. D. 1976. Early intervention: Issues and approaches. In *Intervention strategies for high risk infants and young children*, edited by T. D. Tjossem. Baltimore: University Park Press.

Tredgold, A. F. 1937. *A textbook on mental deficiency.* Baltimore: Wood.

———. 1908. *Mental deficiency.* London: Bailliera, Tindall, and Fox.

Treffert, D. A. 1970. Epidemiology of infantile autism. *Archives of General Psychiatry* 22: 421–438.

Trevarthen, C. 1974. Conversation with a two-month old. *New Scientist* May.

Tulving, E. and Z. Pearlstone. 1966. Availability versus accessibility of information in memory for words. *Journal of Verbal Learning and Verbal Behavior* 5: 381–391.

Tulving, E. and D. M. Thomson. 1973. Encoding specificity and retrieval processes in episodic memory. *Psychological Review* 80: 352–373.

———. 1971. Retrieval processes in recognition memory: Effect of association context. *Journal of Experimental Psychology* 87: 116–124.

Turnbull, A. P. 1978. Moving from being a professional to being a parent: A startling experience. In *Parents speak out: Growing with a handicapped child*, edited by A. P. Turnbull and H. R. Turnbull, III. Columbus, Ohio: Charles E. Merrill.

Turnbull, A. P., B. Strickland, and S. Goldstein. 1978. Training professionals and parents in developing the IEP. *Education and Training of the Mentally Retarded* 13: 414–423.

Turnbull, A. P. and H. R. Turnbull, III. 1982. Parent involvement in the education of handicapped children: A critique. *Mental Retardation* 20: 115–122.

Umbreit, J. and L. D. Ostrow. 1980. The fetal alcohol syndrome. *Mental Retardation* 18: 109–111.

Utley, B. L., J. F. Holvoet, and K. Barnes. 1977. Handling, positioning, and feeding the physically handicapped. In *Educational programming for the severely and profoundly handicapped*, edited by E. Sontag. Reston, Virginia: Council for Exceptional Children, Division on Mental Retardation.

Uzgiris, I. C. and J. McV. Hunt. 1975. *Assessment in infancy: Ordinal scales of psychological development*. Urbana, Ill.: University of Illinois Press.

Vandenberg, B. 1978. Play and development from an ethological perspective. *American Psychologist* 33: 724–738.

VanEtten, G., C. Arkell, and C. VanEtten. 1980. *The severely and profoundly handicapped: Programs, methods, and materials*. St. Louis: C. V. Mosby.

Venn, J., L. Morganstren, and M. K. Dykes. 1979. Checklists for evaluating the fit and function of ortheses, prostheses, and wheelchairs in the classroom. *Teaching Exceptional Children* 11: 51–56.

Vernon, McK. and S. Koh. 1970. Effects of manual communication on deaf children's education achievement, linguistic competence, oral skills, and psychological development. *American Annals of the Deaf* 115: 527–536.

Vygotsky, L. S. 1962. *Thought and language*. Cambridge, Mass.: The M.I.T. Press.

Wahler, R. G. 1980. The insular mother: Her problems in parent-child treatment. *Journal of Applied Behavior Analysis* 13: 207–219.

Waisbren, S. E. 1980. Parents reactions after the birth of a developmentally disabled child. *American Journal of Mental Deficiency* 84: 345–351.

Warren, D. 1977. *Blindness and early childhood development*. New York: American Foundation for the Blind.

Warren, F. 1978. A society that is going to kill your children. In *Parents speak out: Growing with a handicapped child*, edited by A. P. Turnbull and H. R. Turnbull, III. Columbus, Ohio: Charles E. Merrill.

Warren, J. 1977. Early and periodic screening, diagnosis, and treatment. *Educational Researcher* 20: 14–15.

Wechsler, D. 1967. *The preschool and primary scale of intelligence*. New York: Psychological Corporation.

———. 1955. *Wechsler adult intelligence scale*. New York: Psychological Corporation.

Wehman, P. 1977. *Helping the mentally retarded acquire play skills*. Springfield, Ill.: Charles C Thomas.

Weikart, D. P. 1974. Curriculum for early childhood special education. *Focus on Exceptional Children* 6(1): 1–8.

———. 1967. Preschool programs: Preliminary findings. *Journal of Special Education* 1: 163–181.

Weikart, D. P., L. Rogers, C. Adcock, and D. McClelland. 1971. *The cognitively oriented curriculum: A framework for preschool teachers*. Washington, D.C.: National Association for the Education of Young Children.

Weiner, E. A. and B. J. Weiner. 1974. Differentiation of retarded and normal children through toy-play analysis. *Multivariate Behavioral Research* 9(2): 245–252.

Welsh, M. M. and C. S. H. Odum. 1981. Parent involvement in the education of the handicapped child: A review of the literature. *Journal of the Division for Early Childhood* 3: 15–25.

Werner, E. E., M. P. Honzik, and R. S. Smith. 1968. Prediction of intelligence and achievement at 10 years from 20-month pediatric and psychological examinations. *Child Development* 39: 1063–1075.

Westinghouse Learning Corporation. 1969. *The impact of Head Start: An evaluation of the effects of Head Start on children's cognitive and affective development*. Vol. 1.

White, B. 1975. *The first three years of life*. Englewood Cliffs, N.J.: Prentice-Hall.
Widerstrom, A. H. 1982. Mother's language and infant sensorimotor development: Is there a relationship? *Language Learning* 32: 1.
——. 1979. A case study of early language disorder: A developmental-experiential approach to intervention. Unpublished manuscript.
Wiegerink, R., V. Parrish, and I. Buhl. 1979. Consumer involvement in human services. In *Developmental disabilities: The DD movement*, edited by R. Wiegerink and J. W. Pelosi. Baltimore: Paul H. Brookes.
Wihler, L., M. Wasow, and D. Hatfield. 1981. Chronic sorrow revisited: Parent vs. professional depiction of the adjustment of parents of mentally retarded children. *American Journal of Orthopsychiatry* 51: 63–70.
Willis, A. and H. Ricciuti. 1975. *A good beginning for babies: Guidelines for group care*. Washington, D.C.: National Association for the Education of Young Children.
Wilson, J. G. 1974. Teralogic causation in man and its evaluation in non-human primates. In *Proceedings of the fourth international conference*, edited by B. V. Beidel. Dordrecht, Netherlands: Excerpta Medica.
——. 1973. *Environment and birth defects*. New York: Academic Press.
Wing, L., J. Gould, S. R. Yeates, and L. M. Brierley. 1977. Symbolic play in severely mentally retarded and in autistic children. *Journal of Child Psychology and Psychiatry* 18: 167–178.
Winick, M. 1970. Fetal malnutrition and growth process. *Hospital Practice* 5(5): 33–41.
Winick, M. and P. Rosso. 1973. Effects of malnutrition on brain development. *Biology of Brain Dysfunction* 1: 301–317.
Winton, P. J. and A. P. Turnbull. 1981. Parent involvement as viewed by parents of preschool handicapped children. *Topics in Early Childhood Special Education* 1: 11–19.
Wolfensberger, W. 1975. *The origin and nature of our institutional models*. Syracuse, N.Y.: Human Policy Press.
——. 1967. Counseling the parents of the retarded. In *Mental retardation: Appraisal, education and rehabilitation*, edited by A. A. Baumeister. Chicago, Ill.: Aldine Press.
Wolfensberger, W. and F. J. Menolascino. 1970. A theoretical framework for the management of parents of the mentally retarded. In *Psychiatric approaches to mental retardation*, edited by F. J. Menolascino. New York: Basic Books.
Woodcock, L. P. 1941. *Life and ways of the two-year-old*. New York: Dutton.
Woodward, W. M. 1962. Concepts of space in the mentally subnormal studied by Piaget's method. *British Journal of Social and Clinical Psychology* 1: 25–37.
——. 1961. Concepts of number in the mentally subnormal studied by Piaget's method. *Journal of Child Psychology and Psychiatry* 2: 249–259.
——. 1959. The behavior of idiots interpreted by Piaget's theory of sensory motor development. *British Journal of Educational Psychology* 29: 60–71.
Wright, H. F. 1960. Observational child study. In *Handbook of research methods in child development*, edited by P. H. Mussen. New York: Wiley.
Wyne, M. D. and P. D. O'Connor. 1979. *Exceptional children: A developmental view*. Lexington, Mass.: D. C. Heath.

Zaichkowsky, L. D., L. B. Zaichkowsky, and T. J. Martinek. 1980. *Growth and development: The child and physical activity*. St. Louis: Mosby.
Zeaman, D. and B. J. House. 1979. A review of attention theory. In *Handbook on mental deficiency: Psychological theory and research*. 2nd ed., edited by N. R. Ellis. Hillsdale, N.J.: Lawrence Elrbaum.
——. 1963. The role of attention in retardate discrimination loearning. In *Handbook of mental deficiency*, edited by N. R. Ellis. New York: McGraw-Hill.

Zelazo, P. R. 1979. Reactivity to perceptual-cognitive events: Application for infant assessment. In *Infants at risk: Assessment of cognitive functioning*, edited by R. B.
Kearsley and I. E. Sigel. Hillsdale, N.J.: Lawrence Erlbaum.

Zuk, G. H. 1962. The cultural dilemma and spiritual crisis of the family with a handicapped child. *Exceptional Children* 28: 405–408.

Author Index

Yoppi, J.O., 101
Yoshida, R.K., 292

Zaichkowsky, L.B., 115
Zaichkowsky, L.D., 115

Zax, M., 108
Zeaman, D., 34
Zelazo, P.R., 25, 35, 54
Zuk, G.H., 233

Subject Index